BALLOONING

ALSO BY
S. L. KOTAR AND J. E. GESSLER

*The Steamboat Era: A History of Fulton's Folly
on American Rivers, 1807–1860*
(McFarland, 2009)

BALLOONING

A History, 1782–1900

S. L. Kotar *and* J. E. Gessler

McFarland & Company, Inc., Publishers
Jefferson, North Carolina, and London

LIBRARY OF CONGRESS CATALOGUING-IN-PUBLICATION DATA

Kotar, S. L.
Ballooning : a history, 1782–1900 /
S. L. Kotar and J. E. Gessler.
p.   cm.
Includes bibliographical references and index.

ISBN 978-0-7864-4941-5
softcover : 50# alkaline paper ∞

1. Hot air balloons — History — 19th century.
2. Ballooning — History — 19th century.
I. Gessler, J. E.   II. Title.
TL616.K68   2011   797.5'109034 — dc22   2010040878

BRITISH LIBRARY CATALOGUING DATA ARE AVAILABLE

On the cover: lithograph of a balloon over Paris
on June 6, 1874 (Tissandier Collection, Library of Congress)

Manufactured in the United States of America

McFarland & Company, Inc., Publishers
Box 611, Jefferson, North Carolina 28640
www.mcfarlandpub.com

To be a truly successful aeronaut, an individual had to have courage, skill, a craftsman's knowledge and perhaps more than anything else, a burning desire to succeed. Part conjurer, part sportsman, the balloonist was involved in every aspect of the performance, always keeping one step ahead of the game. In that respect, it is not too far removed from being a baseball manager. With that in mind, we respectfully dedicate our book to Dorrel Norman Elvert "Whitey" Herzog, Baseball Hall of Fame 2010.

We would like to express our appreciation to Brian Pearce of Red Jacket Press for scanning our illustrations.

Table of Contents

Preface

We must speak of the ascent once more; It was the most beautiful. Instead of the struggle and violent sweeps which generally follow on cutting the ropes, its progress upward was calm and slow, and grand. As it rose the sun shone out, and a broad gleam of light fell upon its "gorgeous blazonry." There was scarcely an idea of terror in its grand motion: it moved as if at the touch of an enchanter, like MILTON'S Palace, with its music, and its magic, and its multitude:
"Anon, out of the earth, a fabric huge
Rose like an exhalation, with the sound
Of dulcet symphonies and voices sweet."[1]

In the beginning, we never dreamed how utterly compelling a story on aerostation could be. The concept started with one article from the early 1800s that described in vivid detail the ascension of a hot-air balloon. Curiosity piqued, we began searching the archives for more, never dreaming we would find a pathway to an immense phenomenon that consumed the people of the late 18th and 19th centuries.

Tracing the roots of ballooning back through the pages of old, blurry and at times illegible newspaper print, the story quickly assumed a life of its own. We became enmeshed in the techniques of how balloons were constructed, the type of gas used; figuratively bumping shoulders with the multitudes assembled to watch the rise of a manmade globe; held our breath as the frail structure was blown against a chimney or carried out to sea. Seeking more in-depth knowledge, we studied the backgrounds of those who shared from the sky the very earliest glimpses of our world in miniature.

French aeronauts were the first to challenge the realm of gods and winged creatures; in a time span nearly as fast as the flap of a wing, the awe and fascination spread to England, Italy, America and around the globe. With national pride nearly as great a driving force as wonder and adventure, each country claimed to have the bravest aeronauts, the largest aerostats, the fastest machines.

Mankind literally rose to the challenge as they pushed beyond their limits. Some succeeded in breaking newer and greater barriers. Some died horrible and tragic deaths, but others took their places. It did not take long for balloons to accompany armies in the field, those on the sidelines either lauding the new methods of reconnaissance and dropping incendiary bombs on unsuspecting enemies or decrying the barbarism which quickly brought armed conflict to a new and dangerous level.

Balloons and balloonists were present at peace conferences, performing their aerostatic arts as a respite for the royalty and nobility assembled to rewrite the regulations for post–

Napoleonic Europe. And then they were off again, these multi-national aeronauts, performing feats for an ever more fascinated public.

Working our way forward, from the first attempts of the Montgolfier brothers and their paper balloon, we lived the weeks, months, years and finally decades almost as those who had the privilege of being present at the time. We cheered the advent of the science, watching as primitive fire balloons gave way to gas production from mixtures of vitriol and iron shavings. But it did not stop there. Quickly, carbonated hydrogen pumped from factories replaced homemade gas, and just as quickly coal gas and "smokies" emerged on the scene. We raised a fist in the air as de Rosier rose to the heavens, and we suffered his death as the loss of a friend. We followed the start of the celebrated Blanchard and Garnerin and Sadler; we participated, in a vicarious way, as Graham came out of nowhere to ascend at the Coronation, and then came near to ruining his career with The Great Balloon Hoax and Riot.

There were successes and failures; lives championed and lives lost. Stories of men — and women — for uniquely, ballooning was open to anyone with an intrepid spirit and the money to afford an aerostat — who wished to ascend beyond the clouds. Some became folk heroes and others became objects of derision; many lived to write stirring accounts for an adoring public; a few published explanations of why they never got off the ground — and for a select group, which included the celebrated and the unknown — their stories were written by strangers, in the form of obituaries and Coroner's Inquests.

In this book, we have attempted to capture the phenomenon of aerostation as it was witnessed or read about by those who lived during the rise and fall of the Balloon Era. From humble beginnings, a quest for scientific and meteorological discoveries eventually took a back seat to showmanship. Barometers and thermometers gave way to gloriously decorated cars and brightly colored silk envelopes. Free ascensions were replaced by subscriptions and selling seats for flights. Next came tethered ascensions, where ten or twenty passengers could go up together in a relatively safe environment for the cost of several dollars — enough, it was hoped, to compensate the aeronaut for the cost of gas and a little extra to support the family.

In the early years, cities fought over drawing the most famous aeronauts, and it was not uncommon for a single flight to cost $500 or even $1,000. Soon, no 4th of July celebration was complete without a balloon going up, and children of 1830 dreamed of being the next Charles Durant or James Mills, just as young athletes today fantasize of playing shortstop for the New York Yankees or pitching for the Los Angeles Dodgers. A number achieved their goals, and the newspapers were filled with paragraphs detailing the local boy from Philadelphia or San Francisco ascending in a balloon named *Cloud* or *America*.

When every city had its homegrown aeronaut, the novelty began to wear off, so to collect their 25 cents per head at the ticket gate, aeronauts were forced to develop greater thrills for the paying public. As part of the evolving entertainment, dogs and cats were sent down in crude parachutes, then aeronauts ascended on the backs of horses and astride lions or bulls. Balloon races were arranged, fireworks set off and specialties developed where select aeronauts developed a following by jumping from parachutes. Trapeze artists followed, performing daring gymnastics from a bar suspended from the balloon by a slender cord five hundred feet above the ground. As the 19th century wore on, newly expanding traveling circuses gobbled up the aerial performers, exhibiting them alongside the elephants and sword-swallowers.

Balloons went higher and higher until the air became too thin to breathe. Inventors devised clever and bizarre methods of navigation, always with the notion that the heavens could be conquered. Everything from fans and screw propellers to gas engines were used. Headlines written in the 1790s were repeated in the 1890s: "A New, Absolutely Sure Way of Navigating the Skies has been perfected!" Balloon routes from San Francisco to New York or from London to Paris were on the horizon. And, of course, Lowe or Wise or Donaldson or King or any number of others were sure *this time* to succeed in crossing the Atlantic.

If the Napoleonic or Franco-Prussian wars were not enough, aerostats staked their claim in the great American bloodletting known as the Civil War. Whether they succeeded is a matter of debate, but their time was short and their contributions often bitterly contested.

Balloons came in all shapes and sizes. Globes and pear-shaped aerostats ascended beside balloons fashioned after elephants or old ladies. Early gas-inflated balloons became an instant hit with the children of Paris, and in the United States, they were used as advertising gimmicks to sell suits of clothes. Balloons adorned the covers of young adult readers, and little montgolfières were discharged skyward, often landing on hay ricks or thatched roofs and setting them ablaze.

In this work, we have attempted to capture and distill the phenomenon of aerostation as it was witnessed and expressed by those who participated in this great and risky undertaking. Ballooning was an "experiment" and an "exhibition," and those ascending were "aeronauts" or "adventurers" and later "professors." In a larger sense, they were a combination of scientist, showman and sports figure, alternately taking assiduous notes of their barometers and thermometers, while madly waving their flags and rising in wicker baskets covered with silk ribbons. Successful voyages were greeted by adoring multitudes as the following passage from 1811 reveals:

> At half-past nine o'clock, Mr. SADLER and Mr. BURCHAM arrived in a post-chaise and four. The people greeted them with every demonstration of satisfaction. The bells rang in merry peals, and the firing of guns, pistols, &c. announced the welcome intelligence. The populace afterwards drew the carriage with Mr. Sadler, jun. in charge of the balloon, through the principal streets, surrounded by lighted torches. In a few minutes the crowd before the residence of Mr. Sadler became so great, that to satisfy their impatient anxiety, the aerial voyagers exhibited themselves at the windows during a considerable time.[2]

Reports of their exploits were published in minute detail, often several articles on the ascent and aftermath appearing in each subsequent edition of the newspaper. This was no different than the sports writing of today, when a game is typically broken down into a description of the play-by-play, followed by separate articles containing interviews with the athletes, a commentary of what went right and what went wrong, editorial appraisals and a look ahead at the coming schedule.

Every successful ascension was a "win," and each failure a "loss." Just as the contemporary baseball fan can never get enough statistics or quotes from players on his favorite team, subscribing to numerous publications and watching endless re-runs of significant moments, so too, the fans of ballooning had their favorite aeronauts and pored through the newspapers for even the slightest mention of past, present and future plans. Their fanaticism, as well as the history, science and raw emotions of the aeronauts and spectators as they participated, either in practice, or vicariously in the "sport" of ballooning, is what we have attempted to capture with this book.

There were many reasons why individuals wished to "rise to the clouds": for the novelty and excitement, to test their courage, or for the opportunity to be hailed as a "hero," conquering the bonds of human restraint — all in conjunction, of course, with the aim of earning a lucrative living. A number went off in private places, but the vast majority published cards and printed fliers announcing "the day of ascension."

Much like the Mercury and Apollo missions lifting off in glorious clouds of smoke from Cape Canaveral, the earliest aeronauts arose in a magnificent spectacle of fire from grand globes of sparkling flame and flashing colors.

Just as millions gathered in Florida in the 1960s to marvel at the audacity of Man and cheer the conquering of space, hundreds of thousands of late 18th and 19th century people covered the towns and surrounding heights for a glimpse of such an unimaginable sight.

Wonder, astonishment, reverence, awe — a universal fear for the safety of the space traveler — and not a bit of skepticism — is the common thread binding the centuries. Man was challenging the dominion of God — or the gods — lifting off from the earth to soar in regions heretofore reserved for the celestial. It was truly an age of miracles, encapsulating the scientific advancements of the era, and merging adventure with the pitchman's flair for the dramatic.

Neil Armstrong's first step on the moon was a giant leap for mankind, and no one who witnessed this breathtaking achievement will ever forget the chills running down their back, or the tears forming at the corners of their eyes as one human being, representing all of *terra firma*, first touched alien soil. Reading the first-hand accounts of eyewitnesses to the Montgolfier brothers raising their paper balloon off the ground, or witnessing Pilatre de Rosier's ascents elicits the same goose bumps, causes the same awe, raises the same cheers with like enthusiasm. We are with them through the medium of words and the link of a thousand emotions, no different in 1783 than in 1969 or 2010.

French heroes, British heroes, American heroes: one world, teetering on the edge of the final frontier. No one said it would be easy. The 18th and 19th century aeronauts had their causalities. Men and women challenged the limits of the known and some lost their lives in the attempt; just as their brothers and sisters of the 20th century suffered as grievously, offering the ultimate sacrifice. Across the years, we of Earth mourn our heroes, honor their memory, and grow stronger by their example. They were the pioneers to the clouds, the moon and the stars: their stories are the legacy of those who cheer and cry and dare perpetuate the Impossible Dream.

The pages turned, the decades passed; by and large balloonists were relegated to chapters of the past. But their curiosity and indomitable spirit to challenge the limits of this world set the course for those who would follow in bigger and more advanced technologies. One thing will never change, however: the human spirit to reach over our heads. These early aeronauts were the forerunners, and to them we owe a debt of thanks, a wave of the hand and a lingering glance upward at the stars.

Through the words, the thoughts, speculations and sometimes criticisms of the aerostatic arts and sciences, we have attempted to honor those brave and perhaps foolish men and women of varnished silk, heated air and carbonated hydrogen gas.

In summarizing the phenomenon of ballooning, we have compressed an immense amount of data, best described by a paragraph taken from a newspaper in 1888:

> Although it is only a hundred years since the first balloons were made, it would take books enough to fill a good-sized library to record in detail the myriad styles of flying machines and balloons that have been invented, most of them within a comparatively few years.[3]

It is impossible to chronicle all the flights or even mention the hundreds of individuals involved. What we hoped to achieve was a comprehensive text combining the famous and the not-so-famous, always keeping in mind the human element. The story is about people, after all, and the "insignificant" flights often held the imagination long after the great had vanished from the scene and the technologies had been forgotten on the dusty shelves of the Patent Office. We hope this book kindles the imagination and instills the sense of awe and adventure we felt in writing it.

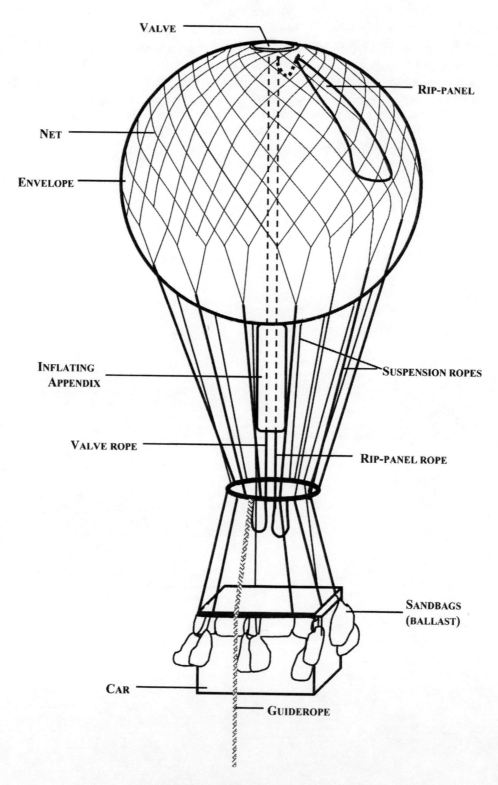

VALVE

RIP-PANEL

NET

ENVELOPE

INFLATING
APPENDIX

SUSPENSION ROPES

VALVE ROPE

RIP-PANEL ROPE

SANDBAGS
(BALLAST)

CAR

GUIDEROPE

Parts of the Balloon, by J. E. Gessler.

1

1782 — In the Beginning:
A *Voador*, a Cock, a Duck and a Sheep

> *AEROSTATION, the art of navigating the air, both in its principles and practice, in aerostatic machines, or air balloons. — No discovery was ever made, which drew after it more general admiration, or excited more extravagant hopes, than the art of aerostation; yet, after the lapse of 40 years, slender indeed have been the additions made to science by its discoveries, while humanity has had to mourn over the loss of several individuals of spirit and enterprise.*[1]

Written in 1829, the above paragraph sums up, perhaps better than anything else, the challenge, romance, disappointment and tragedy of Mankind's ascension through the clouds. Reaching for the temporal heavens on a large scale began, most likely — and appropriately enough — in 1720, with a Brazilian Jesuit named Bartholomew Gusmao. Obtaining permission from Pope John V, Gusmao crafted a hot air balloon in the form of a bird, complete with wings and tail.

Amid a crowd of immense spectators that included the Brazilian royalty, he attempted this first flight contiguous to the Palace. Inflating the balloon by means of a fire contained in the basket to rarify the air, he ascended as high as the cornice of the building. Unfortunately, "through the negligence and want of experience of those who held the cords, the machine took an oblique direction, and touching the cornice, burst and fell."

Failing in his goal of reaching the sky, but undeterred in his belief of the possibilities, the inventor proposed new experiments. According to reports from the time, however, the superstitious commoners charged him with being a "wizard." Terrified of being brought before the Inquisition, Gusmao burned his manuscripts, donned a disguise and fled to Spain. Shortly thereafter, he died in a hospital. The humble monk, called *Voador*, or "Flying-man," deserved credit for his brief ascension, however abortive.[2]

The method by which Gusmao inflated his balloon was rarefied air, or normal atmospheric air heated by means of a fire carried within a basket, or car, of the apparatus. This would become one of two competing methods that would dominate the field for years to come.

Development of Aerostatic Physics

The first successful human endeavor to raise an object off the ground came in the form of kites. Circa 400 B.C. the Chinese experimented with this type of flying machine and grew adept at the art. The kite became important in religious ceremonies and decorative ones were manufactured for the sheer joy of watching the frail objects soar aloft. Later, as larger and more sophisticated kites developed, the inventive Chinese used them to test weather conditions.

In 1790, Europeans, expecting to astonish the Chinese, made a demonstration of the air balloon at *Pekin*. Rather than react with amazement, however, the people "coldly observed it was but a new way of flying a kite."[3]

The history of aerostation in 1784 was described as follows:

> It is asserted for a fact, that the principle on which the air balloon is conducted, was known to the ancients above two thousand years ago. The learned reader will find in the tenth book of Aulus Gellius, chap. 12, a passage to the following purport:—"Archytas, a disciple of Pythagoras, made a wooden pigeon, that could fly by means of *air inclosed within*, which, on the motion being somewhat *rarefied*, kept it aloft, and by the aid of some wheels in the concave part propelled it forwards."[4]

Designing wishful scenarios, great figures of legend were created in the form of Cupid and Mercury to provide man the power of flight. Not satisfied with mere stories, however, people from many countries attempted to imitate birds by constructing wings attached to their arms. Over the course of many centuries, these pseudo-wings, constructed of feathers attached to light wood frames, have been used — unsuccessfully — in an attempt to lift humans off *terra firma*.

In the 1480s, Leonardo da Vinci commenced a study of flight, creating over one hundred drawings to illustrate his theories on bird and mechanical flight. These depicted wings and tails of avians, ideas for man flying by the aid of machines and devices for testing his ideas. The "Ornithopter flying machine," although never actually created, later became the basis of the modern-day helicopter.

Well into the balloon era, individuals persisted in the belief that if only they could find the right formula, human flight with the aid of wings was possible. An 1816 article recounts:

> Expectation was excited at Paris on the celebration of the fete of St. Louis, by a man by the name of GUILLAUME, who proposed to fly from the Champ de Mars. Every preparation was made, and he had his wings attached to his back, but unfortunately his courage failed, or he found his wings would not answer; and this modern ICARUS hid himself in the crowd, from the reproaches and bootings of the populace.[5]

Capturing heat generated by fire into an enclosed vessel and then allowing it to levitate into the atmosphere was practiced by the Chinese centuries before the Montgolfier brothers made the concept one of universal awe and admiration. Realizing that heated air was lighter than cold air, the Chinese trapped gas in an envelope and sent small, unmanned "balloons" skyward. Known as "Kongming lanterns," they were used as signaling devices during the military campaigns, and, incidentally, set the stage for war balloons used by the French, British and later the Americans to reconnoiter enemy positions to some useful effect.[6]

The physics of aerostation, however, began with the Greek mathematician Archimedes (285–212 B.C.), who postulated on the theory of equilibrium: "A body wholly or partially immersed in a fluid experiences an upthrust equal to the weight of fluid displaced." As pertains to balloons, the total weight of the machine (envelope, car, net, mass of gas and passengers) corresponds exactly to the weight of the air displaced by the envelope. All of this was speculation, however, until put to the test.

Another Greek, Hero of Alexandria, examined the idea of levitation from the standpoint of an engineer. Working with air pressure and steam as a source of power, he developed the "aeolipile," using jets of steam to create a rotary motion. Mounting a sphere on top of a water kettle, the heated gas traveled into the globe through a series of pipes. Two L-shaped tubes on opposite sides of the sphere allowed the gas to escape, which gave a thrust to the sphere that caused it to rotate. This engine-created movement would later prove essential in the history of flight.[7]

In the mid–1700s, Henry Cavendish, English physicist and chemist, conducted experiments in the composition of air and water. In 1766, he discovered hydrogen by adding sulfuric acid to iron, tin, or zinc shavings. He identified the two different types of air by calling the first "fixed air" (carbon dioxide) and the second "flammable air" (later called "inflammable air" or hydrogen). Significantly, he demonstrated that the latter gas was lighter than air, a concept that would later appeal to the physician, Jacques Charles, who would become a well-known pioneer in the field of aerostation.

Joseph Priestly continued Cavendish's work on carbon dioxide and in 1777 his paper, "Experiments and Observations with Different Types of Air," was translated into French, making it available to those on the forefront of a new revolution.[8]

Two other gentlemen played a unique role in the early history of ballooning: Dr. Black of Edinburgh suggested the idea that a thin bladder, when filled with inflammable air, must necessarily ascend, and Cavallo, who, in 1782, put Black's ideas into practice. He concluded that a bladder was too heavy, and paper not airtight. Soap bubbles, however, when created with inflammable air, rose as far as the ceiling of his room before bursting.[9]

As developed (1829), the principles of aerostation became:

1. Any body which is specifically lighter than the air, bulk for bulk, will be buoyed up by it, and ascend, till it enters a stratum of the atmosphere in which the weights are equal, and then it will remain stationary, or float horizontally, or descend. A balloon, then, is a machine with less specific gravity than the air in which it rises.
2. Heat rarefies, expands and lessens the specific gravity of air, till its weight is proportional to the heat; 435 degrees of heat will double the bulk of a volume of air.

Therefore, heated air in an enclosed envelope will dilate to such a degree that the excess of the weight of an equal bulk of common air is greater than the weight of the balloon and appendages, and will cause it to ascend. With the cooling and condensation of the enclosed gas, or the diminished density of the atmosphere, the point of specific gravity is reached. Without renewed heat, the balloon will gradually descend.[10]

Men Ascend in a Balloon

The Montgolfier brothers were led to this conclusion by an act of fate. As the story goes, a washerwoman of the Rue aux Juifs, in the Marais, placed a petticoat on a basketwork frame, over a stove to dry. In order to concentrate the heat and to prevent it escaping, she drew the material close together. By degrees the air became rarified, the petticoat began to move and at last rose in the air. As witness to the event, Montgolfier returned home and without loss of time, studied the work of Priestly on different kinds of atmospheres. The result was the discovery of the first modern balloon.[11]

Various versions of this tale surfaced over the years, and as the Montgolfier brothers (Joseph Michel, August 26, 1740–June 26, 1810, and Jacques-Étienne, January 6, 1745–August 2, 1799) became famous, details were added and subtracted. It generally evolved into the story that while watching a fire, Joseph became fascinated by the "force" that caused the smoke to rise. He made a small bag out of paper (or alternately, silk), lit a fire under the opening and watched it ascend. Unfamiliar with the scientific explanation given by the learned men of the day, he believed he had discovered a new phenomenon, and called it "Montgolfier gas." Supposing the powers of the air came from the dense smoke of the material they burned, the brothers persisted in using a combination of damp straw and chopped wool for their aerostatic experiments.

Some years after achieving fame, Joseph elaborated on the above story. He stated that while contemplating an assault on Gibraltar, which had proved impregnable by sea, he wondered at the possibility of an air attack, using troops lifted by the same force that sent embers from the fire upward. He constructed a box-like device (3 × 3 × 4 feet) out of very thin wood, covering the top and sides with taffeta. After he built a fire under the contraption, it quickly rose and struck the ceiling. He is quoted as then writing to Étienne, "Get in a supply of taffeta and of cordage, quickly, and you will see one of the most astonishing sights in the world."[12]

Joseph was the 12th child and Étienne the 15th (the "Jacques" is habitually omitted) of sixteen children. Pierre Montgolfier, the patriarch (1700–1793), was a successful paper manufacturer in Annonay, in the Ardeche, France. Following tradition, he named his eldest son, Raymond (1730–1772), his successor, and sent the other boys away to school to learn other occupations.

Joseph, described as a dreamer, impractical in business and personal affairs, became somewhat of a maverick, while Étienne had a much more businesslike temperament. He went to Paris to train as an architect, but returned to Annonay in 1772 after the sudden and unexpected death of his elder brother Raymond. Taking control of the paper manufacturing business, he incorporated the latest Dutch innovations into the family mills. His practice was so successful that the government of France recognized his accomplishments and rewarded him with a grant to establish the Montgolfier factory as a model for other French papermakers.[13]

In November 1782, Joseph set aloft a small hollow parallelepiped made out of taffeta, with a volume of approximately 40 cubic feet. When the interior had been heated by the burning of paper, it rose rapidly to the ceiling.[14]

On December 14, 1782, the pair successfully elevated a 3-meter balloon over the Vidalone factory in Annonay, again using a combination of damp straw, wool and paper to create the "levity." The upward force was so great they lost control, and the balloon rose to the height of 70 feet, floating nearly 1.2 miles before descending slowly back to earth. Those witnessing the landing subsequently destroyed the aerostat in what Étienne later described as an "indiscretion."[15]

The dawn of 1783, destined to mark a turning point in aerostation, saw the Montgolfier brothers setting off the third of their trial balloons. Consistently creating larger and larger globes, they designed a machine that had a volume of 650 cubic feet. By reason of its extreme lightness, it rose with such force that it broke the ropes holding it down and achieved a height of 100–150 fathoms.

Determined to test their theories on a larger scale, the Montgolfier brothers attempted an ascension on April 3, 1783, but the wind was too brisk, and they postponed the trial. They tried again on April 25th, but the force of the wind on the machine so astonished the men holding it down, that it escaped, landing a quarter of a league away after rising to a height of 200 fathoms. It remained aloft for a period of ten minutes.

At this point, the decision was made to go public with their experiment, and arrangements were made to demonstrate the ascension in Cordillera Square, Annonay. In order to ensure claim to the invention, individuals from the various States of Vivarais and all the notable citizens of Annonay were invited to attend. This set the precedent for all future flights, where the head count of "the nobility and gentry" were often a judge of the exhibition's success.

"According to M. Montgolfier's calculations, the weight of the volume of air the sphere displaced was 2,156 pounds, but since the gas only weighed 1,078 pounds and the sphere 500, this left an excess of 578 pounds to provide the force with which the sphere was inclined to rise."[16]

A letter by Étienne Montgolfier to Faujas de Saint-Fond gave particulars of the June 5th flight. He stated the aerostatic machine was made of linen, backed with paper and sewn on to a network of string attached to strips of linen. Roughly spherical in shape, the balloon had a circumference of 110 feet, with a wooden frame 16 feet square holding it rigid at the base. The various parts of the machine were attached to each other by buttons; two men assembled the apparatus, but when filled with gas, it required eight to hold it down. The balloon rose rapidly, but slowed as it neared the top of its ascent until it reached a height of 1,000 fathoms. It stayed in the air for ten minutes; the loss of air through the buttonholes, the holes made by stitching, and through other flaws in the machine prevented it from staying up any longer. At the time of the experiment there was a southerly wind and it was raining.[17]

The balloon descended in a field and caught fire from the heating apparatus containing the remnants of the still smoldering embers. Nearby peasants, terrified by the apparition, which they believed to be the moon falling from the sky portending the Final Day of Judgment, failed to extinguish the blaze, and the first publicly witnessed balloon was consumed by fire.[18]

In order to achieve official recognition for their accomplishment, Étienne ("the epitome of sober virtues ... modest in clothes and manner ... dressed stylishly in black"), went to the capital to establish the brother's claim to the invention of flight. Joseph (the "unkempt") remained behind with the family.

On July 2, 1783, a report was sent to the Académie Royale des Sciences, including the official report to verify the facts.[19]

Étienne entered into a collaboration with a wealthy wallpaper manufacturer, Jean-Baptiste Réveillon, and together they constructed a 37,500 cubic foot envelope of taffeta covered with a varnish of alum. Influenced by Réveillon, the balloon was colored a sky blue, with golden flourishes, signs of the Zodiac and bright suns. On Friday, September 12, 1783, an experiment was attempted at Réveillon's factory, with members of the Académie des Sciences present. The balloon was successfully inflated and lifted a weight of approximately 400 pounds. However, a brisk wind and a torrent of rain destroyed the paper and linen comprising the vessel, ruining the experiment. A larger spheroid, 41 feet in diameter and 57 feet in height, constructed of linen and calico was inflated the following Thursday, September 18th. It rose majestically and remained airborne for five or six minutes.

Reassured by this success, the following day, Friday, September 19, 1783, was chosen for a public ascent. The apparatus (called the *Aérostat Réveillon* by Étienne) was assembled in the courtyard of Versailles, on a large, elevated platform in the presence of King Louis XVI, Queen Marie Antoinette, the royal court and "among the greatest concourse of people assembled."[20] A fire-pot was let off to inform the spectators when the rarefied air was about

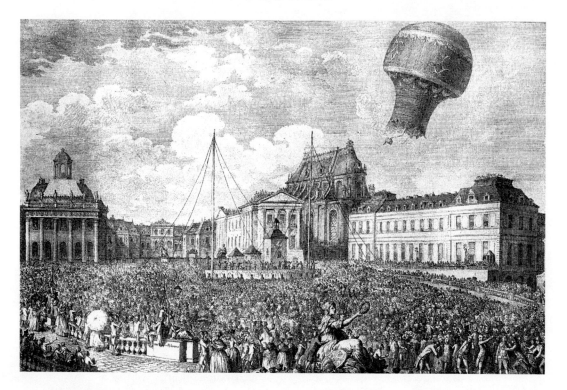

Animal Flight, 1783 (by permission of the National Air and Space Museum, Smithsonian Institution, Washington, D.C.).

to be inserted into the globe, a process that was completed in less than ten minutes by the burning of 80 pounds of straw and 7 or 8 pounds of wool. A second fire-pot announced the completion of the inflation and a final one marked the time of ascension.

There being an understandable concern on how the human body would react to the forces of the upper atmosphere, it was decided to send aloft a sheep (named Montauciel, or "Climb-to-the-sky"), a duck and a rooster in a large wicker basket.

The cord holding down the globe was cut and the balloon rose to a height of more than 240 fathoms, loaded with 200 pounds of weight. Unfortunately, the envelope swayed wildly after ascending, allowing considerable gas to escape. Notwithstanding, it remained aloft 8–10 minutes before descending in the forest at Carefour-Mareclia, two miles distant, so gently "that it did no more than bend the branches of the trees upon which it came to rest and that the animals which were suspended from the machine came to no harm whatsoever."[21]

Pilâtre de Rozier arrived first at the landing site where he discovered the balloon separated from the basket. His presence is significant, in that a month later, he would be one of the two human beings to claim fame as the first ever to ascend in a balloon.[22]

Various accounts report that "the sheep was discovered nibbling imperturbably on straw while the cock and the duck cowered in a corner, not hurt in any way."[23] Other reports stated that the cock broke its neck on landing, and that the sheep lived out an honored life in Marie Antoinette's private zoo.[24]

In any case, the first bipeds to leave Mother Earth by means other than wings, were not human, but avian.

2

1783 — Monsters and Aeronauts

Never has science produced such a majestic and imposing display, and the nation should rightly be proud of a discovery which, only six months ago, we would have discounted and banished into the realm of historic untruths if anyone, even Archimedes himself, were to tell us of it.[1]

Other inventors were simultaneously working on the same principles of aerostation. French physician Jacques Charles and his associates, two French mechanics, Jean and Nicolas Roberts (habitually referred to as "the Roberts brothers"), repeated the Annonay experiment. The date of ascension being advertised beforehand, "never before had a royal review drawn a larger crowd made up of people from all walks of life."[2]

Using hydrogen in place of rarified gas, they staged an unmanned ascension at the Champ de Mars on August 27, 1783, using a balloon 12 feet in circumference. At exactly five o'clock, two cannons were fired to alert spectators of the start of the test. The small sphere, called *Globe*, filled with 60 cubic meters of gas, immediately rose and soon disappeared from sight. Unfortunately, bad weather prevented an accurate estimation of the height obtained, but repeated applause from the onlookers aptly demonstrated their approval. Newspapers promptly credited the glory as belonging "solely to M.M. de Montgolfier."[3]

The sight of the balloon floating over Gonesse caused such a general panic: two carters, suspecting some evil influence, ran from the terrible specter. As luck would have it, the machine landed very near their path of flight. Bounding in all directions, it seemed to follow them, finally forcing the men to turn and defend themselves. Using stones against the beast, they ultimately inflicted "a mortal wound." One erstwhile Don Quixote drove his knife through the breast of the monster, allowing the gas to escape. Thus subdued, the machine was tied to the tail of a horse and dragged through the mud to Gonesse, where it was reclaimed the following day by its owner, who, "with some pain," gave the carters a small fee for their trouble.[4]

So great was the terror of the public, that the Lieutenant of Police was forced to publish an "Advertisement," explaining the phenomenon in the hope of avoiding future embarrassments.[5]

Three days later, all Paris was inundated with etchings of both the arrival and ascent of the balloon, marking yet another point in aerostation history: the hawking of souvenirs.

> Possibly the most famous question and answer sequence ever uttered in the history of ballooning came about immediately after the first ascension. The interrogative was posed: "But what use do these experiments serve? Tell me, what is the point of this discovery which is causing so much disturbance?"

Charles and Robert, First Ascent (by permission of the National Air and Space Museum, Smithsonian Institution, Washington, D.C.).

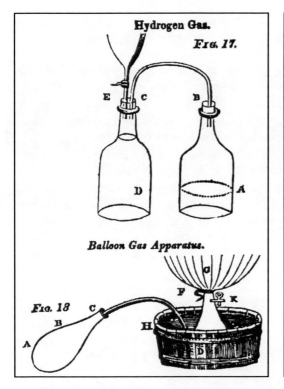
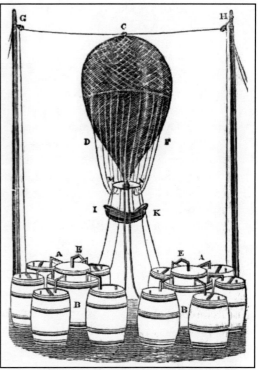

Left: "Making Hydrogen Gas for Balloons." *Right:* "Apparatus for Making Inflammable Air" (both images from Alexander Jamieson, *A Dictionary of Mechanical Science, Arts, Manufactures, and Miscellaneous Knowledge* [London: Henry Fisher, Son, and Co., 1829]).

Benjamin Franklin observed:
"Well! What is the point of the child who has just been born?"
And the Philosopher mused:
"Indeed, this child could die while still in the cradle, could develop into no more than an idiot, but he could equally become the pride of his country, the shining light of his century, the benefactor of humanity."[6]

The above quotations, written after the Roberts' flight on August 27, 1783, became very well known and were still being circulated well into the 1800s.

If the word "rivals" was too strong, there can be no doubt that the Montgolfiers were acutely aware of the competition they had from Charles and the Roberts brothers. Hurrying to be the first "team" to send up a human being, they constructed what was to become known as a "Montgolfière type" balloon, or one basically circular in shape and inflated with hot air.

A private trial, witnessed by about thirty persons, among whom were the Duke de Chartres, Colonel Dillon and "other people of fashion," was held on October 13, in the Montgolfiers' yard. An eyewitness, writing from Paris on October 13, noted the controlled flight was "infinitely more astonishing than all the former." Three persons whom he did not name, although one was undoubtedly the Duke de Chartres, and a second, perhaps, Pilâtre de Rozier, were enclosed in the car. The third individual may have been Étienne Montgolfier, for he is known to have made one tethered ascension against the wishes of his father, whom he had promised never to ride in a balloon.[7]

The trio gradually raised "near as high as the houses," and came down with amazing lightness, notwithstanding a weight of 1,800 pounds fastened to the apparatus to prevent any extraordinary elevation.

The ascent was not without some problems, however, as the valve, "calculated to open and shut at pleasure ... did not answer as well as expected." After the first trial, Colonel Dillon ascended alone and carried the balloon much higher than the first undertaking.[8]

This flight marked the first time humans ascended in a balloon, and although the balloon was held down by cords, it stands by itself as a significant achievement.

Equally important is the mention of the valve malfunctioning. This critical piece of machinery was vital to the success of a flight, and early aeronauts constantly tinkered with the mechanism to achieve a perfect fit and secure closure. Situated on the apex of the balloon, the circular device was made of wood, closed by two semi-circular panels called the "clack." Ropes were run from the top of the fastening hoop through small holes in the clacks, meeting underneath, where the valve rope was attached. Pulling the valve rope lets off gas, forcing the balloon to descend; in cases where the valve failed to seal properly, too much gas was permitted to escape, forcing the machine into free fall. In such a case, the vessel plummeted to earth, leaving only the discharge of ballast with which to manipulate a landing. Many tragic flights ended in disaster because of a faulty valve, or the pilot's inability to use it properly.

A second private trial was conducted two days later on October 15, with Pilâtre de Rozier ascending in the balloon. On October 17, a third tethered voyage was made, and the final prefatory ascension took place on October 19. This time, de Rozier and the Sieur du Réveillon's gardener were "placed in an osier gallery affixed to the machine" and were raised more than 300 feet from the ground. The balloon remained aloft eight minutes before being brought down.[9] Other sources identified the second aeronaut as André Giroud de Villette, a wallpaper manufacturer from Madrid.

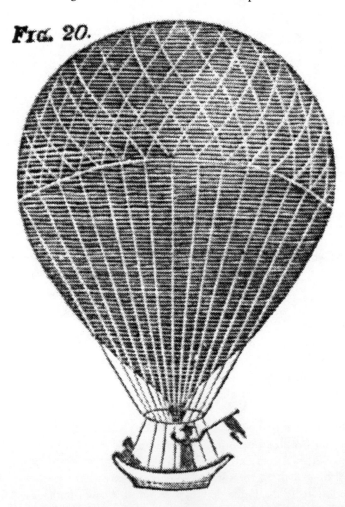

FIG. 20.

"Filled Balloon" (from Alexander Jamieson, *A Dictionary of Mechanical Science, Arts, Manufactures, and Miscellaneous Knowledge* [London: Henry Fisher, Son, and Co., 1829]).

"One Small Step for Man..."

The Montgolfiers constructed the balloon intended to carry the first men aloft in free flight in M. Réveillon's garden, but when informed the Dauphin had expressed a desire to witness the ascent, they removed it to the château de la Muette. There, final preparations were made.

On November 21, 1783, a day described as clear in some places and obscured by cloud in others, with a northwesterly wind, they prepared for what would become the watershed event in aeronautic history.

The first man selected for the flight was Jean-François Pilâtre de Rozier (1756–1785), a professor of physics and chemistry at Reims, who had already experienced a tethered ascension. His companion was the Marquis François d'Arlandes, Mayor de Bourbonnois. The King reportedly suggested two criminals be sent up in their stead, but was convinced that the occasion was of too great an importance to allow the honor to fall on such heads.

At 12:08 P.M. the signal was given to begin filling the balloon, which measured 70 feet in height and 46 feet in diameter, with a volume of 60,000 cubic feet, carrying between 1,600–1,700 pounds of weight. The original plan called for a controlled ascension with the vessel still attached by ropes in order to ascertain the strength of the wind and the precise lifting power of the vessel. The trial was attempted, but the wind proved too strong, and the balloon struck an obstruction in the garden, causing several tears in the fabric, one greater than six feet in length. The balloon was brought back to the platform and repaired in under two hours.

At 2:06 P.M., the balloon was set free and rose 250 feet in the air, with both aeronauts taking off their hats and bowing to the spectators in a style that was to be copied by all future voyagers. The balloon eventually ascended to 3,000 feet, and, still visible to the spectators, crossed the Seine below the gate of la Conference and passed between the Military Academy and the Hotel des Invalides.

The aeronauts determined to descend after a short trip, but being too near the houses of the Rue de Seve, in the Faubourg, Saint-Germain, they increased the production of gas by feeding the fire in the brazier hanging beneath the envelope, and continued toward the outskirts of Paris.

After a distance of 4,000–5,000 fathoms, covering 20–25 minutes, they landed safely in a field beyond the new boulevard, opposite the Croulebarbe mill, with two-thirds of their supplies intact. The historic event was witnessed by the Duke of Polignac, the Duke of Guines, the Comte de Polastron, the Comte de Vaudreil, d'Hunaud, Benjamin Franklin, Faujas de Saint-Fond, Delisle and Lercy from the Académie des Sciences, who put their names to the testimony.[10]

A letter from Paris, dated November 28, stated of this momentous occasion:

> These aerial travelers, for whose lives every spectator was in pain, declared they did not feel the least disagreeable sensation, even when they were at the highest, and their whole journey took up twenty minutes. It was not possible for M. de Rosier to make many observations upon the nature of the fluid which he breathed. The Duke de Chartres, willing to celebrate the day on which the human race first traveled in the air, and returned to give an account of their journey, has resolved to erect a pyramid upon the spot where the ball alighted, and thereon to inscribe the names of Montgolfier, who constructed their airy vehicle, together with those of the two bold travelers, who dared to take a journey to the third region of air.[11]

(De Rozier's name was frequently spelled with an "s" rather than a "z" in contemporary accounts. The "de" preceding the name was also omitted in most newspaper articles.)

"Count" England In

Not surprisingly, word of the wondrous events transpiring in France quickly reached across the English Channel and around the world. With inspiration and adventure in the air, Count Francesco Zambeccari (1762–1812), a nobleman of Italian birth, who had served in the Spanish Navy and fought against the Turks, became fascinated with the idea of balloon flight. He promptly set about constructing his own aerostatic machine, which he accomplished "without difficulty."

In a letter of November 28, 1783, he wrote:

> On the first of this month I succeeded in sending up a sphere, five feet in diameter, from the roof of a certain Biaginni, a trader in artificial flowers who made a financial contribution to the experiment. Although this sphere was sent into the air with no witnesses to the event, and from a purely private location, some amazed person spotted it in the sky and the next day the news had run through London.[12]

Encouraged by the reception, Zambeccari quickly made a larger balloon of ten feet in diameter, constructed of taffeta and decorated with gilt Dutch leaf. On the 25th of November 1783, at the Artillery Ground, he proposed to set off his balloon, the first on British soil. Assisting him in the endeavor was the Royal Family, watching from the terrace at Windsor.

After inflating his globe, a string was fixed with a running knot near the balloon and tightly closed. After the inflation tube was cut away, the string was handed to His Majesty, George III. An eyewitness account related that the King, taking great delight in the process, went under the window where the Queen and Duchess of Portland sat, and dolled out the string until the balloon reached the height of the window. After leaving it there a considerable time, he then went to a second window where the Princess Royal, Princess Augusta Sophia and Princess Elizabeth sat, and let it up again.

Finally he let it free with the words, "Now it goes," and the balloon ascended in a perpendicular direction for upward of three minutes, where the wind blew it around "in visible confusion." It then took a southerly course and was lost from sight.[13]

Zambeccari later noted a desire that would remain the aspiration and the bane of aeronauts from the first ascension to the present day: "I would like to be able to navigate it horizontally and steer it in any direction I wish." It is possible Zambeccari was the "subject of interest" mentioned by the Edinburgh *Advertiser*: "It is well known that a pair of wings and a tail, of the most curious workmanship, are constructing for a person, who, in the spring, is to be sent off upon an air balloon." These wings, each a hefty twenty yards in diameter, were designed to resemble those of a bat, using silk instead of feathers. Attached to a full-sized balloon, it was postulated that a machine so equipped could guide a person wherever he wished to go.[14]

To make matters more interesting (and to add a gambling theme which would recur frequently), a "person of very high rank in Paris" bet five thousand guineas that the foreigner who had undertaken the scheme would make a safe passage from Dover Cliff to Paris. The wings and tail were estimated to cost upward of 600 pounds.

Most Extraordinary Honors

Entrance tickets depicting a round sphere with a basket attached ascending above the clouds with the imprint:

EXPERIENCES
DU GLOBE AEROSTATIQUE
de M.M. Charles et Roberts
1783

were published by the hundreds of thousands, and a reported 300,000 to 800,000 spectators crammed the area around the Tuileries gardens on December 1, 1783, to view the ascension of M. Charles and Roberts, junior. Among those wishing to view the spectacle were the Duke de Chartres, French and foreign princes and nobility.

The air balloon was composed of red and straw-colored taffety (a common corruption of the spelling of "taffeta"), pieced alternately so as to run like meridional lines upon a globe. The upper hemisphere was covered with netting, surrounded at the bottom by a hoop to which the car was suspended by cords, creating equal pressure on all sides. The fabric was covered with a solution of gum elastic, and the envelope filled with inflammable air pressed neatly against the net. Suspended from it was a basket, covered with blue silk and paper, finely gilt, in the shape of a triumphal car, or short gondola.[15]

Prior to ascension a small green trial balloon was sent up to test the wind currents, the honor of setting it free going to M. Montgolfier. After five minutes, the tiny vessel "seemed like an emerald and soon after appeared as a star." After reassuring the crowd on the safety of the voyage a hush fell over the assembly as the balloon began to rise. Once airborne, cheers rent the air and hats were raised. Even the Swiss mercenaries joined in by throwing their sabers into the air.[16]

In this world of aerostation, where everything was new and exciting, the pioneers set another precedent by waving flags to the admiring crowds. (As it developed, aeronauts traditionally carried their native flag, as well as the standard of the country in which they were ascending. They might also display the ensigns of wealthy or influential individuals, always with an eye to future patronage. Once above the crowd the flags were tossed down and greedily collected by spectators).

The philosophers (as early aeronauts were styled), glided along in a steady horizontal tract over the Rue and Fauxbourg St. Honoré, saluting the people as they went. After a voyage covering twenty miles, the balloon descended and Roberts alit. Taking advantage of the suddenly lightened basket, Charles threw out sand ballast and quickly re-ascended. With an eye toward impressing the Duke de Chartres and his party, who had followed the progression of the vessel on horseback, Charles allowed the balloon to reach 1,526 toifes, or 3,052 yards perpendicular, a procedure requiring ten minutes.

Charles descended a second time five miles distant, near the house of an English gentleman. There he spent the night and returned home in the morning. Received as a conquering hero, Charles promised his adoring public to take his balloon to England in less than a month.[17]

To immortalize the event, Charles Robert, Jean Burgatet (vicar of Nesle), Charles Philippet (vicar of Fresnoy), Thomas Hutin (life mayor of Fresnoy), and Lheureux (vicar of Hedouville) attested to the fact the balloon came down between Nesle and Hedouville, nine leagues from Paris, in a meadow at a quarter past three.

It did not take long for the idea of selling tickets to an ascension to take hold, and throughout the era, those involved sought every means possible to raise capital. They were often criticized for their inventiveness and persistence in this matter, but as subsequent events will show, even the most outlandish schemes often left the investors in serious debt.

A summary of the year's momentous achievements was made by the Académie des Sciences on December 23, 1783.[18] Declaring that it would be "reckless" to decide which method of inflation — the heated air used by the Montgolfiers, or the inflammable air used by Charles and Roberts — was the better method, the authors concluded that the ease and speed of the Montgolfier method seemed to give it an advantage, but that the Charles/Roberts method had the advantage of considerably lessening the volume of the balloon while still preserving the same capacity to lift weight. Leaving the discussion for another day, they lauded the new technology as providing a means of studying "meteorological phenomena, which, until now, has remained mysterious."

3

1784 — Big Ascensions

Before today, we were only familiar with inflammable air in Volta's pistols, in india-rubber bottles and in soap bubbles; it was reasonable to suspect that the presence of a large amount of such a rarefied substance could have nothing but dangerous results.[1]

January 16, 1784, was selected as the date when a great new montgolfière balloon, called *La Flesselles*, would be launched by Montgolfier and Pilâtre de Rozier. (When used in reference to a balloon, the proper name was often spelled with a small "m" and an "e" at the end.) Created to hold six passengers, the magnificent envelope was constructed of ordinary linen of an open weave, "such as is used in the packing of comparatively worthless merchandise." Two double thicknesses were stitched together with four sheets of paper lining them to form the basic structure, and the whole was reinforced with pink tape, sewn in diamond shapes over the exterior.

The top of the machine was lined on the outside with white calico, formed in the style of a canopy, the construction of which required more than three hundred ells of material. The sleeve, or inflating appendix, was made out of wool cloth, called Cadis, less prone to catching fire. A wicker basket, 22 feet in diameter on the outside and 17 feet inside, was fastened to it, with the brazier or grill hung in the center, slightly below the base. A mesh or network of ropes was designed to encompass the upper hemisphere to maintain the equilibrium of the base. A small flag was perched atop the crown, and various illustrations decorated the body.

During the night of January 15, a shower of rain and snow blanketed the area. Being left out in the open, the balloon suffered great damage, becoming soaked. By morning a sheen of ice covered the entire structure. This made delay inevitable, and the flight was postponed until Saturday. Conditions were little better and the envelope, now exposed to rain and frost for several consecutive days and nights, lay in a sorry state. Fearing a second failure, the aeronauts decided to attempt an ascent, despite grave misgivings. They fired up the brazier to a greater degree than prudent and began the process of inflation. The top of the balloon began to swell, but in consequence of the damp and the overly hot fire, the envelope split in several places. Within a short time it collapsed over the grill and ignited. Water pumps were used to quench the blaze, but too late to allow for an ascension that day. A swell of immense displeasure rippled through the crowd, who readily blamed the "Physicists" for their lack of planning and foresight.

An announcement was made that a second attempt would go off as soon as the weather improved. By Sunday, the skies had cleared enough to anticipate a flight on Monday, January

19. In spite of the fact they had serious doubts on the wisdom of ascending with the hastily repaired balloon, Montgolfier and de Rozier donned their formal dress and prepared to give it their best shot. Accompanying them on the flight were Prince Charles de Laurencin, and the Comtes de Laurencin, Dampierre and Laporte.[2]

At 11:45 A.M. a mortar was discharged as a signal and the inflation process began. Mindful of the disaster from the previous Saturday, the fire used for inflation was kept to a reasonable level, and by 12:15 P.M. the shape of the filling balloon gave promise of a successful venture. With the wind blowing from east-south-east, the ropes were cut at 1:00 P.M. As the machine rose, a young assistant named Fontaine threw himself into the car. His weight impeded the upward movement and caused the balloon to shudder. To complicate matters, two of the ropes still held fast (another all too common occurrence), causing the entire machine to list dangerously in a westerly direction. Still tethered, yet partially ascended, it careened several yards off the ground, striking the heads of several onlookers. As panic spread, a rope became entangled on a pole and the car struck the side of the enclosure, knocking part of it off.

Amid a near stampede on the ground, the entangled ropes were severed. The sudden release threw off the vessel's center of gravity, and a large fissure split the upper half of the sphere. Too late to do anything but ascend, the aeronauts stoked the fire and the balloon slowly rose in an upright position. It drifted toward the river, where de Rozier was reputed to have said, "Gentlemen, we are going to go down in the Rhone."

To avoid this disaster, the passengers threw wine into the fire as a means of increasing the heat and the balloon finally reached a height of 500 fathoms. With the balloon stabilized for the moment, the company waved their handkerchiefs to the crowd and conveyed their appreciation by means of a speaking tube until too distant to be heard.

When, over the Loge de la Bienfaisance, the flag of *la Renomme* broke away and drifted to earth. After hovering over the Loge for several minutes, the balloon descended. The initial impression of a controlled maneuver was dispelled by the sight of the aeronauts urgently feeding the flames in an attempt to gain altitude. Fearing the worst, a number of terror-stricken witnesses hurried toward where they anticipated the balloon would crash.

Arriving on the scene, these fears seemed well grounded, for they encountered the balloon in flames. Horrified that the men had been burned to death or crushed by the fall, they hurried closer, only to be relieved by the sight of the aeronauts shouting that they had survived. The Marquis d'Anglefort broke a tooth and Prince Charles had a bruised leg, but miraculously that was the extent of the injuries. With rescue at hand, the group returned to Paris, where they were carried in triumph to the Opera.[3]

With this staggering success, the art of ballooning had progressed from unmanned flight, to that of carrying animals, to a two-man ascension and finally one where seven people floated over the earth. Although *La Flesselles* had originally been designed for six, the last — and most fortunate — member of the party was Fontaine, the assistant who had almost fatally jumped into the car at the last minute.

"Count" the Italians In

Impressed with the success of the French in the field of aerostation, Count Paolo Andreani, a wealthy individual from Milan, ordered the construction of a hot air balloon. The men he chose to implement the project were Carlo and Agostino Gerli, two well-known architects. They based their plans on the most recent Montgolfier model, and completed the work in a scant six weeks.[4]

A large platform was built at Moncucco, the seat of the Andreani family, and on February 25, 1784, the brothers Giuseppe and Agostino Gerli and their companion, M. Don Paolo, made the first Italian ascent. The balloon began to rise, then slowly descended. With the aid of workers giving the machine a boost with poles, it continued its upward progress, eventually reaching a height of 600 Milanese brasses — equivalent to 1,100 French feet.

Waving to the 2,000 happy and amazed spectators, the aeronauts, self-described as "drunk as it were, on this delectable sensation" of being aloft, made a serious miscalculation and burned all their combustibles, leaving nothing in reserve for the landing.

Experiencing the "sheer bliss of a voyage in the sky," they eventually reached a point where the balloon began to descend. Shouting through their speaking tube at several "perturbed and stupefied onlookers," they pleaded for help, but their pleas were not understood, due, the brothers confessed, to the fact they had not enunciated clearly, from the fact they were in fear for their lives.

At 100 Milanese brasses from the ground the balloon picked up speed, carrying them down directly over a tree. They hit the obstruction, the car tipped, one of the aeronauts fell out and the other two jumped. Freed from its burden, the balloon began to ascend, but several helpers grabbed the ropes and hauled it back. Pleased with the result, the Gerli brothers and their assistants guided the still-inflated balloon a quarter of a mile back to their point of departure, where they were greeted with tears and shouts of rapture. The brothers gave the eternal honor of being the first in Italy "to attempt and succeed in voyaging through the unlimited pastures of celestial space" to their benefactor, Count Andreani.

Ill-advisedly, the lesson learned by the brothers was that "if one hits a high obstacle when coming down one runs no risk of injury. If one has the wherewithal to feed the fire, one can easily avoid descending in an inconvenient spot and can, in fact, choose the place where one would wish to land." Ultimately, both parts of this statement would prove false, as striking trees or chimneys and the inability to choose a landing site would factor in the injury and deaths of future aeronauts.[5]

Under the Eyes of the Public

Jean-Pierre François Blanchard (1753–1809), in his ascension from the Champ de Mars on March 2, 1784, applied the principles of mechanics to the discovery of the air balloon to demonstrate the practicality of directing the course of an aerostatic machine. Constructing a balloon on the pattern of Charles and Roberts, he added a helm, wings and four tails to his 26-foot diameter envelope in hope of confounding the powers of the wind. He also included an "umbrella," over the car to prevent falling too fast in case of accident.[6]

After issuing an immense number of tickets, a crowd comprised of people from all ranks assembled to watch the marvel. Accompanying Blanchard was a young physician named Dour Pech, a Benedictine of St. Martin des Champs, whose assignment was to make experiments on the atmosphere. At 11:15 A.M. as the moment of ascension approached, Pech seated himself in the vehicle, then brandished his sword in a horrific manner. This action struck the startled spectators as highly inappropriate and they attempted to remove him from the car. The struggle was intense, during the course of which they pressed on the machine, breaking the wings and injuring the balloon.

During the course of the altercation a great deal of gas was discharged, but the efforts proved for naught as the mob failed to persuade Pech from going up. The ascension was attempted, but within a short time the balloon came down, forcing Blanchard to the conclusion there was not enough lifting power for two passengers. This alone forced the Benedictine to resign his seat, although there were calls for the entire experiment to be postponed in lieu of the fact the aeronaut had lost the wings. Blanchard, in the spirit of a Frenchman, said, "I was under the eyes of the public, and my honour was pledged." Rising to an astonishing height, the balloon was pushed by a high wind, carrying it over Paffy. Once there, the machine fell into a perfect calm and remained stationary for a period of fourteen minutes. When the wind picked up, Blanchard re-passed the river and experienced a second calm, this one lasting about a quarter of an hour. Ultimately, a gale sprang up and he was carried with extreme velocity toward Montrouge, tacking four times by means of his helm.

At this point he observed that the balloon was descending from a quantity of air escaping from lacerations in the fabric sustained during the altercation. In order to avoid falling into the river, he discharged his ballast and at length descended on the plain of Ballancourt, having been aloft an hour and fifteen minutes. In his post-flight narrative, Blanchard stated that he experienced extreme heat and afterward, extreme cold, a very sharp appetite and a strong disposition to sleep. Aeronauts soon learned to take hearty meals with them during flights. The propensity to sleep was another common problem, with some passengers actually curling up in the bottom of the basket and drifting off. "Thin air" would become a matter of great interest later in the 19th century.

In regard to a question put to Blanchard as to whether it was possible to direct the aerostatic machines in the air, like the Gerli brothers before him, Blanchard stated that although deprived of his wings, by means of his helm and tails, he was "able not only to withstand the rapidity of the gale, but also to accomplish what none of his predecessors had effected": that of sailing against the wind.[7]

In addition to the actions of the sword-wielding Pech, a number of other balloon stories circulated about soldiers brandishing swords. One in particular described General Dampierre, who reputedly leapt into the car during an ascension in France, waving his sword. When remonstrated for the act, he replied, "If I had fallen and perished, I should have attained celebrity, the very thing I am most solicitous to obtain."[8]

The most common and oft repeated, however, concerned Napoleon Bonaparte. The anecdote had him, when a pupil of the Military Academy at Paris, throwing himself into Blanchard's balloon at the moment of its rising. Once there, he brandished his sword against those who would force him out and did not leave until ordered to do so under express orders of the Governor of the Academy. Although it was wildly believed in France, the British held the story in some contempt, offering numerous other persons as the hero. One fellow so named was the student Dupont, "for whom Viscount *Mirabeau*, who witnessed and admired the boldness of his conduct, immediately procured a commission in the regiment of *Touraine*. This spirited young man is no Republican General, but runs a career far more honourable at the army of the Prince of *Conde*."

The Painter and the Opera Singer

It would be impossible to overstate the fact that 1784 was a year of discovery and invention. Not only did the first men fly un-tethered in a balloon, great advances were made in the science of aerostation, as the thrill of aviation spread around the globe. Of particular wonder was an ascent on June 4 when a balloon ascended from Lyons with two passengers: a man named M. Fleurant, a painter, and a woman named Elisabeth Tible, a French opera singer. The presence of one belonging to the "weaker sex" served as titillation and drew the crowds to witness the flight of *La Gustave*, named after Gustave III of Sweden, who was present for the occasion.

The vessel rose over the houses of Lyons, until the scene below "seemed to us like a shapeless mass of pebbles." After throwing out a second flag, the aeronauts experienced a numbing cold and a humming in their ears, so that they feared they would no longer be able to hear one another. The sensation passed and Mme. Tible sang "La Belle Arsene" ("I am victorious, I am Queen"), after which Fleurant sang the song of Zemire and Azor, "what travelling in the clouds."

The descent went smoothly, but as the balloon touched ground, it burst open at the top and the canvas toppled upon them. Fleurant cut his way out with a knife and went to rescue his "fearless companion," only to find her already out of danger. One of the rescuers refused to believe they all had landed safely, however, as he heard a cry for help. The aeronauts tried to explain the situation, but as he persisted in his belief, an investigation proved him correct. On descending, the balloon had landed on the head of a would-be rescuer, trapping him beneath the car. The man, calling out for help, was freed, and suffered no more than singed clothing from the brazier.[9]

"Marie-Antoinette" Goes Up in Smoke

On June 23, 1784, at Versailles, the grand balloon *Marie-Antoinette* ascended at 4:45 P.M. in a cloud of glory. Among a massive gathering, which included King Louis XVI of France and King Gustave III of Sweden (for whom the vessel had been constructed to mark his visit), the montgolfière-type machine rose to the salvo of three large mortars, musicians playing *The Deserter*, and cries of "Long live the Queen!"

Under the guiding hand of Pilâtre de Rozier, the vessel rose slowly. Everything appeared to indicate a perfect flight, when a gust of wind seemed to snatch the montgolfière "out of human hands," and toss it about in irregular, dangerous spasms. The crowd scattered for fear the vessel would descend on their heads, but de Rozier stoked the fire in the brazier, the balloon continued its upward movement, and disaster was temporarily averted.

Complacency did not last long. Caught in a strong current, the balloon listed dangerously to one side. Joseph Proust, his fellow passenger, was directed to walk around the platform for 8 or 10 minutes to restore balance, then more heat was generated. Responding to the rarefied air, a further altitude was obtained and soon the earth was lost from sight. Clouds soon emptied a layer of snow in the car and dense fog prevented further observations.

Although the barometer had fallen nine inches and the thermometer 16 degrees, the aeronauts determined to reach the maximum height possible. Lifting up the furnace, they stuffed faggots into the fire, making it as hot as possible. Drifting among the expanse of snow, de Rozier determined they had reached a height of 11,732 feet, in a temperature 5° below freezing.

Eighteen minutes after their departure, unable to make any further meteorological observations, the aeronauts decided to lower themselves to a point where they could once more view the ground and ascertain their surroundings. All at once, "as though the curtain hiding nature had been drawn back, we suddenly discovered a thousand different things spread over an area which, to our eyes, almost defied measure," and in the space of one minute they passed from winter into spring.

Writing eloquently of his sensations at such a moment, de Rozier observed that what he beheld was the work of faeries suddenly come to life, creating a world in miniature. "It is in this bewitched state that the soul rises, thoughts are exalted, and follow one another on with amazing rapidity."

Noting that a change of position brought no unsteadiness to the platform, he concluded that previous reports of such a condition were the result of faulty construction of the balloon in question, or panic of the travellers — a comment not likely to endear himself to those who would readily recognize, and be recognized, by others.

Dazzled by the adventure, they descended and rose at will. Having the ability to create a greater quantity of rarified air was a marked advantage of the montgolfière type mechanism; a balloon raised by hydrogen was limited by the gas generated during inflation. Once the valve had been opened to let gas escape, the aeronauts had no power to add more.

Unable to determine their speed except by judging how fast the villages below them disappeared, they arrived at Luzarche and determined to effect a landing. A large gathering appeared below, with hands up-stretched to grab their ropes and pull them down, while animals of all descriptions "fled from our shadow, terrified, as if they had taken the Montgolfière for some savage beast." But upon determining they were too close to the houses, the aeronauts fed their fire and abandoned their dumbfounded would-be rescuers.

In order to avoid the massive forest bordering the Compiegne, and fearing their supply of fuel would run short if they continued further, the aeronauts made a descent at a crossroads in the forest of Chantilly near the Manon road, thirteen leagues from Versailles, at 5:32 P.M. With no ground assistance to grab the ropes, the fierce wind gripped the top portion of the montgolfière and dragged it across the field. Inevitably, this jarring action propelled flames through the grill of the brazier, burning the ropes on the gallery.

Realizing what a disaster it would be if fire spread into the canvas gas-filled envelope, the aeronauts frantically attempted to sever the bindings. With nothing more than a dull knife, they labored for half an hour before de Rozier threw the instrument away in disgust. Thus unarmed, they tore at the envelope, finally managing to shove the unwieldy mass away from the open flames.

Separating the car from the balloon proved more difficult, forcing de Rozier to search for the knife he had so foolishly discarded. Unable to find it and near panic at the thought of fire transferring from the ropes to the inflammable gas, they increased their efforts. Dragging aside the canopy and cylinder that were new and valuable, they might have suffered the ultimate indignation of seeing the *Marie-Antoinette* explode before their eyes, when two men ran up to help. Offered the promise of recompense, the rescuers carried the machinery a safe distance away. What they could not save was the tapering end of the montgolfière that had been used during the first experiments at Versailles and la Muette.

By this time, the aeronauts' struggles had attracted a crowd. In order to prevent a "disturbance," de Rozier distributed pieces of the lower part of the balloon among them as souvenirs.[10] Their flight set records for speed, altitude and distance traveled.

4

Rowing with Wings and Other Oddities

The outcries of the peasants invited us to return; I maneuvered in consequence, and we accosted them at about the height of one hundred feet. Some were clapping their hands together, others kneeling, and the greater part of them running away terrified. The most courageous contemplated us, and exclaimed, "Are you men, or gods?— What are you?— Make yourselves known!" We replied, we are men like you, and here is a proof of it. We took off our coats, and threw them down; they seized upon them eagerly, and began to divide them in pieces.[1]

Early aeronauts fervently believed that their aerostatic machine could be navigated, or directed in any manner they wished, even against prevailing wind currents. Every conceivable method was tried, but the most prevalent system was one that involved the use of oars.

On April 25, 1784, Guyton de Morveau and the Abbé Bertrand prepared for an ascent at Dijon, having prepared the Académie de Dijon's aerostatic machine with oars (two on each side) and a rudder, in order to demonstrate the practicality of aerial navigation. After determining the "specific lightness" of the machine to be 550 pounds, the two voyagers entered the car, along with their meteorological instruments, comestibles and 75–80 pounds of ballast.

When set free at 3:48 P.M., the eddying wind currents struck the church of St. Benigne, creating a whirlpool effect that threatened to fling the vessel against the building walls. Fearful of being thrown against the steeple and toppling into the houses below, the aeronauts rapidly tossed out all their ballast — something experienced pilots would learn never to do at any cost. The decrease in weight had the desired effect, and the balloon ascended at a prodigious rate.

Once above the clouds, the sun heated the inflammable air to such an extent the envelope filled out to dangerous proportions. Realizing the danger of over-inflation could cause the material to burst, the pilots opened both valves in the expectation of lessening the pressure. This did not have the desired effect and consequently a tear, seven or eight inches long, developed close to the appendix. Gas escaped, which the pair erroneously considered a providential occurrence.

At 5:05 P.M., floating over a town they did not recognize, they wrote a note in pencil, tied it to a ball filled with bran and a streamer and dropped it. The missive contained information that the aeronauts felt perfectly fit and provided the barometer reading as 20 inches, 9 lines, the temperature as one degree below zero and the hygrometer at 59 degrees on the M. de Retz scale. According to their watch, it took 57 seconds to reach the ground.

Finding their only complaint a piercing cold biting at their ears, they determined to land after observing the lower part of the balloon flattening. In hopes of descending near Auxonne, they began the experiment of navigation. Unfortunately (a word associated with ballooning nearly as often as "magnificent"), the equipment proposed for this trial had been severely damaged during ascent. The rudder had become dislodged and one of the oars broke away the first time they tried using it. Additionally, the "equatorial oar" on the same side became entangled in the ropes and proved impossible to extricate.

The remaining oars, being on the same side, proved of little use, but they did manipulate them "to some effect" in propelling the vessel in the desired eastward direction.

The once-providential rent ultimately proved a danger, as too much gas had escaped. Approaching the landing site, they had nothing left for ballast but the planks, which they tore from the machine and threw overboard. This lowered them over a copse of trees called "Le Chaignet," belonging to the Comtesse Ferdinande de Brun. After striking the tops, the balloon rebounded, despite their efforts to grab the branches.

Fortunately, the inhabitants of Magny-les-Auxonne came to their rescue, but only after receiving assurances that the aeronauts wished them no ill will. At 6:25 P.M., after the machine was pulled to the ground, the rescuers knelt on the ground in front of the balloon, either in praise to their God for saving them from the aerial monster, or acknowledging divine intervention for the delivery of two men from the clouds.

When news of their safe delivery reached Dijon, a party comprising three quarters of the town went out to welcome the aeronauts and participate in the triumph. The celebrants reached home at 8:45 P.M. on April 26, having installed the aeronauts in a carriage and announcing their arrival with town trumpeters.[2]

Early aeronauts did, indeed, seem to be blessed with inexplicable luck, for the safe landings could easily have turned tragic. Suffering considerable damage during ascensions and hovering over treetops without ballast were recipes for failure. How long such fortune would last was anyone's guess.

"Are You Men or Gods? What Are You?"

Blanchard's third aerial ascent look place on July 18, 1784, from the old barracks of Rouen at 5:15 P.M. His companion for the trip was M. Boby, whose mission aboard the balloon was to take scientific measurements and observations. With 210 pounds of ballast, they arose majestically, saluting the spectators with flags. Continuing upward, the barometer fell four inches and six lines in seven minutes, the thermometer falling 18° in the same time.

Using the wings affixed to either side of the balloon, they were able to turn west out of an air current. After rising a considerable distance and admiring the grandeur of the scene, they endeavored to descend by the aid of wings alone, performing the act so precipitously that those below believed them to be falling. In order to alleviate their fears, the aeronauts threw out a quantity of ballast and reversed course, recording the fact that at 5:32 P.M. the barometer had fallen to 21 inches. At this point they became becalmed and again manipulated the balloon by means of wings.

At 5:56, they reached a point where the barometer stood at 20 inches and the thermometer at 9°. Following a northeast track, they covered much ground, although only a check of his instruments would convince Boby they were not stationary. At 6:06 they found the barometer to have risen to 25 inches and they could hear the inhabitants of Saint Saen calling to them. After saluting with flags they continued on, discharging a portion of ballast in order to ascend.

Coming upon the town of Neufchatel, Boby wished to descend and pay compliments to his friends there *en passant*. Blanchard agreed and they directed their course to that point, passing through a degree of cold that caused condensation in the balloon, prompting a portion of it to collapse.

After drinking to the health of the city of Rouen, the earth in general, and friends at Neufchatel in particular, they tossed an unopened bottle of wine out of the car, watching it fall with such violence "that the liquor escaped like a copious smoke in the form of vapour."

With each man taking one side, they worked the wings forcibly for three minutes, descending near the town of Neufchatel, where they managed to hover as the citizens "made the air resound" with Blanchard's name. Leaving them behind, the pair continued toward the sea, the crossing of the English Channel being Blanchard's goal. The hour growing late, however, he determined to forgo the trial and bring the machine down. Boby opened the valve and they descended rapidly in order to avoid landing in the sea. Bringing the balloon into equilibrium by the discharge of ballast, the aeronauts came over a plain. Dropping lower, the car touched on a patch of trefoil, where the pair encountered a great number of peasants running towards them. Boby immediately divined their purpose as hostile and proposed they re-ascend. Effecting the procedure by means of their wings, they reached a height of nearly 12,000 feet in a calm air.

The cries of the onlookers encouraged them to descend, when the most courageous exclaimed, "Are you men, or gods?—What are you?—Make yourselves known!" After reassuring them they were indeed men by tossing down their clothes, a curious means of establishing kinship with *Homo sapiens*, they pulled away while observing the scene below, a spectacle affording them considerable amusement. Finally convinced the peasants meant them no harm, they lowered the balloon. The men "stretched out their arms toward us, joy was depicted in the countenances of some, while others shed tears of rapture." The balloon descended over a field of corn, stalks supporting its weight. In that manner they skimmed over the top until at last the balloon came to rest upon the earth, having one hundred ten pounds of ballast remaining. The plain of Puissanval where they landed at 7:30 P.M. was fifteen leagues from the place of departure.

In closing his narrative, Blanchard noted that in the course of their journey a lamp would not have been extinguished and thus concluded that sails adapted to an aerostatic machine would never swell.[3]

While it would appear from Blanchard's account that he had considerable success with the wings attached to the balloon, one test could not prove the practicality of the idea. As demonstrated by the trial at Dijon, only a perfect ascent could preserve the fragile appendages from breaking. Nor did Blanchard encounter any strong gales on his flight. Subsequent trials would not prove nearly as successful, and although visionaries would persist in the desire to control the direction of an air balloon, the concept never achieved the desired effect.

There were other "effects" to achieve, however, and Blanchard was acutely aware of the public enthusiasm — and private gain — to be achieved by good relations. After this ascent, he was entertained at the house of M. and Madame Dudonet, where the neighboring nobility assembled to share in the celebrations. In the morning, seeing that the ladies desired to ascend in his balloon, Blanchard invited the Marchioness de Brossond to make a tethered trip with him. After reaching a height of eighty feet, the vessel was drawn down and the navigator graciously gave his seat to Madame de Jean. The two women ascended together, thus becoming the first contingent of all-female passengers in an air balloon.

In turn, the Countess de Bouhers, the Countess de Roquigny, Madame Dudonet, Madame de Vallours, Mademoiselle de Lignemorre, Mademoiselle de Crouteile, Mademoiselle Duquesnoy, and Madam de Milleville all ascended. Blanchard noted the women acted with so much spirit, they would all have made excellent companions on a difficult voyage.[4]

An Overabundance of Ballast

As with most phenomena of popular culture, everyone wanted to take part. The early years of aerostation were filled with reports of balloonists ascending, most from various parts of France, where the movement took hold with great enthusiasm. Along with the penchant for manual navigation developed the obsession of taking scientific observations. Among the first who attempted such an ambitions project were Coustard de Massi, Chevalier de St. Louis and R.P. Mouchet, a teacher of physics at the Oratory, who ascended in their hydrogen gas balloon from Nantes on June 14, 1784.

Under the supervision of M. Levesque, correspondent of the Académie Royale des Sciences, a balloon composed of oiled silk, with a diameter of 30 feet, 4 inches, was prepared. Beside the aeronauts, it carried 245 pounds of ballast and all necessary scientific instruments. The cargo proved too heavy for ascension, rising and sinking twice before gaining sufficient altitude. This turbulence broke their fragile observation equipment, reducing the actual flight to little more than a sightseeing exhibition.

After gaining an altitude of 150–180 fathoms they reached Valette, where the machine began to descend at a precipitous rate. Suffering the fate of others, the aeronauts, having tossed overboard all their ballast, were reduced to lightening their load by jettisoning the only material yet left to them: their speaking trumpets and two bottles. This afforded some relief, but the balloon ultimately struck the earth, bouncing over the landscape. Lacking any means of protecting themselves, a problem that would plague all aeronauts, they were violently thrown about the car as the vessel struck trees and other objects.

At Geste, nine leagues from Nantes, they were finally in a position to leap from the car without serious harm. The balloon, freed from their combined 300 pounds of weight, rose rapidly and in two minutes was out of sight. It was later found in Poitou, a village near Brefenaire, 22 leagues from Nantes.

After the flight, Levesque noted that he considered zinc more suitable than iron in creating hydrogen, being less costly when used with "Goslar's vitriol," one of the earliest "product placement ads" in the history of aerostation.[5]

Awful Grandeur—An American Boy

In June 1784, Philadelphia newspapers ran advertisements announcing the proposed construction of an air balloon 60 feet tall, to be composed of silk and "properly lined, covered, varnished, and painted by the best artists." Subscriptions were open to any wishing to be a part of the First American Ascension. By buying into the flight, they would be aiding the aeronauts in procuring "new proofs of the sublime workmanship of the great Architect of the Universe."[6]

Imagine the shock of the promoters when they learned that an obscure barkeep in

This painting represents the first American ascent in a balloon, June 24, 1784, from Bladensburg, Maryland. Carnes, the creator of the aerostat, was too heavy to be lifted, and so the honor went to a 13-year-old boy named Edward Warren (by permission of the National Air and Space Museum, Smithsonian Institution, Washington, D.C.).

Maryland was well on his way to beating them to the punch. Peter Carnes, an itinerant adventurer known more for his humor than any particular accomplishments, had become fascinated with aerostation after exposure to the experiments of the Montgolfier brothers, most likely through the local newspapers.

Perhaps "fascinated" is too strong a word. Carnes was more closely aligned with the American pitchmen of the mid–19th century than members of the 18th century bar, of which he was a member. With a keen nose for making a profit, it could not have taken him long to realize there was money to be made "in that thar scheme," and he set about constructing his own aerostat. Although Carnes had never seen such a device, his ingenuity must have been great, for on June 24, 1784, "in the Presence of a numerous and respectable congress of people," gathered to witness the "awful grandeur of so novel a scene," he attempted to become the first American to ascend in a balloon.

The place he chose for this momentous occasion was Howard Park, in Bladensburg, Maryland. A number of tethered flights were made during the day, and it was supposed Carnes, himself, had anticipated going up, but his prodigious weight of 234 pounds proved too much for the montgolfière to carry. The crowd might have gone away well satisfied with the unmanned spectacle, but they were destined to witness a far more newsworthy event. Before the last flight of the day, a lad of 13 years named Edward Warren approached the operator and volunteered his services. His offer was accepted, and up he ascended, behaving "with the Steady fortitude of an Old Voyager."

The gathering saluted him with loud applause and as he soared aloft, he politely acknowledged the adoration by a wave of his hat.

"When he returned to our terrene Element, he met with a Reward, from some of the Spectators, which had a *solid*, instead of an *airy*, Foundation, and of a Species which is ever acceptable to the Residents of this *lower World*."[7]

Thus, it happened that a child, similar to the childlike nation to which he belonged, inscribed his name in the history of the United States.

The Unhappy Authors of a Failed Experiment

As early as March 1784, notice was given that construction was underway in France for creation of the largest montgolfière ever made. Subscription tickets depicting a rather bizarre-looking balloon with several flags and peculiar attachments rising above dark, billowing clouds were issued and sold like hotcakes.

The plan was to raise the balloon from the same place it had been built. It measured 112 feet in height and 84 in diameter, with a reported total lifting force of 140,000. So great was the size, that on tests conducted June 17 and 30, the craft held nine people and a staggering 900 pounds of ballast. At that, ten workmen would not have been able to hold it down, had not the inflation process been stopped. Notwithstanding, the volume of the balloon was increased by 40,000 cubic feet, resulting in an increase of 800 pounds lifting power.

On July 11, the machine was removed to the Luxembourg Gardens, and at noon was set out for display. A huge crowd gathered to watch the proceedings and the ascent of Abbé Miollan and Janinet. Among the spectators were the Duke of Chartres, the Marquis de Cassini, M. Jeaurat Mechain, and the Comte de Milli, all members of the Académie des Sciences.

The first signal was given two hours and fifteen minutes later than advertised; the second signal, indicating the lighting of the fire, followed at 3:00. By this time, however, the heat of the day and the hot rays of the sun had created an unfavorably hot temperature and the balloon failed to inflate properly. Desperate efforts were taken to complete the process and several alternate methods were tried, but to no avail. When it became apparent the trial would be a failure, the ire of the public was aroused and they stormed the garden. Madly tearing the fabric of the balloon, they smashed the gallery, chairs, instruments and whatever else they could reach. Eventually the balloon was torched, with the public remaining unsatisfied until everything was burned.

Not content to let the matter drop, the aeronauts were lambasted in the newspapers and many satires, irate editorials and vituperative cartoons were published at their expense.[8]

Things did not get better for the proponents of aerostation. In a letter from Paris, dated July 26, it was reported that Mons. Molland ascended in a 100 feet high and 90 feet diameter balloon, with which he had made an experimental flight two days before near Chantilly. Three persons went up, but after the globe ascended to a considerable height it suddenly burst, falling with great rapidity. One passenger broke his thigh and the other two were greatly injured.[9]

Never Did a More Dreadful Scene Present Itself

The Roberts brothers, together with the Duke de Chartres, prepared an entirely new navigation machine by constructing an exterior set of twelve-foot-long oars, fixed to a ten-foot lever placed at the extremity of the gallery. Additionally, they devised a cylindrical machine terminating in two hemispheres, suspended in the middle of which was a second, smaller balloon containing atmospheric air. A bellows, fixed to the gallery, was used to fill this envelope after it became compressed by the dilatation of the inflammable air in the larger balloon. "By this means they had provided an excess of weight proportioned to the quantity of atmospheric air introduced into this internal globe, and consequently when they had gained their equilibrium in the atmosphere, they could mount or descend at will, without any loss of atmospheric air."

On the 15th of July 1784, the ascension was made from St. Cloud Park. Departing at the early hour of 8:00 A.M., expectations were heightened by having the "elegantly dressed" wives of the Roberts hold down two of the cords attached to the vessel. When the signal was given, the ladies cut the cords and the aerostat rose. Rising with "slow and awesome majesty," the balloon was lost to sight in three minutes.

The aeronauts were carried to an immense height, where the balloon was buried in a dense vapor and spun by powerful whirlwinds. This violent action forced them to abandon plans for navigating with the wings, and in a frantic attempt to arrest their upward progress, they tore away the taffeta.

Never, they reported, did a more dreadful scene present itself than the "ocean of shapeless clouds" which seemed to prevent their return to the distant and invisible earth. With the agitation of the balloon growing worse, they cut the cord holding the interior balloon. Rather than have the desired effect of arresting their progress, the material collapsed, and by its weight "crushed, jammed up, and incommoded them." Using all their strength, the voyagers endeavored to push it away, and at length it burst.

The loss of this secondary balloon did not, however, relieve their distress, as the primary envelope continued to carry them upward. Out of necessity, de Chartres cut two holes, eight feel long, in the lower part of the existing globe. This caused a great escape of gas and the balloon plunged downward. At the last moment, a quantity of ballast was discharged and they were enabled to land without accident thirty feet from a pond.[10]

This trial proved the impossibility of navigating with oars or wings under less than ideal conditions.

As the summer wore on, voyages continued to fill newspapers and draw crowds. On August 13, Blanchard arose in his balloon from Amiens, accompanied by a gentleman and two ladies, marking yet another ascent by the "fairer sex." The aeronauts expected to reach Calais in four hours. In what was to become a standard of aerostatic reporting, the article concluded, "but as nothing has since been heard of those hardy adventurers, the public were under the greatest apprehension for their safety." In this case, their fears proved groundless.[11]

The same month, de Rozier rose from Versailles at 4:45 and landed at Chantilly at 5:32 P.M., having traveled 13 leagues, or 39 miles, in less than an hour. He was reputed to have risen 11,700 feet, and encountered great quantities of snow and hail, finding his thermometer falling to 5° below "congelation."[12]

The month of September 1784, however, belonged to Vincent Lunardi.

5

A Reservation for Hope

To combat the prejudices of a nation, and the incredulity of mankind, especially when deterred by examples of resentment in consequence of deception or misfortune; when awed by the danger incurred in experiment, and the uncertainty of success in the project, must certainly require the greatest effort of human resolution to encounter.[1]

It began inauspiciously. On September 14, 1784, Dr. George Fordee, charged with overseeing the filling of the balloon, remained with the machine until 12:00 A.M., when he retired to his home for a few hours rest. Prior to his departure, he gave strict instructions to the laborers to oversee the creation of inflammable gas with zinc, oil of vitriol and steel shavings.

When Fordee returned at 4:00 A.M., he was greeted with a shocking sight: the workmen had gotten drunk and completely neglected their duty. The balloon was no further along in the inflation process that it had been at midnight. He immediately set about correcting the situation, but the balloon required at least four more hours of filling before it was capable of lifting up the two adventurers scheduled to make an ascent that morning.

The aerial voyage, long proposed by Vincent Lunardi and paid for by subscription, attracted the greatest number of persons ever witnessed within the environs of Moorfield, England. Included among the spectators was the Prince of Wales. After reviewing the apparatus, he and his entourage retired to the Artillery House, joining other persons "who had liberally paid for their admission." Also attending the spectacle were Messrs. Blanchard and Boby, the two celebrated French navigators. "The former, from motives of delicacy, was not in the Artillery ground, but Mr. Boby was present, and gave his assistance in filling and raising the balloon." The King, himself, viewed the proceedings through a telescope from the Queen's Presence Chamber.

Vincent Lunardi, belonging to a good family of Naples, had recently served as principal secretary to Prince Caramanico, the Neapolitan ambassador to England. When asked what he thought of the expedition he was about to undertake, Lunardi replied, "I have an Alexander's *hope!*" alluding to the expression of that warrior who said, when preparing for his famous expedition: "Thus did I dispose of my hereditary dominions, and reserve for myself *hope!*"

Discovering the balloon did not have sufficient lifting power to carry two individuals, Lunardi ascended alone with a cat, dog, and pigeon, safely stowed in little cages. Following two rounds of cannon shot, the aeronaut embraced his friends, assumed his place and ascended at 2:05 P.M. The balloon rose twelve yards and then dropped back to earth. He discharged a portion of ballast, consisting of small bags of white sand, and the machine commenced a most regular and beautiful ascension.

Clearing the buildings, Lunardi saluted the crowd by waving a blue flag from the gallery and took up his oars. This proved a failure, as one promptly broke and fell to earth, alarming the company. Near the same time, the resourceful pigeon escaped.[2] Stabilizing the machine, the aeronaut tacked toward the north, attaining a considerable elevation.

The balloon remained in sight for one hour and twenty minutes until more ballast was discharged and it sailed away. Looking down upon earth, Lunardi wrote, "The stillness, extent, and magnificence of the scene, rendered it highly awful.... It was an enormous beehive, but the industry of it was suspended.... I had soared from the apprehensions and anxieties of the Artillery Ground, and felt as if I had left behind me all the cares and passions that molest mankind."[3]

During the flight, the dog and cat fell asleep and he suffered the same tendency, but fought it off. Twice descending by letting out inflammable air by means of a brass cock, at Hornsby he came so low to earth that he was enabled to speak to people on the ground. Seeing the cat was having difficulty breathing and nearly exhausted, he either "threw it out," "delivered," or "landed the cat" to an old woman.

On re-ascending, Lunardi's water froze, obliging him "to drink freely of the liquor he had in his car to prevent his perishing from cold" (reportedly twelve glasses of Madeira). The thermometer reached six degrees below freezing, and moisture in the atmosphere covered the gallery.

Moving into another strata, the temperature reached 32° where the inflated balloon assumed the form of an oblong spheroid, lacking nearly one third of its full complement of air. Having no valve, he attempted to open the neck of the balloon to expel the rarefied air, but found the condensed vapor around the neck frozen.

Having exhausted his ballast, everything was jettisoned, including plates, knives and forks. After extensive and exhausting labor with the oar, he managed to bring the vessel close to earth.[4] The balloon eventually floated over Collier's-hill, five miles beyond Ware, in Hertfordshire, and at 5:25 he descended at a farm called Collier's End, 26 miles from London, after a voyage of three and a half hours. Upon hitting the ground, the balloon rolled, driving Lunardi against a tree. Quite benumbed by exposure and clothes covered with ice, Lunardi sought help from a girl in the field who was much frightened by his sudden appearance. After he explained the situation, she readily assisted him from the car.

The much worn aeronaut spent the night near Hertford. The balloon survived its voyage in fine condition — albeit without one of its oars.[5]

Lunardi's successful flight earned him the honor of having completed the first free flight in England. Shortly after the voyage he was presented to the King and entertained by the Sheriffs of London at the Sessions House in the Old Bailey.[6] The time was fast approaching when aeronauts would be considered more pests than honored men, but for the moment, there were plenty of high spirits to go around.

Floating in the Air

James Sadler (1753–1828), son of a pastry cook and confectioner, inherited his father's business on High Street in Oxford, but his interests lay in chemistry. These talents skillfully sidelined him into aerostation and on October 4, 1784, he became the first Englishman to ascend in a balloon.[7]

Sadler prepared his "Fire Balloon" (a montgolfière of his own invention) for an ascension at Oxford, creating rarefied air by means of a brazier in the gallery, a process beginning at 3:00 P.M. and concluding at 5:30. On this calm and serene day, he rose into the atmosphere to a height of 3,900 feet. The barometer, which at ground level stood at 29 inches, descended to 24 inches and five lines, while the temperature steadily grew colder.

After viewing the landscape appearing as "one extensive plain," he discharged a portion of air and gradually descended, the globe going through a series of extensions and compressions. He soon struck a light breeze, driving the balloon in a horizontal direction with great rapidity. Quickly approaching a wood, Sadler made extensive use of his oars. Remarking on the effectiveness of the propelling device, which made it extremely easy for him to turn at pleasure — while the air remained calm — he floated for another half an hour before gently descending upon a small eminence between Islip and Wood-Eaton.[8]

His second ascent took place on November 12, 1784, at the Physic Garden in Oxford. Ascending in his balloon before an immense crowd, Sadler was swept rapidly over the Otmoor and Thames. After a brief journey of 17–20 minutes he landed on the estate of Sir William Lee at Hartwell, near Aylesbury in Buckinghamshire. He was unable to secure the balloon, so it was dragged a considerable distance before becoming entangled in some trees.

Sadler's third trip in a balloon came on May 5, 1785, from the gardens of Mr. Dodwell at Moulsey Hurst, neat Hampton-Court. His machine was filled in a scant 25 minutes and rose with uncommon velocity, carrying the aeronaut, one passenger, the Hon. William Windham, M.P. for Norwich, and 3 hundred weight (cwt.) of ballast along with mathematical instruments.

Members of the Royal Society who viewed the ascent "were highly entertained as well as surprised at the various maneuvers performed by the aeronauts, who were hovering about the spot for nearly an hour and a half before the balloon bore away." During the voyage Windham suffered from extreme pain in his ears at the height of two and a half miles.

Their aim had been to reach France, but they were unable to repeat the earlier exploit of Jean-Pierre Blanchard, and were forced to make their descent in an estuary where the Thames and Medway joined. Owing to the difficulty arising when the local peasants came to assist them, the balloon got away and rebounded with great velocity, finally landing three leagues from Nore.[9] Fortunately for the statesman, the will he made before departing Earth was not required.

Sadler completed four more voyages in 1785, two of which were made from Manchester. On the second, he ascended to a height of 13,000 feet and traveled 50 miles before a near-disastrous landing at Pontefract. Again failing to secure the balloon, he was dragged for two miles before being toppled from the car. The balloon sailed away, while he sustained several injuries from his fall.

With pleas from people all over the country for him to make an ascent, Sadler chose Worcester. In September 1785, he made his first successful flight there. A repeat performance the following month, however, proved the exact opposite. As was often the case, he had trouble securing the balloon on the ground after a descent. Without an anchor (later called a grappling iron) in place, the wind buffeted the aerial machine across the countryside for a distance of five miles. Barely able to cling to the car, Sadler was ultimately thrown out and fell a short distance to the ground.[10] He was badly bruised and perhaps worse, once freed from his weight, the balloon arose and was not recovered, a very substantial financial loss.

Whether from monetary reasons or because he had a premonition things could only get worse, Sadler retired from the profession. In 1796, he was appointed Chemist in the newly created Naval Works Department under Sir Samuel Bentham. His time there was apparently an unhappy one as he did not get along with Bentham and carried out few works. He did experiment with the application of steam power to road vehicles and patented a rotary steam engine.[11] Sadler would reappear in 1810, twenty-four years later, and go on to become one of England's greatest aeronauts.

Pilot Balloons, Pigeons and Pickpockets

The English, being notoriously skeptical, were ultimately forced to admit the possibilities and the fascinations of ballooning by recent successes in the Kingdom and abroad. When it was announced, therefore, that Blanchard would make his Fourth Aerial Ascent from Mr. Lochee's Military Academy at Little Chelsea, an immense crowd gathered on Saturday, October 19, 1784, to witness the proceedings.

Prior to Blanchard and his passenger, Mr. Sheldon (a professor of anatomy at the Royal Academy), taking their seats in the boat-shaped gallery, they brought aboard pigeons, a dog and provisions. A small gilt pilot balloon was let off to ascertain the direction and the velocity of the upper air currents. Setting off pilot balloons actually became something of a ritual, and audiences looked forward to these small spectacles almost as much as the marquee event.

Typical of the times, creating inflammable gas and inflating the envelope consisted of equal parts science, experience (or lack thereof) and guesswork. The vessel eventually ascended over the heads of the spectators in the garden, but hardly in "majestic style." It promptly descended a short distance away, bounced, rose a second time, succeeded in mounting (in this sense meaning "rising above") a wall, then sunk again. The aeronauts threw out a greatcoat and some sand bags, finally succeeding in rising with great velocity.

Waving French and English flags, the balloon, constructed of green and light yellow silk ("a mixture which had a poor effect in ascending"), was soon caught in a northeast wind. Remaining in sight for a quarter of an hour, Sheldon employed his time waving his flag, while Blanchard used his efforts to give the balloon direction.

The floating machine passed over Hammersmith, Chiswick and Twickenham, where the aeronauts tossed out a considerable number of cards, meant to acquaint friends and the public of their condition. When they reached their highest elevation, Blanchard dispatched a hapless pigeon with a message, but as the air was too thin and light to support its weight, the bird fluttered in great pain, only with severe difficulty making it back to the vessel. It then piteously hid under Sheldon's seat. When the balloon descended a considerable distance, the bird was thrown out over Hampshire. This time able to fly, it delivered its message to Oxford Street.

Shortly thereafter, the balloon began a gradual descent, and after determining the lifting power of the gas insufficient to carry two men, Sheldon agreed to disembark and allow his friend to continue a solo voyage. Accordingly, a little after 1:00, they touched ground at Sunbury, near Hampton Court, where a number of horsemen who had followed their progress, including the Prince of Wales, greeted the duo. After supping together and taking on more ballast, Blanchard re-ascended, quickly reaching an altitude much higher than previously.

On the morning of the exhibition, the King had sent Blanchard a message, asking that if at all possible, he direct his course toward Windsor. When Blanchard, "with the gallantry of a Frenchman," reached the castle, he wrote a letter addressed to *Monsieur le Roi*. Fastening it to a bladder, he sent it down but due to atmospheric pressure, the bladder burst with a loud retort. When appraised that the balloon was overhead, their Majesties went to the Observatory where, with the assistance of glasses, they watched the aerial progression.

Blanchard finally came to earth at 4:00 P.M. at Rumsey, in Hampshire, 73 miles from London. The journey took less than three and a half hours (subtracting the time spent at Sunbury) and was calculated to have attained a speed of 29 miles per hour. The projected journey had been planned to last longer, but failing light put an end to the exhibition. The descent was completed by means of a rope fastened to the boat and hauled down by bystanders. With the balloon still inflated and Blanchard in the car, he was carried to the marketplace in triumph.

At 3:00 the following day, both aeronauts arrived at Chelsea, where they were met by their committee (generally composed of men who helped arrange the flight) and conducted to town with great pomp and circumstance. The gondola (a descriptive term used alternately with "car," "basket" and "boat") was placed on the seat of a phaeton in which the men were seated. The committeemen, decorated with white wands and blue ribbons, arranged themselves in pairs and escorted them in high style.

A reporter on the scene observed that Blanchard's balloon was "somewhat less than that of Mr. Lunardi's," but as it carried more weight and was filled in considerably less time, Blanchard, "must be allowed to have carried the science to much greater perfection." At the same time, he allowed that Lunardi's effort "had a much grander and more brilliant ascent."

Two addendums in newspaper accounts are worthy of note: the first, that pickpockets had a particularly busy Saturday, relieving spectators of their purses, watches and handkerchiefs. Like pilot balloons and comparisons between aeronauts, the story of pickpockets would be an ongoing one. The second concerned "a good harvest to the practitioners of Westminster Hall," from numerous projected lawsuits by gardeners and farmers who had their fields and crops destroyed by the mobs of people gathering at points of ascension and landing. Although they would later be chided in the papers for their unpatriotic actions, a number understandably took their cases to court.[12]

Prior to the first English flight, the "betts [sic] in this metropolis were one hundred guineas to one guinea that no person would make an excursion on the same principles in England." But on the success of Lunardi, Sadler and Blanchard, 10:1 odds were offered on who and when a man would succeed in crossing the English Channel from England to the Continent and vice versa, within twelve months.[13]

The completion of that wager would have to wait until 1785. But until then, there was always the question of speed. Who was the fastest? It did not take long before sides were chosen and bets began to fly fast and furiously.

On October 22, 1784, the Edinburgh *Advertiser* confidently reported that Lunardi had challenged Blanchard to a balloon race in three heats: the first with the wind, the second across the wind, and the third, who would succeed the quickest against the wind. Odds were laid on each side, and it was "positively declared" that above 50,000 pounds was already depending.

To better assist aeronauts in achieving speed and navigation, many experiments, some outright bizarre, were tried. At the end of September 1784, the "Fore Balloon" was filled in Lord Foley's garden "in order to see how far it was practicable to make it mount." Unfortunately, it caught fire and was consumed. Whether a new balloon on the same theory would rise like a phoenix from the ashes, it was said that "time will determine."[14]

Perhaps the most unique "gamble of the day" came from Paris in September 1784. A merchant in the Fauxbourg of St. Martin discovered a new way to turn the art of aerostation to profit. Joining several small balloons together, he held onto a cord and managed to ascend a slight distance. Adding more balloons to increase buoyancy, he offered to take persons of either sex up with him, so that they might enjoy the pleasure of ascension for a span of several minutes. The cost of this adventure varied by degree of elevation, and it was that at his place of business, "so great is the crowd of people to ascend, that it is with some difficulty he can keep them in order."[15]

Without question, ballooning was expensive and aeronauts often used creative means to raise money. In October 1784, Lunardi arranged with the proprietors of the Pantheon, one of the largest and most successful theaters in London, to exhibit his balloon. For the price of one shilling, spectators were admitted for a view of the famous vessel. By November 27, less than six weeks after his ascension, the aeronaut settled accounts with the proprietors. His share of the profits came to two thousand eighty-five pounds, five shillings and eight-pence, exclusive of what he received from subscriptions to the actual flight.[16]

The currency of England was broken down into the following denominations:

British Currency

12 pence	equaled	1 shilling
5 shillings	equaled	1 crown
1 pound	equaled	20 shillings (in coin form it was called a sovereign)
1 guinea	equaled	21 shillings

From accounts in the newspapers, it is easy to comprehend why so many dreamed of joining the aerostatic ranks. The position not only held the prospect of high adventure and danger, it dangled the allure of fabulous wealth. Clearly, few rose to the heights of Lunardi — and even he had his critics — but his payout from the theater surpassed what a marquee actor or dramatist received — in considerably shorter time.

It would not take long for other exhibitions of balloons, balloon art and balloon theatrics to be exhibited at the Pantheon and other leading theatres.

Surmounting Every Difficulty

November 30, 1784, saw the first public pairing of a duo, destined to inscribe their names at the forefront of aerostation. Jean-Pierre Blanchard and Dr. John Jeffries ("a person of fortune, from America [Boston], of great literary talents") prepared for the ascent of their balloon from Mackenzie's Rhedarium in Grosvenor Square. The process of filling began at 11:00 A.M. and finished by 2:30. The Prince of Wales, the Duke and Duchess of Devonshire and a large party of their friends assembled to watch the exhibition.

A small pilot balloon, decorated with a blue and orange cockade and blue ribbon, was set off by the Duchess. After ascertaining which way the wind blew, and everything now in readiness, the Duchess and another lady cut the cords holding the machine at 2:40 P.M. Dr. Jeffries saluted the crowd with a naval jack sporting the 13 stars of the American republic, while Blanchard carried an English ensign. Two unsuccessful attempts were made, and it was not until Blanchard, the inventor of a pair of oars or wings, worked the device to give added lift that the balloon ascended. When the balloon neared a chimney, ballast was discharged and the apparatus moved upward.

Once above the metropolis, Blanchard used the oars and sails to progress through the hazy but serene sky, granting the onlookers a spectacular view of its passing. Provided with sufficient refreshment, instruments for observation and defenses against the cold and inclement weather, they planned on remaining aloft as long as possible.

The aeronauts crossed and re-crossed the Thames several times, uncertain on which side to land. Making very rapid time, the balloon passed Shooter's Hill and after a voyage of 21 miles, at last descended on a spot called Stone Marsh, a few miles beyond Dartford in Kent. The aeronauts subsequently said that the voyage was terminated due to extreme cold, which they found "very inconvenient and distressing."

This "short, but most noble and enchanting voyage" set the stage for the historic crossing of the English Channel the following year.[17]

Crossing the Channel became the single most sought after goal in aerostation, with considerable fame and fortune at stake. On December 16, 1784, Blanchard sent his balloon and filling apparatus to Dover for the express purpose of such a voyage, and followed it himself on Friday, December 17. On the other side, Messrs. de Rozier and Charles had been at Calais for a week, preparing for their excursion in the opposite direction. With a new balloon, called a "Cafolo-Montgolfière," they were waiting for a fair wind to convey them across the water. The delays must have caused considerable apprehension, not only to the navigators, but to the would-be spectators, as the nobility and gentry filled the various public houses along the route, hoping for a glimpse of history.[18]

It would not be long coming, for the bells heralding in the new year would hardly be silenced before one of these two competing groups won the laurels. And that achievement hardly registered before tragedy hit.

6

Don Quixote de la Manche

Heaven has crowned my utmost wishes with success; I cannot describe to you the magnificence and beauty of our voyage.[1]

On the 7th of January 1785, Jean-Pierre Blanchard and Dr. John Jeffries prepared to cross the English Channel from the cliffs of Dover. Jeffries had paid 700 pounds to help finance the expedition and another 100 pounds for the privilege of accompanying Blanchard.[2] Frost had occurred the night previous but in the morning the wind was calm, coming from the north-north-west. Taking only three 10-pound sacks of sand as ballast, they ascended rapidly, the barometer falling from 29 inches, seven lines, to 27 inches, three lines.

After two descents, and having reached only two thirds of the way across the water, the aeronauts used the last of their ballast, leaving them in a precarious position. At 2:25 P.M., five or six miles from the French coast, the balloon began a third descent, compelling them to "strip our aerial car, first of our silk and finery; this not giving us sufficient release, we cast one wing, then the other, after which I was obliged to unscrue [sic] and cast away our *moulinet* [winch, turnstile]; yet still approaching the sea very fast, and the boats being much alarmed for us, we, though unwillingly, cast away first one anchor; then the other."[3] Next went their greatcoats and trousers. Still fearful of a descent into the water, they put on cork jackets to enable them to float.

Facing the possibility of certain death, Jeffries offered to throw himself into the sea to save his companion. "We are lost, both of us, and if you believe it will save you to be lightened of my weight, I am willing to sacrifice my life." Fulgence Marion, in *Wonderful Balloon Ascents*, astutely commented, "This story has certainly the appearance of romance, and belief in it is not positively demanded."

If lightening the load did not succeed, the aeronauts faced two choices: either "splatter" into the water, or detach the car from the balloon and hang onto the envelope by ropes, in the errant hope they could maintain that position long enough to reach a point over land and jump to earth.

Fortuitously, the balloon began to ascend of its own accord, and the pair "made a most beautiful and lofty *entrée* into France at three o'clock." Arriving over the forest of *De Felmores*, they faced the dilemma of landing, having no ballast with which to secure a safe descent. With the balloon hovering over the trees, Jeffries grabbed hold of the top branches in an effort to stop their progression, while Blanchard worked the valve. With the American's strength nearly exhausted, air rushed out and twenty-eight minutes later enough had escaped for them to push off and fall the remaining distance. At this point, a number of horsemen

Blanchard and Jeffries, an American, made aeronautic history by becoming the first persons to cross the English Channel in a balloon on January 7, 1785. For this achievement, Blanchard was made a good citizen of Calais and presented with the Freedom of the City medal (by permission of the National Air and Space Museum, Smithsonian Institution, Washington, D.C.).

arrived to render assistance and they were taken to the home of M. De Sandrouin, where they received every kind attention.[4]

Blanchard was presented with the Freedom of the City medal in a box of gold and a petition was set forth to make him a citizen of Calais. The municipal officials purchased the balloon with the intention of exhibiting it in one of the churches as a memorial to the first aeronauts who crossed from England to France. Some time later, Blanchard was presented to the King. (Jeffries, like Buzz Aldrin two centuries later, became a footnote to the historic event.) The pilot received an annual pension of 1,200 livres; the Queen, who was at the gambling tables, placed a sum on a card, and presented the aeronaut with her winnings.[5]

Perhaps the greatest honor for Blanchard, however, came in the form of a nickname: *Don Quixote de la Manche* (the Channel).

The First Tragedy

Although he had been working on a new type of balloon expressly for crossing the English Channel, in this case from France to England, Pilâtre de Rozier was frustrated in his attempt to be the first to accomplish the feat. Thwarted in that desire, he nevertheless determined to make the voyage.

Realizing that the basic montgolfière-type balloon would require too much fuel, he requested and received 40,000 livres from the French government to design what was to be called the "Rozière." As constructed, he created a large hydrogen balloon and underneath placed a hot air balloon. By this method, he hoped to combine the best attributes of both styles by omitting the step of discharging ballast when he wished to ascend and letting off gas when desiring to descend.

Despite criticism by Jacques Charles that the combination was too dangerous and that the reverse crossing added the complexity of adverse wind currents, de Rozier continued various trials. None were particularly successful, but the pressure of achieving a substantial success for France, the weight of having taken money for the development, and his own personal ambition drove him forward. National pride also played a role. With Blanchard's success, France, which had led the world in the development of the aerostatic process, was on the verge of losing out on the honors and profits to be derived by such status.

The enterprise was plagued with numerous delays. While waiting for favorable conditions, the balloon was kept in storage and rats gnawed holes in the envelope. When those were repaired, winter tempests kept de Rozier from flying. Finally, at Boulogne, a date for departure was announced. Again, the weather failed to cooperate and for weeks in succession, trial balloons blew back over the coast, making it impossible to contemplate a journey against the current.

The grand balloon was finally inflated January 13 but, with results of the pilot balloons remaining unfavorable, was left inflated through the 14th. Finally, on January 15, 1785, at four o'clock in the morning, the pilot balloon landed perpendicularly to where it had been launched, and the aeronauts prepared for flight.

Several hours later, de Rozier and his brother, Romain (alternately spelled "Romaine," and variously described as a passenger of no relation, or one who had been instrumental in designing the machine), prepared for their momentous ascent. A nobleman by the name of De Maisonfort offered 200 louis to join them but de Rozier politely refused, explaining the attempt was too dangerous to risk the life of a third person.[6]

With the sound of cannon signaling departure, the balloon rose at seven o'clock at an angle of 60°. Reaching a height of 200 feet, it was caught in a southeast wind and carried out to sea. At this point, 700 feet above sea level, the balloon reached a new current and was pushed back toward the French coast after being aloft twenty-seven minutes.

Those on land witnessed the two aeronauts displaying signs of alarm, and they "seemed suddenly to lower the grating of the Montgolfière." But a column of flame had already darted upward into the area of hydrogen gas. Almost instantly the entire machine was ablaze and after shuddering several times, began a rapid and violent fall to earth. The balloon crash-landed in front of the Tour de Croy, a league from Boulogne, 300 feet from the sea.

Pilâtre de Rozier was killed instantly, his body found burnt in the gallery, many of his bones broken. Romain was still alive, giving slight recognition of his surroundings, but died within a few minutes.[7]

Another account related that when rescuers reached the scene, they found the balloon intact, "having been neither burned nor even torn."[8]

Tragically, the doomed aeronauts fell only a small distance from where Blanchard and Jeffries landed after their historic crossing. Pilâtre de Rozier was thirty-one years of age at his death.

It is said that a young English woman whom Pilâtre met shortly before his final voyage suffered a convulsive fit and followed him to the grave eight days later.[9] Other accounts state that she may have committed suicide. A commemorative marker was placed at the site of the fatal crash and the King had a medal struck in de Rozier's honor. His family was given a pension in recognition of the service rendered France.

In October, 1786, in the church-yard of Wimille, a village in the neighborhood of Boulogne sur Mer, a small monument to the memory of Pilâtre de Rozier and Romain was erected, the funds raised by subscription. On it was depicted an overset and burst balloon, and around it several French and Latin inscriptions, alluding to the fatal catastrophe. An eminent engraver also prepared a print to be exhibited by Blanchard's pillar near Calais, and Pilâtre's tomb.[10]

The Parachute

Leonardo de Vinci made sketches of a parachute, but credit for designing and testing the first actual device is generally attributed to Louis-Sebastien Lenormand (May 25, 1757–December, 1837), a French monk. He is also credited with the origin of the word "parachute," taken from the French "parasol" (sun shield) and "chute" (to fall).[11]

His first attempt consisted of two modified umbrellas. Using them to break his fall, he demonstrated the utility by jumping from a tree. On December 26, 1783, he leapt from

Photograph of the actual gondola, or boat, used by Blanchard and Jeffries on their flight across the English Channel. The photograph was taken while the boat was on display at the Exposition Internationale de Locomotion, 1909 (by permission of the National Air and Space Museum, Smithsonian Institution, Washington, D.C.).

An attractive programme has been arranged, and among the special features will be

A GRAND BALLOON ASCENSION

The parachute went through many modifications and became an integral part of balloon acts throughout the 19th century (*Athens Messenger* [Ohio], August 15, 1889).

the tower of the Montpellier observatory using a 14-foot parachute with a rigid wooden frame. Joseph Montgolfier was among those in the crowd watching the experiment. The intended use of the device was to enable persons trapped in burning buildings to escape unharmed.[12]

The death of Pilâtre de Rozier and his brother Romain was the first tragedy to strike those who dared challenge the limits of gravity, but the suddenly underscored danger did not deter the movement from proceeding. After a period of mourning, Blanchard, now the most renowned aeronaut, prepared a new balloon, this time with an added dimension.

On August 26, 1785, he and the Chevalier de l'Epinard made an ascent from Lille. After the balloon had been filled at 9:45 A.M., a test was made of his parachute, created along the lines of those invented by Sebastien Lenormand. At 10:45, the aeronauts entered the car to the hearty cheers of spectators on the esplanade. Ten minutes later the ropes were cut and the balloon, painted with the arms of the town, ascended. After four minutes, Blanchard released the parachute, to which a dog was affixed. A whirlwind interrupted its descent, and bore it above the clouds. The balloon and parachute afterwards met again, and the dog, recognizing his master, began to bark. Just as Blanchard was going to seize it, another whirlwind suddenly carried it beyond his reach.

Drifting for three quarters of an hour in sight of Lille, the machine eventually floated southward toward Paris. The flight lasted until 6 P.M. when the vessel came down at Servon, in the region of Clermont, having traveled 157 miles in 7 hours. The parachute came down 12 minutes afterward with the dog perfectly safe.[13]

The following day, Blanchard and l'Epinard were escorted to Saint Menehould, where they were greeted by the municipal officers and the Knights of the Arquebus in full armor. After honoring them with a draught of wine, the men were led through a cheering crowd to the town hall, where they feasted.

Prior to the ascent Blanchard was awarded 1,200 pounds (French) and on his return to Lille five days later, was offered the choice of a matching sum, or a gold box worth a similar value, decorated with the insignia of the town and carrying a suitable inscription.[14]

August 26, 1785 (other sources put the date as June 29), Lunardi flew over London with George Higgin and Mrs. L. A. Sage, the first English woman to fly in a balloon. After a short trip he soared on alone, setting a new record by flying 162 miles in 4 hours. On November 20, 1785, Blanchard made the first ascent in Belgium at Ghent.

7

Destinies Played Out

When Pilâtre de Rosier, who was a man of enterprise and approved science, received so melancholy a death in an aerostatic experiment, it might naturally be supposed that such men as Lunardi, even after three failures, would have given up a pursuit, to which he was so manifestly unequal.[1]

By 1776, pigeons, cats, dogs and a variety of barnyard animals had been sent into the atmosphere. Men had ascended alone and in tandem; two of them had died. Balloons had risen attached by cords; they had been set free to sail over boundaries and water. An American boy had reached the sky and a number of women had braved the unknown. Professors, scientists, soldiers and opera singers had added their names to the growing list of aeronauts. So it was no particular shock that a brother-sister team should try their hand at aerostation.

Mr. and Miss Drury, of Ranelagh, Ireland, put together enough money to finance a balloon adventure, and on Tuesday, April 20, 1786, a large gathering of spectators waited patiently for the inflation to finish. Their combined weight proved too heavy and Drury prevailed on his sister to quit the car. Very reluctant to do so, her good-faith gesture proved in vain for the balloon remained stationary.

"Impatience now slashed in Miss Drury's countenance, and being considerable lighter than her brother, she prevailed on him, in turn, to quit the car [and] with joy and agility leaped into it, and with the utmost intrepidity, and amidst an universal shout of applause, ordered the balloon to be liberated." The balloon rose, but immediately dashed against the temporary orchestra, constructed at a slight elevation to assist in the preparations. The stove tipped and came close to spilling hot coals on the wooden structure. The netting entangled with the top of the orchestra and tore off the carved Irish crown strongly attached to the top. Unwilling to admit defeat, Miss Drury made two more futile attempts before quitting the car "with inexpressible regret."

Realizing the day could not be saved in any other manner, the brother and sister ordered the balloon and car adrift, "as a humble sacrifice to a disappointed public for their abortive undertaking."

All was not completely lost, as the balloon soared majestically into the heavens, eventually landing on the lands of Gammonstown, near Naas. Having retained so much gas, it skimmed along the surface of the earth for a considerable time, "affording an entertaining chase to the gentlemen of that part of the country."[2]

By the Skin of His Teeth

Another private ascent, this time from the garden of Mr. Lockwood behind the Lyceum, in the Strand (London), had better luck. Two naval officers, Blake and Redman, apparently using their own funds, constructed a balloon from which they intended to make a voyage as far as the current would take them. Without advertisement or any intention of profiting by the experiment (already an irritant among newspaper reporters), the adventurers ascended on June 3 in grand style, with only a select company of "fashionable persons" present.

The balloon lingered overhead for a considerable time before floating off on the wind. Two hours later it descended at Maidstone, in Kent, where the fellows took in more ballast and provisions and re-ascended, planning on traveling through the night. If their gas permitted, the pair promised to continue the journey for two or three days.[3]

The following account is of another small and hardly noted ascension, this time from the Castle-Yard at Exeter. Like the Blakes and Redmans of the world, this aeronaut, by the name of M. St. Croix, acquired a balloon. Much like the sandlot ballplayer dreams of playing in the Major Leagues, possibly some, if not all, these aerostatic minor leaguers imagined themselves standing before huge concourses, waving flags and tipping their hat to the royalty, the gentry and the people of fashion who flocked to watch the Blanchards and the Lunardis.

Most were out of their league, both in the science and the art of ballooning. Copying diagrams published in any of the texts and pamphlets popping up like mushrooms, they gathered together a small supply of chemicals and filled an envelope, not of expensive silk but of linen covered with resin or gum. Since most accounts did not bother to give a physical description, it is easy to envision globes decorated by the hand of the pilot. Invitations spread by word of mouth rather than engraved invitations; a notice in the local weekly bulletin rather than a huge spread in the *Times* alerted their friends and neighbors.

They were the Everymen — and Everywomen — whose lives were put in equal or greater danger as they dared challenge the sky. Most were simple merchants, or dreamers, always seeking that spark which would ignite their souls. A handful were undoubtedly fortune hunters: those who lusted after the gold and the pensions dolled out to those of higher stature. Some, perhaps not so oddly, began their erstwhile careers as passengers, falling under the spell of the glamour and the thrill of adventure.

It could not be said these wistful participants were the backbone of the early balloon craze, for they were not. They were the adjuncts, the asides, the fringe decorating the galleries of the great and mighty. That they alternately entertained and disappointed there is ample proof; that they underestimated the risks and over-rated the rewards is likewise true. Some settled for seeing their name in print. A few sacrificed their lives for the glory of the moment, achieving in death a perverse posthumous fame. Few of these backyard rookies can be said to have truly succeeded. But more often than not, their stories carried an emotional impact as true as any noble heart.

Entertained by an excellent band of music, the crowd assembled to watch St. Croix, cheering as the balloon ascended in a slow and even manner. Admiration mingling with terror, awe with incredulity, the farmers and shopkeepers, with their wives and children, from as far away as Cornwall, offered the aeronaut the praise he sought. How long that lasted is a matter of conjecture: perhaps until the balloon was out of sight. Did that matter to St. Croix? Unlike the notable and the famous, he never wrote a narrative.

What is known, is that the balloon continued in flight for half an hour following the course of the wind before it descended too rapidly and burst. Clutching for dear life literally by his teeth, he hung on until the crippled craft reached a point low enough for him to jump. "Very fortunately," the Edinburgh *Advertiser* of June 27, 1786, notes, he "came down unhurt."

Was St. Croix one of those who, once having tasted fame, could not get enough? It is certain that three months later, an extract of a letter from Salisbury, dated September 11, observed that on Tuesday, September 5, one of the large bottles containing spirits of vitriol meant for an ascension from the market-place was unfortunately broken, "whereby a bale of serges and corduroys was nearly destroyed, and other goods much damaged," the loss estimated at a full 50 pounds. Perhaps that deflated his chances for another flight.[4]

Puffing Himself into Notice

Blanchard's ascent at Ghent at the latter end of 1785 may not have been the inspiration for Lunardi to seek other aerial skies to conquer, but it was to his personal and financial benefit to spread his fame as far and as high as possible. The March 14, 1786, edition of the *Daily Universal Register* (London) printed a rather tongue-in-cheek notice that Lunardi had applied to the India Directors for permission to practice his profession in Bengal. When the petition was denied, the newspaper concluded, "the *flying* report of the day is, that he means to *sail* thither in spite of them in an *air balloon!*"

The comment ending the article gave a slice of the temper of the times: "*Lunardi's* request to the India Company was rather unapropos [sic] — there are too many *high flyers* in India already!"

The same newspaper of April 20th reported that while they had no particular argument with the Magistrates of Edinburgh conferring honours, as the Freedom of the City given to "that most scientific of philosophers, Mr. Lunardi," they ignored Mr. Burke, the author of the *sublime and beautiful*, during his short stay in that city. (The reference is to Edmund Burke [1729–1797], Irish essayist and politician, who, by this date, had already published his famous work, "A Philosophical Enquiry into the Origin of Our Ideas of the Sublime and the Beautiful," 1756.)

Five days later, the *Register* pursued the topic, again with Lunardi the example, by declaring that while he "traveled to the clouds for *excitement*" (italics added), and Dr. Graham buried himself underground for the same purpose, "Pitiable, indeed, is the fate of those men who cannot get a livelihood on the *face of the earth*."

Still not finished with Lunardi, the *Register* of July 8 made reference to the infamous mystic by observing, "*Cagliostro* takes tolerable pains to puff himself into notice, and probably will presently raise contributions by shewing his person like renowned Lunardi."

The Edinburgh *Advertiser* ran an article more to public taste by announcing that Lunardi planned, weather permitting, to do all in his power to gratify the people of that city by ascending on July 20 in a new balloon decorated with his Majesty's and the Prince of Wales' Arms. The newspaper also kindly added that an Account of these Voyages, written by himself in a series of letters to his Guardian, Chevalier Gheraray Compagnt (Prince Caramanico), and embellished with his portrait, the balloon and apparatus in two plates, was now available at Mr. Chrench's bookshop, price five shillings.

This last, an attempt to capitalize on fame by publishing a narrative, was one of the ways aeronauts raised funds needed to continue in their newly created livelihood. Pamphlets and other merchandizing — selling seats in their car during ascensions, displaying their balloons before and after voyages, hawking tickets which provided the holder with an up-close view of the inflation process — added to their income, but did little for the reputation of the profession. Although they were, first and foremost entertainers, the appellation would come to haunt them when they attempted to step out of that mold. A century later, T. S. C. Lowe would have a difficult time dissociating himself from the reputation of being a "showman" when he tried to organize a Balloon Corps for the Union Army during the Civil War.

On July 27 Lunardi made his sixth ascent in Scotland. For this voyage the Royal Balloon was inflated at Heriot's Garden, with Castle and Calton Hills covered with a genteel company of ladies and gentlemen. The balloon rose very high but owing to a lack of wind soon became almost stationary. At 5:30 it descended in a field near Duddingston Mill about a mile and a half from Edinburgh. The aeronaut returned that evening and was carried through the streets in triumph.

The following month found Lunardi in York. On August 23 he gratified his audience, who cared more for his reputation of ascending on time than for any profession of scientific or literary achievements, by rising in his Royal Balloon from Kettlewell's Orchard behind the Minster. He ascended to a "prodigious height" and took a N.E. direction. At a great distance from the earth, the aeronaut experienced very inclement weather, assailed by rain, snow, hail and an electrical storm.

Descending when the neck of the balloon froze and "quite benumbed with cold," he landed safely at Greenock, in the parish of Bishop Wilton, twenty miles distant.[5]

A Melancholy Account

On September 5, 1786, Lunardi proposed to ascend from Newcastle upon Tyne, and the weather being agreeable, a large number of people assembled in the Spittal-ground to view the proceedings. The balloon was filled from a large wooden cistern sunk in the earth. A tube ran from a large cask, carrying the inflammable air into the neck of the balloon where it was secured to prevent leakage.

The process went forward without problems and the globe filled as expected. Reaching near its proper height, the ropes attached to the poles supporting the top had to be removed, as they were too short to be of further service. In order to accelerate the process, a quantity of acid was added to create more gas. In a few minutes a considerable effervescence was perceived. In order to test its force, Lunardi drew the plug from the funnel. A great quantity of gas escaped, making a loud noise, startling the men holding the ropes near the cask.

Although no danger existed, the sound frightened the assistants and they dropped the ropes and fled to the opposite side. The balloon lurched upward, tearing the neck where it joined the barrel. This increased the quantity of escaping gas, adding to the confusion. Despite Lunardi's assurance of safety and his pleas for the men to return to their posts, the balloon was released. Disengaging from the barrel, it rose with great velocity.[6]

According to another report, the vitriol began to burn, creating smoke and flames. Ralph Heron, one of the assistants who had either retained his hold or had his arm entangled in the rope, was lifted off his feet and carried away with the balloon as it ascended. The crowd reacted in terror as they witnessed the man, suspended by his arm, hanging from the netting. His identity was soon ascertained as his father, mother and sisters were standing on the scaffold when the tragedy occurred.[7]

Heron was carried to a height of 300 yards, twisting in a horrific manner as he tried to free himself. This effort caused the balloon to invert and either the cord broke or the victim disengaged himself. At the same time, the fire, which had spread to the envelope, caused an explosion and burst in mid–air. Heron was thrown down and landed in a tree before plummeting to the ground 20 feet from where he ascended. He landed semi-erect in a soft loam flowerbed, where he sunk to his knees. The balloon, torn to pieces by the explosion, left a great cloud of black smoke in the air as it burned.

Heron died within two hours of the accident. He was between 21 and 22 years of age, and still a clerk under his father, who was an attorney and the under-sheriff for the county of Northumberland.

Lunardi was also much burnt, and was subsequently seized with a fever. Newspaper accounts observed they did not know what happened to Lunardi, but "fancy he made as good a retreat as he possibly could, for fear of the fury of the enraged populace." It concluded:

> If Lunardi had shared the fate of his balloon, Folly might have wept over her victim, while pity would scarce have designed a sigh; but the catastrophe of Mr. Heron demands the tears of compassion; and while it is shed over him, does it not become the good sense of the nation, by its future discouragement, to prevent the possibility of a similar misfortune.

The incident accelerated several days later when a letter written by Lunardi to a gentleman in London contained the following paragraph (italics in the original):

> Before this unhappy accident, I had taken notice of the young gentleman, and twice untwisted the fatal rope from his hand, begging him to leave it loose, and give free expansion to the balloon, which was now filling apace.—*But I think it was his destiny, and his appointed hour was come.*[8]

The letter was subsequently released and did not find favor with the public. A comment by one of the gentlemen hearing it read aloud perhaps summed up the popular feeling: that if the Italian should again ascend in a balloon, "he might have occasion *to go in mourning for himself*" (italics in the original).[9]

The *Register* did not let the subject go. Three days later it ran a second article chastising Lunardi and remarking that the feelings of the public have been so thoroughly aroused by the death of Mr. Heron that this, if nothing else, would probably stop him from renewing "his nonsensical exhibitions."

It is impossible to know whether Lunardi took such predictions to heart, but as the old year passed into the new, he had turned his attention to other pursuits, for which he received far kinder reviews.

The Poltroon, the Virgin and the Public Ballooned

In an odd article published 60 years after the fact, an account of Blanchard's non-ascent from Liège on December 11, 1786 (published in the United States), was given in great detail. The story purports that amid a great gathering that included the "Prince, Bishop, and all the municipal officials," Blanchard readied himself to lift off, but at the moment the rope was cut, he leaned over to accept a bouquet of flowers from Madame de Berlnimont. The sudden jerk of the machine tossed him from the car and he fell to the ground, stunned by the fall. The Prince, forewarned that the aeronaut would try such a trick, warned him that if he did not ascend in another balloon, "he would be handed over to the arm of justice and loose [sic] your head like a common robber."

The tenetless balloon came down at the village of LaRoche where the impoverished villagers were attending a religious ceremony. Seeing the "enormous globe of resplendent hue" descend, they deemed it a present from the Virgin and at once cut the balloon to ribbons, using the silk to clothe her statue.[10] It is impossible to conceive that Blanchard would have feigned a fall, but it is interesting to note how his reputation in the United States had disintegrated to the point of being called a coward.

The advertisement ran:

THE TWO AIR BALLOONS WILL POSITIVELY ASCEND
THIS DAY, the 1st of AUGUST, at TWELVE o'Clock.

On the entertainment side of aerostation, whenever a newspaper advertisement or handbill contained the word "positively," a red flag should have gone up in the consciousness of those planning to attend. Times were equally suspect.

Considering that the fascination of ballooning was tantamount to the thrill of a modern World Series game, it is not surprising spectators arrived early for the chance of participating in the mounting excitement of the day. That said, there were too many variables involved in the sport to permit any more than an educated guess or a hopeful estimate. Statements such as "positively," "at 12:00 sharp," or "absolutely at 4 P.M." only caused frustration, which easily transferred into annoyance and finally violence when promises were not kept.

Aeronauts quickly learned to provide entertainment to cover long lapses where nothing significant transpired. They employed marching bands, solicited local militia to parade, even encouraged vendors to sell refreshments and cool drinks. In the decades that followed, the more famous gentlemen, whose operations were then organized by committees, actually paid cities and towns to hire additional peacekeepers. But there was only so much these limited officers could do before tempers flared. Once incited, no amount of help could stop a mob. Such was the case with the unlucky — and possibly willfully — unnamed aeronauts who put out the above advert.

The two gentlemen (later to be styled "professors") set up their trial in the yard of the Oil of Vitriol Works (which conjures images of Ambrose Bierce's "Oil of Dog" factory), Tooley Street, Southwark. Stating that the ground was spacious and well-adapted for the purpose, they begged "those Ladies who intend honouring their exhibition" to be under no apprehension of rain, for there was sufficient shelter for upward of 2,000 people. The price for admission was: Galleries 3s. 6d. and 5s. Grounds 2s. 6d.

Both balloons were to be launched at the same moment, "in order to ascertain the extent of the circumambient air, as to height, celerity, &c.&c. produced by the difference of size and gravity." The larger balloon was 17,157 feet and the smaller 9,023 feet.[11]

The "doors" opened at 9 A.M. and at a very early hour an amazing concourse of people collected. The usual delays prevented an ascension at noon and by 1:45 P.M. the impatient mob made its way into the area surrounding the platform. They tore the larger balloon to shreds; someone threw a tile, striking the smaller and making a large incision. Somehow freed from its ropes, the balloon went up and soon disappeared in a northeast direction.[12]

Two days later the same newspaper included a brief remark that the Magistrates should have done more to prevent the public from being *ballooned*, and the "consequence of this *bubble* was, *full* ale houses and *empty* shops — and, in general, idleness among the manufacturers."[13]

That type of comment, too, would come to haunt the exhibition of balloons throughout its 18th and 19th century practice.

8

Balloons at War

The day was, therefore, ours; we returned to Charleroi expiring with hunger and fatigue; the balloon had been aloft for ten consecutive hours, and without wishing to make any ridiculous claim that its presence was the direct cause of the victory, one cannot deny its material and moral effect.[1]

There is some irony to the fact that by the 1790s, with war a constant threat, death became intertwined with life, and fatality reports from various sources were lumped together in a somewhat causal manner. In the same paragraph, a balloon explosion at Champ de Mars, injuring and killing several bystanders, was given alongside the report that an overladen boat had sunk; nine ladies of fashion were lost, while the gentlemen were saved by boatmen.[2]

With the idea of conflict almost inevitably swirling around England and France, a letter from a gentleman at Boudreaux shed some sanity, if not specifically some truth, on the subject:

> While you probably imagine the people of this country are planning the destruction of the British empire, and equipping fleets and armies, a visitor perceives them as a much more harmless amusement, and, from their eagerness of pursuit, would suppose it to absorb every idea of war and politics. I allude to their air balloons, which are in every quarter either flying, constructing, or the subject of conversation. Had this aerostatic contrivance been the minister's, and intended to divert the inhabitants from all reflection upon any distresses which the late hostilities may have produced, his genius would have merited immortality.[3]

Ten years later, however, France began a protracted war with much of Europe and not surprisingly, the use of balloons was contemplated. In 1794, Napoleon established the Committee of Public Safety, composed of Monge, Bertholette, Carnot, Poucroy and Guyton de Morveau. The latter put forth an idea of using captive balloons as observation posts where troop layout and movement of the enemy could be observed. The physicist Jean-Marie-Joseph Coutelle held the first trials at Meudon.

The first true military ascent took place at Maubeuge, then besieged by the Austrians. On June 23 a balloon was brought to Charleroi where observations were taken; the Battle of Fleurus was fought on June 26.

Inflating a balloon near the scene of battle proved a difficult and time-consuming process, posing problems never completely overcome. At Charleroi, two reverberatory furnaces were constructed and seven cast iron tubes from le Creusot were filled with filings and iron turnings. The tubes thus filled and sharpened at each end were placed in the furnace. At one side of the furnace a long, elevated tank was situated, from which, by means of specially modified little pipes, water was supplied to each tube. At the other end of the furnace another square tank held a saturated lime solution through which the gas passed, extracting carbon as it went through. The hydrogen thus created then passed into a rubber tube and entered the aerostatic sphere. The operation of inflation required from 36–40 hours.[4]

Moving the inflated balloon *L'Entreprenant* to the village of Gosselies, it ascended with three aeronauts: Captain Coutelle, an adjutant and a general. Coutelle used a series of signals to convey his observations to General Jourdan below. When more detailed messages were required, hand-written notes affixed to small bags of ballast were sent down tether lines. The enemy soldiers "looked dumbfounded on our enormous machine borne aloft with no visible means of support [the tether ropes being hidden from their view]; some were prepared to throw themselves on their knees and worship it, while others, waving their fists at it, declared in their own languages: 'Spies, spies, you'll be hung if you're caught!'"[5]

The experiment nearly proved fatal as the enemy, warned beforehand of the ascent, directed battery fire against it. The first volley went too low but a second passed between the bal-

Aeronautic military reconnaissance was done from a captive balloon several hundred feet in the air. The cable was played out by means of a windlass.

loon and the car.[6] After sustaining serious losses it appeared the French had lost the battle and the aeronauts prepared to descend before the swelling ranks of the enemy overran them. But fortune turned, and at the last, the Austrians failed to hold their ground and retreated. History later attributed the victory of the French over the Austrians on the plains of Fleurus to the information garnered by the captive balloon.[7]

War news filled the newspapers of the 1790s and understandably, the English feared that once Napoleon conquered Europe he would turn his attention to the British Isles. Rumors of every type swirled through the pages, and methods of destruction of various practical and impractical descriptions were put forth as a means of conquering the enemy.

Humanity Forbids the Practice

With tension daily growing, it was reported in the summer of 1794 that French "Chymists" had discovered an explosive powder capable of leveling the strongest fortifications. The British had also conducted experiments along the same lines, postulating that a "fire balloon" might be filled with such material and projected toward enemy ships where it would burst into flame, readily consuming sails and rigging. Although "humanity forbids the practice," both sides were eager to gain advantage.[8]

French war balloons ascending from Herve and Liège were described as being elliptical, 29 feet in length, 19 feet in diameter and 57 feet in circumference. Composed of yellow taffeta gummal (possibly referring to a gummy lacquer used to make the material airtight), they were covered with a network of strong threads, by which were attached cords holding the aerostat to earth.[9]

Ascensions were all "captive," or tethered flights. Without any appreciable means of directing the course of a balloon, the danger that aeronauts would be forced to land behind enemy lines prohibited free flight. Balloon usefulness was also limited by atmospheric conditions. If a battle were fought during a period of high wind, ascensions were not possible; rain, mist and cannon smoke also obscured the plain of view. Not until the American Civil War were any free reconnaissances attempted, and these were few in number. The use of a balloon was primarily limited to reconnoitering standing armies during a siege or periods of inactivity.

While the French used a variety of signals to convey troop movement and T. S. C. Lowe pioneered the use of a wired telegraph in 1861, the means of getting news in a timely manner to the commanding generals remained a debilitating problem.

The Treaty of Campo Formio on October 18, 1797, temporarily ended the war between France and Austria, allowing Bonaparte, the new Commander-in-Chief of the Armée d'Angleterre, to turn his attention to the conquest of England. Rumors of extraordinary new weapons drove the British to look to not only the seas, but the skies, when a report in December revealed two supposed plans for invasion: a project for sending the army to England in balloons and the other a "submarine project" for sending troops across "under the Sea, in Diving Machines."[10]

Fueling the flames, on December 3, 1797, *L'Etoile de Bruxelles* announced that a vast montgolfière was being constructed to carry 100,000 men across to England to effect its conquest. Although little more than a ploy, it inspired others to propose additional schemes. An advocate by the name of Thilorier proposed a montgolfière designed to cross the Channel by night, with an enormous oil lamp hanging beneath the platform to keep the air hot.[11]

While it may seem difficult to imagine such a manner of invasion occurring in the late 18th century, ideas such as these were actually tested, and while they proved impracticable on a large scale, these early efforts at a forked prong of attack set the groundwork for later and more successful underwater and aerial invasions.

The British press continued to report on French plans, stirring up a great deal of animosity and fear. On June 15, 1798, the Edinburgh *Advertiser* described a continuation on the theme of aerial assault by advising that onboard the Teulon Fleet were 300 pupils of the Polytechnic School, called "Geographical Engineers." They reportedly had with them a complete library, maps of Africa, India and other places of interest, as well as "several Aeronauts, with the Balloons of 30 feet in diameter." Actually, Napoleon himself had little enthusiasm for the idea of a balloon corps, although they had seen service in the Campaign of 1794 and in the Egyptian theater. In 1794, he closed the École Nationale Aéronautique.[12]

Citizen Garnerin Makes His Appearance

Andre-Jacques Garnerin (January 31, 1769–August 18, 1823), who would later become one of the most celebrated aeronauts of his time, first appeared in British newspapers in 1799. A soldier in the first Napoleonic Wars, Garnerin was captured by British troops, handed to the Austrians and held prisoner at Buda, Hungary, for three years. Returning to France, he became a student of ballooning and devoted considerable time to the development of the free-form parachute, eventually being appointed "balloonist to public entertainment" in his native country.

In early 1799, Citizen Garnerin presented a plan to the French Directory by which he proposed to send dispatches to "Buonaparte" via balloons. Another claimant came forward, professing to be "the first projector" of the idea and stating "that the merit of the original invention is warmly contested in the French papers!"[13]

On October 22, 1797, Garnerin made his first jump with a silk parachute over Parc Monceau, in Paris, descending 3,000 feet from a hydrogen balloon. Lacking an air vent at the top of the parachute, however, the device oscillated wildly, but the aeronaut managed to land safely half a mile from his ascension point. This marked the first time anyone had used a parachute to break a fall from such a high altitude.[14]

Making improvements, Garnerin ascended with a balloon on June 22, 1799, from Paris. He detached himself "from a prodigious height," deployed the parachute and after 20 minutes alighted in a garden with perfect ease and security.[15]

England was not attacked by air, but Napoleon was not through with his plans of world conquest, and in 1812 he brought the French Army to Moscow. Rumors circulated on how the Russian government would defend itself; primary among them were stories of an immense exterminating machine designed to destroy the invaders.

Curiosity was most acute in France, where word spread that Rostopchin, the military governor of Moscow, had ordered the construction of a grand aerial machine, meant to annihilate the French army. This balloon reportedly had the capacity to carry 50 men armed with rockets, hand grenades and canister shot. All experiments were said to have failed but word came out that "the Russians were as usual indebted to their allies, the *English*—and perhaps the *English* General Wilson, who was lately in Moscow," acting as the engineer for the "wicked" plot.

The fright of such a device, "reprobated by civilized nations," persisted, and it was later alleged that after the balloon failed to ascend, the factory was converted to the manufacture of fireworks which were ultimately used by the governor to burn his own city.[16]

9

Playing Catch-up

[T]hose who were thrilled by the ascent and who at the time expressed the whole-hearted wish to add a supplement to the amount they had already donated, will by this gesture reply to the question of whether this courage is amply rewarded by M. Blanchard's method of recompense.[1]

Civilian ballooning necessarily fell off during the long period of the Napoleonic Wars but never completely vanished. Among the most prolific and successful of the aeronauts during this period was Jean-Pierre Blanchard. He made numerous ascensions, but none perhaps more dangerous and thrilling than that made from Basle on May 5, 1788.

A huge crowd gathered to watch his balloon, but for various reasons it proved impossible to fully inflate. Blanchard removed the basket and ascended with nothing more to support him than four ropes. The landing was, of necessity, extremely hard, and he was badly injured, requiring a fifteen-day recovery.

Proving that little would stop these hearty adventurers, Blanchard traveled to many foreign countries, introducing the spectacle of ballooning to an admiring world. On May 8, 1788, he appeared at Basel, Switzerland, and on September 27 he ascended from Berlin before a gathering that included Frederick the Great and his Queen. Despite the wind being near gale force, Blanchard managed to lift into the atmosphere.

After "scudding" along at great speed he attempted to descend by opening the valve, but the cord broke away and fell into his hand. The balloon, "like a maddened horse," became uncontrollable and carried him toward a nearby forest. In order to arrest his progress, Blanchard attempted to cut a hole in the middle of the balloon. Unable to achieve sufficient escape of gas, he prepared to tear the envelope when a group of horsemen following his course caught his attention. He threw out the anchor cable and the balloon was hauled down by brute strength in spite of lively pressure from the gusting wind.[2]

On August 31, 1798, the Edinburgh *Advertiser* ran the following announcement:

Among the Aerostatic novelties of Paris, is the ascension of a man and horse in a balloon. This we should suppose to be the most expeditious mode of travelling possible, and to exceed greatly our flying wagons, flying dillys, and flying coaches.

Citizen Testu-Brissy undertook the ascent at Bellevue although it was not quite as uncomplicated as implied by the *Advertiser*. After numerous delays, the balloon was inflated, but insufficiently to carry the enormous weight required. The vessel failed to clear the wing of the castle and was thrown back against a chimney, tearing a large hole in the envelope.

The aeronaut and horse, equally "calm and undaunted," were pulled safely back to earth. Testu wished to repair the rent and have another try, but the public did not favor the plan.

"Whatever the result of the experiment," noted *Le Moniteur Universel*, Paris, October 16, 1798, "citizen Testu proved nonetheless that those who had thrown doubts on his courage were mistaken."

Two Sorcerers from the Clouds

Who wouldn't want to see the ascension of the Temple of Olympus and its Fifteen Great Gods? All of Paris and the surrounding countryside did, for a crowd estimated at 7,000–8,000 gathered in and around the Tivoli Gardens on August 3, 1800, to watch Garnerin and an eighteen-year-old woman go up in a mechanism so decorated. While the ascent was majestic, it did not take place until late in the afternoon and was soon lost from sight, diminishing the wonder.

Although the aeronaut had contemplated reaching Luxembourg Gardens, complications arising from uncontrollable sparks scattering in all directions threatened the gigantic balloon with imminent destruction. Garnerin was forced to make an unanticipated landing at the Rue de Tournon, a street fortunately wide enough to accommodate the breadth of the envelope. Had he been unable to achieve the descent where he did, narrower streets on either side would have compressed the envelope, possibly igniting a huge conflagration.

Two police officers and several firemen rushed to the spot and were able to assist the travelers out of their montgolfière. The lady "remained calm in the midst of the danger," and Garnerin escaped with his life and reputation intact.[3]

While Jean-Pierre Blanchard went to America to avoid the conflict of the Napoleonic Wars, Garnerin became the premiere aeronaut of Europe. As tensions between England and France lessened, he arrived in London to take up his occupation. The first notice of his planned excursion appeared on June 16, 1802, when it was reported that Garnerin and his wife, Jeanne-Genevieve, would ascend from the middle of the Thames in a balloon decorated with the colors of every nation in honor of the peace.[4]

Once announced, fantastic enthusiasm was generated. People were desperate for the innocent pleasures of peacetime, and the topic of balloons dominated everyone's thoughts. On Saturday, June 26, the Duchess of Devonshire, a devotee of aerostation, held a breakfast at Cheswick attended by no less than the Prince of Wales, another fan of ballooning. The highlight of the pre–ascension festivities was to be a fete offered by the *PicNic* Society,[5] but as the Season was still early, the "Regatta Fete" did not go as scheduled.

Five hundred of the *Beau Monde* remaining in town assembled on June 28 at the Garden where the grand and colorful green-, pink- and yellow-striped balloon was filled with inflammable air. The envelope measured 30 feet in diameter and 45 feet in height with the car measuring 6 × 4 feet, 2½ feet deep with a seat at each end. Ballast was hung from the extremity of the netting.[6]

Garnerin chose R.C. Sowden (incorrectly given as "Sotheron") to accompany him, reputedly because the latter paid £800 for the honor.[7] No explanation was given why Mrs. Garnerin was not included, but the presence of a strong wind, which Garnerin later noted would have postponed the flight had he not pledged his honor, was a likely cause. A "female, either a relation or his wife," entreated Sowden to abandon the project but he ignored her entreaties and leapt into the car, which made for good theater, if nothing else.

The ropes being disengaged, the machine rose slowly, requiring the discharge of two sand bags. Due to a torrential rainfall, it was lost to sight in ten minutes.[8] The balloon safely landed at Colchester at 5:45 P.M. after covering 54 miles in three quarters of an hour. Local farmers thought the aeronauts sorcerers, "it being rather an unusual thing to see two men coming down post–haste from the clouds."[9]

For his effort, the PicNic Society paid Garnerin 500 guineas, a hefty reward and certainly an incentive for him to have attempted the voyage, torrential rains, high winds and honor notwithstanding.

If anyone were ever said to make the most of their fifteen minutes of fame, then Captain R. C. Sowden was the man. Apparently a loquacious gentleman, he attended numerous parties after the ascension, became somewhat of a character and a fixture. His lengthy and detailed account of the voyage received intimate scrutiny and not a little jesting, as some of his remarks were "opposite to all past experiments of the same nature; but this is the age of wonders, and why may not the air have its revelations as well as earth?"[10] Sowden's description that Epping Forest appeared "no larger than a gooseberry bush" became a catch phrase and was quoted by various aeronauts and in the papers on numerous occasions.

While Captain Sowden was basking in the afterglow of a 45-minute balloon ride, Garnerin was in somewhat less pleasant circumstances. Due to the inclement weather, he had been unable to descend in his parachute, a loss acutely felt by the paying public. In order to rectify the situation, he scheduled an ascent for Saturday, July 3. However, some malicious person, supposed to have been a Frenchman, cut the balloon in three places. Repairs were made and the trial was to go off as scheduled, but torrential rain prevented the ascension. This did not sit well as the much-irritated mob hissed as the balloon was removed to the Pantheon.[11]

It was expected Garnerin would make good his promise at the first opportunity, but "being quite unprepared for a simple ascension with his Balloon, on account of the hardships he experienced in his last excursion (in grounding)" he was unable to promise a second ascension until Monday, July 5.

Running a notice in the *Times* of the same date, Garnerin "anxiously and confidently" trusted that his apology would be accepted by "a liberal and discerning public," pledging his honor that nothing would prevent his ascension, weather permitting, at Lord's Cricket Ground at 4:00 precisely. The cost of First Seats were 10s, 6d; Second seats 5s. If contrary weather prohibited him from descending in his parachute, "he will nevertheless and most certainly ride and travel in the air with Capt. Sowden."

"Most certainly" being another euphemism, it appears Sowden did not sanction his name being used in the advertisements, causing some embarrassment. A man giving his name as "Brown" (later identified as Edward Hawke Locker) was chosen, instead. Casks containing materials from which the gas was to be extracted were brought out and before 3:00 the balloon was filled. At this point it began to rain.

Constables kept the curious away, although they were helpless to prevent the "flagrant and atrocious acts of plunder and robbery" committed by gangs of thieves and pickpockets. Nor could they control the large numbers of spectators gathering on hastily constructed viewing sites. Before the ascent a scaffold collapsed, crushing several persons and killing a child.

Likely unaware of the tragedy, the Prince of Wales, accompanied by the Duchess of Devonshire came forward, expressing sorrow at the unfavourable weather. Garnerin asked and received a signed statement from the Prince attesting to the time and place of departure and the final signal was given. After a fifteen-minute flight covering seventy miles, the aeronauts landed safely in Essex. Garnerin returned immediately to Paris, being engaged to be present at the Fete, on the 14th instant. Both of his balloons and the (unused) parachute were taken to the Pantheon and put on display.[12]

With the British Isles alive with talk of Garnerin and balloon mania raging at fever pitch, popular culture burst at the seams with everything aerostatic. New books reached the stalls, including one called *Aeronautica*, beautifully embellished with a color plate "descriptive of five of the principal Balloons made in France and England."

For those visiting the Royal Amphitheatre, the "inimitable Pantomime of the Phoenix" showed the ascension of Garnerin's Balloon, complete with the actual car used by the aeronaut and Captain Sowden. The Intermezzo at the Royal Circus featured the Aerial Candidates, or "Both Members Returned," displaying the passage of Garnerin's balloon over London, designed so that the globe appeared to grow smaller in size as it passed out of sight.[13]

Nothing surpassed the actual event, however, and Garnerin was swift to capitalize on his fame. On August 3, he and his wife ("a very pretty and elegant woman"), dressed in white muslin, prepared for ascension, using the same balloon from Lord's Cricket Ground although enlarged by another circle.

The balloon was placed on an elevated platform, requiring five hours to inflate by means of an air pump and tubes. Five minutes into the flight Mrs. Garnerin let down a parachute holding a kitten in a basket with a note attached that read, "This kitten ascended in a Balloon, and whoever will bring it to Madame GARNERIN, No. 55 Poland-street, shall receive one guinea reward." The animal, although in "great consternation, and a little bruised," was rescued by a waterman.[14]

The balloon soared over the Thames between Milbank and Westminster Bridge, hovered over Hyde Park for twenty minutes, then continued in a northerly direction, finally descending in safety at 8:00 P.M. on the west side of Hampstead. While her husband secured the balloon, Mrs. Garnerin, making her ninth ascension, was conveyed back to Vauxhall, where she arrived at 10 P.M. Unable to speak English, her description of the flight was translated for those remaining to hear the gladsome tidings.[15]

10

The Sad Tale of Francis Barrett
and the Great English Balloon

*It might have been presumed from the rapidity with which Balloon Exhibitions have
lately succeeded each other, that by this time novelty would have in a great degree
ceased. Yesterday was however a proof to the contrary.*[1]

Garnerin's take from his ascent at Vauxhall — £250 plus one third of the gate, added
to what he received from the proprietor of the Pantheon[2] — was a fortune by anyone's standard. One dreamer who hoped to outdo him was Francis Barrett, a chemist and professor
of Occult Philosophy at East Greenwich. ("Occult" in this case meant hidden; thus, the
study of what was not clearly known, as opposed to the more narrow reference to the supernatural.)

Barrett's emergence prompted great press from the expectation that an Englishman
was finally in a position to challenge the French aeronauts. With a globe much larger than
Garnerin's, Barrett's success would be a matter of British pride. Adding to his newsworthiness
was his associate, the "*ingennous* [sic] Captain Sowden, whose wonderful discoveries and
observations, are so well known to the public." For whatever reason, the London *Times*
became fixated with Barrett's enterprise. From start to finish, they never let go.

The *Times* initial notice of Thursday, August 12, 1802, advised the public that these
two gentlemen proposed a trip to France, weather permitting (a grandiose scheme at best)
and concluded with its own brand of sarcasm, noting that if the pickpockets had the smallest
degree of gratitude, they would donate to the subscription set on foot, as aeronauts were
their best friends; adding that surgeons might contribute upon the same principle.

The balloon was to be inflated from the grounds of J. Andrade, Esq., Greenwich, but
by 2:00 when the aérostatic machine had not been brought out, considerable anxiety arose
that no ascension would take place. Such proved to be the case, the explanation being given
by a hellman and hand-bills that the business hired to supply the tubes and other machinery
for the process "disappointed" the aeronauts. Barrett promised that at 3:00 the following
day the flight would most certainly take place. People went away content with the explanation
and even the *Times* remarked that Barrett's preparations were "in every respect complete,"
and that the tubes intended for use were made of tin, following the Lunardi plan, as opposed
to the material used by Garnerin.

By 9:00 P.M. the same evening preparations did not seem promising for a morning
ascent. A private meeting between Barrett, Andrade and a committee interested in the

success of the "English Balloon" met to discuss the situation. The majority determined that in consequence of the poor workmanship manifested that morning, the entire operation ought to be postponed.

The decision did not sit well with Andrade, who feared his character might be compromised by the ire of the spectators. Having some knowledge of Barrett and aware he was anxious to rival a foreigner in the science of Aerostation, Andrade resolved to offer everything in his power to make the trial a success. Yet facing a potential public relations disaster, he wished to "relinquish any further interference in the business" until Captain Sowden arrived.

Sowden appeared at 9:30 P.M. and after examining the balloon, pledged that if he were "suffered to superintend the arrangements," the balloon would most certainly ascend at the proper time. On that promise, preparations went forward. At 10 P.M. several tailors and carpenters were hired to assist in readying the machine and the envelope was filled with common air by two pair of large bellows in the hope it would be sufficiently filled by 1:00 the following afternoon. Sowden sat up all night supervising the process and everything appeared in readiness for the flight.[3]

The Smile of Approbation or Contempt

Friday morning brought with it an even larger gathering than that of Thursday; some wished to see how Barrett would manage the balloon, while others appeared more fascinated by the prospect of a riot, should the ascent not take place. At 2:00 Andrade's ground was filled. Spectators also gathered atop a large shed that soon collapsed. A great calamity was anticipated but no one reportedly suffered more than bruises.

At 3:00 the balloon was brought out and placed on a platform similar to the type constructed at Vauxhall Gardens for Garnerin. The inflation tubes were connected and the inflation begun. Eventually the envelope began to swell, although it was apparent the ascent, should it take place, would not happen for a considerable time. Eventually the mob grew noisy, and a band of musicians was provided to quell the discontent. At 4:00, a diversion of another sort was occasioned by the appearance of Mr. and Mrs. Garnerin. "The French Aeronaut viewed with great attention the balloon, while filling, as well as the casks and other utensils used on the occasion; a smile was perceivable on his countenance, but whether it was a token of approbation or contempt" remained unclear.

Captain Sowden earned praise, the *Times* noting that he deserved the thanks of the public for his exertions, night and day, in forwarding the completion of the balloon, "being no otherwise interested in the event than wishing to retrieve his countrymen from the disagreeable situation in which he was placed." Considering Sowden proposed to be a passenger, it is supposed he had other motives than merely retrieving his countrymen.

At 5:00 fresh vitriol was put in the casks. Sowden thought it inferior to that previously supplied and wagers were bet on whether the balloon would ever rise. The temper of those in the crowd turning sour, the Artillery was called in to maintain order. The effort proved ineffective, and a surging mass of humanity stormed the area around the platform. Nearly one hundred got past the gate before some semblance of order could be restored.

To make matters worse, gas began escaping through the valve. Garnerin kindly advised the attendants to wet it, which they did. The procedure had a positive effect and prevented further loss. By 7:00 the ire of the spectators reached another boiling point and fights broke out. Order was temporarily lost and the situation appeared grim. By 8:00, with the clamor reaching the desperate stage and the balloon only half filled, it was determined that some attempt be made to ascend. Accordingly, Barrett, Sowden and Mr. Madox, described as a brewer of Tooley-street, got into the car. When it became readily apparent the balloon would not go up, the two passengers left Barrett to try it alone. Success proved elusive.

Barrett quitted the balloon. Determined to salvage something from the botched trial, he removed the car and substituted a child's cradle. Two flags were put inside, the cords let go and the balloon ascended. It remained in sight ten minutes, slightly appeasing the crowd. Information was soon conveyed to those remaining that the machine had descended in some marshes near the river, three miles distant. There was no report on what Mr. Chandler, the gentleman discovering the contrivance thought, upon seeing an empty baby cradle in the marshes.

As a fitting end to the stressful and hardly triumphal day, it was discovered that Mr. Madox, while on the scaffold, had his pocket picked of five guineas.[4]

The London Times' Pet Irritant

Whether from embarrassment that the Great English Balloon and its master, Francis Barrett, proved a disaster, or from a sense of irritation, the London *Times* refused to let the failed aeronaut go in peace. On August 18, only four days after the debacle at Greenwich, it published the following searing comment: "Several of our Quacks have blown themselves higher than this occult Philosopher was able to send up his empty cradle."

On August 31, Barrett's name re-appeared in a one-sentence report that he had repaired to Preston to ascend in his balloon during the Guild festivities. It never came off. Two weeks later, in an expanded two-sentence report, the *Times* mentioned that a great many staunch Englishmen were determined to support Barrett because they wished one of their own to triumph over the French aeronauts. The *Times*, predictably, less than optimistic, concluded, "We commend their love of their native ground, in which the Balloon fully partakes with them."[5]

The following month, the *Times* dug in deeper by reporting: "Mr. BARRETT, it is said, intends converting his balloon into a diving machine, which has been suggested by its antipathy to mounting. The best Philosophers are of the opinion it will dive with great alacrity, particularly if he attaches his cradle."[6]

Francis Barrett refused to surrender. Packing up his wife and child, the family traveled to Swansea for a vacation, leaving a trusted servant to bring his balloon on to Wales. Having plenty of leisure, he assembled a montgolfière made from tissue paper, measuring 12 by 18 feet. Word spread that he intended to let a cat down in a parachute from his toy aerostat and 1,000 people gathered outside the Ball Court of the George Inn to watch the proceedings. The weather proved uncooperative, and the test should have been postponed, but as an informant suggested he might gain two or three hundred pounds for his trouble, Barrett plunged ahead.

A large hole just below the middle of the envelope caused problems, but as it maintained just enough buoyancy to lift the balloon, he gave the order to "cut away." The machine ascended but complications from a malfunctioning pulley caused it to burn, entirely consuming the balloon.

Feeling the failure "severely," Barrett went about constructing two more montgolfières, using common printing paper "much too heavy" for the purpose. The first measured 12 by

15 feet and the second 7 by 7 feet, both designed after Garnerin's cylindrical balloon, the tops being spherical.

Holding another public display (fortunately without animals), he began by firing off two dozen good maroons (fireworks), then set off the first balloon. It rose 4,000 feet and remained in the air until the fire burned out, after which it descended 200 yards away and was brought back "very much torn." An hour later he sent up the second. It rose 1,200 feet, falling in nearly the identical spot. After discharging several more maroons Barrett left the court, presumably satisfied with his night's work.

Several days later his servant arrived with his full-sized balloon. Unfortunately, the pipes were "shook to pieces" and had to be repaired. Barrett noted, "I found that the town seemed rather dissatisfied; but I began to think that as the sight of a proper aerostatic machine, with its apparatus, must be an entire novelty to some hundreds of the inhabitants, I concluded that to attempt an ascent would still be more satisfactory, and, in some measure, make amends for the disappointment occasioned by the non-ascent of the first Montgolfier."

Swansea, situated in a very windy area with no covered buildings or convenient place to inflate the balloon, Barrett was forced to attempt the inflation from the Ball Court, "which was high enough, but exposed to the atmosphere." The first experiment ended in abject failure. After "half a day's puffing and blowing with a small pair of forge bellows, which had twenty holes in them," he managed to get the balloon "seven-tenths" full. This was either considered insufficient or the weather proved disagreeable, for at dark he pressed out the air and removed the balloon to his apartments. For the day's exhibition he earned twenty-two shillings.

The second experiment a day or two later had similar results. The wind proved too high and again he pressed out the air and brought the machine back to his lodging. His receipts amounted to four shillings and his expenses totaled four pounds, twelve shillings and two-pence halfpenny. Having only eleven shillings with which to pay his debt, he was left in arrears to the workmen and the owner of the Ball Court. Speculating on whether "it would not be more profitable to cut up my balloon, and set up a manufactory of bathing caps, umbrellas, and hat-covers, of which I could soon have produced a plentiful stock," he nevertheless determined to press forward. He published handbills, and solicited a subscription to the amount of £70.

With the added monetary assistance of Mr. Russell and another gentleman, Barrett ordered a fresh supply of vitriol from Bristol and Neath, and set a new date for his ascension.[7]

"A Bad Beginning Often [But Not Always] Makes a Good Ending"

October 6, 1802, was chosen as the Day of Ascension. Advertisements were circulated to every part of the Principality, drawing a crowd estimated at 20,000 persons.[8] Peculiarly, Barrett himself stated there were "about 300 people assembled."

The process of inflation began at 8:00 A.M. and proceeded very slowly. Owing to a misunderstanding, the gas condensed while Barrett waited for another delivery of vitriol, creating a delay. By 11:00, after consuming eight carpoys (bottles) of the chemical, it was clear he would not be able to fully inflate the balloon. More vitriol was required, but the chemist who had already provided six hundred weight, refused more until paid in cash.

Barrett "was on the point of haranguing the audience," and had just begun with the opening, "Ladies and Gentlemen…" when part of the stage broke with a tremendous crash. Barrett, his balloon and several persons fell, many of whom were seriously hurt, including a boy who fractured a leg bone. The aeronaut hurt his thumb and later acknowledged "some measure" of responsibility for the child's injury, promising to pay for the setting of his leg out of the subscription money.

Recovering from the disaster, Barrett attempted to address the audience, laying blame for the disappointment on the chemist, "but he could not be heard for hooting and howlings." Seeing that the mob was getting violent, he begged them not to destroy the balloon and they permitted him at last to take it away.[9]

Bitterly ruing that the day's business yielded him nothing but chagrin, and that the proceedings were incorrectly, "not to say malicious or ill-natured," reported in the newspapers, he concluded a published narrative by writing that his consolation came from the old adage, "that a bad beginning often makes a good ending," and before long he should be able to hold his head as high as any aeronaut, French or English.

News of Barrett's misfortunes spread across the British Empire. On October 12, 1802, a letter to the Edinburgh *Weekly Journal* began, "It is strange that our countrymen will persist in making fools of themselves, that they will not allow the subjects of a very near relation of the *Prince of the Power of the Air* to possess the undivided empire of that element." The author continued by writing that a man named Barrett made his "fourth, fifth, or sixth attempt to ascend in a balloon," but failed because the chemist who supplied him was aware that the "Aeronaut possessed a marvelous alacrity in sinking, but very little in rising." The letter finished, "We sincerely hope that this *earth* balloonist will not escape a good dunking the next time that he tries a similar experiment."

Unfazed, or at least undeterred by the criticism, Barrett pledged his balloon and apparatus on the promise he would make a triumphal ascension. A new subscription was created with the help of two locals and plans were made for another experiment.

After spending five days re-varnishing the balloon with elastic gum varnish in an open field as weather permitted, the date was set for what would prove to be his final trial. On October 15th, the process of inflation began at 9:45 A.M. and by 12:30 it was deemed sufficient, although barely so, to sustain Barrett's weight. At this point, a cask holding vitriol and water exploded, causing a delay. This damage being cleared away, a breeze came up, tearing a hole in the lower part of the balloon. A great deal of gas escaped but the rent was repaired.

At 1:30, eager for his long delayed success, Barrett went to his lodgings to get some mutton to sustain him on the voyage. Returning fifteen minutes later, he found no further inflation had occurred. As he had no more vitriol, he accordingly gave orders for the car to be "slung," and entered, taking with him his dinner, a bottle of brandy, fifty pounds of ballast and his flags.

The balloon failed to rise. Barrett threw out everything but the bottle, "and that went soon after," enabling him to clear a hedge in which the balloon had become entangled. The populace came to his assistance, bearing the balloon on their shoulders to the end of the field. This seemed to do the trick, for the machine began to ascend, and for the first time in his life Barrett felt "abandoned to a new element."

The cheers of 10,000 people and the prospect of viewing the town from the environs of space thrilled the aeronaut, but his joy was short-lived. To his great mortification and disappointment, the balloon descended, lightly touching earth four fields distant. Over the next fifteen minutes it re-bounded from field to field, sometimes reaching the height of the trees and at others skimming the ground.

Barrett finally got out and opened the valve. Lightened by 130 pounds, the balloon ascended with great velocity, descending three hours later in the middle of a field four miles distant, having been in sight the entire time. The country people promptly cut the envelope through the middle, supposing they were rescuing the hapless aeronaut.[10] The *Times* had a different explanation, recording that the balloon was taken up by two laborers, "who, thinking they could make a better use of it than Mr. Barrett, went through the simple operation of cutting it in two, each taking his half." The summary advised, "he ought not to persevere in what to him at least must be an idle and useless speculations."[11]

Francis Barrett was through with ballooning, but not without a struggle. On November 8, 1802, in accordance with his pledge, the creditors came knocking. They were forced to break the lock on Barrett's door and overpower the aeronaut before finally taking away his literal and figurative dream. Barrett was left without a shilling "wherewith to bless himself," and still in debt to the tailor, the cobbler and numerous other merchants.[12]

The final time the unfortunate Barrett's name appeared in the newspapers is perhaps a fitting one, as he finally became synonymous with aerostation, albeit in a negative perspective. A letter from Petersburgh, dated October 29th, says:

> Professor CZERNY'S ascent in the air has had the fate of Mr. Barrett's. All was yesterday in readiness. An immense multitude stood in eager expectation. The EMPEROR and the whole Court were present; but a deficiency of the materials from which the gas is generated suddenly disappointed every hope.[13]

11

The Skies Belong to Garnerin

The reason why Englishmen are not calculated for aerial celebrity is their want of volatility. A Frenchman is often in the clouds without a Balloon.[1]

With the demise of Francis Barrett's Great English Balloon, André-Jacques Garnerin resumed his celebrity status as the première aeronaut of his day. Pursuant to his own goals of successfully exhibiting a descent from a parachute, he announced on August 23, 1802, that he had obtained permission to use St. George's Parade ground, Grosvenor-Square.[2] To augment interest, the balloon and parachute were displayed at the Pantheon,[3] while at the Royal Amphitheatre, an "exact representation" of Garnerin and Sowden's Appearance over London, "in the Real Car, presented by Mons. Garnerin to Mr. Astley" (the manager) was exhibited "Under the Patronage of their Royal Highnesses, the Prince of WALES, and the Duke of York." The ascent did not come off and advertisements immediately went out that he would ascend from Bath.[4]

On September 6, 1802, Garnerin and his passenger ascended from Sydney Gardens, Bath, at 5:30. Upon their ascent the barometer read 30° degrees and the thermometer 62°. By 5:50 the temperature dropped ten degrees and the barometer indicated 26°, indicating an elevation of 3,420 feet.

At 6:12 the temperature dropped to 46° although the altitude had not significantly changed, which Garnerin explained by the presence of a dark, thick cloud floating over the balloon. Fearing it was electrically charged, and not wishing to "meet the fate of Icarus," Garnerin ascended above the danger. Reaching a high point of 5,420 feet with the balloon in a state of considerable dilation, the aeronauts prepared to descend. At 7:20 P.M. they made a safe landing in a field near Mells Park, 16 miles from Bath.[5]

Having often disappointed the public in his promised descent with the parachute, Garnerin returned to London for the express purpose of making good his pledge. Advertisements appeared as early as September 17, with Garnerin promising to explore, through the medium of the air, as much of the Island as possible, hoping to add "his mite to the attainment of so many desirable objects which could derive from his exertion." Ticket prices were set at 5 shillings. Those wishing a close view of the balloon and parachute might see them beforehand at the Pantheon for the fee of 1 shilling.[6]

If that were not enough to satisfy the craving for all things balloon (and incidentally, as a competition to the Pantheon), interested parties could patronize the New Sadler's Wells Theatre, where, under the patronage of H.R.H. the Duke of Clarence, they could hear Mr. Davis sing a new Comic Song called "Notorieties, or Opinions on the Balloon, Parachute,

Invisible Girl, Wet Ducks, and Preston Guild." As a reference for comparison, boxes for the performance cost 4 shillings, the Pit 2 shillings, and the Gallery 2 shillings.[7]

On September 22, an immense crowd flocked the area of St. George's Parade, North Audley Street, to witness the ascent. With numerous Bow Street officers and constables in place to defeat the "light-fingered gentry," order was maintained, although many Ladies were kept away from closer observation from fear of being trampled.

At 1:00 the balloon was brought to the ground to be impregnated with inflammable air. In all, there were thirty-six casks filled with vitriol and other materials to produce the gas. These communicated to three other casks called "general receivers," to each of which was fixed a tube that emptied into the main artery attached to the balloon. In this manner it began to fill with regularity.

At 5:00 a pilot balloon was set up, disappearing after ten minutes. Proving satisfactory, the balloon was raised several feet and the parachute attached to the bottom of the netting by a rope used to support the aeronaut's weight when in the apparatus. It ran through a thin tube to prevent it becoming entangled with other cords. The basket, made of leather, was designed to resist any severe blows sustained in the descent, and contained a quantity of sand for ballast.

With everything in readiness, word was given and the balloon ascended. After eight minutes, the machine was nearly out of sight. At this point, Garnerin cut the rope and detached himself in the parachute. The device expanded and began a gradual descent, but almost immediately its agitation became so great spectators feared for his safety. Pitching forward and backward with tremendous velocity, Garnerin eventually disappeared behind intervening houses.

On coming to earth in an enclosed hold near the Small Pox Hospital at Paneras, he struck with great force. Quickly rescued, he was put on a horse, but due to fatigue and faintness he was barely able to ride. Greatly imperiled by the thousands who surrounded him, the horsemen acted as a bodyguard. When the crowd at the Tottenham-court road obstructed their passage, Garnerin's entourage detoured up Portland Road.

In what might have been a comic tragedy, the procession was stopped at the turnpike when the toll attendant refused to let them pass without paying the fee. Several "knock-down arguments" took place before they were allowed to continue, and they reached Baker Street, Garnerin's destination without further incident. The balloon was later recovered near Farmingham[8] and a subscription taken up "in the same manner as his Pilot Balloon was sent aloft to try the current of the air." Additional revenue was obtained by another showing of the balloon and parachute at the Pantheon.[9]

Intelligence from the Skies

Garnerin arrived in Hamburg in April 1803 and went on to St. Petersburg by sea where he had been invited to ascend as part of the ongoing celebrations for the Emperor's mother's birthday.[10] As part of the festivities on July 3, two air balloons "of transparent fire" costing 3,000 roubles rose from the edge of the water. Sparks shot off a glorious spectacle of fireworks until they exploded in a grand finale.

Garnerin's first flight, made with his wife, Jeanne, earned him 15,000 roubles, 12,000 of which he lost at the gaming table. To cover his losses, for his ascent on July 30 from the Garden of Cadets, he upped his asking price to 20,000 roubles plus a generous portion of the gate receipts, "which the public, who are really generous, have taken very ill." The balloon remained aloft for an hour, landing three German miles (18 English miles) from Krasno Selo.[11]

In August 31, 1803, a startling report stated, "Garnerin, the Aeronaut, has taken his last flight, and become the victim of his aspiring character. His balloon is supposed to have been unable to resist some electrical influence, and was destroyed; when he, of course, was dashed to pieces by the fall which followed."[12] As was often the case, it proved false.

Zambeccari Makes a Reappearance

Francesco Zambeccari devoted his life to the study of aerostation after escaping as a prisoner of war from the Turks. He originally believed he could direct the course of a balloon by using the flame of a lamp fueled with spirits of wine. An early trial nearly proved disastrous when his balloon crashed into a tree, upturning the lamp. Flames quickly engulfed him which he managed to quench, but not before frightening his wife and children who witnessed the accident.

He subsequently received 8,000 crowns for experiments made at Milan. They proved unsuccessful "in consequence of the inclemency of the weather, the treachery of his assistants, and the malice of his rivals."[13]

September 4, 1803, was set for Zambeccari's aerial excursion from Bologna, but circumstances prevented him from ascending. After another failure on September 5, preparations were made for an October 7 voyage. The large size of the balloon required an unduly long filling time, prompting speculation that this attempt, too, would end in disappointment. The crowd, which to this point had been well controlled, became annoyed. With many foreigners present, whose money was greatly prized by the local businessmen, the authorities prompted Zambeccari to hurry.

The inflation process required two basins, one surrounded by seventeen tanks of iron filings and the other by sixteen tanks of zinc filings. Five of them were used again for the decomposition of the substance, there not being enough tanks capable of holding a sufficient quantity for the production of the gas. The residue remaining in the small tanks was emptied by means of eight cisterns, some of which were thirteen feet deep. The proportions used were:

200 pounds of iron filings
6,000 pounds of zinc filings
8,500 pounds of sulphuric acid
A quantity of water five times greater, producing 14,000 cubic feet of gas.

By the time enough gas was produced, night had fallen. Zambeccari wished to delay the flight until morning. His request was denied and near midnight, Zambeccari, Dr. Grassetti of Rome, a doctor of physics and Giovanni Andreoli entered the car. After rising to a height of forty feet, with the balloon still anchored, the aeronaut descended three times by the use of oars, begging that the free flight be postponed. Fearing a morning ascension might be delayed by escape of gas during the night, the cords were cut at 12:14 A.M. and the balloon rose, narrowly avoiding a sixty-foot tree on the way up. The few remaining spectators cheered the ascent and tracked it for ten minutes before it was lost from sight.[14]

Once aloft, the lamp intended to increase their ascending force "became useless."

Numb from cold, Zambeccari and Grassetti sank into "a kind of insensibility and a very deep sleep," the former ascribing this to "weariness and hunger arising from my having neglected to take nourishment for twenty-four hours [and] the vexation that embittered my spirit." Andreoli remained awake, "no doubt because he had taken plenty of food and a large quantity of rum."

At 2:00 A.M., hearing the sea off the coast of "Romagnia," he awoke his companions with difficulty, but too late to prevent a descent into the water. In a near panic, they threw out everything they had to lighten the load and the vessel rose with great rapidity. The sudden change in altitude caused Zambeccari to vomit and Grassetti to bleed from the nose; both were short of breath and "felt oppression on the chest." Additionally, they suffered frostbite from the cold and found themselves covered by a thin sheet of ice.

Some time after 3:00 the balloon was driven by the wind back to the Adriatic Sea and the coast of Isteria. The half-submerged car skipped over the water for five hours, putting the passengers in imminent danger of drowning. At full light they were spotted by a number of boats and anticipated rescue, but the unfamiliar and terrifying sight of a half-filled balloon frightened the seamen away. Finally, at 8:00 A.M. they were rescued near the harbor of Veruda in Isteria. The balloon, lightened of its weight, ascended and was lost in the clouds.

The three aeronauts were taken to Ferrara and from there carried to the nearby port of Pola. Grassetti's hands were badly mutilated and Zambeccari's fingers were amputated to save his life.[15] The distance from the coast of Romagnia to Isteria was 120 miles.

Zambeccari made another ascent in December 1803, in the balloon recovered from the Bologna flight. This time his machine dropped on a chalet near Zara, in Dalmatia.[16]

Zambeccari's Fondness for the Adriatic Sea

Nearly a year later, on August 23, 1804, Zambeccari and Andreoli made another ascent from Bologna, rising in their balloon, *Aeromontgolfière*, at 9:00 A.M. After reaching the neighborhood of Mermorta in two hours, Zambeccari determined to descend. He dropped anchor but the resulting shock spilled a lamp filled with spirits of wine. The inflammable substance splashed over his clothing, on the fabric of the balloon and the car ropes, instantly igniting them. Zambeccari poured water from a flask over his head, extinguishing the flames on his hair, but when he looked for his companion, discovered he had vanished. With no other explanation, he supposed Andreoli had either jumped out to escape, or slid down the rope to earth.

Lightened of Andreoli's weight, the balloon tore away the anchor and soared upward. It reached such a great height that the aeronaut suffered from the stinging cold and soon his hands were frozen and useless. The balloon, pushed by the wind, reached the area of Porto di Magnavacca, but by this time, night was falling. Understandably unwilling to touch down in the water, Zambeccari attempted to tie himself into the car so that he might sleep without fear of being tossed out. He attempted to use the silken anchor rope, but discovered he could not pull it free. Having no knife to cut it, he broke the glass in his spectacles and holding a fragment in his teeth, succeeded in severing it.

During the night the balloon was blown further out to sea, despite his attempts to use the oars and row. In the morning several vessels witnessed his plight but none came to his aid until three o'clock that afternoon. Two fishermen eventually rescued him and he was brought to Comacchio, where he was hospitably received and given a chance to recover.[17]

Around the World in 80 Days

The Russians were very much taken with the idea of aerial ascension and in the summer of 1804, Professor Étienne Robertson (born in Liège, 1763, and the father of aeronauts Eugene and Dimitri) visited Riga for the purpose of putting on a demonstration. Opening a subscription to secure the necessary expenses, he had no trouble finding gentlemen of wealth willing to put up 100 rubles.

Announcing an ascent for August 30, 1804, the citadel at Riga was decorated for the occasion and filled with a great multitude. For the price of one dollar or a gold ducat, seats close to the proceedings were offered, while those less fortunate crowded the ramparts, roofs and chimneys of surrounding buildings. Nobility and peasants from the surrounding country joined the festivities and despite a cloudy, drizzly day, the experiment went off as promised.

Robertson's balloon rose to a height of 4,200 feet and he descended three leagues away from the city. Notwithstanding prior admonitions from the pulpit, the country people fell to their knees in wondrous astonishment to witness the descent. They did not, however, without earnest pleas, render him any assistance in landing. One farmer was reported to have intended shooting the balloon, taking it for a species of rare game.[18]

Flush from his successes in Russia, Robertson proposed an "extended and romantic plan"— that of creating a gigantic balloon capable of circumnavigating the globe by going over the tropics by the aid of the trade winds. His proposal, possibly the inspiration for the novel by Jules Verne, was to create a balloon of strong taffeta, 136 feet in diameter and capable of raising a weight of 33 tons. A boat, substantially built and weighing 8½ tons, was to be used in place of the common wicker basket, and divided into several apartments, capable of accommodating fifty persons. Robertson planned on including bedchambers, a kitchen, washhouse, observatory, two workshops, a chapel, academical saloon, card and concert rooms. He anticipated the machine capable of traveling at all elevations and in every type of weather.

Robertson went so far as to apply to the different Learned Societies for contributions, offering in return that each subscribing Academy have the nomination of two aeronauts. The estimated cost of construction was a staggering £40,000.[19]

By 1806, the dimensions of Robertson's proposal had grown to 732 feet in diameter, capable of carrying 37 tons and supporting fifty people. He added to the plans "a mast, sails and every other article requisite for navigating at sea, in case of accidents, and provided with a cabin for the aeronauts, properly fitted up, gallery for cooking, proper stores stowing provisions, and several other conveniences."

In order to ensure safety, he planned on including a smaller balloon "and a parachute, which would render the descent perfectly gentle, if the outer balloon bursts." Scaling down previous estimates, Robertson now calculated the flying machine to be enabled to stay aloft for several weeks.[20] Next to air navigation and flights across the Atlantic, this type of aerostat was probably the most common pipe dream of the 19th century.

On a related theme, the following appeared in the London *Times*, September 25, 1817:

> On the 20th, the Edinburgh Royal Charlotte Balloon blew up as it was passing over the Fyne, at the height of 703 feet from the bursting of the steam-engine which directed its course. There were 32 passengers on board; but owing to the balloon being furnished with one of Aircastle's improved parachutes, the whole of the party descended in perfect safety, and experienced no other inconvenience than that of being a little wetted by their falling into the river Fyne.

This, too, might have come from the pages of a Jules Verne novel. Actually, it was part of an article entitled, "A Peep into Futurity," a look 100 years distant. Mixing air flight with the notoriously explosive steam engine then in common use on steamboats and ocean liners, the author painted a not overly exaggerated view of 21st century mass transit.

In October 1804, the celebrated Blanchard advertised in Marseilles that he would ascend with his wife in a car drawn by three balloons. His plans did not go as promised and he went up alone in a simple balloon that came down again in a span of ten minutes, "to the no small disappointment of the public."[21]

Things did not go much better for Blanchard on his 61st voyage, this one taking place at Rotterdam. Ascending on August 2, 1807, with his wife, who was making her eleventh air trip, the balloon left the ground at 7:30. Unfortunately, it struck the iron wire on which it had previously been attached. Shaking violently and out of control, the envelope collided with a tall tree, receiving a hole in the fabric. Blanchard was thrown from the car, struck the roof of a house and then fell to the ground, receiving a large contusion on his head; Mrs. Blanchard fainted dead away. The balloon fared worst, being torn to pieces in the descent.[22]

Descending into Disfavor

The Coronation of Emperor Napoleon was cause for extravagant celebrations. Garnerin, who listed his titles as "privileged aeronaut of His Majesty the Emperor of Russia, and ordinary aeronaut of the French Government,"[23] was placed in charge of the aerial demonstrations. Five decorative balloons were sent up from the Place de la Concorde, the largest of which bore the representation of an eagle with outspread wings; in its talons were two large flags bearing the name of Napoleon.[24]

Garnerin's responsibilities also included management of the magnificent, unmanned Coronation Balloon that ascended on December 15, 1804, carrying an Imperial Crown. In the basket he placed a note, asking that whoever found the aerostat notify him of its place of descent. A letter from Cardinal Caphara, by order of Cardinal Consalvi, Secretary to the Holy See, dated at Anguillors, near Rome, December 18th, informed him the balloon had fallen into Lake Brasciano and been secured by some watermen. A second note included information that the balloon had crossed France, the Alps and passed over a distance of three hundred leagues in twenty-four hours, making its velocity fifteen leagues an hour. Additional reports reached the Emperor that the balloon had grazed the tomb of Nero and left part of the crown on it. As this portended ill tidings, Garnerin fell out of favor with Napoleon and his position was given to Madame Blanchard.

Three years later, Garnerin again was invited to take part in the French celebrations, this time for the anniversary of the Battle of Jena. He completed two nocturnal ascensions, the first on October 14, 1807, where he rose in his balloon from the Gardens of Tivoli at 11:00 P.M. His car displayed both the French and Russian colors and was decorated with 120 lamps to make it visible in the darkness. Reaching the height of 3,000 toises (nearly 4 miles), it landed safely 45 leagues from Paris.

The second ascent proved far more dangerous, as he encountered an aerial tempest encompassing the envelope in thick clouds. On attempting to descend, the balloon became entangled in the trees, was dashed against a mountain and plunged to the bottom of a precipice. Unable to land, the balloon alternately rose and fell until the anchor finally hooked in a tree. Garnerin was brought down by some peasants, being in a state of utter exhaustion and near insensibility. The distance covered was 100 leagues.[25]

On August 16, 1808, Garnerin suffered another near-disaster. After a night ascension, his balloon fell on the morning of the 17th at Manoncourt en Voevre, in the district of Toul. When the machine was discovered, the aeronaut was missing; the only remnants remaining were some shirts marked "A.G." and a pair of gloves.[26] Garnerin was later found and lived for many more years.

A Tragedy "from Want of Prudence"

In cases of misadventure or the death of an aeronaut, it was common practice to seek the opinion of others from the same profession. Thus, when M. Mosment died in a balloon accident on April 7, 1806, André-Jacques Garnerin was solicited for comment. Although not present at the tragedy, he boldly asserted that the cause "did not result from any of the inconveniences which are connected with aerostatic aeronauts, but merely from want of prudence."[27]

April 7 dawned remarkably fine with an uncommon serenity. Mosment ascended in a balloon made of silk and filled with hydrogen gas. An hour after departure, the balloon disappeared from sight. Shortly after, his flag was discovered on the ramparts, causing great concern for the sole passenger. An investigation was immediately set afoot.[28] The balloon was found intact between Charlesville and Charleroi, with no damage to the car or the cords that held it to the basket. Inside, searchers discovered a pistol, a small loaf of bread and some meat.[29]

The body of Mosment lay in a nearby ditch, bruised and bloodied. Garnerin deduced that the car in which Mosment ascended was too shallow and the cords affixing the car to the balloon spread too far apart. He supposed that when the aeronaut leaned over to let an animal drop in a parachute, he lost his balance and fell.[30] Rumors persisted after the fatal flight that Mosment had foretold his death.[31]

Elaborating on the imprudence of other tragedies, Garnerin noted that "every one foresaw" the danger into which de Rozier had placed himself when using both a montgolfière and a balloon filled with inflammable gas, adding that balloons covered with gilt or silver were likely to attract electricity from the clouds. Zambeccari, "who employed those means, sustained several accidents, and it is only surprising that he escaped at last."[32]

Elevated Warfare on a Small Scale

Perhaps the most astonishing — and ridiculous — event concerning balloons took place at Paris in July 1808. M. Grandpré and M. LePique quarreled over a celebrated opera dancer, "who was kept by the former, but had been discovered in an intrigue with the latter." Being men of "elevated" minds, they decided to settle their quarrel in a duel — fought in balloons. Each attended with his second, they ascended from Thuilleries at 9 A.M. carrying loaded blunderbusses, "as pistols could not be expected to be efficient in their probable situations."

Keeping within eighty yards of one another, LePique fired first and missed. Grandpre returned the shot, putting a hole in the other's balloon. LePique and his second plummeted to earth where they landed on a housetop and were dashed to pieces. The victor "then mounted aloft in the grandest style" and landed safely seven leagues from the place of ascension.[33]

The year 1809 closed out manned aerostation with a flight by Bittorf of Wurtzbaugh. Making his 21st ascension on October 1, he flew from Leipzig in a paper balloon 48 feet in diameter. After reaching a considerable height, he passed over the city and landed a league and a half distant.[34]

12

James Sadler and the
Real Great English Balloon

*This intrepid aeronaut has now become apparently so well acquainted with the
English atmosphere, that a voyage through these perilous regions seems to him only
an ordinary excursion.*[1]

Although Francis Barrett tried hard to become the Great English Aeronaut, the honor
went to James Sadler (1753–1828). Sadler was the second individual given credit for ascending in England after Lunardi, and perhaps more significantly to the British, he was the first
Englishman to reach the heavens in a balloon when he went up from Oxford on October
4, 1784. After retiring in 1785 to pursue his vocation in chemistry he reappeared on the
aeronautic scene in 1810.

A native of Oxford, Sadler was well known in the area, where his brother worked as a
pastry chef. In order to raise money for his grand return, friends placed handbills all over
town advertising the proposed ascension and stating "his much-to-be-regretted misfortunes,
and his ancient patronage." It was felt these efforts, as well as the money received from the
gate would put him on stronger financial ground.[2]

James Sadler's balloon ascent was to be the grand finale of Celebration Week in Oxford,
held in honor of the installation of Lord Grenville as chancellor of the university. Displayed
in Merton Fields on July 7, the balloon was decorated in green, red and yellow with black
margins above, bearing an inscription dedicated to Lord Grenville and the date of his Chan-
cellorion Election. Underneath were stripes of red and yellow and below all, a beautifully
shaped and decorated car.

Placard promises notwithstanding, the balloon required a lengthy filling process and
did not arise until 2:15 P.M. With his son as passenger, Sadler's balloon floated over the college, Sadler dropping a white and then a blue flag, bearing the inscription, "Protected by
the Conqueror of Bonaparte, the Hero of Acre, Rear-Admiral Sydney Smith."

The dimension of the spherical balloon was 30 feet diameter, with a capacity of
14,137 cubic feet, or 86,721 gallons. It had a surface of 314 square yards, with the envelope
consisting of 566 yards of lustring silk. The size was "considered larger than a hay rick two
ton weight."

Soon after it rose, Sadler let out some ballast, Sir Sydney Smith's bag and a cat in a
parachute. The cat was picked up at Headington, two miles distant. The little animal had
on a red collar and the basket contained a note to Miss Robarts, daughter of the coach-

proprietor in High Street, Oxford. The countryman took the cat home as directed, but along the way made an exhibition of "Puss, at a premium."[3]

Communicating their progress by means of a little white signal balloon, the "airship" passed into a cloud and was temporarily hidden from sight. In all, those with telescopes were able to view the machine until 2:45 P.M.[4]

The balloon descended at 4:14 P.M. in a field near Newport Pagnell, 50 miles from Oxford. At the time a number of hay-makers were at work and although hailed by the travelers for assistance, were too terrified of the apparition to come to their aid. In consequence the balloon skimmed the field, rebounding forty feet into the air and clearing a hedge before their grappling iron caught on a quickset hedge bordering Buckinghamshire and Bedfordshire. Here they were more successful in procuring help, and the father-son team were safely brought out of the car.[5]

The Sojourners in Air

On Monday, September 24, 1810, Sadler made another spectacular ascent, this time from Bristol. With "the whole of the Bristol volunteers" on duty to keep the peace, Sadler proposed to ascend with his daughter, but the state of the wind being too violent, her seat was offered to another. Upon clearing the city, the "sojourners in air" let down a cat in a parachute. It fell upon Leigh Down and was rescued by a lime-burner. The local medical man to whom it was delivered adopted the creature and gave it the name "Balloon."

The velocity of the wind blew the vessel toward the coast of Wales, but after attaining considerable altitude it struck a fresh current and was cast back on the coast of Devon. After a difficult and exhausting flight, the aeronauts found they were losing altitude and discharged the last of their ballast. Unable to check their fall, everything else went overboard, including a barometer given Sadler by the celebrated Dr. Johnson, for which he had once been offered two hundred guineas.

At 4:15 the machine descend with astonishing precipitancy into the sea, six miles from Lymouth. Had the day not been remarkably clear, no one would have witnessed the accident and the two would have drowned. Fortunately, a boat was dispatched and the aeronauts were brought aboard in "in an extreme state of fatigue," Sadler being unable to stand, having been some time in the water before rescue. The balloon traveled one hundred miles in the short space of three hours.[6]

On July 3, 1811, Sadler ascended from the Great Court of Trinity College in a spherical balloon 34 feet in diameter, equal to 20,530 cubic feet when inflated with hydrogen. The envelope contained 3,692 square feet of lustring silk and was varnished with caoutebone (a solution of India-rubber). The colors were arranged in perpendicular stripes, the upper hemisphere sky blue and white, the lower crimson and white. The two hemispheres were connected by a band of "garter-blue and white," in horizontal stripes. The car was decorated with the banners of the Chancellor and Lord High Steward and the arms of the University and town.

Offering to sell the second seat for 100 guineas, it was found the balloon did not have enough ascending power for two, compelling Sadler to go alone. The aerostat ascended and moved steadily south, cheered by the spectators who paid 5 shillings for admission into the Great Court. Having previously determined to fly no more than 48 minutes, Sadler brought the balloon down in a field near Stanstead, in Essex, 23 miles from Cambridge.[7]

On August 13, Lieutenant Paget (also referred to as "Captain"), who lost his seat on the July 3 flight, got his chance. Going up in a balloon navigated by James Sadler, Junior, they departed from Hackney. After packing the car with a barometer, thermometer, compass, two grappling irons, a telescope, refreshments and 130 pounds of ballast, the machine soared upward to a height of 300 yards before heading in an easterly direction.

Coming upon London, the officer opened a bottle of Madeira and they drank a bumper to the health of the Prince Regent. Either the height or the wine affected Paget's view, for he took the capital for a small village and could not be persuaded otherwise until the four bridges of London — London, Westminster, Blackfriars and Battersea — were pointed out to him. After passing Gravesend, they determined to land before being blown out to sea. A brisk wind came up and the machine was blown over several fields, skimming over hedges and ditches. Eventually the grappling irons caught on the clothes of a laborer, who became so entangled the shirt was torn from his back.

During one of the shocks sustained as the balloon rebounded, Paget was thrown from the car but had "sufficient presence of mind to catch hold of its rim," by which he managed to hold on until help arrived. Having been aloft for an hour and 13 minutes, the aeronauts touched *terra firma* and were assisted from the car. Paget sustained a serious injury from his fall, but admitted only an extreme pain in his ear when the balloon was at its greatest height.[8]

The Mermaid Tavern was destined to become synonymous with English balloon ascensions. Situated in Hackney, it hosted numerous events, providing an open lawn or garden for the inflation and ample space for numerous spectators to gather.

On August 29, Sadler made his second flight there with a gentleman named Beaufoy. At an early hour the roads leading to the area presented a solid line of carriages, "and every thing that could be strained into the name of a vehicle was pressed into the service of the City amateurs."[9]

On ascending, the "thickness of the London atmosphere" soon obscured the land from the aeronaut's view, an interesting note on the perennial fog surrounding the city, and surprisingly the first of its kind in a balloon article. Presumably, the description of "thick clouds" referred to the same condition.

Passing Romford, Brentwood, Ingatestone and the intermediate towns, the vessel arrived over Chelmsford. In the name of science, Sadler threw out several hapless pigeons, which invariably returned to the balloon. At 5,961 feet Sadler repeated the experiment. The innocent bird "made the strongest efforts to recover its situation in the air, but ultimately failed, and sunk down towards the earth."

Traveling through a hailstorm during which the balloon sustained several severe shocks, prudence required a descent, which was made by allowing gas to escape. Moving downward with remarkable rapidity, the aeronauts threw out their grappling irons and landed safely in a meadow near the village of East-Thorpe, Essex.[10]

A Hoax and a Perilous Voyage

In an incident proving that people have not changed much over the years and that a good joke (to the perpetrator, at least) was worth the effort, a "mischievous person" sent invitations to the leading citizens of Birmingham, purporting to be from the Reverend T. Edgell, Master of the Academy in the Green Lanes, "requiring their attendance in their various avocations." The date selected was October 7, one day before Sadler's scheduled ascension.

In consequence, at the appointed time of 11:00, no less than eight chaises and two coaches approached the gentleman's house. Among them were four tailors for measuring the young gentlemen of the academy for new suits in honor of the coming event; several drapers, shoemakers and hatters came for a similar outfitting, while a butcher with a large quantity of meat arrived to feed them. A doctor and dentist appeared to cure their bodily ills and the postman brought up the rear with a large sack of spurious letters addressed to the students.

The road to the Academy being narrow, the lane was quickly jammed, causing loud disputes and quarrelling among the merchants. "The scene of confusion and disappointment … may be easily conceived."[11]

The hoax notwithstanding, the area near Birmingham was crowded with spectators for the 21st ascension of Mr. Sadler. At 2:20 the balloon arose with the aeronaut and his passenger, Mr. Burcham, carrying with them nearly 200 pounds of ballast. In several seconds they were obscured from view.

Continuing east, they reached their greatest elevation of two miles and a half, but coming into a current of air threatening to carry them out to sea, Sadler deemed it prudent to descend. In consequence of the grappling irons "being ineffectually thrown out," the machine struck earth with extreme violence. Sadler, who had hold of the valve line was thrown out, receiving several severe contusions to the head and body.

With only one person aboard, the balloon quickly ascended to a height of 100 yards and traveled a mile and a half before the grappling iron caught fast. The balloon struck a tree, leaving Burcham shaken and bruised.

With no one near his landing, Sadler was forced to walk to a nearby mill. Having lost one of his shoes on his expulsion, he begged a replacement from the miller. The man charged him 7 shillings for an old one, "though it was not worth two-pence." Later, after the aeronaut made it safely to town and told his story, the miller was recognized in the crowd and forced to refund the charge. At Heckington, the lost companions were reunited, each fancying the other killed. "The interview was scarcely less that *ludicrous*. They *flew* into one another's arms, with such expressions of joy, as cannot be conceived by those who have not been in circumstances nearly similar!"[12]

13

The Women of Aerostation

*The beauty, the majestic motion, and the spirit of adventure, connected with a bal-
loon, naturally attract the multitude, while men of science may not unworthily
admire the skill and science which prepare this singular machine for the command
of an element that seems of all others the most uncontrollable.*[1]

Traditionally, in the history of the human race, challenges of great magnitude and danger were the province of men. Even if women were physically, artistically, and intellectually
capable of such undertakings, their forced subservient position as the "weaker sex" prevented
them from achieving international fame. In the 19th century, when the highest attainment
for women was motherhood and females were revered for their chastity, beauty, frailty and
attainment of household virtues, it is all the more remarkable that they were intricately
involved in ballooning almost from the very beginning.

It is difficult to fathom exactly why women were permitted to participate in this new —
and potentially deadly — sport. While it is true that the early female pioneers were brought —
or perhaps it is more accurate to say allowed to participate — by husbands, fathers or other
male relatives, the fact they were accepted by the "paying public" is astonishing by itself.
Had a female displayed prowess as a jockey or a cricket player it is highly unlikely she would
have been permitted to race a horse in competition with men or join an otherwise all-male
team. Hundreds of articles would have been written on how such participation would
destroy her chances of ever having a baby (a notion which carried over well into the 20th
century), weaken her bones or even challenge her intellect.

Women were forced to write under male pseudonyms, practice medicine as midwives
and educate themselves solely for the edification of their husbands and sons. If they dared
stray from their accepted role, they were chastised, classified as "manish," or charged with
witchcraft. Even reigning queens were supposed to be led by their consorts or councilors,
and then, as now in England and Japan, the rule of firstborn quietly omits daughters unless
there are no blood males anywhere in the line.

How it came to pass that women took their place beside men in the dangerous and
always potentially deadly adventure of hot air ballooning can only be surmised. Perhaps it
stemmed from the fact aerostation was more entertainment than sport, and women were
accepted as actresses and singers. Or possibly, because the entire concept was so new and
uncharted, no rules applied.

Certainly, the appearance of women on the platform was a cause of astonishment, and
always with an eye toward finance, an ascension promising a female aeronaut brought in

the crowds. Women quickly learned how to use this to advantage and became as adept as men at showmanship. That said, their contributions were far greater than mere moneymakers. They flew solo flights, traveled around the world giving performances (often before royal audiences) and several became more adept in the art of parachuting than their male counterparts.

For whatever reasons, the inclusion of women gave aerostation a dimension far more elevated than other sports and offered girls of the 1800s a legitimate reason to wish upon the clouds. Not all their dreams came true, of course, but then neither did every boy — or man — get his share of the limelight. Perhaps for some women, just knowing the opportunity existed was enough; but for others, the brave, intrepid women explorers became celebrities, worthy of having their likeness hung from the wall with pride.

The two early standouts representing women's liberation in the heavens were Jeanne-Genevieve Garnerin, wife of André-Jacques Garnerin, and Marie Madeleine-Sophie Blanchard, wife of Jean-Pierre Blanchard.

The Garnerin Women

Jeanne Garnerin was the first woman ever to make a parachute jump, when she descended from a balloon in 1799. It should be noted that ascending in a balloon was, in and of itself, a monumental feat; to actually risk one's life by detaching from the relative safety of the car and plunge into the air with only an experimental parachute was a risk few men dared take.

Garnerin had already made eight flights when, on August 3, 1802, she ascended with her husband at Vauxhall. That same month, the Garnerins went to Greenwich to watch the (failed) ascent of Francis Barrett. Easily recognized in the crowd, the famous pair were received as celebrities.

Eager to keep the aerostatic tradition in the family, Garnerin's niece, Elisa (also spelled "Eliza"), learned the trade and made an ascent from the bowling green at Tivoli on September 20, 1815. Only twenty years of age, her flight brought forth "a number of persons of distinction, among them the King of Prussia and the Prince Royal, his son." Although the wind blew with considerable violence and a small pilot balloon was rapidly carried off, she eagerly threw herself into the car and was applauded by the acclamations of the spectators. Rising quickly, Elisa prepared her parachute; at eleven and a half minutes into the flight she separated from the balloon. The parachute was observed to be revolving rapidly "and the descent effected majestically and without danger." Or, more appropriately, the descent was effected majestically and with considerable danger, performed with consummate skill and considerable courage. The descent required more than five minutes and the young aeronaut landed without accident near Meudom.[2]

A year later, on May 2, 1816, Elisa rose into a calm and serene atmosphere. The wind being from the southeast, she was carried over the Seine and passing the river, disengaged from her car and alighted without incident in the Bois de Boulogne. Lightened of its load and without direction, the machine continued to rise, reaching an air current that took it toward the plain of Montrague.[3]

For the fete of St. Louis on August 25, 1816, Elisa and her sister were invited to perform. Pre–publicity announced that the Garnerins would ascend in their balloon, Elisa singing verses in honor of the King and Royal family while accompanying herself on the harp.[4] The proposed flight did not go off as planned. The women attempted three ascensions but the balloon would not rise. In order to allay the crowd that had become "seriously angry," Mademoiselle Elisa ascended alone. The flight was of short duration and she descended fifteen minutes later near the Bois de Boulogne (also spelled "Bologne"). The newspaper noted, "More fortunate than M. Guillaume [see below], M. Garnerin, the father [actually, her uncle], had not his chair broken, and his barriers remained untouched."[5]

Madame Blanchard, also an invited performer at the fete, ascended in her balloon from the Champ de Mars amid cheers from the masses.[6]

Interestingly, on the same day a gentleman named Guillaume had proposed to fly from the Champ de Mars by the use of wings attached to his back. Unfortunately, "his courage failed, or he found his wings would not answer; and this modern ICARUS hid himself in the crowd, from the reproaches and bootings [sic] of the populace." The disappointment was, in some measure, compensated for by the ascent of a balloon with the aeronaut Augustin "and an adventurous young lady, aged 14."[7]

The next mention of Elisa Garnerin came on June 28, 1818, from Boudreaux. At the hour of 6:00 P.M. the young aeronaut prepared to ascend when a strong wind kicked up, agitating the balloon and fears for her safety. She entered the car "and with an intrepid countenance, and waving a white flag," acknowledged the applause of an immense multitude.

The balloon was driven violently toward the south and the crowd moved toward the harbor, where precautions had been taken against accident. In a few minutes she separated from the vessel in a parachute, but was caught in a crosscurrent and pushed into the middle of the river where she was obliged to descend. Two boats were on hand and picked her up; the account states "she was very much terrified when the boats came to her assistance."[8]

Madame Blanchard

Marie Madeleine-Sophie Armant (known as "Sophie") married Jean-Pierre Blanchard in 1804. She made a number of balloon ascents both with her husband and solo, earning the great distinction of being appointed by Napoleon as the official balloonist of France in 1804 when Garnerin fell out of favor. In 1809 M. Blanchard suffered an apparent heart attack in the Hague while in his balloon. He fell to earth and died several weeks later from his injuries.

Sophie continued her own career, and by September 1810 she had already made fifteen ascensions. Her 16th ascent at Frankfort was one long to be remembered. Delayed in the morning for want of vitriolic acid, the first attempts failed as the balloon would not rise. By 7:00 P.M., alarmed that she should disappoint the public, Madame Blanchard got into the car. In spite of those who felt the attempt too dangerous, she ordered the cords cut to a cry of universal acclamation.

Despite a brisk wind from the northeast, the ascent was very fine and she was soon carried out of sight. Until word of her landing arrived "there was reason to fear lest she should be the victim of her courage, or rather her temerity," but all turned out well. She descended at 9:00 P.M. in a wood near Sternfisbush, ten leagues from Frankfort, and returned to the city at 4:00 the next afternoon.[9]

On June 23, 1811, for the fete of St. Cloud, the public was invited to attend a grand celebration. As became the official aeronaut of France, Madame Blanchard ascended in a gilt balloon to highlight the festivities.[10]

This undated poster advertises Madame Blanchard's balloon ascent from Milan, Italy, August 15, 1811. Married to the celebrated aeronaut, "Sophie" became a famous balloonist and parachutist in her own right, proving that women were equally and — in many instances — more adept than men in the developing and dangerous sport (by permission of the National Air and Space Museum, Smithsonian Institution, Washington, D.C.).

On July 30, 1811, the London *Times* reported that Madame Blanchard, in one of her late ascents from Paris, was caught in a storm of hail and rain. On ascending to a greater height, she was lost from sight and did not alight from her balloon until 7:00 A.M., when she landed near Vincenners. "In consequence of the prodigious height the balloon ascended, Madame Blanchard fainted, and continued insensible for some time. Her ascension occupied fourteen and a half hours."

It was not unusual for an aeronaut to suffer from extreme sleepiness at high altitudes, and numerous accounts were given of men dropping off to sleep without being able to fight the effects of thin air. (See M. Blanchard's and Lunardi's flights of 1784 and Zambeccari's flight of 1803 for similar remarks about sleeping.)

Not surprisingly, one feature peculiar to women was that they frequently flew alone, without companions to aid them, either in the physically demanding aspects of landing or to wake them should they nod off. While some of this may be ascribed to the fact many chose to be parachutists (by far the most dangerous of the aerial trials), and thus needed no companion, others opted to fly alone by choice. Whether they chose a solo adventure in order that any fame might not be erroneously credited to their male counterparts or for other reasons is not clear. But certainly in Madame Blanchard's case, ascending alone deprived her of the lucrative business of selling the second seat in the balloon. For a woman making her living in aerostation, this must have been a financial hardship.

Again in October 1811, Madame Blanchard was attributed to have become "the victim of her intrepidity." A violent wind came up immediately before her ascension, but did not prevent her from going up. "Not withstanding all her presence of mind," was she able to command the vessel. The balloon was dashed against the tiles of houses and then thrown against a tree, where it caught. Rescuers came to her aid and dragged her from the gondola, "but not before she was dead." The balloon immediately arose and was lost in the clouds.[11]

Three days later the same paper reported that Madame Blanchard was not killed by the accident but "she was much bruised." Happily, the two-sentence notice informed the public, "she has completely recovered."

Alive and well in 1814, the aeronaut was in Paris, performing for the King. "The balloon reclined for an instant on the statue of Henry IV, but shortly rose in the direction of the Palace of the Four Nations." After attaining sufficient height, a number of white pigeons were set free, "and, like the dove of the ark, flew to communicate to the provinces that the storms and tempests of France were at an end."[12]

On September 21, 1817, she made her 53rd ascension at Nantes. Despite violent winds in the environs of Paris, the flight was a successful one and she descended four leagues from the place of her departure.

Sophie's career came to a tragic end on Tuesday, July 6, 1819, during her 67th ascension. (Some accounts gave the date as Monday, July 5; see the London *Times*, July 12, and the Edinburgh *Advertiser* of July 13.) Her ascent, long announced to be part of the extraordinary fete at Tivoli, attracted a large crowd and the aeronaut, dressed in white and wearing a white hat decorated with feathers, entered her car at 10:30 P.M. Her balloon was constructed of luminous material and was illuminated by Bengal fire-pots, creating a spectacular vision. Inside were placed artificial fireworks meant to be discharged in a series of explosions, filling the sky with sparkling light.

The machine rose slowly, presumably due of an excessive load and caught on the outer branches of trees surrounding the enclosure. Madame Blanchard jettisoned ballast, causing it to ascend more rapidly, then saluted the gathering by waving her flag. Everything appeared normal except for several small containers of spirits of wine that were overturned during the initial ascent.

The balloon entered a light cloud, completely extinguishing the fire-pots. At this point, she ignited the fireworks, producing the desired effect. Some of the fuses were observed to move perpendicularly toward the envelope, but the bystanders, "enchanted by the sight, paid no attention," until a vivid light alerted them to the fact something terrible had happened, "leaving no doubt of the deplorable fate of the aeronaut."

The fire began at the base and quickly spread. On the ground, cries of agony burst forth in every direction; "some women fell unwell, and the terror which such a tragedy instills in the hearts of witnesses, soon spread throughout the assembly." The gendarmes instantly galloped toward the place where it was presumed she would fall and it was soon learned that she had plummeted 400 feet, landing on a housetop in the Rue de Provence. The roof was broken to the extent of four or five feet circumference and the inhabitants of the house report hearing dreadful cries. She afterward fell from the roof onto the street, "and this last fall was that which appears to have caused her death."[13]

Another account stated that her body was discovered in the car, being caught by the cords that attached it to the balloon. When taken up she was heard to utter several sighs, and she was conveyed with all speed in a chair to Tivoli, where physicians attempted to restore her to life, but their efforts proved futile. Although her body was badly crushed, there was no disfiguration, and another guess as to the cause of death was proposed that, as her clothes were not burned and "the head was intact as were the legs, so it seemed that the principle cause of death was asphyxiation.

"Many suggestions have been put forth as to the cause of the fire on board the balloon. One cannot doubt that the personages chosen by Mme. Blanchard, who presided over the ascent, did not do all that was possible to ensure a successful issue."

Speculation centered around the supposition that Blanchard wanted to descend in close proximity to where she rose, and had not closed the appendix through which the gas had been introduced and through which it subsequently escaped. "Wishing to light another firework attached to a small parachute which she was meant to throw out of the balloon, the taper which she held ignited the escaping gas."[14]

"The different reports agree in saying that Madame Blanchard, commonly so courageous, was agitated by sinister presentments. At the moment of her ascent she said to a person near her, 'I know not why, but I am not easy to-day.'" Among her papers was found a will, leaving her property, amounting to 50,000 francs, to the eight-year-old daughter of one of her friends.[15] She herself had no children and her age was estimated at 45 years.

After her death was announced, all amusements for the fete were immediately stopped and the proprietors gave notice that the admission money would be given to the poor woman's children. Ladies and gentlemen stood at the gate to receive subscriptions for the family.[16] By July 16 it had already reached 3,000 francs.[17]

Two months after the tragedy of Madame Blanchard, Elisa Garnerin announced a magnificent fete at Orleans in which "the least splendid ornament was to be the ascent of a balloon of 1,000 feet." The venue was to be the old burying-ground of the town where a scene of most beautiful exhibition would take place. The venue and timing proved to be a bad omen, for the inhabitants, furious at not finding the wonders promised in the advertisements, reported the aeronaut to the magistrates. Instead of "mounting with glory into the ethereal regions," Mademoiselle Garnerin was conducted, amid the hisses of the people, "to a vile prison, where she will be brought before the Tribunal of Correctional Police!"[18]

Wilhelmine Reichard the "Ballonfaherin"

Wilhelmine Reichard *née* Schmidt was born April 2, 1788, in Braunschweig and died February 23, 1848, in Dresden. During her career as an aeronaut she made 17 balloon flights between 1811 and 1820, the first taking place on August 6, 1807. She married Professor Johann Carl Gottfried Reichard (occasionally misspelled as "Reichardt" or "Richard"), and dedicated herself to aerial exhibitions after the manner of Madame Blanchard. In the expanding field of aerostation, her exploits were apparently of less interest to the newspapers of Britain and France; her first mention came on August 7, 1816. The brief article, taken from Berlin sources, merely mentioned that she ascended in a balloon, "in presence of the Prince Royal, the Princess William, Prince Charles of Mecklenbourg, Prince of Radziwil, and a numerous concourse of spectators."[19]

That same year the *Times* reported that Madame "Richard," who lately went up in a balloon from Hamburg, landed at Mulheim, half a league from the frontier of Mecklenburgh.[20] The ascent was "attended with some remarkable circumstances." After a rapid rise in her balloon from Hamburg she traveled over a space of 110 English miles in three hours due to a very violent wind. At one point she was on the verge of being pushed over the Baltic, when the machine fell into a different wind current and blew her away.

At 7,000–8,000 feet she found the atmosphere very agreeable with a warmth of 15°, "a temperature of the air without parallel." The highest elevation reached was 10,000 feet. Reichard attempted to descend several times without success, but finally managed to bring the vessel down. Unfortunately, it became entangled among some trees and was blown from one to another. The aeronaut finally managed to break away a thick branch in order to disengage herself and then landed in safety.[21]

An End to War Celebrated with Balloons

In 1818 the major powers assembled to negotiate the peace and put an end to the Napoleonic Wars. With so many dignitaries assembled, they necessarily needed entertainment to take the edge off the serious business of diplomacy. Among brass bands, concerts, fireworks and banquets, balloon ascensions were one of the main attractions.

What makes this particularly remarkable is that the two aeronauts invited to perform were both women — Madame Reichard and Mademoiselle Garnerin. Adding to popular interest, the "feud" between the two performers, not an uncommon ploy in the very competitive world of aerial showmanship, made good press.

On October 11, Madame Reichard ascended in her balloon at Aix-La-Chapelle. Prior to the ascent, the King conversed with her some minutes before the fastenings were cut. "She displayed the utmost courage and indifference in making the preparations for so dangerous an experiment, and entered the basket with the greatest composure and some grace." At 4:30 P.M. the balloon arose, Madame Reichard scattering flowers over the spectators and waving her flag. She alighted safely in a garden about 15 miles on the road to Cologne.[22]

The following day another voyage was perfectly well executed, although Reichard was late getting off. Accompanied by her husband, "both acquitted themselves exceedingly well." At the height of 150 toises, she threw out a small parachute, "which very well answered the purpose of exhibiting its effect."[23]

The date of Mademoiselle Garnerin's ascent from Louisberg was set for October 20, at 3:00 P.M. The heights at the north end of town were crowded with spectators, with the coffeehouses reserved for those willing to pay one franc for the privilege of a closer view. Between the height of two mountains a platform was raised for the balloon; admittance here to view the lady and her apparatus cost between five and ten francs. A "sufficient number" of Prussian soldiers were stationed to keep the 6,000 onlookers in order and to prevent admission without payment.

By 4:30 the Prussian King became impatient for Garnerin to ascend, but numerous small holes in the balloon caused delays. The aeronaut became "rather alarmed," and when she did make the attempt, the balloon rose and fell twice, "making what the French would call *a chute sans parachute*, and showing an 'alacrity at sinking' greater than Falstaff's."

On the third attempt, "either by accident or design," the ropes holding the *nacelle* (boat) came loose. The car fell some distance while the balloon ascended without her. Amid the shouts and jeers of the company she was carried away in the car by the Prussian troops, completely overwhelmed by the humiliation.

The spectators demanded restitution for the 6,000 francs collected. To avoid a riot, the police seized the money, announcing it would go into the Prussian treasury.[24] The balloon, found in the commune of Nieotrastad, was a total loss.

The opposing factions supporting the aeronauts came to a low point when those supporting Reichard announced Mademoiselle Garnerin would make fresh ascent "as soon as she acquires courage, and has recovered her balloon and her health." M Garnerin responded by writing an editorial, stating: "*If there is a single person in the whole world* who can count, like Mademoiselle Garnerin, 14 ascents, and, which are things unheard of, 14 descents in the parachute, *let him be named*: she will then renounce willingly, in his favour, the credit of being still the most *able and most intrepid aeroporist, that ever existed.*"[25] (italics in the original).

The final mention of ballooning from the summit merely stated that Madame Reichard ascended "today" in her balloon. "The fine though cold weather favoured the enterprise, which was completely successful."[26]

Although the events surrounding the Peace Conference brought Madame Reichard to world attention, few of her subsequent ascents were deemed newsworthy in the British and French newspapers. What was perhaps her last balloon flight occurred at Munich in October 1820. After a successful ascent she arose to a height of 3,000 feet, at which point she opened the valve to let out some gas and the machine plummeted at least one thousand feet. "The spectators no longer feared for the courageous woman," and watched with interest as she then threw out some ballast and rose again to a great height.

Skillfully manipulating the balloon in order to avoid landing in some trees, she safely alit in the Keferlohe district.[27]

Other Early Women Pioneers in Aerostation

Mrs. L. A. Sage was the first Englishwoman to fly in a balloon when she ascended with Vincent Lunardi on June 29, 1785. The first all-female pair of aeronauts were Madame de Jean and the Marchioness de Brossond, who ascended in a tethered balloon under the supervision of M. Blanchard on July 19, 1784. Miss Drury attempted to become the first Irish woman to ascend, when, on April 20, 1786, she and her brother planned an aerial experiment, but unfortunately they were unable to succeed.

Another woman who took up the profession in order to support herself was Madame Bittorf. The "mechanician, Bittorf, from Manheim," presumably her husband, suffered a fatal accident on July 7, 1812. After rising to a considerable height, he perceived, too late, that the balloon was damaged and opened the valve. As the machine descended with great velocity, the inflammable air caught fire and the envelope exploded, sending shreds over the aeronaut's head and breast, severely burning him. The vehicle struck the roof of a house and he died the next day in extreme agony.[28] Madame Bittorf went on to make a number of ascensions and was depicted on a popular print of the times.

On September 9, 1821, Mademoiselle Cecelia (also spelled "Cecilia") encountered an event that nearly proved fatal. In attempting an ascent from Marseilles, the balloon struck against the mast (used to hold the envelope upright while inflating). It lost the power to clear a neighboring house and hit the balcony. The aeronaut received a violent contusion on her side and a severer injury to her head. Fortunately, "she was indebted for her safety to her unshaken courage."[29]

À la Marie Stuart

During festival week in Paris, August 1823, Mademoiselle Garnerin was the aeronaut invited to perform. The envelope, not permitted to fill more than two-thirds to prevent the balloon traveling any distance, was of plain varnished silk and the parachute from which the artist was to descend, of blue and yellow. The basket, weighing only a few pounds, also presented a simple appearance. The netting held a ticket containing Mademoiselle Garnerin's address in order to secure the restoration of the machine wherever it chanced to fall.

The aeronaut, described as about 40 years of age, wore a white dress with a hat *à la Marie Stuart*. At 8:30 P.M. the attendants attached the car and Garnerin took her seat. The cords were then cut away and two persons dragged the vessel up to the balcony occupied by the Duchess de Berri. After exchanging pleasantries, the pilot, "having been turned round and round by the action like a fowl upon a spit, took her leave of the august personages."

A few minutes before 9:00, the balloon rose and went off toward St. Denis. When at a height of 300 yards and nearly out of sight as darkness settled, Garnerin let herself out and descended in the parachute, landing in safety at Bourge, three leagues distant. The successful adventurer returned to the Champ de Mars by 10:00 but the spectators had already disbanded, many state of anxiety as to her fate. Inquiries were made at her residence and receiving no word, it was "consequently inferred that she had broken her neck." Not until morning did the public learn the contrary.[30]

Perhaps the most fascinating female aeronaut of the 19th century was Sophia Stocks. Her astonishing story is given in Chapter 17.

14

(Mostly) Magnificent
Balloon Ascensions: 1812–1819

*Amongst the several applications of science to the arts, which we have witnessed in
our own times, that of ballooning appears to be one of the most imperfect and
unpromising.*[1]

Until the emergence of Charles Green in 1821, James Sadler remained the darling of
British aerostation, although difficulties in landing—typically the most dangerous part of
a voyage—continued to plague him.

On June 29, 1812, Sadler ascended from a yard adjoining St. George's Fields, Manchester, and descended at Oak Woods, six miles east of Sheffield, having traveled 51 miles
in 48 minutes. The landing site being a barren moor, the grappling irons found nothing
on which to secure, continually breaking away from the loose material on the ground. The
machine rebounded several times and in consequence became much torn and the car greatly
damaged. Sadler himself sustained several severe bruises, but eventually walked away from
the scene.[2]

Various words were used to describe "minor" injuries sustained by aeronauts and typically little was made of "several bruises," "shaken up," "a bump on the head," or "quite
exhausted" in the newspapers. Unless the fall was fatal, balloonists were absolutely expected
to keep their next appointment. Almost without exception, they did, no matter how badly
injured they may actually have been.

The reason was basic: aeronauts were primarily entertainers, well aware there was always
some upstart willing to assume their next engagement. While the stars of the profession
were household names and their announced ascensions drew large crowds, no amount of
fame was likely to hold back an irate mob which found itself disappointed.

That meant the men and women of aerostation learned to live with their contusions,
concussions, stitches, bumps, bruises and even broken bones and work through the pain.
And pain there was, for even landings described as "gentle" or "safe" more than likely occasioned any number of hurts along the way. Hard jarrings in the car when the machine was
beaten by contrary currents; enormous raising or precipitous drops in altitude caused serious
ear problems; frostbite from extremes of temperature; twisted ankles sustained in a parachute
drop; the rebounding of the aerial machine once, twice, half a dozen times before coming
to a standstill were all the day-in and day-out hazards of the occupation.

It took a hearty constitution and a considerable amount of stamina to be an aeronaut.

The obvious reference to "courage," used so casually in the periodicals of the day, referred to putting their life on the line, and so it was. But contending with stiff muscles, headaches, sinus troubles, earaches and fractures while keeping a schedule were the un-lauded but equally trying demands placed on these individuals.

In order to survive the rigors of the profession, the wealthier aeronauts had whirlpools constructed in their homes so that they might try and soak away the aches and pains. Those of the lower orders were required to tolerate pain and suffering as they might. But in any case, the fortitude and extreme physical endurance required were often lost on the public.

Consequently, Sadler did not have long to recover from his bruises. By August 1812, he was in Liverpool, where his appearance had been long awaited and much anticipated. "At twelve o'clock the town was nearly deserted; and the shops being almost universally shut, it wore the aspect of Sunday, but with scarcely a person in the streets." Good for aeronauts, not so good for local businesses: One of the most common complaints about balloon exhibitions came from local merchants ruing the fact no one made their usual shopping trips on days when the balloonists performed.

The operation of filling the balloon commenced at 10:00 on August 12 and finished at 2:30 P.M. The wind took Sadler in a southeast direction, where he reached his highest elevation in twenty minutes. Remaining in sight the entire time, the balloon descended in Knowsley Park, four miles from Liverpool.[3]

Sandwiched between Sadler's flight from Manchester and his ascent from Dublin in October, the aerostatic community suffered two tragedies. The first came on September 21, 1812, when Francesco Zambeccari, accompanied by a friend named Bonoga, ascended in a balloon from Bologna. The flight itself was smooth, but on descending the vehicle became entangled in the branches of a tree. Before it could be disengaged it caught fire, forcing the men to jump. Zambeccari was killed on the spot, but Bonoga survived, although sustaining several broken bones.

The second loss came from Manheim, where the aeronaut Bittorf died after falling out of his descending balloon.[4]

Aerial Voyage Across the Irish Channel

Despite the fact two fellow aeronauts had died horrible deaths within recent months, James Sadler took his balloon to Ireland and ascended from the Belvidere House, Dublin, on October 1, 1812. Amid a collection of "rank, fashion, and respectability," including the Duchess of Richmond, a devotee of ballooning, he rose at precisely 12:48. In 35 minutes he had sight of the mountains of Wales, and continuing in that direction, reached the Isle of Man by 3:00. An hour later Sadler reported seeing the Skerry Lighthouse and held out hopes of a swift arrival at Liverpool.

The wind shifted, however, and blew him away from land and back over the water. While no aeronaut ever desired to land in the sea, he spotted five vessels bearing down the Channel and in hopes of their assistance, lowered the machine. In this critical position he discovered that none of the vessels paid the slightest heed to his plight, obliging him to throw out a quantity of ballast and re-ascend. With night coming on and having no other choice, he once more descended into the sea near Ormshead at 5:00 P.M. Unfortunately, wind currents skimming the surface of the water caught the balloon and hurtled him away from a nearby boat. In a panic, he tied his clothes to the grappling iron and tossed it overboard in an effort to create drag. This proved ineffectual, forcing him to expel gas from the envelope. The ensuing propulsion actually sank the car, leaving him nothing but the netting on which to cling.

Sadler's perilous condition and the fear of getting entangled in the netting kept the herring fisher *Victory* away until it became apparent the man would drown if they did not help. Heeding his entreaties to run the bowsprit through the balloon and expel the remaining gas, they completed the operation and threw out a line. Sadler grabbed it, wrapped the rope around his arms and the rescuers dragged him a considerable distance before finally being able to pull him aboard, "quite exhausted."

Captain John Lee, out of Douglas, Isle of Man, conveyed the aeronaut to Liverpool. As he was unprepared for the immense crowd of spectators waiting for him on shore and lacking clothes, the fishermen placed him on board the frigate *Princess*, where he was politely received and accommodated with a wardrobe.[5]

Blowing up a Hurricane

The ascent of James Sadler at Cheltenham was scheduled for Monday, the 6th of September, 1813, but owing to the boisterous wind and the torrents of rain, the experiment had to be put off until the following day. Acutely aware that his reputation lay at stake, Sadler determined to ascend on September 7, despite the fact the wind was still powerful enough to pose a threat to his safety.

The balloon, made of white and crimson silk, in the shape of a Windsor pear, was filled, but its power was not deemed sufficient to raise the aeronaut. At the last minute, Wyndham Sadler (also spelled "Windham"), James' son, aged 16 or 17 years, took his place in the car "with all the firmness which his veteran father possesses." At 4:45 P.M. a signal was given, the ropes were loosened and the youth ascended with great fortitude.

The machine remained in sight for seven minutes, with the sire and his older son, John, following its progress on horseback. Wyndham encountered a thick fall of snow, but managed to reach a field near Chadington Bridge, where he landed in safety. The first man who approached him was armed with a pitchfork and cried, "Lord, Sir, where have you come from?"

Significantly, although the assemblage of people witnessing the ascent was great, comparatively few paid for admission, "and there is, therefore, reason to suspect, that Mr. Sadler, unless indemnified in some other way, will rather be a loser than a gainer by the exhibition."[6]

Ballooning Season was typically limited to the warmer months when atmospheric conditions were less severe and tourists gathered at the more fashionable ascension sites. Desirability did not always coincide with practicality, however, especially when the aeronaut needed money to pay his creditors. Thus, on November 1, 1813, James Sadler made his 28th voyage, this time from the Canal Company's Wharf at Nottingham. After a voyage of 50 minutes covering a distance of 44 miles, he descended with ease near Stamford.[7]

By the summer of 1814, when the weather again permitted safe travel, Sadler had "the honour to acquaint the Nobility and Public in general" with news that he would make his 29th ascension from the Burlington House on July 15.[8]

Sadler's car was of slight construction, made of cork (usually used when any possibility of landing in the water was apprehended) and wicker-work, painted with the Royal arms

and British flags at both ends; the balloon was handsomely painted with figures of the cardinal virtues in compartments of columns, the upper part striped with pale orange, and the
lower resembling clouds.

The inflation process, by means of silk tubes connected by brass fixtures to the gas vessels, was slow, although the vats from which the gas issued were of a large size, ten feet high,
unremittingly pouring out a stream of vapor in a state which required a constant effusion
of cold water to keep the conductors from violently overheating. The inflation was completed
at 3:00 P.M. Sadler and his son entered the car and lifted off at 3:15 P.M. After suffering from
intense pain in the ears[9] the aeronauts brought the machine safely down in the parish of
Great Warley, in Essex, 18 miles from town.[10]

On July 23, the newspapers announced that Wyndham Sadler had obtained permission
from the Duke of Devonshire to re-ascend from the Burlington House on Friday, the 29th.[11]
After a skillful ascension, he maneuvered in the air and then manipulated his descent so as
to be visible to the same crowd that had gathered for the lift-off. Setting down safely at
5:00 P.M., the only inconvenience he encountered was "several hundred persons wishing to
offer assistance."[12]

The following years were primarily consumed with the Napoleonic wars. While there
were certainly civilian balloon ascensions in the British Isles, few merited mention in the
newspapers. The next time Sadler's name appeared came in 1816. This time, he ascended
from Cork, Ireland. After discharging an unmanned parachute he sought a landing at Ringa-
bella. Striking ground in a grass enclosure and rebounding, the grappling irons caught in
a hedge, enabling him to secure the balloon.[13]

Two months later, on Tuesday, November 5, 1816, Mr. Sadler, Junior (presumably
Wyndham), accompanied by Mr. Livingston, ascended soon after 3:00 P.M. from Richmond
Barracks, Dublin. The pair descended between 4:00 and 5:00 P.M. in Tickneven Bog, near
Edenderry, 30 miles from Dublin.[14]

Conquering the Irish Sea

The momentous crossing of St. George's Channel was accomplished by Wyndham
Sadler on July 22, 1817. Ascending from the Cavalry Barrack near Dublin at 1:40 P.M., the
aeronaut descended in safety about a mile and a half from Holyhead at 7:00 P.M., having
crossed the Irish Channel in five hours and twenty minutes.

During the voyage he simultaneously felt hot and cold, the sun being inconveniently
warm on the upper part of his body, while his feet required additional coverings to restore
circulation. During the trip he encountered a snow shower, which transformed to rain
before it reached earth. He descended in a cornfield within a mile and a half of Holyhead
and was borne in triumph to the house of Captain Skinner. After spending the night, the
young aeronaut, not yet twenty-two years old, visited the new pier being constructed at
Holyhead. Seeing the Diving-bell, he expressed his desire to go down in it, remarking, "I
am just come from the *Clouds*, I should now wish to visit the *Deep*." The bell was prepared
for him and he went down to a depth of several fathoms, remaining underwater a considerable time.[15] An ascent of "Mr. Sadler's Balloon" went off at Dublin on August 20, 1817.
The aeronauts were Mr. Livingston (also spelled "Livingstone") and Miss Thompson. The
balloon ascended at 3:30 P.M. and after "a short but beautiful voyage through the air,"
descended three miles from town in the shrubbery.[16]

Mr. Livingston, now partners with Sadler, and an aeronaut in his own right, ordered the construction of a balloon larger than any which had gone before, being 32 feet in diameter and 38 feet high. It contained 31,600 cubic feet of gas with an ascending power of 1,100 pounds. The form of the car was oval, the ground an azure blue painted with clouds, having on either side the Star of the Orders of St. George and St. Patrick, and at each end the Regent's plume. It also possessed a gilt handrail and trelliswork from which were suspended festoons of flowers for the flight. The envelope was of blue and yellow satin.

Prior to the day of ascent the magnificent machine was displayed at the Music Hall, raising expectations for a wondrous flight. On Tuesday, September 28, 1819, the weather was dull and overcast with dark clouds threatening rain, dashing his hopes of crossing the Channel to Ireland.

Dr. Traill conducted the process of inflation and as the sky brightened, the balloon, carrying Livingston and Sadler, arose amid the congratulations and benedictions of the spectators. Between 3 and 4 o'clock the vessel was observed over Skipton, in Yorkshire, about 50 miles in a straight line from Liverpool, and it was conjectured the pair had determined to cross the island. Such did not prove to be the case, however. They had not traveled much further before deciding to descend at Tees Bay, eventually coming to ground at 4:00 in the neighborhood of Blackburn, within eight miles of the sea, having traveled approximately 35 miles in little more than an hour and a half.[17]

The year 1819 was rounded out in Lisbon on Sunday, December 12th, where the citizens succeeded in inducing Mr. Eugene Robertson (son of the aeronaut Étienne Robertson), who had recently "ascended in the presence of the first Nobility," to descend in a parachute. He rose in his balloon to the height of 1,200 French feet and then separated himself from the machine in a double parachute his father had invented in 1804. The parachute expanded majestically and deposited the intrepid traveler in safety about half a league from Lisbon after a descent of about 25 minutes.

For his trouble, Mr. Robertson's take for the performance exceeded 6,000 piastres. After the success, Robertson declared his intention to set out immediately for Madrid where he proposed to repeat his experiments.[18]

"Fire Balloons and Children's Toys"

"Fire balloons," as the term came to be applied, represented any number of small, inexpensive toy balloons, which were sold to children by the hundreds. Fire balloons were raised by the formation of hot air and sent skyward, their owners having no idea how far the wind would take them. Most consumed the straw or paper fuel before descending, but occasionally residual embers were hot enough to start a conflagration once the apparatus struck ground.

As early as 1802, a fire balloon fell on a haystack near Cannongate, setting the dried material ablaze. A newspaper decried, "The consequences which may follow these trifling and childish exhibitions, are of such a dangerous nature, that the Magistrates have, with great propriety, issued a proclamation prohibiting them in future."[19]

Proclamations and public outcry served little purpose as these toys continued to plague England and Scotland, causing considerable damage and threatening lives by the fires they created. In 1822, Edinburgh magistrates were prompted to issue new rules concerning various public dangers: "No Snow Balls or Squibs shall be thrown, nor Foot Ball, Shinty, or other Game played, nor shall any Kite or Fire Balloon be set off in any of the streets, squares, lanes, or passages, within the bounds of Police, under the penalty after mentioned."[20] The law proved ineffective.

It was inevitable that fire balloons made their way to America. In August 1855, the Terre Haute *American* reported that one such device landed on the house of a Dr. Clippenger and came close to destroying the structure.[21]

Aside from being dangerous, fire balloons also had the power to terrify. In June 1857, a German philosopher predicted a comet would destroy the world. Citizens in Janesville, Wisconsin, were therefore justly horrified to see an apparition with a "very red and fiery appearance" moving across the sky. While they "prepared themselves for a passage to another sphere," the horrific sight was revealed to be no more than a fire balloon some juvenile had sent skyward. The frightened ones forgot their folly "and sinned as before."[22]

Thirty-eight years later, a toy balloon ignited a fire at a copper and iron mill in Silver City, New Mexico, completely destroying the uninsured property worth $100,000.[23]

15

For the World Is Green and I Have Touched the Sky

The only person of importance or notoriety attending the ascension was Mr. Hunt, although a number of pickpockets thought proper to mingle in the spectacle, and to employ themselves in their usual avocation.[1]

With the Regency Period coming to a close, political unrest, still stirred by the upheavals of the French Revolution, Napoleon's conquests and the war with America remained on the minds of ordinary citizens.

The death of the "mad king," George III, in 1820, along with preparations for the coronation of George IV, relieved the outward anxiety of the public, and balloons — symbols of all that was light and airy and optimistic — became an integral part of the proceedings.

The entertainment story of the festivities was the splendid Coronation Balloon, piloted by the unknown aeronaut, Charles Green, who was to ascend on the 19th after the ceremony. As early as 1:00 A.M., a huge gathering assembled in the vicinity of Westminster, the gates of the Abbey were thrown open at 2:00 A.M. and the ceremony commenced at 10:00 A.M. The king was crowned at half past 1:00 P.M. while in another quarter preparations were being finalized for the grand balloon ascent.[2]

Green's balloon cost £280 and measured 31 feet in diameter, "as near the size as possible of the one with which Lunardi first made an ascension in England." At 8:00 A.M. it was brought out and the operation of filling began. Employing a new and revolutionary idea, it was filled with 1,200 cubic feet of carbonated hydrogen gas supplied from the main pipes of the original chartered Gas Company.

While the crowning of a king marked the beginning of a new era in England, this simple change in the inflation process marked the transition from the old methods of hot air ballooning and the laborious fuss and bother of creating hydrogen.

The Gas Light and Coke Company

The Gas Light and Coke Company (also known as the Westminster Gas Light and Coke Company) was located on the Horseferry Road in the Westminster district of London. Chartered on April 30, 1812, it became the first company to supply Londoners with coal gas and operated the first gas works in the United Kingdom. Offices were soon established in Pall Mall with a wharf at Cannon Row. By 1818 the company had established a tar works in Poplar and expanded their works at Brick Lane and Westminster. A gas works was installed at the Royal Mint in 1817 and by 1819 nearly 290 miles of pipes had been laid in London, supplying 51,000 burners.[3]

At 1:00 P.M. the ropes of Mr. Green's magnificent balloon were unfastened and the balloon ascended in a nearly perpendicular manner. Feeling no sensation of movement although "the balloon had a rotary motion, and turned about four times in a minute," the oscillation prevented him from reading the quicksilver in the barometer. Green could not be certain of his height, but estimated it at 11,000 feet. After experiencing an extreme of cold and fearful of being driven toward the sea, he put on his cloak and opened the valve. The gas escaped in considerable quantity and the vessel descended very rapidly.

Still anxious, Green let out more gas and fell into another current, taking him over land. He ate some sandwiches with a good appetite and at 12:40 P.M. descended in a field four miles beyond Barnet in the parish of South Mims. The car struck the earth with great force. Stunned from the effect, he still managed to cling to the hoop of the balloon as he was dragged on his back along the ground a considerable distance before help arrived. The aeronaut estimated that he traveled altogether, in various directions, upward of 50 miles.[4]

An instant celebrity, Charles Green quickly scheduled a second ascent, this time from the Belvedere Tea Gardens, Pentonville, a place destined to witness many future balloon voyages. Long before the appointed hour of 1:00 P.M. an immense crowd gathered to see the "Coronation Aeronaut." Sums ranging from 6d to 2p were paid for seats on the outskirts of action, depending on their proximity to the balloon. The means of inflation was the "common carbonated hydrogen that is used in lighting the streets."

Green ordered the balloon to a more favorable situation so that upon rising it would not strike nearby trees. Ascending alone after his passenger cancelled, the balloon arose in a straight line. Experiencing the extremes of heat and cold, Green then opened the valve "to its utmost extremity," and descended "most rapidly." At 3:30 P.M. having traveled 14 miles in 20 minutes, he landed in a field two miles from Ilford, Essex.[5]

Striking while the iron was hot, Green made a flight from Portsea toward the end of August or early September and being so well received, made a second ascent on September 6, 1821. Advertised as the aeronaut flying the Coronation Balloon, a crowd estimated as 25,000 persons gathered at the Duke of York's Bastion to witness the event. Inflation of the balloon took a mere hour and a half, being filled under the superintendence of Mr. Onthett, engineer of the gas company. Assuming his place in the car at 1:30 P.M., Green took a glass of wine in salute to those who had aided him, and was then paraded around the ring before ascending.

After reaching a height of 4,500 feet he discharged a cat in a parachute. The unfortunate animal must have suffered greatly, for it plunged downward at great speed for 300 feet before the parachute distended. It reached the earth nine minutes later. A further ascent brought Green to 10,000 feet, and knowing this to be the greatest altitude he could reach with safety, he set about making several philosophical experiments. Finishing this, he descended at 2:30 under a heavy rain shower. Water-soaked, the balloon began to fall, requiring the discharge of ballast to break the rapid downward velocity.

Striking the earth with considerable violence, the balloon rebounded, and it was only with the assistance of some men working in the fields that he was enabled to bring it under control. Green reached Portsea the following day, after an aerial voyage of nearly 43 miles in 45 minutes. In his post–flight narrative he thanked the gentlemen of the committee who, after "paying me the sum stipulated, … voluntarily surrendered the overplus of the money for the use and benefit of my only child." He also thanked the brothers Barlow for their gratuitous supply of gas.[6]

This was generous, indeed, but may be considered the exception that proved the rule, for money was very jealously guarded and seldom dispensed with such charity, except in cases where the aeronaut perished. The mention of gas being supplied free of charge would also prove an anomaly, for later aeronauts were burdened with heavy bills incurred during the inflation of their balloons.

A Dunking and a Dreadful Accident

It could not be said that any of the aeronauts, no matter how celebrated and lauded for their skill, had a career devoid of accident and perhaps mischief. On Tuesday, October 2, 1821, Charles Green ascended from the Gas Works at Brighton amid a collection of 30,000 persons. The aeronaut entered the car and directed the band to play "God Save the King" before setting out.[7]

The balloon rose slowly, taking a southeasterly direction.[8] Pushed rapidly over water at an altitude of two miles, he noticed two vessels nearby and determined to make a descent. Plunged by the force of the wind into a tremendously heavy sea, the balloon "drifted rapidly, assuming the appearance of an immense umbrella before me; the car striking the water on its side, its ornaments and coverings were presently destroyed, and it instantly filled with water."

Having previously put on his life preserver, it unfortunately became entangled in the cords and consequently of no use. In this perilous situation, with the car repeatedly turning over so he was alternately under water, Green continued for many minutes until it occurred to him to cut the cords that entangled the preserver. He accomplished this with a knife, which enabled him "to hail a boat humanely sent to my assistance by Capt. Clear, of the *Utility* packet, whose humane and active exertions I shall ever feel proud to acknowledge."

After being dragged in the water a distance of two miles, he was brought on board with much difficulty, his distress "so great as to render it absolutely necessary to strip me. I continued for some hours insensible." After his recovery, Captain Clear informed him that the balloon was "literally torn to ribands [sic]," and that his philosophical instruments and apparatus were all lost or destroyed.[9] For his exertions, Green received £100 and lost a balloon worth £300.[10]

On July 30, 1822, Charles Green ascended with Mr. Griffith of the Cheltenham *Chronicle* from a yard at the back of the London Hotel, Cheltenham. At 1:00 P.M. the spacious yard was nearly filled with ladies and gentlemen, and the balloon was slung up to a rope near 50 feet in the center, when the inflation commenced under the direction of Mr. Spinney, the superintendent of the Gas Works. The weather was very favourable, and by 3:00 it was filled, and displayed a most delightful transparent globe, quartered in alternate colors of blue, red, and yellow, in size beyond anything ever seen in England.

At 3:30 P.M. the aeronauts entered the car, which was of most costly and elegant structure (a gift to the aeronaut by Colonel Reddell of Cheltenham), when it was discovered that some "most wicked person" had cut one of the cords that suspended it from the network. When urged to have the cord repaired, Green replied, "I'll not hazard the cutting of another cord—I do not depend upon one line only, unloose the ropes." The cords were loosened and the balloon ascended in the most majestic manner.[11]

In consequence of the rope being cut, an arch was formed in the network, which from the unequal pressure continued to give way several times during the flight. Within a mile and a half of Salperton the aeronauts determined to descend, the car being at the time only held by one side of the balloon Their grappling irons came in contact with a wall into which it was fastened by some country people, but it was speedily torn away, and they were dragged for the distance of four fields, knocked from hedge to hedge, till at length the car became entangled in a tree. The ropes gave way and the balloon ascended. In the process, the men were flung to the ground from a tremendous height.

A report reached Cheltenham that Green had perished, causing distress "beyond description" to his wife and son. Fortunately, it proved in error, as the aeronauts, after lying insensible, were rescued by Mr. Day of the King's Head, Northleach. Accompanied by his son, they had fortunately ridden over to witness the descent. Finding the men in acute distress, they placed them on horses and accompanied them to Northleach. Green sustained a severe contusion on the left side of the chest and Griffith received a severe injury of the spine. A subscription was opened for Green to replace his £500 balloon.[12] The aerostat was later recovered at Woodstock.[13]

Interestingly, Green was of the opinion that the cord had been cut by black legs from London, "as not less than £20,000 was betted on the event at Cheltenham, besides great sums in London. The severed cord appeared to have been cut by some instrument as sharp as a razor, and the operation must have been effected with great dexterity to avoid notice in the presence of such numbers."[14]

Two weeks later, sufficiently recovered from his injuries, Green traveled to Worcester to ascertain whether an ascent in his balloon would be advisable. Finding, from the want of sufficient notice, there would be little hope of remuneration, and having several pressing offers from other places, he has declined a voyage, at least during the present season.[15]

Before departing from Dublin on August 5, 1822, Mr. Livingston inquired of his assistant, James Sadler, Jr., whether his balloon had enough gas to carry him across the British Channel. Sadler replied it was "scarcely sufficient," to which Livingston vowed, "I am finally resolved to make the attempt, and whatever may be the consequences, I shall cross the sea."

Receiving a flag bearing the arms of Dublin, Livingston ascended "in slow but awful sublimity." After a scant twenty minutes it landed at Caninteely (Ireland), far short of his intended destination. To make matters worse, reports surfaced that money had been exacted from Livingston in consequence of some corn being injured by the balloon when descending. Reviewing the flight, the London *Times*, August 6, 1822, added, "we hope, for the character of our country, this is not true."

The *programme* of amusements for the Preston Guild festival presented something for everyone, from processions, to plays, races, to the Mayor's Ball. On the final day, September 9, 1822, Livingston's balloon was the crowning exhibit. Scheduled for 11:00, the ascent did not take place until 3:00 in consequence of a want of gas. Livingston's voyage lasted 20 minutes, when he came to land in a field between Stonyhurst and Blackburn. After dreadful rebounds, the aeronaut was thrown from the car at the height of 18 feet, falling upon his side.

Relieved from his weight, the balloon ascended and drifted toward the German Ocean, 120 miles distant from the border of Yorkshire.[16] A balloon of yellow and black, the "size of a hay-stack," with a pink car lined with yellow, length 6 feet, was discovered flying over

Manthrope, 6 miles east of Selby. The grapples were hanging from the car but the irons were turned the wrong way so as to prevent them from fastening. Several men grabbed the ropes and brought it down. "When secured there were several sand bags in it, also some biscuits, and a few sheets of blank paper, with an address card of a firm in the woolen trade in Dublin."[17]

Gooseberry Bushes

The 7th ascent of Mr. Green from a balloon was advertised for June 3, 1823, from the Mermaid Tavern, Hackney. Patrons were thereby notified that the exhibition of the balloon and car, currently in the assembly room of the tavern, would close the evening of June 2.[18]

The weather being unfavorable, the inflation did not begin until after 12:00 P.M., and by a mismanagement of the cords, no attention was given the valve, through which the gas passed into the balloon. It was left open and enough escaped that it became necessary to restart the filling process. Bets were "offered and taken to a considerable amount," that Mr. Green would not ascend. Both sides had a claim on the winning hand as the balloon finally went up, but at so low an altitude it was unable to clear the trees. Consequently, more gas escaped and the envelope required another turn at the gas pipes.

Rising a second time, the balloon hovered so close to the tower that several persons were able to reach out and shake his hand. Discharging ballast, the machine reached an altitude of two and a half miles, where Green suffered so extensively from cold that his fingers were paralyzed. With a nod toward his "important and notorious" predecessors, Green's post-flight narrative stated:

> Epping-forest, as I passed over one part of it, appeared of a triangular form, and resembled a coppice covering two acres of land, the trees of which did not appear to my visual organs to be higher than gooseberry-bushes. I mention this to explain a statement made by Captain Sowden, who passed over the same forest with a balloon, in company with Mr. Garnerin, "That although Epping-forest did not appear larger than a gooseberry-bush, he could distinctly see the ruts and furrows in the fields." I have no doubt but that gentleman mistook cross-roads and lanes for ruts and furrows, which any person on a first ascent would be likely to do; and I conceive that his observation as to the gooseberry-bush referral merely of the height of the trees.

He determined to descend early, having pledged to return to Hackney the same night. The balloon came down in the lead-mill marshes, Laytonstone, Barking Side, in a cloverfield belonging to Mr. Staines at Nore-hill. Green was prevented from keeping his promise, however, being detained by Mr. Staines, "who, very illiberally, as I conceive, forcibly seized my balloon, because of some trifling injury that had been done to his clover by persons who ran into the field to witness the descent, and whose natural curiosity inducted them to witness a close inspection of the aeronautical machine."[19]

Mr. Green's ascent from Oxford on June 14, 1823, was delayed by an accident to the poles by which the balloon was suspended. After repairs, the balloon went up with the aeronaut and his passenger, a young gentleman from London named Sparrow, who paid £50 "to be allowed to encounter the perils of the voyage."

Sparrow described the sensation of ascending "as if we were impelled upwards, not unlike the feeling excited by the action of a swing." The car struck the chimney of the gaswork, temporarily giving it a vertical movement" before righting itself and rising in "a retrograde and sometimes angular motion." Sparrow avoided the sensation of fear by gradually accustoming himself to the view, taking in more distant objects first, then slowly observing those on the surface.

During the voyage the aeronauts discovered the cap at the neck of the balloon had come off, compelling them to tie a silk handkerchief around the opening to prevent the too rapid escape of gas. As the balloon fell, Green ordered Sparrow to cling to the hoop to mitigate the shock of striking ground. He complied, but after a violent crash and rebound, he was thrown from the car. Recovering quickly, Sparrow grabbed a dangling rope and with the assistance of a dozen strong fellows, succeeded in bringing down Green and the balloon. Although the car was dashed to pieces, and the event not "well graced with nobility as on former occasions," a large sum was collected at the gate as compensation.[20]

Mr. Henry Simonds, a deaf and dumb gentleman of Bond Street, accompanied Mr. Green on his ninth voyage, this time from Reading on August 1, 1823. In order to ensure a proper remuneration for the aeronaut, hurdles forming a barrier were constructed, through which an admission fee had to be paid.

The balloon measured 107 feet in circumference, and contained 136,280 gallons of gas. Drawn between two poles for support, the envelope comprised 700 yards of oiled silk in alternate stripes of blue, red and yellow. The aeronauts ascended at 4:53, Green bowing to the crowd and Simonds waving his flag. Although they suffered a slight giddiness from the rotary motion of the balloon, the flight went well until it came time to descend. Afforded "not a minute of preparation," the balloon collided with the ground, rebounded several times and dragged them over a hedge and through a field, "with their sides to the ground, and their faces toward each other." The wind eventually propelled them into a cart road five feet deep before striking a tree.[21]

16

Candidates for
Aeronautical Distinction

The LARGEST BALLOON in the WORLD is now EXHIBITING.... Mr. GRA-HAM has the honour to announce, that he has just completed a magnificent BAL-LOON, far exceeding in magnitude and splendour any aerostatic machine hitherto made or exhibited in any part of the world, in which he intended to ASCEND on Monday next.

"August 18, from the gardens of White Conduit-house, Pentonville, where he will be assisted in the inflation and process of ascent by Messrs. Sadler, the well known and celebrated aeronauts; in consequence of which powerful aid, and his having spared neither pains nor expense in the formation of his stupendous machine, he has no doubt of affording to his friends and the public an extraordinary and interesting exhibition."[1]

In this manner, George Graham was introduced to the world of aerostation. The notice added that the dimensions of his aerial vessel were "unparalleled in the annals of philosophy, as it forms a globe, 60 feet in height and 40 feet in diameter," capable of carrying up 9cwt (900 pounds), and containing 33,500 cubic feet, or 250,600 gallons of gas, which, on this occasion was to be furnished by the Imperial Gas Company. Tickets to view the inflation and ascent were priced at 3s 6d each.

In consequence of the "ostentatious placards... industriously circulated throughout the metropolis," an immense multitude gathered at the White Conduit House, Islington, to see the extraordinary machine. That said, the paying company going to inspect the novelty was "neither very numerous nor very select," either from the fact the balloon had been shown during the week for the small price of one shilling, or owing to the heavy price of three and six-pence demanded at the "Cerberus gate" for a close-up view of the inflation.

Inflation began at 10:00 but by 6:00 that evening, it had not been completed. Various excuses were offered, including the large size of the envelope and the fact it was constructed of cotton rather than silk and tended to leak. When those explanations were rebuffed, Graham observed that the supply of gas was not so great as it ought to have been. Various opinions were then delivered on whether the spectators ought to blame the aeronaut or the Gas Company. The majority sided with Graham, citing the recent ascent of Green from Hackney (June 3, 1823) and the failure of the Gas Company in that instance.

The remaining spectators declared that if the balloon did not go up immediately, they would burst into the garden and discover the reason why. The threat had its effect — not in making the balloon inflate faster, but to prompt Sadler, Jr., to cut the ropes and send the balloon up without car, parachute or aeronaut.

"Ridicule itself," wrote the *Times*, could not "paint any thing more ludicrous than the manner in which this rickety, half-filled bladder of painted cotton rose into the air." Sadler's act converted disappointment into "perfect phrenzy." The mob screamed for an appearance by Graham, frenzy quickly turned to rage, and the mob sought out the car in order to smash it. Fortunately, it, like its proprietor, had vanished into the tavern during the time all eyes were fixed on the ascent. The general cry became, "Give us back our money–we'll not be swindled in this way for nothing." Although the majority had paid nothing, it did not make their wailings less vocal.

The owner of the tavern achieved a temporary lull by promising that the fees would be returned; that lasted only until it was discovered the money-taker had absconded with the cash. Friends of Graham came forward, warning that any who broke the law would find themselves in a scrape. That proved the fuse that lit the explosion. A volley of stones was thrown in his direction and in a few short minutes the palings of the garden were broken and various acts of outrage committed.[2]

The dilapidation of the White Conduit House was judged to be great. Aside from 150 yards of fence and several small trees torn down, the shrubbery was destroyed and glass panes to the summerhouse where the car had been stored were entirely smashed. The damage was estimated at £200.

Mr. Graham's "hoax" continued to be a topic of discussion for weeks afterward, the London *Times* blaming the porous envelope, while ordinary citizens cast a finger at the Gas Company. To defend itself, a spokesman asserted that although their contract stipulated they would not supply gas after 5:00 P.M., they had continued to do so in order to prevent disappointment.[3]

It appears likely that after Graham's humiliating adventure, neither the Sadlers nor Green wished to be associated in the public's mind with failure. Consequently, they quickly arranged ascents of their own. As luck would have it, neither was attended with sterling success.

Oscillating and Waving and Lost Balloons

Moving with alacrity, Sadler arranged for an exhibition from Leeds on September 4, 1823, promising to ascend at 5:00 P.M. The weather proved uncooperative and at the scheduled time the envelope had not been half filled. Realizing circumstances were against him, Sadler abandoned his usual trappings and entered the car with the balloon little more than half filled. Unable to carry two people, the aeronaut stood alone in the car as the wind whipped the 80-foot balloon in circles over his head, "oscillating and waving like a mast of a ship in a storm." After several false starts, Green assisted him in getting airborne. In twelve minutes the aeronaut and his floating machine passed from sight "in the bosom of the air." He arrived safely back at Leeds on Friday morning.[4]

The following day Green made his own ascension at Leeds from the yard of the White Cloth Hall in a magnificent balloon 37 feet high. The process of inflation consumed a mere hour and five minutes, allowing Green to hold back his departure until the yard was filled with paying spectators. The ascension was described as being more imposing than Sadler's, "though Mr. Green's car had few ornaments."

The aeronaut waved his hat and flag for a considerable time, then sat down and let out a rope for the purpose of preventing the rotatory motion so often observed during lift-off. The dragline (or drag rope) was Charles Green's own invention and represented a significant improvement in the control of the aerostat, subsequently employed by all balloonists. The dragline not only stabilized motion, but altitude, as well. The end of the rope dragged over the ground when the machine came close to earth, reducing the weight carried and slowing its descent. On ascending, the considerable weight of the rope (often used as ballast) gave the aeronaut control over the height he achieved without sacrificing gas.

Forty miles from Leeds, Green discovered a ground wind "blowing a hurricane." His grappling iron did not hold and the machine was violently thrown against a rail, stunning him. The rope snapped, heaving him onto the ground. Severely bruised, he could do nothing to prevent the balloon from escaping.

Although considerably injured, Green made it back to Leeds, offering a £10 reward to anyone who recovered his balloon "without its having sustained very material injury."[5]

The balloon (made of silk and bearing the arms of England) was subsequently recovered at sea by some fishermen near Wych-op-Zee and carried to Texel.[6]

Once more reunited, Graham, Green and the Messrs. Sadler went to work at Soho, trying to discover why Graham's balloon failed to inflate on August 18. On September 3 they removed it from the Pantheon where it had been on display and filled the envelope with common air to ascertain if any gas would escape. Discovering none had, they exonerated Graham from any blame, anonymously providing this information to the newspapers.[7]

A private ascension was scheduled for the 5th and at 2:30 P.M. the car, "made of wicker and tastefully painted, with the inside lined with pink velvet and red curtains," was brought out. Mrs. Graham was originally scheduled to be the passenger, but at the last minute her place was taken by a young gentleman named Harris. This seemingly innocuous change would greatly affect Harris' fate. Enamored by the thrill, he recruited a committee, secured a balloon and joined the aerostatic community. (See chapter 17)

Determining their speed by tossing out bits of paper, the pair gradually descended toward a turnip field between Stroud and Rochester. Jettisoning three bags of ballast, they skimmed over a wood. The grappling iron failed to take hold and they were carried over four acres, the car occasionally touching earth until, by holding down the valve line, they managed to discharge enough gas to land.[8]

"It Will Be in the Recollection..."

"...of our readers, that about three weeks ago Mr. Graham advertised his intention of ascending in a balloon of varnished lawn [a fine sheer linen or cotton fabric], and was prevented by the occurrence of several circumstances ... it is unnecessary we should repeat at present." Thus began Mr. Graham's re-emergence on the aerostatic scene.

On September 12, 1823, the "idle and curious of London" assembled at the White Conduit-house (also spelled "White Conduit House") but the crowd attracted was by no means so great "as might rationally have been anticipated," owing to the fear of again being disappointed. Those paying for a close view of the inflation were estimated at four hundred and the crowd outside ten thousand.

At 3:00 P.M., the time appointed for the ascension, the balloon was not half full and the complaint arose that the Gas Company had not supplied sufficient product. This caused a general anxiety, but a few minutes after 5:00 P.M. the car was taken out and attached. Graham and Sadler, entered but a further delay was occasioned by "the foolish obstinacy with which several well-dressed persons, who ought to have known better, thronged about Mr. Graham and his bold associate." Cries from the crowd and efforts by the constables proved vain, finally requiring the use of their "staffs of office" to clear a small space. Lift-off was then achieved.

All was not destined to go smoothly. As was too often the case, a rope attached to one of the poles used to hold the balloon while inflating was not withdrawn. Several persons attempted to extricate the balloon, but by excessive force, so the pole broke. Rebounding with great violence against the envelope, it cut a hole in the surface nearly a yard long. A cry went up that the aeronauts not try so dangerous a flight, but the constables "seemed to hold a different opinion" and kept back the surging masses as the balloon ascended. It did not go far.

On account of gas escaping from the hole, the balloon listed back to earth. Spectators rushed upon it, attempting to force out the remaining gas. Sadler jumped out and "by threats and entreaties," induced them to desist. Without his added weight the machine gave every indication of rising. Graham "pulled off his coat, flung it to one of the by-standers, and very gallantly ordered his friends to leave hold of the ropes." They obeyed and the aeronaut ascended alone.

The vessel proceeded slowly toward the northwest but after five minutes was observed to descend very rapidly. Fearing the worst, the mob ran toward the supposed spot of landing, but happily found Graham's balloon in a gravel-pit near Barnbury Park. One of the men employed in labor there "proceeded to roll himself up in the balloon in a very foolish but at the same time a very destructive manner," and was threatened with severe punishment if he did not stop. For his part, Graham implored the company to preserve his property, "just as he had risked his life for the satisfaction of the public." His cries were heeded, the balloon packed up, and the aeronaut, fatigued from the quantity of gas imbibed during the short flight, returned to the White Conduit House where he was loudly cheered.

In a somewhat qualified but nevertheless surprising tribute from the editors of the *Times*, who were better known for their acerbic comments than a tip of the hat, came the following conclusion:

> We join heartily in this tribute of applause to Mr. Graham, because his conduct of yesterday richly deserved it. Indeed, the alacrity with which he forwarded all the preparations leads us to suspect that we were somewhat mistaken in the views which we attributed to him on a former occasion. If he shall again attempt to sail into the bosom of the air, we wish him better luck than that which has hitherto attended him. At present he stands upon record as one of the most gallant but unfortunate of aeronauts.[9]

It is interesting to conjecture why "several well-dressed persons" thronged around Mr. Graham's balloon, preventing him from ascending, or why a rope had been left hanging between two poles "which certainly ought to have been withdrawn." Considering the large amounts of money habitually wagered on whether a flight would come off or not, it is not improbable that any number of notorious blacklegs were involved in a scheme to hedge their bets.

Nor is it surprising that Mr. Graham risked his life "to avoid giving the public a second disappointment." Had he failed in this attempt (disregarding the private success on the 5th), his career would certainly have been ruined.

Blame the Gas Company and the Weather

With the advent of using coal gas supplied in pipes directly from the manufacturer, the new scapegoat of aerostation became the "Gas Company." W.W. Sadler advertised an ascension from Sheffield on September 12th, 1823, "but owing to the failure of one of the pipes laid by the gas company in bringing gas from their works, and to the heaviness of the gas itself," he was unable to fulfill his promise. Sadler announced a flight the following day but again he was delayed, "partly by the wetness of the weather, and partly by the bad quality of the gas, which, from neglect at the works, had been much mixed with atmospheric air."

To prevent a third disappointment, Sadler determined to erect an apparatus for the formation of hydrogen gas and with the leave of the gas company, erected a reform in the contents of their gasometer. September 18 being an extremely fine day, he filled his balloon with 9,000 feet of hydrogen and 11,000 feet of carbonated hydrogen and achieved a magnificent ascent at 2:05 P.M. After reaching a maximum altitude of 2¼ miles, he descended at 3:15 in a grass field a mile south of Tickhill, seventeen miles from Sheffield.

This flight is noteworthy for several reasons. First, it displays how soon aeronauts became dependent upon carbonated hydrogen to fill their balloons. The extreme effort Sadler went to in preparing an apparatus for the formation of supplementary hydrogen gas, only lately the gold standard of the profession, earned him the acclamations of the public and press. It is also important to remark that with the development of the new technique, it limited major balloon ascensions to places near gas works. The ease of inflation quickly superceded the desire to perform in smaller, out-of-the-way locales not served by gas companies, depriving those citizens of viewing the more celebrated and experienced balloonists ascending in their own backyards.

A comparison between the review of Sadler's ascent and that of Graham's "hoax" is also revealing. Wyndham Sadler was a well-known aeronaut with ties to Oxford. His family had been associated with aerostation since 1784. Graham, on the other hand, was new to the press, and his pretentious claims to have the "most wonderful balloon" set him up for dire consequences. Thus, Graham's failure to ascend was lambasted in the newspapers and his character questioned, while Sadler's two failures were passed over as a matter of moment.

On September 22, Sadler made another ascent, this time from Toft Green, near Micklegate Bar. Due to stormy weather, he might have been "dashed out of the car against the Bar walls, but he dexterously suspended himself in the basket by the cords, and thus escaped." A vast concourse had assembled to watch the flight and the "ascent was a very good one."[10]

Two days later Graham, having previously postponed a flight on Monday, ascended on Wednesday from the Royal Oaks Inn, Oxford. The supply of gas proved sufficient; by 2:00 the envelope was inflated enough to display its shape and by 4:00 the car was affixed. Watching the process near the balloon was the Duke of Buckingham and a party of friends who waved on Mr. Graham from their chairs. Despite the easy inflation, the machine ascended with difficulty, knocking off slates from a nearby house before descending in the middle of a main street. The crowd paraded the car to an open area where Graham's passenger was required to quit his station.[11]

The flight proved a very cold one. Upon entering a thick cloud Graham could scarcely see his balloon and was much oppressed with pains and noises, particularly in his ears. In descending, the grapnel failed to hold, dragging him along for nearly a mile, spilling out the contents of the car and Graham's pockets, including watch, book and small telescope.

He kept his seat, however, and eventually the vessel caught between two trees. He alit, very cold and much exhausted.[12]

Other Forms of Inhospitality

The process of inflation commencing with "the greatest regularity," Mr. Sadler's balloon at York ascended at 4:30 P.M. amid the loud acclamations of a countless multitude. The balloon passed away in rapid progress and glided toward Selby. At the height of one mile the aeronaut experienced a very severe shower of snow. He descended safely at Kellington near Spaith at 5:05 P.M. but not before two prongs of his grappling-irons (each one inch in diameter) had been snapped in two by the combined force of the wind and the balloon.

On his return to town, the aeronaut remarked that "never had he received such inhospitable treatment as from the inhabitants of Kellington; their indifference to assist him, and their rapacity, more resembled a Cornwell wreck-hunter than the general well-known liberality of a Yorkshireman; not a crust of bread nor a draught of water was offered."[13]

The qualified success of these flights was viewed less hospitably in France, where "ultra-Royalist augurs" viewed them as means of preparing for the relief of Cadiz. "Mr. Canning, according to their hypothesis, is to accompany the [balloon] expedition, to give a new constitution to Spain."[14]

Proving once again that luck often rivaled skill in the success of a voyage, Sadler ascended from Liverpool on September 29, 1823. Being over-heavy, the balloon rapidly sank, striking the side-building of a nearby residence. Fearing "the certain destruction of the adventurers," the crowd raced 200 yards to a field, but were unexpectedly rewarded by seeing the balloon re-ascend, but this time without the passenger. Sadler made a safe landing, "actively lent aid by several persons having followed the flight of the balloon."[15]

An early November voyage brought a bit more excitement. After ascending from Derby, Sadler passed so low over Selston he was enabled to speak to the people with his trumpet. A young man named Samuel Waterall reportedly went home expressing his regret "that he had not had his gun with him, that he might have fetched that huge thing down, for he might as well have had it as any body else!"[16]

Closing out the year 1823 was the holiday performances at the Covent-Garden Theatre. Among the numerous presentations were the depiction of a balloon, which seems to have brought down the house:

> But the grand effort of the whole piece, which really is a very curious one, is the ascent of the balloon from Vauxhall, and its journey to Paris. The back scene descending as the ropes of the balloon are cut, produces entirely the sensation that the audience, as well as the machine, are rising; and in this way a moving panorama (in bird's eye view) is presented—first, of the city of London, the river and the suburbs—next, of the line of country bearing towards the coast—then the sea, with the moon rising-passage of the balloon through clouds, rain, &c.; and last, its arriving over the coast of France, hanging for a time above Paris, and descending in the gardens (illuminated) of the Tuileries. The whole getting up of this scene—which takes up several minutes in exhibition—does the highest credit to the invention and liberality of the house; and there can be no doubt that the pantomime, generally, will bring money.[17]

The year 1823 had been an exciting one for aeronauts. Spectators witnessed the continued success of the celebrated Charles Green, Elisa Garnerin ascended from Paris, further inscribing her name on the honored rolls of aerostation, and George Graham made his appearance, surviving the infamous "Balloon Hoax and Riot." James Sadler and his sons made magnificent ascensions and the public taste for such spectacular exhibitions showed no signs of abating. So popular were all things related to aerostation, that a British coach was named the "Balloon Nottingham."[18]

Charles Green opened the season on April 19, 1824, ascending from Halifax (York) on Easter Monday. Due to the holiday "the spectacle became an object of general interest," and at 3:45 P.M. an immense crowd watched him carried from the earth in his magnificent balloon. He descended in safety after an hour's voyage at Richmond, in North Riding, having traveled 64 miles.[19] What came next would change the entire scope of the year.

17

Mr. Harris and Miss Stocks:
The Journey Unforeseen

On entering the car, Sophia stated she felt no nervousness, but "Mr. Harris was rather frightened, and that his fear increased as he ascended."[1]

Mr. Harris was one of those fortunate people who made his way onto a balloon flight. On September 5, 1823, he ascended with Graham from Berwick Street, Soho, presumably "paying his tuppence" for the honor. As a Master Cabinetmaker in the neighborhood of Wells street, Oxford road, Harris (no first name ever given) presumably made a good living; certainly enough to expend a considerable amount on a balloon trip.

Clearly taken with the idea of being an aeronaut, Harris subsequently put together a Committee to finance the construction of a balloon. Harris and members of the Committee, none of whom had actual flight experience, made changes to the valves used to control the amount of gas in the globe during its time aloft. Since the mechanics of valve opening and closing could not accurately be tested on the ground, their effectiveness had to be confirmed on the dangerous premise of trial-and-error while the balloon was aloft.

The story of Mr. Harris' flight began on May 25, 1824. Where it took him and his obscure passenger, no one could have foreseen.

The "Royal George"

Mr. Harris constructed, under his own immediate direction at the Tennis-court in Haymarket, a "stupendous and magnificent" balloon. Several months in preparation, the envelope was composed entirely of silk and the vessel named the *Royal George*, this title being inscribed in large gold letters. The car was of an oval shape, elegantly constructed. The covering of the body was of crimson silk with an intermixture of deep green and yellow silk, "prettily festooned and fringed with the same material."

The balloon and apparatus were moved on Monday, May 24, to the gardens of the Eagle Tavern at the early hour of 5:00 A.M. A large gas-pipe was laid from the main pipe belonging to the Brick-land Company, and the stage from which it was to ascend being completed, the envelope was lashed on. By 11:00 A.M. the process of inflation began.

The aeronaut had given so little advance notice of his planned ascent that by 2:30 P.M. the time appointed for departure, the number of persons gathered was comparatively small.

Harris opted to wait another hour and by 3:30 the gardens were nearly filled with well-dressed persons to the number of 1,000.

The second seat in the balloon was offered for fifty guineas. Three gentlemen applied, each offering thirty, "but for some private reasons, these offers were declined by Mr. Harris." It is speculation to presume Harris' motives, but inasmuch as none of the men met the stated price, he was unwilling to charge less. Or, perhaps more to the point, 50 guineas may have been the sum he paid Graham for an ascension and to accept less would have been an insult to his youthful sensibilities.

Harris returned from the committee-room to dress for the ascent when a young woman, appearing about 18 years of age, approached, intimating that she was willing to accompany him. She did not have any money, but impressed with her courage, Harris accepted her offer. "Miss Stocks was then introduced to some female friends of the committee, who with great propriety asked if she did not wish the attendance of some of her family? She replied, that her mother, who was outside the gate, had consented to her ascent, but had declined entering the gardens. She was then induced, with much persuasion, to take a glass of wine, but would not accept the offer of additional covering, which some persons thought necessary, as she was dressed in white, without a shawl."[2]

Why did Harris take Miss Stocks, who was unable to pay anything? Notoriety is the most obvious answer. The presence of the "fair sex" was always good copy for the newspapers. If Harris intended on making a living as an aeronaut, and from the expenses incurred it appeared he did, he would need publicity. In order to ensure that his name and details of his voyage reached across the British Isles, having a woman passenger was a good place to start. It would also have been embarrassing to ascend alone, making it obvious he had been unable to sell the seat. A mystery woman would solve that dilemma. His judgment proved correct.

A strong degree of interest was elicited by the announcement that a young lady would accompany the aeronaut. The young adventuress soon made her appearance, accompanied by Harris, two other ladies and several of the Committee of Gentlemen. "The universal cry was, "Who is she? What is her name?" She was identified as "Miss Stocks," although her situation in life and family were studiously concealed. She wore a white muslin gown, straw bonnet with a wreath of roses, and a small green shawl, with her hair tapered back upon the temples and braided. Bearing a delicate frame and complexion, her "appearance altogether was extremely interesting."[3]

At 4:00 P.M. Harris, who had superintended all the arrangements in person and "directed them with the greatest possible coolness and judgment" took his place in the car. He was "dressed in a jacket, waistcoat, and trousers, of deep blue, ornamented with gold lace in profusion, and buttons with the anchor and crown upon them, and wearing a white hat." The naval attire likely stemmed from his earliest appointment as mate of an Indianman and perhaps it was his way of playing Admiral.

Leaning on his arm was "the Lady." (Quote marks in the newspaper article indicate the reporter took her for a serving girl, which she was.) The committee and several ladies brought by the rear to the accompaniment of a band playing a slow air. Miss Stocks displayed "but a slight appearance of fear in her manner, and was instantly greeted with the warmest cheers from the spectators. She curtsied in return," and received an affectionate farewell.

Amid cheers of "Bravo!" Harris gave the word to cut the cords and the immense vessel ascended swiftly for a short distance but suddenly stopped when it was discovered one of the four ropes had not been loosened from the pole and the balloon could ascend no further.

A violent shock, stemming from the abrupt cessation of movement drew the car into an almost horizontal position and the young lady, "whose end of the car was downwards, was seen clinging to the sides, and seemed with difficulty to keep her seat." A cry of, "Cut the rope; for God's sake cut the rope!" went up from the spectators, but the assistants would not do so until given the order by Harris. He subsequently waved his flag, the rope was severed and the balloon, finally freed from all restraint, ascended most majestically.

Regrouping quickly, Miss Stocks joined Harris in waving a flag as the balloon took off in a southwesterly direction. The cause of the near disaster was soon explained as a pre-determined event by order of the aeronaut. It appeared that he invented the ploy to afford "an additional and prolonged gratification to those who might attend to witness his attempt. The fourth rope was so contrived as to reach an enormous length, and then to arrest the balloon in its progress, so long as Mr. Harris chose, when, by a hand signal, it could be in a moment severed without the least danger." This idea would seem to indicate inexperience and recklessness on Harris' part. He did not calculate on the car tipping, a fact more worldly aeronauts would certainly have considered, risking an early and disastrous end.

The weather turned against the adventurers by the time of ascension. At 2:00 P.M. the wind had increased, the sky became cloudy and several rain showers fell. But as the machine floated away, there was every expectation of an uneventful journey.

"It Is Too True"

Prior to assuming his seat, Harris appeared in high spirits when taking leave of his wife and friends. Preparatory to ascending, he promised to return to the Tavern in two hours.[4] As the story developed and perhaps became more exaggerated, this was expanded to Harris laying a wager with one of the gentlemen of the Committee on his time of return.[5]

However that may be, his arrival was anxiously anticipated but when the time passed and no intelligence reached the town, "a gloom seemed to pervade the assembled party." Mrs. Harris, however, expressed satisfaction that nothing ill had befallen her husband. Unfortunately, a courier finally arrived at 10:00 P.M. with secret information for Mr. Rossiter, a member of the Committee. Without saying a word he instantly set out in a post chaise to the Plough Inn at Carshalton.[6]

As details were slowly revealed, the only eyewitness to the entire voyage had this to say:

> I ascended the balloon in good spirits, and in consequence of the persons below holding the ropes, the car was a little on one side; Mr. Harris said he would remedy it, and he threw out some ballast. In a short time we ascended most rapidly, and we found ourselves going through the clouds, which looked like mountains of snow. Mr. Harris asked me to hold the string, and he looked at his watch. He told me that we had been up a quarter of an hour, and said that he had got two pigeons. He then again asked me to hold a string, and then threw out a piece of paper. And, as far as I recollect at this moment, he said the balloon was falling rapidly. After throwing out more ballast, we again ascended, and got through another cloud, when I felt myself extremely cold. He said, "Dear girl, don't let your heart fail; I hope we shall sup together, and wish that you may, for your courage, be connected with my family as long as you live." He then said that we were again descending, and desired me, if the balloon should incline on one side, to lay hold of the other. I heard the balloon go "clap, clap," and he said he was afraid the balloon was bursting; at which information I fainted, and remember nothing more till I found myself in bed.[7]

Further details were supplied by Anthony Geary, a gamekeeper. He stated at around 5:00 P.M. he heard a loud rumbling noise as of thunder and saw a balloon rapidly falling. The machine struck against a tree 40 feet from him, carrying away a branch. "It was then driving very rapidly in an elongated form." He laid hold of the car that was partly covered with the balloon, by then nearly emptied of gas. Hearing a moan, he uncovered Miss Stocks, who asked, "Where am I?" With the assistance of others, he lifted her out and laid her on the grass with her head on a cushion. Harris was then discovered in the bottom of the car, "quite dead."

Mr. Wallace, a surgeon of Beddington was sent for and promptly attended, but was unable to restore Harris to life. Miss Stocks was carried insensate to the Plough public-house at Beddington and put to bed. The body of Harris was also carried there, placed in an adjacent room and partially stripped of his naval uniform, "neatly embroidered with gold."

Before the Coroner arrived, members of the press and the Committee were permitted to see Miss Stocks and cautiously interrogate her. At this time she stated that after the balloon had "got through the clouds, Mr. Harris desired her not to be alarmed, for they were going to descend; she had not the least alarm, but she thought Mr. Harris seemed to be alarmed. He gave her a drop of brandy, and soon afterwards said, 'Oh God, look out,' which so affected her, that she turned, and remembered nothing further until she was carried to the Plough."[8] On coming to her senses, she was informed of the fatal event.[9]

At 4:30 on the morning of May 26, Miss Stocks' father appeared at the gate of the Eagle Tavern to make anxious inquiries about his daughter. Some members of the Committee "answered him with proper caution," and he went away to work, apparently satisfied. Mr. Stocks was a millwright and lived at No. 14, Henrietta Street, Vinegar Gardens, City Road. He had six other children.

At 6:00 A.M. the Committee met a gentleman from Beddington. "His feelings overcame him, and bursting into tears, he could only say 'It is too true,' and sunk upon a seat."[10] The melancholy intelligence of her husband's death was communicated to Mrs. Harris at 8:00 A.M. May 26. "She was deeply affected, but became tolerably composed after the first shock."[11]

The Coroner's Inquest

It was the law in 19th century England to hold an inquest after a suspicious or unusual death to determine probable cause and culpability, if any. Notably, Miss Stocks was not called to offer evidence. Instead, George Graham, the aeronaut, was summoned as an expert witness. It was convened May 27 at 4:00 P.M. William Sullivan, bootmaker, deposed that he witnessed the ascent, stating the Gas Company considered the balloon to be the "most perfect machine that ever was put into their hands." Anthony Geary, gamekeeper, testified he saw the balloon descend and aided the passengers; John Wallace, surgeon, remarked that he first attended the woman, who was "in a very low state, scarcely able to speak, but not senseless; she complained of severe pain in her back, stomach and legs. He examined the deceased at the tavern. He found a fractured breast-bone, a fracture of three ribs on the left side, "which were sufficient to produce death." He could not pronounce the lady out of danger.

W. Kervill offered facts on inflating a balloon. He was of the opinion the accident resulted from lines leading to the valves becoming entangled or the deceased was inexperienced; "he was more inclined to think the latter." He stated Harris "perfectly capable of managing a balloon in every other respect, but he was unable to manage the new valve." Mr. Sullivan then added that after Miss Stocks fainted, Harris allowed too much gas to escape "in his great anxiety to reach the earth to obtain assistance for her."

Graham testified that with several lines leading to the valve, "the accident arose from the wrong line being pulled, which opened the large valve instead of the small one." The Jury returned a verdict of "Accidental Death."[12]

The Recovery Phase

The father of the deceased, who appeared to be about 60 years of age, arrived in Beddington with his 13-year-old son on Wednesday afternoon, the 26th. The jury viewing the body at the time, preventing him from seeing the remains, so took the opportunity of visiting Miss Stocks.

Immediately after the inquest, the body was laid out and put into the shell by order of the churchwardens. After going in and out of the dead man's room several times, the elder Harris took a seat at the bar of the tavern and was heard to say that he had repeatedly warned him he was building a machine of his own destruction, to which his son answered, "Never mind that, father; but go and attend to your own business."[13]

Miss Stocks spent a bad night in her room at the Plough, continually moaning. She reported the whole affair was "too much for her to bear, and prayed God relieve her." She often said her recovery "is impossible." On Friday, however, she woke in better spirits, expressing a great desire to see the mother of the deceased or some of her own family.

The same day, demand for pieces of the tree the balloon struck was so great that two station men were placed near it to prevent it being torn up by the roots. The pigeons that Harris intended to release were luckily saved and by Thursday were nearly recovered from the shock of the fall.[14]

Facts concerning the fatal voyage continued to fascinate the public and the curious gathered around her home, hoping for a view of the suddenly famous young lady. They discovered that Sophia had lived, since she was old enough, in service. Her last situation was as an attendant in the shop of a pastry-cook in Barbican, which she quitted only on Saturday evening last, in consequence of a love affair "not in the smallest degree discreditable to either party" with a young man. She was said to have a "romantic turn of mind."[15]

On her arrival home, Mrs. Stocks, Sophia's mother, had in her possession a piece of whalebone from her daughter's stays. The thick bone was shattered from the violence of impact and had the stays not been over the girl's stomach, "the blow must have proved fatal." She also brought with her the frock in which her daughter was attired, torn to pieces and covered with the brandy that she spilled after fainting. Mrs. Stocks additionally stated that her daughter was always possessed of considerable courage and frequently expressed a strong inclination to ascend in a balloon, but never had an opportunity of closely examining one. "Although courageous, and possessed of excessively high spirits, her character was always exemplary"[16]—an important fact to state for the record in 19th century England.

The Committee sponsoring Mr. Harris came to the conclusion that the accident resulted from the valve being too spacious, causing an excessive emission of gas. They reclaimed control of the balloon and astonishingly announced "another ascension very shortly."

One of the gentlemen who offered Mr. Harris 30 guineas to ascend with him was reputed to have "liberally come forward to present that sum to the unfortunate girl." A subscription was also set on foot for Mrs. Harris and Miss Stocks, reported to be "rather liberal."[17] Three days later a follow-up to the story discounted the gift of 30 guineas as a "hoax," and added not £5 had been collected for the parties concerned.[18]

The Surprising Addendum

True to their shocking promise, Mr. Harris' Committee announced that Mr. Rossiter (a member of the committee and by some accounts an uncle of the late aeronaut) had volunteered to ascend with the same balloon "for the sole benefit of the unfortunate widow and family." The Imperial Gas Light Company refused to supply gas until all chance of accident was removed, so the valve was reduced to 20 inches and worked with one line instead of two.

The ascent was scheduled for Thursday, June 24, at the Bedford Arms Grounds in Camden Town and it was advertised that Mr. Rossiter would be accompanied "by a young nobleman, who on that day will become of age, and who has made the widow [Mrs. Harris] a present of sixty guineas." The flight was later postponed until Wednesday, June 30.[19]

Long before 4:00 P.M. persons gathered on the Tottenham Court Road and around the Bedford Arms Public House to witness the spectacle, most on the cheaper sides of the walls. Mr. Rossiter, dressed in a plain suit of deep mourning, took no active part in the preparations and no sign of his intended companion evinced itself, speculation being that his "Lordship, upon reaching his full age, attained at the same moment his age of discretion." A Frenchman named St. Auben, who had made one previous aerial excursion with his father at Nantes, was selected by Mrs. Rossiter "for his experience." St. Auben was a gentlemanly looking young man of 20–22 years of age.

The process of inflation commenced at 2:00 P.M. and finished at 5:00. Rossiter stepped to the edge of the platform, thanking the spectators on behalf of Mrs. Harris and the late aeronaut's friends for their kind support. He added that he felt great pleasure in exhibiting "a most beautiful piece of mechanism," and trusted he would be able to demonstrate its beauty was equal to its security.

Rossiter shook hands with those nearest, and then took leave of his children, "particularly the younger ones." St. Auben mounted the car at the same time, his cheek appearing to blanch a moment before he recovered his intrepidity. No sooner had the balloon quitted the platform when it fell to the ground. Ballast was immediately discharged, and it rose a little but struck the corner of a house. Additional sand was jettisoned and the balloon rose again, this time striking one of the poles. It was soon disengaged and rose majestically to a considerable height. The machine remained in sight for six minutes before disappearing.

At half-past six o'clock a pigeon arrived at a house on Old Street, St. Luke's, with a note stating that a safe descent had been made at Havering Park, three miles of Rumford. The owner of the house brought the note and the bird to the Bedford Arms, where it was received with loud cheers. At 10:30 P.M. the two adventurers arrived back at their place of ascent in a post–chaise with the balloon strapped on top.[20]

And finally, the story came to America:

> *Fatal Aerial Excursion.* A *Mr.* Harris and *Miss* Stocks, new candidates for aerostatic fame, ascended in a balloon near London. When about 2 miles from the earth, owing to some

mismanagement in letting the gass [sic] off, the balloon descended with so much rapidity that *Mr.* Harris was instantaneously killed, and *Miss* Stocks materially injured.[21]

In the end, the local tale of Mr. Harris' ascension and subsequent death sailed far higher, and three thousand miles further, than the passenger-turned-aeronaut himself, becoming, by its publication in the United States, an international incident. It was not the first aerostatic story to travel that far, and it would not be the last to bear sad tidings, but it stood as a connection between the hopes, ambitions and fates of those bold adventurers from the Old Country to the New. It was no longer armed conflict (the War of 1812 was a scant baker's dozen years past), but the conquest of the unknown, the challenge of the heavens, the expansion of scientific and mechanical knowledge, and, ultimately, the pursuit of fame and fortune, which united the continually evolving world of the 19th century.

18

The Aftermath and Beyond

The death of a Matador in Spain is always sure to give a fresh zest and to assemble additional crowds to the next bull-fight.[1]

If anyone supposed the untimely and unsavory death of Mr. Harris would put a damper on what might be called the "blood sport" of ballooning, they were wrong. On the contrary, those aeronauts who had already established their credentials were quick to take advantage of renewed public interest in the majesty — and, not incidentally, the danger of the pursuit — to immediately schedule their own flights.

Sadler ascended on May 27, 1824, from Liverpool, accompanied by Mr. Peel of the 3rd Dragoons Guards. Never exceeding a mile in height, they reached ground safely at 5:35 P.M.[2]

The Edinburgh *Advertiser* took exception to the timing. On June 4th it published a letter expressing a dire view of aerostation. The opening paragraph stated, "We observe, notwithstanding the sad disaster which has lately arisen from Balloon voyages, that another has been made from Liverpool…. If these voyages were made with any view to Science, a ready excuse might be found for them; but as they are undertaken merely as a medium of making money, we do not see that either the public grounds and walks which adorn a city, should thereby be put in peril of destruction, or that the properties of persons around should be exposed to ruin, merely to gratify idle curiosity on the one hand, and the love of money on the other, while the experiment, as we have just seen, is fraught with the utmost danger."

On June 2, 1824, when Graham and his wife ascended from the White Conduit House near Pentonville, the London *Times* expressed its distaste, remarking, "Scarcely is the coroner's inquest over on the deceased, and the survivor recovered from her bruises and terrors, when the public is called upon to witness another ascent of the same kind. The time even seems to have been purpously [sic] chosen when the event was recent and public attention awake, to make this renewed attempt: Mr. Graham and his friends calculating very justly, that the curiosity and interest which such enterprises excite, and always in proportion to the hazards which accompany them, and the boldness required for their execution."[3]

After succumbing to its public duty, however, the remainder of the article was full of praise. Remarking that after his first unsuccessful voyage last year, Graham took every precaution to guard against failure and never, added the reporter, had he seen "a more handsome and magnificent balloon."

Mrs. Graham chose to accompany her husband on the flight and both appeared to be in high spirits "as if undertaking the jaunt of the honeymoon." The lady appeared ill-dressed for the rigors of the occasion, but her husband, "who had before made the excursion, was the best judge of the matter."

At 5:25 P.M. the pair ascended, the balloon remaining in sight nearly twenty minutes. The balloon was a new one, constructed of silk, thickly varnished, colored crimson, blue and bright stone, in the shape of a pear. It measured 37 feet in diameter and containing 30,000 cubic feet of gas, supplied by the Imperial Gas Company, "who are said (we know not on what authority) to have made a demand for it proportioned to the expected pecuniary proceeds of Mr. Graham's expedition."

One of the "most singular consequences" of the ascent was the postponement of the House of Commons when the members went out to view the passing balloon.[4]

The aeronauts descended at Cuckfield, in Sussex, 40 miles from London, at 6:55 P.M., having been in the air one hour and 20 minutes.[5]

In a cruel twist of irony, Graham's balloon passed over the mourners coming from the burial of Mr. Harris. "Mrs. Harris, whose face was completely concealed by her hood, appeared to be deeply affected on taking a last view of the coffin in the grave, but seemed more composed on the return till within a short distance of her home, when the shouts of the populace announcing the ascent of Mr. Graham, revived her extreme grief."[6]

Graham made another ascension from the White Conduit House, Pentonville, on June 17. The balloon was "of oiled silk, in red and yellow stripes and without decoration, except for a broad band of black silk around the circumference." Likewise, the car "was gorgeously painted and gilded and hung with purple velvet and furnished with cushions of the same material."

Captain Beaufoy, a "person of very genteel appearance" was announced as Mr. Graham's *compagnon du voyage*. In the first such mention of the oft-copied, theatrical technique, "Mr. Graham continued standing up, kissing his hand to the spectators" as the balloon rose.[7] After a voyage of one hour the pair began their descent from the highest point of two and a half miles. Suffering from a pain in the head, Graham threw out the grapple and they landed at Tunbridge, 33 miles from London. "Here I also discovered the great utility of strong iron spring hooks, which I had fastened to the hoop; to these the ropes of the netting were looped, and thus avoided, not only the dangerous, but destructive work of cutting the ropes to obtain my liberation from the car."

Captain Beaufoy described the peculiar sensation of seeing "every object appear as flat as on a map, even the hills seemed to be sunk on the same level with the valleys." When the balloon revolved, he suffered from a slight sickness and experienced a "disagreeable noise in the ear, what is commonly called 'singing,' which continued the whole time after, and did not leave me till this morning."[8]

A Bumper to Absent Friends

Everything was on "tiptoe" for the intended ascent of Wyndham Sadler. The Governors of Heriot's Hospital having granted permission for the experiment to take place on their Green, Sadler fixed upon a spot westward of the front gate and preparations began on Friday, running through the weekend for the Monday flight. Workmen set the poles and laid pipe from the Coal-Gas Company's main in the Grassmarket up to Heriot's Bridge. On Sunday the approaches to the Castlehill were fenced off, requiring the public to pay sixpence for a close view of the inflation the following day. This, however, did not prove very lucrative, for the crowd forced the barriers nearly two hours before the process began.

Following the custom of the day, a flag was hoisted on the tower of the Hospital and a gun discharged to announce the ascent would take place as advertised. Ascending with Mr. Campbell, the balloon took a southerly direction, then fell into a new wind current and turned north, passing down the Frith, until disappearing after an hour and 34 minutes.[9] The balloon descended near Leven, a small fishing village on the coast at 5:00 P.M. within eight miles of the spot where Lunardi alighted.[10] The aeronauts returned to the city at 1:15 A.M. where Sadler announced his immediate departure for Glasgow, where he intended to ascend on Thursday. A number of persons who had not had the opportunity of contributing toward Sadler's heavy expense were offered that chance by boxes being placed by Sadler "in situations to be afterwards notified."[11]

Coal Gas

The coal gas used for filling Mr. Sadler's balloon on Monday, was selected by the Gas Company here of the highest quality that is manufactured at their works, having been made on purpose from an inferior sort of coal, and the due quantity having been allowed to collect in the gasometers from the last hours of each charge of the retorts, for several days previous to the ascension. This gas was found by Professor Leslie to be only two-fifths lighter than common air. Its buoyant force, therefore, is but slight, amounting only to 1 lb. averdupois for every 33 cubic feet of gas; so that if there were 24,000, or what is perhaps more probable, 25,000 cubic feet in the balloon, it would have an ascensional power of about 760 lbs. But the weight of the balloon and car is 260 lbs., ballast 120 lbs., and the joint weight of the passengers may be estimated at 300 lbs., in all 680 lbs., leaving a buoyancy of only 80 lbs., a degree of force which accounts for, and agrees pretty well with the slow and gradual ascent that was observed, and which has been estimated at the rate of eight or ten feet per second, or about five or six miles per hour. With such a load, however, and so heavy a gas, the balloon, even though the wind had been more favourable, could not have risen to any great height, as the air becoming continually lighter gradually checks and at last stops altogether its farthest ascent. At the height of about 2700 feet the air is 1–10th part lighter than at the surface of the earth, and here the ascentional force of the balloon, though all the ballast had been thrown out, would, on that account, have been reduced 20 lbs.; add at a little greater height and considerably below the usual region of the clouds, the balloon would have remained suspended and floating about, but incapable of raising itself any higher; a single person might have gained a much greater height, but still nothing equal to what balloonists have attained with the purer and lighter species of hydrogen. In the celebrated voyage undertaken in France, for scientific objects, by M.M. Biot and Gay Lussac, those distinguished philosophers, rose to the height of 13,000 feet; and in a second ascent, Gay Lussac, by himself, gained the astonishing altitude of 23,000 feet, being 1600 feet beyond the highest summit of the Andes. Such ascents, however, are only adapted for the purposes of science, and one like the present is better calculated to gratify the public curiosity.[12]

After the flight, a spirit dealer on the Castlehill brought action in the Justice of the Peace Court on Monday, July 5, against Sadler. He alleged that in consequence of the railings erected as barriers placed across the street from his tavern, customers were denied access and requested compensation of two pounds. The Judge declared the dealer had "over estimated the proceeds of his trade, and dismissed the action with costs."[13]

Not insensitive to the real or supposed damages to property during aerial exhibitions, Magistrates in Glasgow refused permission for Sadler to ascend in that city unless he agreed to "indemnify the inhabitants for whatever damage might ensue to their gardens and other property."[14] The aeronaut refused, offering instead to hire police protection. The compromise was rejected and Sadler published his ire in the newspaper: "I submit to the public to judge if I, as a stranger, have not to regret a visit to Glasgow which has so terminated."[15]

Green, Graham and Sadler

On July 8, 1824, Green ascended in his Coronation Balloon from Northhampton. The envelope contained 700 yards of silk, had a circumference of 103 feet and required 16,000 cubic feet of gas to fill, although the gasometer only reached 8,000. While Mrs. Green collected admission money (the first time an aeronaut's wife had been mentioned as performing such an act) preparations were completed. Green went up alone, and the balloon remained visible for 22 minutes, pursuing a course toward Kettering and Stamford.[16]

On a more charitable note, Graham ascended from the Sydney Gardens, Bath, on Friday, July 16, for the benefit of the Bath General Hospital. He took with him a friend from London named Mr. Adams, leaving at 6:30 P.M., "clearing the trees in gallant style, and soaring aloft in a manner at once stately and majestic." On attaining a good elevation Graham noted an object that had the appearance of a crawling animal, "something like a crab, and afforded considerable merriment." This "extraordinary phenomenon" was later revealed to be "nothing less than a horse with a man on its back!" They descended at 8:15 P.M. near Hamsbury, Wiltshire, 46 miles from Bath.[17]

Without assigning rank, but merely listing him in order of ascensions for the month of July, the third of the trio of celebrated aeronauts performing in Europe with any regularity, James Sadler went up with his balloon from Coburg Gardens, Dublin. Accompanied by friend and associate Mr. Livingston, an immense crowd witnessed the perfect lift-off amid the performance of bands, discharge of cannon and "shouts and acclamations." The machine remained in view half an hour until descending in a potato field between Rush and Sherries.[18]

On Thursday evening, July 29, 1824, Graham made his 10th ascension from the Gas Works at St. Philip's, Bristol, accompanied by Mr. Saunders. Graham took the precaution of having his car lined with cork in the event of its falling into the Channel, and offered £10 to the first person who should arrive to his assistance.

After a perfect ascent, the balloon floated over the Severn. Along the way he attached several notes to the middle feathers of the tail of his pigeons, providing observations such as, "We fear we shall not go far; we are in a complete calm. God bless all our friends and enemies." The pair eventually descended into a quarry upon Itchington Common, Glocestershire (thus saving Graham his ten pound reward), 11 miles from Bristol. The remaining two pigeons were dispatched and the balloon packed up.

Charles Green ascended from Shrewsbury on August 23, 1824, on a fairly routine flight. What made it especially interesting were the preparations beforehand.

Carbonated Gas Inflation

Early in the morning the process of inflation commenced. In the center of the yard, a cistern of something larger in circumference than the balloon, and about 15 feet in depth, had been sunk to receive a new gasometer, and in this the balloon was placed, secured by the net-ropes, which were attached to small weights; in this position it slowly underwent the process of inflation by means of a tube, which passing from the gasometer under ground, came out at the bottom of the cistern, and was there inserted in the mouth of the balloon. On the back of the cistern were inserted two posts, to which pulleys were attached, through these a rope passed over the top of the balloon, which was made fast to the ground, and thus completely fixed its position. As the balloon expanded, and waving in the cistern, seemed to struggle to release itself from its hold, the small weights below became insufficient to hold it, and several men descended into the cistern, who, by leaning on the lower extremity of the net, kept it steady till the whole process of inflation was completed, which was about four o'clock. Mr. Green then descended, and began to attach the car. This was but the business of a few moments, and stepping into the car, he gave orders to the men to let go, and in a few minutes he cleared the cistern, without experiencing the slightest difficulty.[19]

Green also took a pigeon with him "for the purpose of ascertaining the power of the wing in a rare atmosphere." At the elevation of 4,000 feet, he opened the basket and the bird got out on the edge of the car, "and there remained until the aeronaut, attempting to catch hold of it, moved off the edge, and fell down rapidly; but it soon recovered the use of its wings, and after moving to the right and left for a few moments, it darted off in the direction of Shrewsbury. Though it is likely that it has arrived in the town, it has not yet been found."[20]

The "experiment" with a pigeon was oft tried and certainly by this point added little to science. The trial likely was performed for the benefit of publicity, Green having refused to take up any scientific men without their paying "a pretty round sum," for which he was lambasted in the press.[21]

What Goes Around, Comes Around

Mr. Graham attempted his eleventh ascent from Taunton, Devon, England, on the 16th of August 1824, but owing to the oil-gas (as opposed to coal gas) provided by the gas works in Holway Lane, was unable to achieve sufficient buoyancy, the gas proving too heavy for use in balloons.

On account of this embarrassing failure, Graham announced that the fields surrounding his second attempt would be thrown open to the public gratis, "and that he should rely on the voluntary contributions of those assembled." To further stress his sacrifice, he issued a "particular statement of his expenses, by which it appears that his disbursements amounted to upwards of [£]300."

Abandoning all hope of using the available carbonated hydrogen, Graham determined on using pure hydrogen gas for the first time in his career. "His materials of iron and vitriol were therefore brought from Bristol at a considerable cost, and Mr. Graham is indeed entitled to the greatest credit for having spared neither pains nor expense in redeeming his reputation from the disadvantage occasioned by his recent failure."

The creation of gas was performed in four hours, but in consequence of 5,000 cubic feet escaping through the valve, not enough material remained to re-fill the envelope. What remained proved sufficient for only one person to ascend. The flight was successful and Graham landed in an oat field near Upottery, Devon, 12 miles from Taunton.[22]

It is interesting to note that this was the first time in Graham's career that he was compelled to go back to the roots of ballooning and use the "old" standard of vitriol and iron shavings to produce hydrogen gas. What is not surprising is that he went to "the most extreme exertions" to make this flight a success, as it saved his reputation and prevented his name from being derided in the newspapers. More importantly in the short term, it kept the anger of the crowd at bay.

19

The Case of the Pastry
Cook and a Grand Tragedy

*The worthy Magistrate, having consulted Hall, the chief constable, on the regulation
which he should adopt for the preservation of the peace on the occasion, requested
that Mr. Smithers would send him three or four tickets of admission to the above
gardens, for himself and friends to witness the ascent.[1]*

Thus, for the bribery of several tickets, Mr. Smithers, aeronaut aspirant, achieved permission from the Court of Assistants, London, to ascend from the Montpellier Gardens, in aid of the Greek nation "in their desperate struggles against the Infidel."

An advertisement on September 1, 1824, stated that Mr. Smithers' ascent in a splendid Balloon would take place on Monday, September 6, from the Mermaid Tavern, Hackney, Mr. Sparrow, the proprietor, "having very handsomely given the use of his elegant and spacious grounds for the occasion."[2] Despite pleas to generous Londoners, only 350 "Spaniards" appeared to pay the ticket price of 3s.6d. It may have been just as well, for no one connected with the project appeared before 3:00, although the gas pipes had been laid well ahead of time. Finally, an old, patched balloon was brought out, recognized as having once belonged to George Graham and derisively called "the lawn balloon" for its previous failures to ascend.

The pipe conveying gas from the Imperial Gas Company's works, Hackney, was applied to the opening and the process went on well for a time. The crowd being so thin, Smithers was asked to postpone the performance, but as he had paid the Gas Company forty guineas, "and on no future day could they promise him a supply on any terms," having lately obtained the contract for lighting the Essex road, he determined to continue at all hazards.

Smithers, a pastry cook, appeared completely intoxicated, eliciting disgust from the crowd. There seemed to be plenty of disgust to go around, "for during the process of inflation, it was often found necessary to stitch up and patch the material of this old balloon," the smell of the gas was "very offensive in the gardens." The car was on a par with the balloon, being an old wicker-work basket, lined with faded velvet, "that might once have been a purple colour, and a little bit of orange fringe round the top."

At half-past six o'clock talk of a hoax was loudly spoken of, and although the supply of gas was kept up, it became evident the balloon was diminishing rather than growing larger. At 7:00 the Secretary of the Imperial Gas Company declared that instead of the usual 20,000 feet of gas needed for an ordinary balloon, this one had consumed 50,000 feet. He added that if he had known it was the old lawn balloon "which they had over and over refused to fill upon any terms, they would not have had any thing to do with it."

When Smithers refused to be dissuaded, his friends took the car away by force and ultimately let the gas escape. There was no "row" at the termination, "as few had lost their money." The *Times* concluded, "We sincerely hope that the present attempt to create an interest in the Greek cause may not operate on public opinion as an omen, for should it be considered in such a light, miserable indeed will be the hopes of the well-intentioned towards that ill-fated country."[3]

If this were not ludicrous enough, the "lawn balloon" found itself in the Court of Common Pleas, May 27, 1825. In a convoluted trial punctuated with laughter, facts revealed that after the non-ascension, a Mr. Courtney housed the "lawn balloon" for Smithers, who had purchased it for £140. A lien was then placed on the balloon by individuals to whom Courtney owed money. Smithers claimed Courtney's problems should not be visited upon him, and demanded its return. Since he was not in a position to pay the boarding charges, the balloon fell to Courtney and by order of the court, passed into the hands of Courtney's creditors.[4]

Things did not get better for aeronauts. Graham planned an ascension from Worcester on September 11 but the gas company was unable to supply sufficient gas. Mrs. Graham, weighing considerably less that her husband, volunteered to go up, but even her scant weight proved too heavy. The country people, some having traveled thirty miles to witness the spectacle, turned violent, one cutting the silk pipe off the balloon. They were eventually dispersed and the machine "secured within doors."[5]

A second try was made on September 20. After striking a house and dislodging several bricks, the balloon gradually reached an altitude of two and a half miles and descended in a field five miles from Evesham.[6]

While Graham had his problems in Worcester, Wyndham Sadler was at Wigan. On Wednesday, September 22, 1824, he went up from the great yard of the gas works. The balloon mounted with extreme rapidity and quickly disappeared. Within half an hour the aeronaut found himself near the Irish Sea and determined to descend. He made a safe landing within three miles of Liverpool, having traveled a distance of 19 miles.[7]

Death of Wyndham W. Sadler

The notice of Wyndham Sadler's fateful journey began with the following words: "It is our painful task to have to record another fatal accident, arising from the dangerous and useless practice of ascension."

On Wednesday, September 29, 1824, W.W. Sadler ascended from the yard of the Bolton Gas Works, accompanied by an Irishman named Donnell, who had been employed in the Liverpool gas yard under Sadler, where he was engaged in the establishment of the works. The ascent was majestic and all went well until attempting a descent thirteen miles north of Bolton. Sadler threw out his grappling iron, but the rope broke. The wind carried the balloon several hundred yards, alternately dragging the car and dashing it against whatever happened to be in its way. At length the car struck the chimney of a cottage, which it knocked down. Sadler was thrown out, one foot entangled amongst the cords with his head downwards. The balloon rose again and Sadler was precipitated from a height of 25 yards to the ground.

Rescuers found the aeronaut in a state of insensibility and carried him to a neighbouring public house. Surgical aid was sent for, and on examination, his skull was found to be terribly fractured, a considerable portion of it compressing the brain. Some of his ribs were broken and his body was much bruised. Mr. Barlow, of Blackburn, performed a surgical operation on his skull, removing several loose pieces of bone. All was in vain; he lingered speechless, in a state of great suffering, until 8:00 on Thursday morning, when he expired.

Donnell remained in the bottom of the car after Sadler's fall and was carried four miles northward to Whalley where the balloon struck a fence. He was thrown out by the shock and broke his left arm. The balloon again rose, borne northwards toward Yorkshire.

Sadler, twenty-three years old at the time of his death, was best known for his perilous enterprise of crossing the Irish channel. Having made over thirty successful flights, his death was "owing to one of those accidents, against the danger of which it is not probable that either intrepidity or skill will ever suffice to prevent those who venture on this hazardous mode of travelling." Sadler fixed his residence in Liverpool (where he had an establishment of warm, medicated vapour baths) and, "by the excellence of his disposition and character, had obtained the esteem and respect of a numerous circle of friends."

Being informed of her husband's accident, Mrs. Sadler traveled to Hollitroyds, finding that he had been dead many hours. She was left with one child and in an advanced stage of pregnancy. Being in dire pecuniary circumstances, a subscription was opened for her benefit.[8]

The Coroner's Inquest was convened on October 1, with the Coroner, John Hangreaves and the jury proceeding to view of the body, finding the face livid and the eyes of a dark purple, the head presenting a "frightful spectacle." Eyewitness testimony was taken, one stating that as the balloon rebounded, "Sadler appeared most intense; he and his companion were lying flat on the car calling out to me, 'Get hold of the rope, get hold of the rope.'" After failing to do so, the balloon soon disappeared. Another testified he saw Sadler strike several chimneys before falling, and these concussions, rather than the fall, killed him. The surgeon concurred and the verdict came back "Accidental death, by being struck against a chimney."[9] As in the case of Mr. Harris' death, the passenger accompanying the deceased was not called to testify.

As it was after the tragic death of Mr. Harris, the more notable aeronauts hurried to make ascents, presumably to assure the public of the safety of the sport. Graham wasted no time announcing a voyage from Brighton on October 6, about as far away from Bolton (north of Manchester) as he could get in England.

Rain and a brisk wind caused the balloon to flap violently and "many persons wished Mr. Graham to desist." Remaining "cool and collected," he stated his determination to ascend "if it was the public wish." Clearly calculated to elicit a protest, he acknowledged significant danger presented itself. The crowd cried, "God forbid a man should risk his life for our amusement!" and Graham was enabled to postpone the adventure while still saving face.[10]

After two successive days of disappointment, Graham ascended in his balloon from the new cricket-ground. Having previously solicited the company whether they preferred a lengthened voyage or a descent within sight of Brighton, the general opinion favored the latter. Willing and perhaps glad to accommodate, the aeronaut and his companion sailed the short distance of three miles before descending near Lord Chisholm's lodges in perfect safety and well within view of those on the heights at the cricket-ground.[11]

Graham returned to the vicinity of London where he intended making an ascent from Hammersmith. Early in the week he busied himself making preparations and on Wednesday, the 13th, he required the balloon set up to finalize the arrangements. Finishing the work at

6:00 P.M., he and two friends, Mr. Adams (a picture-dealer in Duke's-court, St. Martin's-land) and Mr. Fargues (a respectable tradesman of St. James's parish), returned to town in a cart. In coming through the Hammersmith turnpike-gate, they paid the toll and received the usual ticket to pass them to Hyde Park Corner. With Adams driving, they came upon the Kensington turnpike-gate, but the gatekeeper "seized the horse's head, and drove the cart back against a heap of stones, so as nearly to upset it." Adams jumped out, attempted to show the ticket, and received a blow that "leveled him in the dust."

Fargues was also attacked, and after ascertaining the gatekeeper's name, the three drove off to the nearest magistrate's office to press charges. A warrant was issued against George Noble, the toll-taker, who was dragged off and deposited in the watchhouse of St. George's for the night. The case was brought to trial the following morning, where Sir George Farrant, the magistrate, declared this being no ordinary case of assault, Noble must pay more than the ordinary bail. "He must, therefore, find two respectable housekeepers in [£]30 each to bail him, and his own recognizance in [£]60."[12]

With his legal entanglements behind him, Mr. Graham "announced in the public prints of Saturday, and by means of innumerable gaudy placards," that he would ascend from the grounds of the Windsor Castle Tavern, Hammersmith, at 3:00 on Monday, October 18. His companion was to be his friend Mr. Adams, who had previously voyaged with him from the Sydney Gardens, Bath, on July 16, 1824. Unfortunately, the Gas Works at Brentford failed to supply the requisite amount and the smallness of the conductors (three inches in diameter at the bore) further limited gas flow. The aeronaut, "who appeared to view the possibility of a disappointment with a very sensible uneasiness," was ultimately forced to call for a postponement. Addressing the crowd, Graham explained that in consequence of extreme frost, an earlier commencement of inflation was impossible and that from the small-ness of the main and the distance the gas had to come, the balloon could not fill. He asked for forgiveness "that he could neither contemplate nor control," and promised those who had paid admission money would receive money-checks at the door for the next day's ascent. The announcement was passively received.[13]

The passivity did not last long. On the morrow (October 19th) the process of inflation resumed at 9:00 A.M. "but a recurrence of disappointment took place." Unable to fill the balloon, the ascent was called a "hoax" and the crowd became ugly. A friend of Graham's came out and gave "an exordium upon the state of the weather," and asked the crowd whether they wished Graham to expose his life for their amusement. Having already heard this story once, the spectators hinted that as they had had no "amusement," it was only fair that the aeronaut return the admission money.

Demand for remuneration finally brought out Graham, who stated the oft-repeated line that as he had no way of determining who actually paid and who had entered gratis, he could not offer any reimbursement. The balloon continued flapping, the argument on both sides reached the vociferous point, and after an hour a "sort of compromise took place" by Graham promising once again to admit all in the audience free at the promised voyage next day.[14] No mention of a subsequent flight made it to the newspapers.

Excuses and Wafting

Charles Green proposed to ascend at Portsea on October 16, but notwithstanding every preparation, the committee was of the opinion that the high wind, blowing from the northward, would have "wafted the balloon over the British Channel, to the imminent risk of the life of the aeronaut." The population behaved "with becoming moderation," unlike "the riotous disposition" shown in other places.[15]

After a delay of nine days, Green again announced his intention to ascend on the 25th,[16] The balloon set off at 3:10 P.M., rising to a height of a mile and a half, remaining in sight 26 minutes before disappearing in the clouds.[17]

After a 35-minute voyage the aeronauts arrived at Heyshott, two miles from Midhurst, where the balloon struck several trees, tearing away 60-pound limbs. After narrowly avoiding the chimney of the Heyshott church, a young man came to their assistance. While attempting to secure the balloon, the grappling iron caught hold of his shirt, requiring the help of several additional men to extricate him. Green reported him as "not much hurt," and for his trouble he was given a sovereign to repair his clothes.

The aeronaut commented that the people of the village, never having seen a balloon, were so alarmed they ran into their houses, their fear preventing them from offering help that would have rendered the landing "more easy." The balloon was left at the Swan Inn, Chichester, where Green planned another ascent, and returned to Portsea at 9:15 P.M.[18]

The anticipated flight from Chichester went off as scheduled on November 9th, as Mr. Green made his 25th aerial voyage from the Gas Works near the Barns, South Gate. The gas apparently being better here than in most small places, the inflation finished ahead of schedule, requiring Green to hold off "in order, no doubt, that no one should be disappointed by being a little too late after the stated hour."

The balloon, "giving the effect of a bright ball of gold on an azure field," went in and out of clouds before it "dwindled into a mere speck." The landing, at a field in Henfield, was carried off in safety.[19]

Closing out the hectic year 1824 came news that the celebrated aeronaut Mademoiselle Garnerin made a balloon ascent on the 20th of December, at Rome. A great multitude, including the Prince and Princess of Lucca and the foreign ambassadors, assembled on Monte Pincio, where the preparations were made. When she had been a quarter of an hour in the air, Mademoiselle Garnerin cut the rope of the parachute, and descended safely in an enclosure of the Villa Borghese."[20]

20

An Astonishing Resurrection

The inflation of the balloon commenced at an early hour, and was skillfully con-
ducted. Little art, however, is now required in this process, which has been rendered
extremely easy now that the coal gas has been brought to so much perfection.[1]

While it can fairly be said there were many novel and astonishing human-interest stories connected with the art and science of aerostation, perhaps the most shocking came in April 1825 with the sudden and unexpected reemergence of a person no one would have guessed would come within a league of a balloon.

In a review of Mr. Green's flight from the bowling green of the Eagle Tavern, April 4, 1825, the London *Times* of the following day noted, "Among the individuals present on the ground, was Miss Stocks, the companion of Mr. Harris in his first and fatal excursion from the same place; she was, of course, an object of considerable attention. Her complexion was pale, and her appearance rather delicate, but her countenance evinced no remarkable quality." The paper continued, "She is desirous, it is said, of making a second ascent. She was leaning on the arm of another young woman, and bore the gaze of the crowd with great composure."

Nothing further was mentioned of her, and Green made the ascension in his "Coronation Balloon," accompanied by one of his brothers." This was the first mention of Green's brother. It is important to point out that due to the fact first names were seldom used, it is presumed, unless specifically stated, that the Green referred to here and in subsequent paragraphs is Charles Green. Charles made an estimated 249 flights by 1838, and at the time of his death in 1870, was credited with 526 ascents. Charles Green was synonymous in the minds of most Englishmen as being the aeronaut who "reduced ballooning to routine," and he made more flights than anyone of his era.[2] There were two other Green brothers, Henry and George, both of whom became aeronauts. Presumably Charles' companion on this voyage was George. Henry did not make his first ascension until 1827.

In a moment of reflection the writer added, "The number within the grounds, although very unequal to that without, was by no means considerable, but both within and without the assemblage was much more numerous than select, and perhaps the scene was the more gratifying as affording innocent recreation to an industrious class of persons at a time when they were enjoying one of their infrequent periodical relaxations from labour, rather than to those infinitely less important members of the community whose whole lives are devoted to the prospect of amusement."

Although advertised as the "Coronation Balloon," Green actually ascended in an "altogether new one and very inferior to the other upon observation." After the aeronauts entered the car, the machine rose to a moderate height, hung over the city for half an hour, seeming to bear "two of the inhabitants of a distant planet." It took a direction toward Crordon and made a safe landing.

Green and his brother made a second flight from Nunn's Field in the center of Newcastle on May 11[3] and on Monday, May 30, they made a third voyage together, this time reaching Pottoe, forty-eight miles away.[4] One of the pilot balloons they sent up fell at Red Chesters, 25 miles from Newcastle. It landed on a bank side and rolled into a brook, where it was "burst by the country people pelting it with stones, under the error that it was some portentous being, come among them with a mischievous design.[5]

It is certain that between April 4 and June 9, someone told Charles Green of Miss Stocks' appearance in the audience, and the two of them got together. Acutely aware of the publicity surrounding the young lady, he must have invited her to fly with him, for on the latter date they ascended from the Cloth Hall at Leeds. Since Leeds was a considerable distance from London (although closer than Newcastle, which may explain why she did not accompany him on those voyages) and presumably she did not have the wherewithal to pay for transportation, he surely brought her there.

In any case, they had a successful voyage and descended after 33 minutes at a small village near Leeds.[6] So great was her fame, that news of her trip made at least two American newspapers, the *Torch-Light and Public Advertiser* (Maryland) July 26 and the *Republican Compiler* (Pennsylvania) on August 3. Both ran a duplicate article, stating, "Mr. Green, the Aeronaut, has made his thirty second aerial ascent, accompanied by Miss Stocks, the young lady, who some time since ascended with Mr. Harris, from London, and fell with him from a great elevation in consequence of the sudden escape of gas from the balloon."

Five days after the Green/Stocks ascension, Graham went up with two young ladies from Camden Town in what would seem to be a display of "one up-man-ship." Interestingly, less than two weeks later, the showmen got together and ascended from the White Conduit House on June 23 (see details of the flights below).

Miss Stocks must have relished the adventure and the attention (and so must have Green), for she accompanied him to Stamford, 100 miles from London. On Saturday, July 2, the aeronauts ascended on what was Green's 36th voyage. This being the first exhibition of its kind in that part of the country, among the persons of rank and fashion attending the festivities were the Marquis and Marchioness of Exeter, Lord T. Cecil and Miss Poynzt. The flight went well and Mr. Green lowered the balloon in the vicinity of Thorney.

Grounding the machine by means of the grappling iron in a field of wheat, he advised his companion to alight, "which she did with great promptitude." At this point, he ordered a laborer who had hold of the rope to let go. Either the man misunderstood the command or got caught in the cord, for as the balloon rose, it pulled him ten or fifteen feet in the air. Finally managing to extricate himself, he dropped to the ground, stunned but otherwise unhurt.

Green and Miss Stocks were reunited, a chaise was procured for them and they returned to Stamford at 9:30 P.M. The brother of the Marquis of Exeter invited him to the Burghley-house. Reports stated Green cleared £140 by his voyage.

The real winner would seem to be Miss Stocks. A servant girl by trade, her status rose considerably by becoming an aeronaut in her own right. While the article specifically states the brother of the Marquis invited "him" (Green) to the Burghley House, Sophia surely was treated to some form of congratulatory supper. Presuming she went back into service during the weeks of preparation between flights, her status must have been considerably elevated, not only among her own "caste," but with the master and mistress.

On Tuesday, July 5, 1825, George Green ascended from the Palace Green, Durham, apparently alone. Although the "magnificent" balloon was not more than two-thirds filled, it rose in grand style and took an easterly direction. After a short voyage of 13 minutes he descended safely in a cornfield about four miles distant.[7]

Green and Miss Stocks ascended together on Wednesday, August 11, from Leicester, situated near Stamford, the site of their previous voyage. They descended in less than an hour in perfect safety at Atherstone, a distance of 20 miles.[8]

Miss Stocks disappeared from the newspapers until a year later, when circumstances had radically altered. An ascent from the White Conduit-house, Pentonville, generated considerable interest when it was advertised that two woman — Mrs. Graham (wife of the aeronaut), to whom management of the balloon was entrusted, and Miss Stocks — were to go up alone.[9]

How Sophia came to be associated with the Grahams is a matter of conjecture. She had already established her credentials with Charles Green. What happened to make her change sides from one competing showman to another? Although it was not unprecedented for Graham ascended with a female companion (see August 23; he also made occasional voyages with his wife), the change appears striking. Green continued to fly, at one point (March 23, 1826) ascending with his son, and at another with his brother and "Master Green." Yet there were no further references of him taking a woman passenger between his last flight with Sophia and her proposed ascent with Mrs. Graham in June 1826.

Did Graham finally determine Miss Stocks' celebrity had waned? Possibly; by August 10, 1825, her presence merited a scant two sentences in the Edinburgh *Advertiser*. Was he forced to sell his passenger seat to the highest bidder? Although he needed money more than most (see Chapter 21), he ascended with family members on a number of occasions and they certainly did not pay for the privilege. Without further details, it is reasonable to assume Green and Stocks merely went their separate ways.

June 28, 1826, the day selected for the voyage, proved that the best-laid plans were often thwarted by nature. With the time of departure being announced as 5:30 P.M., a violent storm came upon the grounds at 3:00, postponing the inflation. An hour later, the skies cleared, orders were given to continue filling the balloon and the aeronauts appeared in high spirits, "only eager for the moment to arrive when they could make their departure."

After Graham assured himself everything was in order, he departed on horseback in the direction he supposed the machine to take in order to be present for the descent. No sooner had he left, when it was discovered the balloon was not sufficiently inflated to carry both occupants — a peculiar mistake on the part of an experienced aeronaut.

Sophia being compelled to relinquish her seat, Mrs. Graham took her place in the car and rose alone, waving her flag. The machine scarcely cleared the surrounding trees and sank into a nearby field before reaching the low altitude of 130 feet and floating in the direction of Hackney. She descended in safety at Stoke Newington, "but tranquility could not be restored until the arrival of Mr. Graham himself, at nearly ten o'clock, when he publicly informed the company of Mrs. Graham's safety."[10]

This marked the last mention of Sophia Stocks. A woman of unusual character and courage, she survived near-death injuries to forge ahead in the field of aerostation. One wonders if she went on to lead a happy life, telling and re-telling her adventures to an enthusiastic crowd, or if thirty years in the future, when ballooning had all but faded from the European scene, her grandchildren failed to appreciate her remarkable accomplishments as a woman pioneer.

"The Public Taste for Ballooning"

Concurrent with Miss Stocks' summer of re-emergence, Graham busied himself with his own ascensions. A month after Green's first flight with Sophia, Graham went up from the gardens of the Star and Garter Tavern near Key Bridge. For a quarter of an hour the aeronaut was visible waving his cap and flags as the balloon floated southeast, in the direction of Kingston, Surrey. He descended at ten minutes past six at Oaksco, a mile and a half from Claremont in Surrey.[11]

In May, when Green and his brother were in Newcastle, Graham had returned to the gardens of the White Conduit-house, Pentonville, ascending on Wednesday, May 11. During the course of the preparations, several gentlemen who were "anxious to share with him the pleasures and perils of an aerial voyage" made offers for the passenger's seat, but none were thought worthy of acceptance until Captain Currie of the 3rd Dragoon Guards put into his hand a cheque for £40. The price proved agreeable and Currie quickly assumed an active part in the proceedings.

At 5:40 P.M. Graham entered the car to rousing cheers and Currie followed, enjoying the notoriety. Escaping a brush with nearby trees, the machine rose at 6:15 P.M. Taking a northwesterly course, it remained visible for nearly an hour and a half. They reached an altitude of two and a half miles before descending in a field at Waltham Abbey about 7:15 P.M.[12]

The London *Times* offered a slightly less flattering account: "Yesterday was announced by Mr. Graham, the aeronaut, that he would be making his seventeenth ascent with his balloon. He selected for the occasion a spot which seems to be a favourite of aeronauts to ascend from — namely, the Gardens of the White Conduit-house, Pentonville, where he had three times before exhibited an ascent and twice the contrary. The public taste for ballooning."[13]

Graham made his promised balloon ascent from the gardens of the Bedford Arms, Camden Town, accompanied by two ladies, "whose names were not suffered to transpire." Several hours after the announced time, an elderly gentleman, said to be their father, conducted them to the platform. "They were dressed alike, in nankeen habits, seal-skin caps, and white veils; and seemed to be sisters, about 20 and 23 years of age."

The women stepped into the car without betraying the slightest timidity; one's cheeks glowed "with the flush of delight," while the other's were paler, but both talked and laughed merrily. Graham entered and positioned himself between them, the fastenings were undone and the aeronauts waved their flags to the multitude, which cheered them as long as they remained within hearing.[14]

Choosing the White Conduit-house as the site of his 25th voyage, "if he did not enter 'the heaven of heavens,'" Mr. Graham, Mr. Green (presumably Charles) and another gentleman watched as "the huge machine, which had previously presented a very unwieldy and misshapen appearance — like a well-grown Alderman after a grand civic fete — now assumed a grand and majestic form."

The aeronauts descended in Essex, returning to Graham's residence in Poland Street at 11:30 P.M. The paying crowd was not large and it was presumed Graham's voyage to be an unprofitable one.[15]

Graham wasted no time making his 28th ascent. Moving his balloon and apparatus to Cambridge, a locale deprived of an ascent since James Sadler went up on July 3, 1811 (see chapter 12), he was compelled to use the "old fashioned" method of manufacturing hydrogen gas. Although the process was scheduled to begin early in the morning, the van with the sulfuric acid overturned 18 miles from London and did not arrive until noon.

The spectacle on July 5 drew a paying crowd of 3,000 (which explains why he went to the bother), while the area surrounding Mount Pleasant was filled with numerous spectators. At 6:30 P.M. despite a deficiency of gas requiring the aeronaut to leave behind his grappling irons, the assistants attached the car. The balloon rose in majestic style and shortly after, he threw out a parcel of newspapers. Six minutes later he discharged a second set of newspapers that were "exactly seven minutes reaching the ground." A third batch of papers landed at New Town. Aeronauts frequently took copies of the latest editions "hot off the press" as a means of proving to country folk at the point of landing where they had come from and at what time they departed. Often, these newspapers were used like ballast.

In an interesting observation, Graham noted that the balloon, which rose with great rapidity, required no small degree of skill to manage, there being "so much difference between hydrogen and carbonated gases." Reaching an estimated height of three miles, he utilized a new technique of discharging gas and using the deflated envelope as a parachute, by which means he reached Babraham, seven miles from Cambridge.[16]

Friday, July 15, Charles and George Green ascended for the fourth time from Nunn's Field, Newcastle, in their magnificent balloon.[17] The brothers' other flights from this locale were on April 4, May 11 and May 30, 1825.

Not to be outdone, Graham arose from Norwich on July 30, 1825. After entering a cloud and becoming "invisible," the multitude was almost "breathless with anxiety till it passed through the intervening medium." After twenty minutes the machine began to descend and Graham made it safely to earth a mile from Ocle.[18] A week later, on August 10, Graham again ascended from Norwich. Due to a tremendous storm of thunder and lightning, the ascent was delayed until 6:00 P.M. The balloon took an easterly course and remained visible as it traveled along the line of the Yarmouth Road. Not long afterward, the storm returned with renewed violence, the frequent flashes of lightning making the flight "peculiar and awful" for the aeronaut.[19]

Somewhat surprisingly, on the anniversary of his Majesty's birthday, celebrated August 12, 1825, neither Graham nor the Green brothers managed to secure a commission to ascend during the festivities. Instead, an aeronaut named Mons. Boyour advertised his proposed flight "in a most splendid Balloon, containing 6,000 cubic feet of air." He also promised to descend in a parachute 50 feet in circumference "on the plan of Mons. Garnerin." A grand display of fireworks at the Jamaica Tea Gardens, Germundsey, would follow.

Possibly the promise of adding a fireworks display gave Boyour the upper hand; the price of admission was also extremely inexpensive, underbidding what the more celebrated aeronauts typically charged. In consequence, Graham hustled his apparatus across the country from Norwich on the far eastern coast to Kendal in western England (not far from Scotland), to make an ascent. Failing to satisfy the residents, the pair made a second voyage from the gas works there, on August 23, landing at the foot of Murton Pike, 29 miles from Kendal.

After alighting, several gentlemen expressed a desire to ascend by means of a rope. As the balloon was still sufficiently buoyant, Graham complied with their request, "to the no small gratification of the persons assembled."[20] Returning to Kendal, Graham expanded the entertainment by offering tethered ascents to anyone willing to pay a fee of 5 shillings. This allowed his passengers to enjoy the thrill of an aerial voyage at the height of 500 feet without danger. The idea proved so successful, he stayed two days, gratifying the public and filling his purse.[21]

Charles Green was apparently of the same mind. After a successful flight at Worcester, he re-inflated his balloon and spent several hours conveying persons aloft in his captive aerostat for the same fee of 5 shillings. Again, the rides were highly popular.[22]

Although selling tethered rides reduced the idea of ascending in a balloon to dog-and-pony status, the idea was not new; before a manned flight was ever accomplished, the earliest aeronauts practiced the feasibility of ascension with tethered ascents and in 1784, while Jean-Pierre Blanchard offered such attached trips to a number of ladies and gentlemen, he did not charge them for the privilege. (See chapter 4.)

The idea rapidly crossed the Atlantic, where aeronauts were also desirous of earning extra income. On September 5, 1825, before his ascent from Castle Garden, New York, the celebrated aeronaut Robertson (incorrectly spelled "Robinson") permitted a lady wearing a bridal gown to take her station in the car and be led around by cord-bearers, reaching a height equal to the heads of the audience seated around the garden.[23]

After an unsuccessful ascent from Chelmaford when his insufficiently inflated balloon failed to carry up two persons and sustained some injury, Graham was forced to cancel another flight from Norwich. A make-up announcement advertised a flight on August 30 with John Harvey, Esq., High Sheriff of Norfolk. The balloon could not be inflated sufficiently to carry two persons, so Colonel Harvey offered to go alone. Fearing the life of so valuable a man, the crowd refused the proposition. Reluctantly giving up his seat, Graham took his place and immediately ascended. The vessel never reached any considerable elevation and descended in a turnip field a mile from the walls of Norwich.[24]

Crossing over into Scotland, Green ascended from Carlisle Castle on September 29, accompanied by William Ramshay. After floating for an hour and a half, a descent was effected in a pasture near Beatock Bridge. The balloon struck earth with such violence, Ramshay was thrown from the car. In consequence, the machine rose to a considerable height. Green eventually managed to get it down, but lacking sufficient gas, the car crashed into the ground, considerably hurting him. "He is however in a convalescent state, and will probably regain his strength in the course of a few days."[25]

If that were not bad enough, Green followed that trial with a balloon ascension from Richmond Castle in northern England. The day being tempestuous, however, he descended after traveling 20 miles in 14 minutes. There being no one near the landing site, he was unable to secure the balloon, "and it flew onwards it is supposed, towards the German Ocean."[26] The wayward balloon, with half a car and grappling irons dangling, nearly caught on a gig, but fortunately the passengers were able to avoid the irons as they passed over their heads. They presumed it eventually came to land in the North Sea.[27]

21

Notwithstanding, Notwithstanding, Notwithstanding...

Ballooning has, of course, progressed no farther than to afford amusement to spectators and assist scientific research.[1]

The announcement of an ascent by Mrs. Graham had the public in Plymouth on the tiptoe of expectation for some weeks prior to the actual date. However, the weather failed to cooperate and cancellations were made on November 7 and 10 due to "ungovernable circumstances"—the wind blowing out to sea. Monday the 14th dawned with no better luck, but Mrs. Graham, strangely accorded the status of "principal attraction and decision-maker," resolved to proceed, taking with her both her husband and Mr. Grillis of the Plymouth dock-yard, "who had paid handsomely for a trip to the upper regions."

The balloon was inflated in the marketplace, Stonehouse, gas supplied from the Millhay gasometer. The Earl and Countess of Morley patronized the festive scene and a Committee of Gentlemen supervised the proceedings, which they completed shortly before 3:00 P.M. Their efforts proved inadequate, however, and it was declared that the machine had not enough buoyancy to carry three persons. To administer more gas was considered too dangerous "from the impossibility in such case of managing the progress of the balloon," and Mr. Grillis was left behind.[2]

The large, elegant balloon ascended in imposing style but did not remain long in the air. Being blown, as expected but not desired, out to sea, Graham discharged gas in the hope of landing near the Mew Stone seven miles distant. "In this, he was most unfortunately disappointed."[3] As the machine dropped, Mrs. Graham put on a cork waistcoat and Mr. Graham a copper life preserver around his waist. The descent became so rapid the aeronauts felt a tremendous rush of upward air, and the noise of the waves seemed to be all around them. The balloon floated on its side while the car remained completely under water, with every wave passing over the heads of the two unfortunates. They remained clinging to life in this manner for half an hour before the Royal Marine boat, commanded by Sergeant White came to their rescue.[4] In the confusion, the ropes of the balloon became entangled with the masthead, and they were in imminent danger of being thrown from it into the ocean, when one of the crew pulled out a knife and cut the ropes; the balloon proceeded towards the French coast. When placed in safety by the exertion of the seamen, Mrs. Graham, overcome by agitation of the mind, had every appearance of a corpse. Mr. Graham, too, was evidently in a state of utter exhaustion."[5]

Two of the seamen were injured cutting the balloon free and were handsomely rewarded. On return to the Admiral's Hand, Stonehouse, Mrs. Green was bled and recovered nicely.[6]

Opening the aerostatic season of 1826 on March 23, Charles Green ascended from the Bowling Green of the Eagle Tavern, City Road. Not surprisingly for that early time of year, the wind blew lustily, causing fears that the machine would be blown against the surrounding houses. To prevent such a disaster, Green ordered the envelope inflated "considerably beyond the extent originally intended," hoping to gain an ascending power that would take him up rapidly in a perpendicular direction.

The ploy succeeded and he quickly passed up and through the clouds, the temperature rising from 50° to 70° in a matter of minutes. The rapid change in temperature expanded the gas and the balloon continued to ascend, despite the valve opened to its greatest extent, eventually reaching an altitude of two miles in 17 minutes. During the flight, he perceived in the clouds opposite the sun a most beautiful and perfect reflection of their balloon and its appendages, encircled by two haloes, presenting, with the utmost vividness, all the various colours of the rainbow. The illusion did not cease during the whole time he remained at that height, affording the aeronaut an easy mode of ascertaining direction.

Green then performed yet another "experiment" with pigeons. Releasing three, the birds betrayed symptoms of fear and soon become exhausted, owing to the rarity of the air, but kept flying in all directions around the balloon before finally being lost to sight.

Crossing the river into Essex, he effected a safe landing near Barking. Using a valve of new construction purported to exhaust the balloon in one-tenth the time previously required, the aeronaut packed up his apparatus and returned to town. Happily, in the course of the evening, the pigeons returned home "without appearing to be the least exhausted."[7]

On March 30, Green made a second ascent from the Eagle Tavern, accompanied by his brother and Master Green,[8] and on May 16 he completed a third voyage. This one had unfortunate consequences, as several persons were severely injured by the fall of a scaffold erected outside the gardens. Nine persons were carried off to St. Bartholomew's Hospital, three or four of whom subsequently died.[9]

"One of the Most Magnificent Ascensions in Aeronautic Annals"

So wrote the editor of the New York *Evening Post* in describing the voyage of Mr. P. Cornillot and T. H. Joliffe, Esq., from the Eyre Arms Tavern, St. John's Wood, England.

The inflation of the handsome *Aeolian Pegasus* was completed without "the usual hub-bub and confusion," although the process proved lengthy.[10]

The machine was purported to have the ability to move horizontally but this was not ascertained during the time the balloon remained in sight. Scientific experiments were carried out, however, on "a brace of birds and pigeons" and some frogs. At two miles elevation the eyes of the birds appeared more prominent and their heart beat with greater rapidity. No mention was made of the frog's condition.

After descending to a more moderate height, the aeronauts distinguished the environs of Seven Oaks where they had made their first balloon ascension last year, and after a flight of fifty-five minutes, landed in a field near the village of Sonbridge, within three miles of Seven Oaks.[11]

On Wednesday, June 28, Mrs. Graham ascended from the gardens of the White Conduit-house, but the machine became entangled with the coping of a nearby house. Failing to rise, it passed down the street so low as to be on a level with the second story windows, imperiling her life. After discharging ballast, it floated twenty minutes, neither rising nor falling. It eventually passed over the New River before landing at Newington Green, "where the balloon was seized by some brickmakers and was nearly cut to pieces, because a sufficient quantity of beer was not distributed among them."[12]

Nearly as quickly as the balloon went down, Mr. King, the proprietor of the Green Man Public House brought charges against Mr. and Mrs. Graham. He "complained of sundry breaches of the peace; and breaches in the premises, occasioned by Mrs. Graham's unlooked-for descent in his neighbourhood on Wednesday evening last."

Interestingly, Mr. King was unable to attend the court proceedings held on Monday, July 3, but sent his daughter to stand in for him. It appeared the major complaint was an unpaid bar tab of £5 that Mr. Green incurred when ordering beer distributed to the crowd. Green had demurred payment and countered by complaining his balloon had been confiscated by King, although after two repeat visits (and much disturbance) he succeeded in regaining possession. In "a warm and rather irregular discussion," King wanted Graham charged with causing a riot, and Graham demanded restitution for damages done to his balloon.

Mr. Osborne, the Magistrate, ultimately informed the parties that it was a case in which he could not interfere.[13]

The Night Balloon

"An experiment, never before attempted in this country," was made at Vauxhall Gardens on July 21, 1826, by Mr. Green. Announcements went out well ahead of the proposed date proclaiming a nighttime ascent, and the aeronaut, "who must be by this time as familiar with the clouds as he is with his own threshold, having visited them no less than 55 times," had everything in order by 9:00 in the morning.

A magnificent balloon, considerably larger than witnessed before, was constructed for the occasion, possessing a car capable of accommodating four or six persons. At nightfall, Green and his two sons ascended into a black, moonless sky, the light from the stars enabling spectators to keep the balloon in view. "The danger attending the enterprise seemed to be felt by every body except the intrepid aeronauts themselves." They landed safely at Richmond and returned to the Gardens by 2:00 A.M.[14]

The success of his nocturnal adventure prompted Green to make a second on July 28th from the same location. This time, his advertisement drew not less than twenty thousand persons. Two passengers, paying £50, ascended with Green. The balloon remained in view half an hour and descended safely at Merton, in Surrey. Due to the lateness of the hour, no conveyance was available, compelling them to walk back, reaching Vauxhall Gardens at 3:00 the following morning.[15]

After three nocturnal adventures, Green was decidedly of the opinion that there was less danger or difficulty in making an ascent on a calm, moonlight night than at any other time. The temperature being more equitable, the balloon was not exposed to alternate variations and condensations that, in daylight, cause much trouble. At the same time, he offered his opinion that navigating a balloon against moving air with any velocity was "utterly impracticable." He had, however, constructed a machine, weighing 19 pounds, designed to discharge 70,000 gallons of air in eight minutes, which would operate like a bellows in moving the aerostat forward. He hoped to test his machine at the first possible opportunity.[16]

A month after this interview, on September 11, he ascended from Bolton, in Lancashire, descending safely at Chadderton, near Oldham.[17] No mention was made of any navigational experiments.

On October 3, 1826, Green scheduled ascent from the Potteries, Hanley. His balloon, having made but few voyages, contained 1,000 yards of silk, arranged in alternate stripes of crimson; when attached to the car, the entire machine measured 60 feet high. The car was of an oval figure with seats at the ends, each capable of containing one person. The inside was lined with crimson and yellow hangings; outside, the covering contained allegorical paintings of Aurora and Aeolus; Fame and Victory occupied the two ends of the car. The entire aerostat cost upward of £700.

Pipes of six inch bore were laid down from High Street, Shelton, for the purpose of conducting gas from the British Gas Light Company. Sixty thousand people poured into the area, the majority of which had never seen a balloon. In order to secure the aeronaut a sufficient remuneration, the balloon was hidden by an enclosure, excluding those who could or would not pay an entrance fee. Even the workmen were charged one shilling for a close view.

Cords attached to the netting to hold down the machine were fastened to 20 half-hundred weights and brought up to the circular frame, to which the car was fastened by strong ropes. With the Reverend B. Vale as his passenger, Green made a tethered ascent, sending down a cat in a parachute before being brought back down. The aeronauts were presented with flags, the ropes detached and they proceeded on a free flight.

Back to the Law Courts

Not surprisingly, a memorial, "very numerously signed, from the inhabitants of Kennington and its vicinity," was presented during the Michaelmas Quarter Sessions, Surrey Sessions, Kingston, on October 17, 1826. Besides complaining of the "greatest disorders, and often gross indecencies" shown by citizens attending fireworks displays and balloon ascensions (introduced last season), the events caused the public houses to be kept open at all hours of the night. The memorialists considered that, without wishing to put any undo restrictions on the proprietors of such places or those putting on such events, "something was necessary for the public protection," and they prayed for interference by the court.

After some give-and-take on the possible liability of those involved, the motion was ordered to stand over.[18]

The court, in effect, tabled the motion. The action is not surprising, considering previous petitions of a similar nature were presented with like result. Fireworks, however noisy, and balloon ascents, however bothersome, drew the crowds and added greatly to the pocketbooks of local merchants. No magistrate wanted to stand in the way of money-making ventures.

Charles Green performed his 66th ascent from the Golden Eagle Tavern (mistakenly called the "Royal Eagle Tavern") on the Mile-end Road in the eastern part of the city on April 17, 1827. Mr. M'Taggurt of the British Gas Company's works on Ratcliffe Highway supervised the inflation. (It was a common practice of newspapers to abbreviate names beginning with "Mc" as "M'.") With inflation completed before mid–day, the aeronaut spent the rest of the afternoon and the whole of the preceding day (16th) providing tethered rides to small parties.

The balloon contained 141,364 gallons of gas and was composed of 1,200 yards of silk "of a peculiar texture," worked in alternate stripes of crimson and gold. Continuing his performances of the previous year, Green made one tethered flight, letting out a fine tabby cat in a parachute before the main event. Taking with him Messrs. Fox and Mercer, the balloon headed north.[19] They quickly encountered a snowstorm that filled the car with water. Fortunately, Green had recently invented a means of releasing the water, and they were able to proceed, eventually landing safely at Fulham.

Pursuing a busy schedule, Green left London and ascended on May 16 from Chesterfield. In attempting a landing in a field near Tidewell, he was thrown out of the car and fell 30 feet to the ground. Being much hurt, he "was obliged to be bled and put to bed." Lightened of his weight, the unmanned balloon sailed away.[20]

The absence of George Graham from the ballooning season was explained in a court of law, May 7, 1827. Being that he was in debt to three gentlemen (William Maton, Morton Grafton and Mr. Brooker), a writ of execution was placed against him. Brooker took possession of the balloon and arranged to sell it to Maton and Grafton for £70 with the stipulation Charles Bailey (Graham's partner) was to be indemnified from £361 he owed. Graham, himself, was not to be excused his debt to the purchasers. When a question of ownership arose, Brooker sued Maton and Grafton.

Considerable wrangling occurred over the actual value of the balloon. Margaret Graham, George's wife, testified that it required four or five weeks for her husband to make the aerostat, the total cost being £260–270. Without preparation, the 1,018 yards of silk alone was worth £203, the netting £15 and the car £3–4 more. She stated it was worth that sum to an aeronaut but to no one else. Besides her husband, only Mr. Green, Mr. Brown (see October 6, 1827) and a Frenchman named Cornillot (misspelled "Cornetlleu" in the transcript) would have any use for it. She testified that her husband sold his share in the balloon to Mr. Bailey for £20 and the discharge of an £83 debt, actually making Bailey and Brooker the owners. Since (at least) November, Graham had been in custody at Birmingham for the debt owed Bailey.

The jury awarded damages of £50 to the plaintiffs.[21]

With their only significant competition safely out of the way, the Greens became the biggest name in the business. Charles Green's second voyage since leaving London occurred at Newbury on May 24. Described as his 59th ascent (counts were notoriously inaccurate), he was accompanied by Mr. Simmons, a gentleman "who had been deaf and dumb from his infancy." This was Simmons' second flight with Green (see August 1, 1823, chapter 15; spelled "Simonds" in those reports.)

A tremendous storm of hail, rain and thunder blew over the area, scattering the crowd and threatening to destroy the balloon, "which could scarcely be kept down, although loaded with two tons weight of iron, and the united exertions of nearly one hundred individuals holding to the net-work." With the wind continuing in unabated fury, Green opted to ascend and the balloon bounded off "with the velocity of lightning."

Assailed by contrary air currents and horrific thunder, the pair finally descended in the parish of Cranley, Surrey, 58 miles from Newbury.[22]

Charles Green apparently had no problem risking his own life, but he did not take any chances with his brother. When it came Henry's turn to make his first voyage from the Bull Inn, Rochester, on June 7, 1827, he engaged Mr. Bailey, George Graham's former business partner, to assist in the management of the balloon. Mr. Bacon, engineer to the Rochester Gas Works, supervised the inflation, completing it in under two hours. The ascent was made under adverse weather conditions, the wind hurling the balloon against a nearby building. Three long tears were made in the envelope and the machine was dashed to earth. Determined not to lose his chance, Henry called on Bailey to re-ascend with him, "which he reluctantly did."

Stemming from whatever cause, Bailey, upon whom so much reliance was placed, curled up in the bottom of the car and could not be roused. Left entirely to himself, Henry managed to avoid being blown out to sea and brought the balloon down at Rainham after 35 minutes aloft. He declared the journey "pleasant," but for the disaster which occurred at the outset.[23]

Near disasters notwithstanding, Green (presumably Charles) made another ascent, this time from Stockport, on June 18, 1827.[24] On July 11, the idea of charging for short, tethered balloon ascents having "taken off," Green appeared at Maidstone (in Kent, southeast of London), offering rides "to a considerable distance above the houses." After four hours, the balloon was fully inflated and he completed the exhibition by making a free ascent. Flush from success after a difficult landing, the aeronaut expressed his opinion that he was so convinced of the safety of aerial expeditions, "that he would at any time prefer a voyage to the upper regions to one on the ocean."[25]

It seems a bit of bravado on Green's part, considering the number of aeronauts who had lost their lives in performance of their sport. Certainly more people drowned from sea accidents but the account of deaths from the air and water were disproportionate. His comment was particularly misplaced in light of the fact he panicked during the descent, letting out too much gas and thus causing the envelope to collapse.

Green's next flight came at Warrington on July 29 where he ascended with his son and a ship's captain. After an uneventful flight, the aeronauts landed at Greenhead near Lees, about nine miles from Manchester.[26]

Crossing the country to Ipswich, Green ascended on October 12. A number of gentlemen offered the meager sum of £10 for the privilege of occupying the vacant seat, "but whether by accident or design," there was not enough gas to accommodate a second adventurer. In another dangerous descent, Green's grapple failed to catch and the balloon was dragged four miles before coming to a stop at Hollesley White Post after a 20-minute flight. The balloon was much damaged during the landing.[27]

Selling the passenger's place for his ascent at the Eagle Tavern, City Road, on Monday, November 19, did not get any easier, as an advertisement for the late-season event on the 17th remarked: "A seat in the car is still vacant.[28]

While the Greens were dominating aerostation, several others continued to make headlines. In June 1827, Mademoiselle Garnerin ascended in Turin in the midst of an immense concourse of spectators, including the King and Queen of Sardonia. After rising with extreme rapidity, the intrepid aeronaut detached herself from the vessel in a parachute; "The descent was dreadful, and the destruction of Mademoiselle Garnerin appeared inevitable." The parachute finally opened, recovered its horizontal position "and put an end completely to the fears of the spectators." She landed in safety and returned to the palace where she was presented to their Majesties.[29]

"Mr. Brown," mentioned by Mrs. Graham during her husband's trial, advertised an ascent up from Wakefield on October 6, 1827, but in consequence of sudden illness, his youngest brother fulfilled the engagement. It did not go well. Shortly after rising, the balloon was seen to make a rapid and uncontrolled approach to earth. Brown's frantic voice was heard in "fearful exclamations," and the balloon collapsed, "presenting no longer a sphere or rotund appearance. The gyrations or whirlings of the balloon and car were frightful in the extreme, and the worst apprehensions were entertained."

The descent was completed two miles from Wakefield. The aeronaut was pulled out from underneath the envelope before the noxious gas pouring out threatened his life. He sustained a gash on the head and a fractured foot. The accident was attributed to the inexperience of the young aeronaut," and the extremes of weather."[30]

Henry Green, another inexperienced aeronaut, ascended with his balloon from Greenwich on April 8, 1828, descending safely in Hertfordshire after a flight of half an hour.[31] A month later at Boston (Lincoln, England), C. Green, his son, a youth still in his minority, ascended on May 21. After remaining airborne three hours, he landed safely near Sleaford.[32]

The month of July was a busy one for Charles Green. He advertised that on July 9 he would make his 98th ascent in a balloon partially inflated with pure hydrogen gas, generated from a "chymical process" from the decomposition of water.[33] On July 17 he ascended from Manchester, but after a flight of an hour and a quarter, while leaning over the car to throw out the grapnel, he was nearly thrown out. Managing to keep hold of the edge, he remained in that precarious position some time before a sudden jerk caused by the breaking grapnel precipitated him to the ground, seriously injuring him.[34]

A Pegasean Flight

As balloon flights became more common and the take at the gate diminished, those in the aerostatic entertainment business were forced to promote and actually perform more grandiose and risky flights. On July 29, 1828, Charles Green pulled off what has to stand as one of the most outlandish events in the history of the sport. While preparations were made for his ascent from the Eagle Tavern, City Road, a large crowd gathered to witness Mr. Green's *passenger*. In what many considered a hoax, a Shetland pony of small stature and the most extraordinary docility was paraded out for viewing. "Decorated with blue satin housing, bridle and ribbands," it was put through a handful of tricks, including bowing to the ladies and offering its foot to the gentlemen. Green, who owned and had trained the animal, stated that it was accustomed to walking up and down stairs, to lie on the hearthrug at the command of its master and drink tea from a cup.

After the balloon was inflated, the apparatus on which the pony stood was brought out. "It consisted of a round wicker platform, resembling a scale, and of sufficient width to contain the four feet of the pony; to its edges were attached six ropes, intended to support it from the netting, after the manner of the car, and kept separate by a hoop affixed to the upper end, from which hoop the grapnel and ballast [250 pounds in 11 bags] were all to be slung."

The wind at the time blew up a small hurricane and the spectators believed Green would use that as an excuse not to ascend. Undeterred, Green brought out the pony and placed it in its stall under the balloon. Quickly mounting, the assistants, one of whom was his son, set the balloon free. "The pony evidently disliked the excursion, and plunged violently at the moment of ascent," but after a short time after being petted and coaxed, it became "somewhat reconciled" to his situation and remained comparatively quiet.

Keeping his place in the saddle, Green fed the pony a handful of beans to keep it passive. Making a short journey, the aeronaut hung out his grapnel and dismounted to discharge ballast. Finding that his weight on one side of the platform upset the equilibrium and discomposed the pony, he resumed his seat and attained an elevation of a mile and a quarter. At that height they experienced a snowstorm, requiring a descent to a lower altitude where the precipitation turned to rain. After half an hour they landed "without the slightest injury" in a clover field in the parish of Beckenham, Kent.

Green gave the weight of the balloon as follows:

Balloon and appendages (including grapnel, platform, cables, ballast	508 pounds
Weight of the pony	250
Weight of myself	148
Total	906 pounds

Finding a considerable amount of gas left in the balloon, Green made a second flight, unaccompanied by pony or passenger, descending after half an hour on Bromley Common, five miles distant.

After being visited by hundreds of individuals, the now-famous pony returned to his old quarters, "safe and sound, being the first of his race that (the wooden horse of Pacolet excepted) ever traversed the regions of the air."[35]

The weather continued boisterous, forcing Green to cancel a second "Equestrian Balloon Ascent" on August 13. After a delay due to weather, Green made his reported 100th voyage from the White Conduit Gardens, Pentonville, on Friday the 15th. Considerable apprehension owing to the state of the weather caused many to fear he would only go up "in the ordinary way," but Green brought out the pony, put it through its paces, and secured it in the stall. On the signal, "Away," the balloon "bounded off with the velocity of lightning." Again the poor animal seemed much alarmed, causing the spectators to fear for the travelers, "although every one seemed highly gratified with the novelty of their situation."

"Every one" apparently did not include the newspapers, as the following attests:

> Balloon ascents have long ceased to have any philosophical or useful purpose attached to them; and have become mere puppet-shows, the more or less attractive as the fools who go up with them run the more or less risk.[36]

Regardless, Green substituted a different type of novelty for his next voyage, made from Dover, by declaring his intention to cross the Channel into France. Forty-three years had passed since an aeronaut ascended from Dover and the inhabitants readily collected a subscription of £40 to reimburse Green for his expenses. On August 10, 1828, making his "103rd aerial voyage," the balloon shot up with amazing velocity; once airborne, he discerned Calais and a good part of the French coast, but encountering gale-like conditions, the balloon quickly descended ten miles from Dover. The machine struck a tree and rebounded with great violence before help arrived.[37]

Onward to the End of the Decade

After repeated disappointments, Mademoiselle Garnerin ascended from Brussels on August 17, 1828. Following two minutes of rapid ascent, she detached her parachute from the car and for a minute appeared to drop with frightful speed. Spectators on the ground typically had this impression as the rapid upward movement of the balloon, coupled with the descent of the parachute, gave the impression of the aeronaut falling faster than what actually occurred. The parachute descended with very little oscillation and within two minutes she once again stood on *terra firma*, to the great joy and applause of the witnesses.[38]

On September 19, 1828, George Graham made his first appearance in the newspapers since the trial over his finances a year earlier. His balloon ascended from Baker's Millyard, Southampton. The cords became entangled with a chimney, but they were soon unfastened and the balloon remained in view of the nearly 10,000 spectators for nearly two hours. He landed safely at Norman Court near Salisbury and immediately announced a second ascent from town the following week.[39]

True to his word, the Grahams made two more ascents in that neighborhood, the second from the Chichester Gas Works, where Mrs. Graham and her passenger, Mr. Pickering, went up on October 21. After a difficult lift-off, where all the ballast and grappling had to be jettisoned, they soared for 11 minutes before attempting a descent. Being without grappling irons, however, the balloon rebounded nearly 300 yards and again descending, came in contact with a walnut tree.

During an evening parade, the still-inflated balloon was paraded through the streets. Unfortunately, the network caught on the pinnacle of a cross, seriously injuring the envelope. The city paid for the repairs and "the receipts, under the management of a committee, who greatly exerted themselves, cleared all demands, and satisfied the aeronauts."[40]

On June 11, 1829, Green made his second flight from the Albion brewery, Bristol. Forced to ascend alone due to insufficient buoyancy, he had trouble getting at the valve and was forced to cut holes in the silk to effect a descent. In accomplishing this, the grappling rope broke and he was dragged across two fields, sustaining very considerable damage to his right knee and wrist and a serious fracture of his thumb. After traveling 50 miles in 40 minutes he was helped from the car; a subscription was set on foot to "remunerate this spirited aeronaut" for his injuries.[41]

On July 2, 1829, George Green made his 71st ascent from the Golden Eagle, Mile-end Road, accompanied by a young lady. She subsequently wrote, "Having been present at most of Mr. Green's metropolitan ascents, I felt a strong desire to accompany him, placing implicit confidence in his skillful management of the balloon, and being well assured that if there had been the slightest danger he would not have permitted me to accompany him."

Apparently the lady did not realize that the greatest danger lay in *descending*, but fortunately the pair landed in safety.[42]

Later that month, things did not go so perfectly. Green, having already disappointed the people at Devices, made an unsuccessful attempt but "on account of its unfinished state," the balloon would not inflate properly. A mob destroyed the balloon with knives and other instruments and it was only by the prompt intervention of the magistrates that Green was saved from personal injury. Such was the fury of the people of Wilts that to preserve his life, Green, his wife and a friend "were compelled to secrete themselves in a dark hole until 11 o'clock at night."[43] The decade closed with some sidebars to ballooning. On August 3, 1829, a young man named Charles Durant ascended with Eugene Robertson, recently returned to France from the United States. As a 19-year-old native New Yorker, Durant had witnessed Robertson's first American ascent on July 9, 1825, and become enamored of the sport. Meeting the aeronaut later, he was invited to accompany him on his voyage to Havana in 1828 and was later sent to France to study aerostation under Étienne Robertson. Following a self-styled heroic voyage in which he climbed up the netting to secure a broken cord, he spent two years on the ground learning the craft from the famous family.[44]

22

Ballooning in the Americas

A New York paper, of August 24, mentions the second ascent of a balloon in the shape of an elephant of the largest size.[1]

By 1820 ballooning was not new to the United States. As early as 1784 a boy had ascended in Maryland in a montgolfière (see chapter 4), marking what was to become an American love affair with ascension. Twenty years into the new century, small balloons were already used by ship owners, being launched as a means of communicating with those on shore.[2]

As with the sport, crowds everywhere differed little from one another. In Philadelphia on October 14, 1820, Charles Guille ascended from Vauxhall Gardens, fortunately surviving the mistaken interference of many people attempting to assist him. In consequence, the envelope lost a considerable quantity of gas, requiring five minutes to rise 1,000 feet. Considering it dangerous to disengage himself in his parachute, Guille abandoned the idea.

Having no valve to regulate ascension, he reached a height of 35,000 feet, much higher than he otherwise would have gone. Suffering from great cold and fatigue he fell asleep, but luckily, the wet condition of the silk acted as ballast, weighing down the balloon and preventing further ascent. By the time he awoke the machine was descending so rapidly his parachute opened. Reaching an open field 40 miles from Philadelphia, Guille attempted to land, but lacking grapples, he was dragged some way before assistance arrived. The locals secured the balloon and helped him from the car after a flight of one hour and a quarter.[3]

On November 23, 1830, Guille made another ascent from Vauxhall Gardens. Ascending at 3:00 P.M., he quickly reached a predetermined elevation and set off his parachute containing a monkey, "which gradually and safely descended to the earth." After a short journey he descended near Schuylkill without incident.[4]

Independence Day in the United States rivaled the British celebration of the King's birthday, and on July 4, 1824, the famous aeronaut Eugene Robertson (one of two brothers, sons of the European balloonist Étienne Robertson) made his 18th ascent from Castle Garden, New York. Rising to the height of *three miles*, the aeronaut remarked he had "never passed through the clouds before, having always until now, had clear weather." He reported that while over Long Island he was very much annoyed by the firing of cannon that shook the balloon "like an aspen," causing great apprehension.[5]

Displaying an early penchant for balloons of various shapes, on August 24, 1824, the balloon *Eclipse*, representing a man on horseback, was let loose from the Castle Garden, Vauxhall, New York. The Brooklyn *Star* joyously wrote, "Eclipse against the world."[6]

In Honor of General Lafayette and Brides

Never forgetting its war heroes, Robertson's flight on July 9, 1825, from Castle Garden had the honor of entertaining generals Lafayette, Fish, Lewis, Morton and Governor Ogdon. Ten thousand persons gathered to watch the proceedings under the trees while another 5,000 were comfortably accommodated within the spacious amphitheatre.

"Within a line surrounded by a strong rope and guarded by peace officers," Mr. Robertson had arranged his apparatus, consisting of "wooden buts or pipes, tin conductors," and all material necessary for making gas. The process of inflation was slow and tedious. The balloon was "of a moderate size, and of dark silk thickly varnished.... The car was made of wicker; it was in fact one of those wicker cradles, the size of the balloon not permitting any thing heavier."

After disengaging the inflating pipes, the intrepid aeronaut, "dressed in a blue coat, embroidered collar and cuffs, chapeau, &c." took his seat with American and French flags in hand. On being released the balloon struck against the flagstaff, grazed the top of the saloon and the heads of the spectators and nearly caused Robertson to fall from the car. After throwing out "bags of sand, his flags, hat, bottle and every thing he had," the grapnel and cords soon followed, finally lightening the machine enough to permit its slow ascension. The balloon headed for Long Island as the aeronaut "employed himself in throwing out slips of paper." He eventually reached an open field after a journey of 55 minutes. Without grapples, however, the machine struck a fence before the rebounding could be checked and brought safely to ground.[7]

Hydrogen continued to be manufactured for balloon ascensions long after its use had fallen into disfavor in Europe. In fact, coal gas lighting of street lamps (and consequently of inflating balloons) was slow coming to the United States. By 1850, only 8,144 of 15,007 street lamps in New York City were lit by gas, and most of those were either downtown or located in the wealthier neighborhoods.[8]

Like his European counterparts, Robertson (frequently misspelled "Robinson") was not above a little showmanship and perhaps a chance to pad his remuneration. Prior to his second ascent from Castle Garden on September 5, 1825, a lady dressed as a bride took her station in the car and was paraded around the heads of the audience. Afterward, additional gas was added and the "ingenious Aeronaut" began his voyage in front of 7,000 persons in the garden and three times that number in the Battery. The newspaper account added, "it is honorable to the people of New York, that the most scrupulous decorum was observed."[9]

America's First Lady and First Gentleman of the Air

On Thursday, October 20, 1825, Madame Johnson became the first American woman to fly when she ascended from Castle Garden. Wearing an elegant dress and waving a beautiful white French flag, she calmly examined the cords fastening the car to the balloon, being the only one present who "seemed to remain undaunted and unconcerned."

Making no display or affecting "the least parade or show," she arose from the ground seated in the car, waving the American flag in her left hand and the French flag in her right. After throwing out ballast, she passed over Brooklyn where great fears were entertained that she would be blown out to sea. However, Madame Johnson landed safely in a salt marsh near Flatlands, 200–300 feet from the sea, descending so gently and easily that she made no use of the grappling. After returning to the garden, she embraced her children and sister, noting that during the voyage she had not experienced any inconvenience from the cold, but that the atmosphere grew warmer as she ascended. She felt no difficulty breathing, finding respiration as free and easy as when on earth.

The report concluded, "Thus has this intrepid woman most completely fulfilled her promise and undertaking with the public, and vastly exceeded all expectation, for never before has there been in this country so successful, so perfect an ascent."[10]

On July 21, 1826, Green made the first nighttime ascent in England. News traveled rapidly, for in September, Robertson announced his intention to make a similar flight from Castle Garden. Perhaps to do the Europeans one better, he added a fireworks display to the proceedings.

At 8:15 P.M. a pilot balloon of considerable size was sent aloft; to it was attached a parachute which was disengaged at a great height by a slow match. At the same moment, by the same means, a brilliant Bengola light placed in the car of the parachute was fired, illuminating the sky with brilliance. Robertson's balloon then ascended with another set of fireworks suspended 150 feet below his basket. Reaching the proper height, the fireworks were set off, the glare of rockets and wheels of fire causing those below to hold their breath for the safety of the pilot, whose life might, at any moment, be extinguished by a spark igniting the gas. When the display burned out Robertson had disappeared from the sky as if by magic. He descended at 10:30 P.M. at Flatbush.[11]

Taking his show on the road, Robertson traveled to New Orleans where, on May 29, 1827, he made the second of his ascensions. Accompanying him was "a lady attached to the New-Orleans Theatre." The balloon descended on the opposite side of the river and the aeronauts returned to the city after an absence of two and a half hours.[12]

Robertson's fortune turned on September 18, 1828. Back in New York at the Castle Garden, the aeronaut began his ascent, flourishing his banner and bowing to the crowd of 2,000 within the Garden and 15,000 without. Unfortunately, the vessel had been released directly windward of the flagstaff (which Robertson had requested be taken down), with which it came in violent contact. The netting became entangled with the pole and the car turned nearly upside down.

Robertson was flung out, but managed to retain a position by hanging to the netting, face downward, feet upmost in the car. Suspended 100 feet from the ground and vibrating in every direction, a large rent was made in the silk, causing him to descend another 15 feet. Though "nearly black in the face," he held tight as a man climbed the rope for his relief. He came within 15 feet of the aeronaut before his strength failed and he was obliged to descend.

Maintaining his precarious position, at times by his feet and at others by one hand, Robertson at length caught the rope, cleared himself from the car and the entanglements of the cord and descended forty or fifty feet before dropping to the ground. After receiving the congratulations from his friends on the perilous escape, he retired to a private apartment, hands blistered and excoriated by the rope. He also lost one of his front teeth by having seized a cord in his mouth as he threw himself from the car.

The balloon was taken down before dark, but was entirely ruined.[13]

A month later, Robertson, in possession of a new balloon, ascended from Castle Garden on October 22. This time he took a young lady as passenger, and the two arose in majestic style, she waving a white flag with the name of "LAFAYETTE" inscribed and kissing her hand, while he held the Star-spangled Banner. Among the 30,000 spectators was a delegation of Winnebago Indians. "Never was astonishment more perfectly personified, than in the faces and actions of these children of the forest. They seemed gazing at an exhibition of supernatural powers.... They were also apparently lost in wonder at the immensity of the throng of human beings collected on the Battery."[14]

The balloon fell into the river between Bushwick Creek and Williamsburgh, 150–300 yards from shore. It was discovered by a number of boats in the vicinity; crews rushed to the aeronauts, secured them and the balloon and landed them safely at Williamsburgh. Robertson later explained that the gas became exhausted before reaching Long Island, and despite the fact he threw out all his ballast he could not prevent it from falling into the water.[15]

Mr. Durant, the "Great Brave," Makes a Name for Himself

Using a French-made balloon, constructed of green silk and featuring a portrait of Governor DeWitt Clinton, holding 10,000 feet of hydrogen, Charles Durant made his American debut on September 9, 1830. Advertised as the "First Native Citizen of the United States That ever Attempted an Ascension in a Balloon," the "pupil of Eugene Robertson" set off from Castle Garden in front of 20,000 people.

After passing out copies of his poem, which included, "Good bye to you-people of Earth, I am soaring to regions above you. But much that I know of your earth, Will ever endure me to love you,"[16] he made a successful flight of two hours. Halfway across the Bay he released one of his carrier pigeons that followed the balloon a short time before landing on the steamboat *Bolivar*. Failing to secure the bird, it flew on to Bedlow's Island, a short distance from the boat.

Crossing Staten Island, the balloon approached so near the earth that Durant was able to speak to the inhabitants before discharging ballast and crossing Prince's Bay. Soon afterward, he completed a successful landing in South Amboy, New Jersey.[17] Mr. Marsh, the Castle Garden booking agent, took advantage of the success to schedule a second voyage on September 22. After a delay occasioned by two tears in the balloon, Durant completed a successful trip, dropping a line one mile south of Hackensack, and was towed by admirers into town.

Durant stated that in a span of three minutes he traveled three miles, making a speed of sixty miles per hour. At this rate he supposed that, given a fair wind, he could traverse "the whole continent of America from New Orleans to Portland," in the short space of 21 hours. The "great brave," as he was called, supposed that he could be propelled 100 miles per hour by a gale. Such a wind would carry him from Louisiana to Maine between sunrise and sunset.[18]

A year later, on August 23, 1831, Durant again ascended from Castle Garden, with spectators urged to "pay for the trouble, experience, and danger" of the aeronaut. He rose perpendicularly in a balloon "beautifully ornamented with flowers."[19] After letting out a rabbit in a parachute at 2,000 feet, Durant landed over the Buttermilk Channel, where a boat crew towed him back to shore.

The flight cost $1,000 to arrange and brought in $1,200, which the aeronaut dismissed by saying he was "happy to make 30,000 people happy."[20]

Durant made a fourth voyage on September 10, this time earning enough to buy a house at Paulus Hook and establish a candy shop. With grand plans in mind for 1832, he varnished silk for a new balloon with a combination of turpentine, linseed oil and gumelastic. Unfortunately, "spontaneous combustion" rendered the material to ash,[21] ending his season before it began.

With a new balloon "entirely of his own construction," containing 600 yards of Levantine silk, 47 feet in diameter and 28 feet through, featuring 37 major seams double-sewn with a backstitch and a disposable lift of 200–300 pounds.[22] Durant ascended on May 30, 1833, from Castle Garden. In "twelve seconds" he was completely out of sight, due to a dense fog.

In 39 minutes he reached an altitude of 16,000 feet, encountering a temperature so extreme his flagstaff became too cold to touch. Taking a course over New Jersey, he crossed the North River and made for Westchester, 11 miles from New York City. Assisted by three African American men, he landed in safety.[23]

Durant's sixth flight took place on June 14, 1833, with several unusual witnesses: the famous Indian chief Black Hawk and his party. Arriving at 5 o'clock in a steamboat, the vessel was rounded to, and the "children of the forest" exhibited "greater astonishment on this occasion, than on any other upon their journey. Black Hawk, in speaking of the Aeronaut, said, 'he must be a very great brave,' and seemed to think that 'he could go to the Heavens — to the Great Spirit.'"[24] Also in attendance, however briefly, was President Andrew Jackson, who bowed to the spectators from the Saloon before retiring.

With 5,000 persons in the garden and 30–40,000 without, the balloon ascended,

ONE CENT A MILE
TO THE GREAT
DAKOTA FAIR
AT MITCHELL
SEPT. 24th to 28th.
EXCITING RACES.
A Larger And Better Stock Show Than Ever.
PROFS. HUNT
AND
PRICE,
—OF—
CLEVELAND, OHIO
The most celebrated balloonists in the world have been engaged at great expense to make two balloon ascensions and two parachute jumps from a height of Five Thousand Feet.
ON THE WAY DOWN
Read the Program and Come with your Friends.
PROGRAM:

In the early years of ballooning, animals were dropped from parachutes, or particularly brave aeronauts dared leap from their basket. Over the decades, as audiences became bored with simple ascensions, parachute drops became the norm. Newspapers of the 1880s were filled with articles describing failed attempts and dire outcomes (*Mitchell Daily Republican* [South Dakota], September 17, 1888).

but the cords that fastened the car to the balloon struck the saloon and the machine had to be drawn back. After being cut loose, the balloon moved in the direction of Long Island. Durant released a carrier pigeon with the words "all's well," and attained an altitude of 3,736 feet before descending on Long Island.[25]

This voyage netted the young man the staggering sum of $12,000 and added much to his prestige. After a wildly successful flight in Albany on August 8, in which the aeronaut's share of the gate receipts amounted to $1,300,[26] it was announced his next ascent would be at Baltimore, where he required "a ton and a half of oil of vitriol" to inflate his balloon.[27]

On September 26 Durant ascended from Federal Hill, but not without incident. At the moment the balloon was cut free, the crowd in the amphitheatre surged forward, causing the makeshift seating over the saloon to collapse. Fortunately no one was injured.[28] After setting out a rabbit in a parachute, which fell without injury in Old Town,[29] he completed a scientific experiment for a local gentleman, and arrived over Bel-Air, settling his grapples down 200 feet from the Courthouse.[30]

In his journal, Durant made extensive mention of those who assisted him and included details of a tea party and the presentation of a very old bottle of wine, but failed to include information that subsequently made the newspapers. Many involved slaves who, upon seeing the "dreadful messenger" in the sky, flew home in order to escape the Devil.[31]

The citizens of Baltimore madly collected money for a second flight and numerous committees took up the work of preparing the grounds, so that Durant had little pre–flight preparation, and on October 14, five thousand spectators paid $1 each to fill the amphitheatre on Federal Hill. Again using sulfuric acid from Ellicott's Chemical Laboratory, it "bore full 66 Raume," which is a high degree of concentration. Lacking a sufficient quantity of iron, he purchasing a few hundred pounds of nails, "which rather improved the decomposition, as they were free from oxyd, and furnished a purer hydrogen." He ascended at 4:30 P.M., scattering the garden with copies of his verses and waving the national flag.[32] After passing a few words of condolence to his "physiological" rabbit, he set it out by parachute. He also tried an experiment with the magnetic needle for Mr. T. Edmonson and a second of a geological nature.

Setting down briefly in a field to chat with two gentlemen, Durant then continued toward Chestertown. With night approaching, he noted the steamboat *Independence* on her way to Frenchtown. Dropping his cords, the passengers hauled him down and Captain Pearce provided a fine meal.[33]

Durant made three more ascents in 1834, all from Boston. On the premiere flight from Boston Common on July 31, 1834 (the first ascension there since 1821), he arose before 50,000 persons. His intent had been to reach Cape Ann, but finding it difficult to maintain a proper altitude over the water, he resolved to drop 300–400 feet of cable and let his anchors trail below. As they skipped over the surface, the balloon undulated to such a degree that it was plunged into the water. He anticipated that being of open wicker, the car would not fill, but it was drawn with such force it soon sank, leaving him partially immersed. In order to prevent further sinking and retard its progress, Durant spread a sheet, which he carried to fold the balloon, across the car.

The *Miner*, a schooner under the command of Captain Spaulding, came abreast and threw him a halyard, which, with the boat to wind, had the effect of drawing him 800 feet into the air. He descended with great velocity and the process was repeated, this time to a height of 300 feet before a "flaw of wind upturned the balloon so as to exhaust the gas." Untangling himself from the cords that had gotten caught in his gum-elastic life preserver, the captain came for Durant in a small boat and took him aboard.[34]

He flew again on August 25th and made his final voyage September 13, 1834. Thereafter he retired from the sport, apparently on the request of his bride.[35] Although completing only thirteen flights, Durant captured the imagination of a nation, and well into the century he was regarded as America's premiere aeronaut.[36] He died at his home in Jersey City on March 1, 1873, from pneumonia. At the time of his death he was working on a text of astronomy.[37]

The Daring Undertakings of James Mills, Nicholas Ash &C

Fresh on the heels of Charles Durant came a young Baltimore mechanic named James Mills. Having already made at least one successful ascent in 1831, the "new aeronaut" appointed Wednesday, April 3, 1824, as the day of his official introduction to aerostation. Owing to a heavy wind and his over-anxious friends, who "pressed around him too closely, confused him and even disarranged his machinery," the inflation from Federal Hill was not completed until 4:50 P.M., when he ascended to the cheers of 30,000 spectators. Throwing out three bags of sand, he waved his flag until out of sight.[38] Mills made a safe landing at Magothy,[39] having traveled 16 miles and reaching an elevation of a mile and a quarter.[40]

Mills' second flight came on May 1, from the Fairmount Gardens. It was calculated he traveled 50 miles in three hours and that he crossed the Chesapeake Bay, a distance of 14 miles, in 17 minutes. During the flight the constant rotary motion of the balloon rendered his compass useless.[41] While aloft he encountered a violent snowstorm and the temperature plunged to 34°. The precipitation drenched him and the clouds obscured the sight of earth "altogether!"[42]

Successfully descending at North Point, the Baltimore *American* declared that this young mechanic, "self-taught, and dependent alone on his own unaided efforts — may fairly take rank with the most successful aeronauts of the age."[43]

Mills announced that before his next ascent on May 26 he would permit passengers to ascend in the tethered balloon free of charge. Unfortunately the event was rained out,[44] and on June 25, "the celebrated Baltimore Aeronaut" left the city with his balloon and fixtures in the steamboat *Kentucky* for Philadelphia.[45]

"Unquestionably one of the most fearless and skilful aeronauts who ever ascended from this city" rose in "One of the most beautiful balloon ascensions which we have ever witnessed," gushed the U.S. *Gazette*, speaking of James Mill's flight from Philadelphia on June 26. Passing over the city at a low altitude, he threw out some printed verses, crossed the Delaware and passed Camden at the height of two miles. Nearing the sea he quickly descended, throwing out his anchor. Having it torn away and violently rebounding, he was finally tossed out.[46]

Although sustaining injuries to the left side of his face, left arm and right foot,[47] his regret was the "disappointment of losing his old companion the balloon," which disappeared out to sea along with his fine barometer and compass.[48]

The people of Philadelphia raised a fund to compensate Mills and on September 16 he ascended from Broad Street, landing 16 miles away on the Lancaster Turnpike. On October 6 he ascended from Camden. On this voyage he released a rabbit in a muslin parachute and descended near Moorestown.[49]

Mills made one more voyage that year, ascending from Lancaster on November 1. Passing close to a house, some white people hailed him, asking, "Who are you?" to which he replied, "Where am I?" They answered, "Go back where you came from." The flight lasted two hours, covering one hundred miles. Mills table provides some interesting flight data:

Time	Barom.	Therm.	[Wind]
2 54	29.8	54	W.
3 5	27.5	44	N.W.
3 15	25.0	46	N.
3 20	22.2	34	E.N.E.
4 0	19.9	31½	S.E. by S.

The method used for estimating force and direction of the current was "A feather of sufficient size to be visible at a distance, leaded in such a manner as to fall slowly."[50]

Nicholas J. Ash blew onto the scene with an advertisement in the Baltimore *Visitor*, announcing that he had constructed a silken balloon "of six different colours, the largest that has yet been made."[51] On June 2, he attempted to make an aerostatic name for himself by ascending at the Observatory Gardens. Failing to sufficiently inflate the balloon, Ash set it free. Ascending "something in the form of an umbrella, or parachute," the unmanned vessel made a two-mile journey before falling into the water near Fort McHenry.[52]

A second attempt on July 7 at Fairmount Garden proved marginally successful, the balloon making it into the air after striking a nearby chimney. Fifteen minutes into the flight the rotation twisted the cords so badly, Ash mistakenly pulled the valve line, plummeting the machine onto the top of a house. A gust of wind ultimately dropped the contrivance onto Lexington Street.[53]

On July 30, he became the first aeronaut to ascend from the District of Columbia, where he managed a successful flight of two hours before descending four miles from Georgetown. He quickly advertised a repeat performance, but fell ill, ultimately canceling the endeavor.

Baltimore remained the hot bed of ballooning but things did not always go as planned. The proposed ascent of two aeronauts on July 28, 1834, ascending simultaneously in separate balloons, drew huge crowds. When it became obvious there was not enough gas to fill both aerostats, George Elliott and William A. Woodall, Jr. (occasionally spelled "Woodal"), cast lots to determine who should be entitled to the honor. Woodall won and ascended at 6:30 P.M., making a complete circuit around the city at a low altitude. He descended an hour later seven miles distant.[54]

August 11, 1834, saw George Elliott ascend with a six-year-old boy named John Quincy Adams Redman[55] from the Observatory Garden. Reaching an elevation of "six miles," Elliott found respiration extremely difficult, "especially to the child." After passing over a lightning storm, the machine began to fall. Elliott could not check the rate of descent "in consequence of the cord having a splice, which became fast to a piece of tin placed by mistake in the neck pipe of the balloon."

Violently landing in the water with the child in his arms, the shock broke the valve cord, closing it. Waist deep in water, he bade Redman wave his hat to a passing steamboat; they were noticed and Captain Taylor took them safely aboard.[56]

Elliott's next flight did not have equal fortune. On August 25 he attempted an ascent on the Jersey side of Philadelphia (Camden) with a woman. Ten thousand people crossed over to witness the spectacle but owing to a lack of gas the balloon failed to rise. "The mob became exasperated, tore down the fence, and deliberately cut the balloon to pieces. Mr. Elliott was not injured."[57] Woodall's luck proved no better. On September 6 he intended a voyage from Frederick, but the balloon failed to ascend.[58]

Following his unsuccessful flight at Camden, George Elliott traveled to Charleston, where he ascended on October 22 before few paying customers. After a voyage of nearly two hours, he experienced problems landing "on account of some difficulty in opening the valve," and descended in perfect darkness into the water. Captain Albert of the *Cora* rescued him after 30 minutes.[59]

Elliott made a second flight on November 3, reaching an altitude of two and a half miles over the course of 45 minutes. Twenty miles from Charleston the balloon rebounded, dragging the aeronaut one mile before lodging him in a tree. Forty Negroes lent a hand in disentangling the aeronaut, "some asking if it was true that he was a living man, and all regarding him as a supernatural monster."[60]

Hugh Frazier Parker made his appearance on November 8, 1834, when, "for the benefit of his brother aeronaut Mr. Ash, who had been ill for some time past,"[61] he ascended from the Square north of the President's house, in Washington, D.C. A light wind carried the balloon off and he landed safely in St. Mary's County, having traveled 80 miles in one hour and ten minutes.[62] The tumultuous aerostatic year 1834 came to a violent close on December 28 when George Elliott made an ascent from New Orleans. The balloon was let loose during a violent wind, moving horizontally and striking benches of spectators, some of whom were injured. Moving slowly upward, the machine then struck a chimney in the enclosure, fracturing Elliott's thigh bone. He was driven through an upper story window, and his face and hands were cut.

The balloon managed to clear the building but, passing over water, became entangled in the rigging of two ships. Finally rescued, it was seen his broken thighbone had been forced through his drawers and pantaloons and he was placed in the care of doctors.[63]

Enthralled by the idea of flying, Americans wasted no time preparing for the season of 1835. As early as February 9, an announcement gave details of James Mills' next flight, using wings and sails attached to a conical balloon in the expectation of guiding the vessel.[64] Ascending on May 4 from Fairmount Garden, the balloon stuck an apple tree in Peach Bottom Township, York County, while descending. He managed to extricate himself and the balloon was secured without damage.[65]

In June, Mills ascended from Lancaster with a handful of jewelry presented by some ladies, and enjoyed a "romantic and novel" voyage through the clouds until the balloon became "violently agitated, swung to and fro, rotated rapidly, and immediately took a direction opposite to the old one."[66]

He next advertised an ascent from York on Saturday, June 27. The necessary expense was $800, which a committee was appointed to raise.[67] Mills made his tenth ascent from York on Saturday, July 25. Tickets to the event cost 50 cents.[68] He landed safely near Columbia on the Susquehanna River.[69]

His eleventh voyage was scheduled for August 22, but sadly Mills never made it. On August 15 he complained of feeling ill. Friends later found him lying on the floor by the balloon he had been repairing, apparently dying without a struggle.[70] Baltimore newspapers reported he had burst a blood vessel, but it is equally likely he died by asphyxiation from the varnish used on the balloon.[71]

Richard Clayton was a native of England, "a gentleman of respectability, about 27 years of age, of considerable scientific acquirements, [who] understands perfectly the science of Ballooning."[72] Long established in Cincinnati, he made an ascent in his *Star of the West*, on the promise of "remaining in the air as long as his gas would sustain him." Taking his departure from the amphitheatre on April 8, 1835, after "some delay," he set out on the hoop entirely above the basket. After reaching a certain height, he launched a 20-pound dog in a basket that floated safely to earth in a parachute.[73] After reaching a height of two and a half miles, Clayton crossed the Little Miami River. He finally landed at Stinson's Knob, Virginia[74] having traveled 350 miles in 9 hours, "the longest voyage, by far, ever performed by any person in a Balloon."[75]

The Cincinnati papers duly noted, "Mr. Clayton has signally revived the flagging interest of the public in Balloon ascensions," and proudly announced his second flight, which the aeronaut hoped would take his "Aerial Ship" as far as the Atlantic Ocean.[76]

"The unrivaled Aeronaut" attempted to make good that promise on May 14 from Cincinnati. Unluckily, Clayton fell out of the car after it broke away from the attendants, injuring his right hip and sustaining a cut on his arm. Amid shouts of "he is killed," the balloon ascended without him and soon disappeared. A committee assembled for the purpose of devising measures to remunerate Clayton of his loss: the balloon valued at $900 and the cost of inflation $400.[77]

The "fugitive balloon" was found on May 16, 15 miles from Cincinnati near the Licking River in Kentucky. "It is so much damaged as to be unfit for use, except for patching old balloons."[78]

Independence Day saw Mr. Clayton ascend from Cincinnati on his fourth voyage. The *Star of the West*, an uncommonly handsome balloon made of silk of various colors, arose in grand style.[79] After the release of a little dog by parachute, the machine rose to an altitude of two miles, where Clayton discovered the neck had become entangled between the cords, preventing surplus gas from escaping and over-inflating the balloon.[80] Another account attributed this to neglect.[81]

In attempting to liberate the valve cord, the neck and cord were pulled away and the upper portion of the balloon burst with tremendous noise. Dropping a mile in four minutes, the balloon struck ground with a severe shock, rending the fabric to "a mass of ribbands."[82]

In December, Clayton made the first American balloon flight using carbonated gas provided by the New Orleans Gas Light and Banking Company works, owned by James H. Caldwell. The flight was a complete success, the aeronaut traveling 25 miles from the city to the island of "Chef de Menteurs" (Petit Coquille), near Fort Pike.[83]

Zebulon Mitchell, another of the Baltimore aeronauts, made an ascent on March 23, 1835, for the benefit of the local seamstresses. On a bizarre note, September 14, 1837, he was about to enter his car at Fairmount, Baltimore, when a lady named Jane Warren stepped out from the crowd and politely insisted on taking his place. The spectators seconded her wish and she "went up rapidly to a great elevation." The machine flew over the city where the aeronaut was seen "calm as a summer's morning," waving her handkerchief.[84] She landed two hours later on the eastern shore of Maryland.

In October, Warren made a second ascent, landing in Chesapeake Bay. Her plight was completely ignored by a passing schooner and she was finally rescued by a boat of surly fishermen. On her return to Baltimore, she voiced her displeasure at the "brutes in britches."[85]

John Wise Emerges onto the Scene

John Wise (family name Weiss) was born in Lancaster, Pennsylvania, in 1808. An apprenticed cabinetmaker, he first developed an interest in ballooning when he was fourteen years old. By 1835 he had paid for and constructed his own aerostatic machine; lack of funds forced him to use lacquered muslin instead of silk, and his wicker basket measured only 2 feet in diameter, with a depth of less than four feet.

He made several flights in 1835 and 1836. Earning enough money to construct a new balloon, this one made of silk, which he christened the *Meteor*, it had a pear-shaped appearance and measured 24 feet in diameter. Wise ascended with it on May 7, 1836, from Lancaster. The flight itself varied little from the routine of the day and he descended very gradually. After throwing out one of his anchors it caught in a fence and in a short time he had discharged enough gas to alight from the car. Wise wrote:

It being dark, I called for help, and soon received the assistance of some negroes from the farm upon which I descended.... As I was engaged in folding up my balloon in the car, there being still more gas in the upper part of it, which I was pressing thro the valve at the top, a negro approached behind me with a lighted candle. I did not observe him until within a few feet of the balloon, when I repeated the command I had given at first, not to come too near the balloon with a candle, when at that moment, the stream of gas issuing from the valve, took fire and exploded with a loud retort, injuring the top of my balloon considerably, and scorching my face and hand very much. The negroes were very much frightened at the accident, rushing against each other in their confusion to get away, whilst their heads being in a blaze, presented a truly ludicrous appearance.[86]

While there were more individual aeronauts trying their hand at public entertainment in America, just as in Europe, the favorites garnered most of the press. Richard Clayton continued to dominate the newspapers throughout 1837 as he made several ascents from Cincinnati. On May 1, after discovering the balloon lacked sufficient power, he detached the car and made a seat of cords by tying them together. He rose 20 feet, but finding further ascent impossible, deliberately cast off all the un-inflated part of the envelope, leaving an open space at the bottom, more than ten feet in diameter. This gave him added buoyancy and he floated away, waving his hat to the crowd. In what was styled "the most thrilling ascent he has yet made in Cincinnati," the aeronaut landed 15 miles from the city[87] on the top of a beach tree.[88]

Clayton's next ascension came on July 31, 1837, at the Woodland Garden, Louisville. The aeronaut made his first landing after 45 minutes, descending on the farm of Mr. Churchill, four miles south of Louisville. In the morning after the sun's rays evaporated the dew from the balloon, he ascended again. After sailing over Louisville, he came down at dinnertime, supped with a local farmer and then took off again at 3:30 P.M. At suppertime he landed for the final time near Bardstown, having covered not less than 100 miles. From this experiment, Clayton concluded he could travel in the *Star of the West* ("which is the best that was ever constructed in the United States") several thousand miles and remain a week in the atmosphere.

Clayton flew from Allegheny, Pennsylvania, on August 31, experiencing extreme cold and suffering from a dousing of water condensed from the gas which ran down his neck and froze on the silk and gas cord. Descending in a thunderstorm, the wind carried the balloon through trees and over rocks, eventually entangling him fifteen feet from the ground. Being taken for a "monster" by the locals, they refused assistance, forcing him to escape by himself in the morning.[89]

Despite the not entirely new insult of being taken for a monster, Clayton made one more ascent from Allegheny on September 13, descending safely four miles from Brownsville.

23

The Europeans Continue
to Make Headlines

*A late London periodical says: "Balloons now start almost every evening from various
parts of the town—and men, women and monkeys are to be seen ascending and
descending. We have less commercial and other distresses, probably in consequence
of the world's looking up."*[1]

Aerostation in the early part of the 1830s belonged to America, but in Europe, the old favorites continued to make ascensions, albeit with less fanfare and fewer newspaper reports. After his ascent with Charles Green from Chelmsford on April 30, 1831, Dr. Forster made an interesting observation. After experiencing "pressure on the tympanion of the car, arising from the rarefaction of the atmosphere," which became so painful they had to descend, the doctor thought an ascent might cure some kinds of deafness. "Sounds, however loud below, soon become perfectly inaudible as they ascended."[2]

The years of relative obscurity ended in 1836 with a historic flight destined to garner the attention and admiration of the world.

In a pre–flight test for the voyage of his life, Charles Green ascended from Vauxhall on the 9th of September 1836. The balloon, holding 70,000 cubic feet of gas, measured 157 feet in circumference and stood 80 feet high. The envelope contained 2,000 yards of crimson and white silk, exceedingly thick and woven "in a peculiar manner." The gores were united by a cement invented by Green, so tenacious as to prevent all chance of separation.

The inflation was supervised by Mr. Hutchinson and cost £70. Accounts reported that the highly rarefied gas was sufficiently buoyant to carry 20 persons. On this occasion, however, besides 336 pounds of ballast, nine persons ascended.[3] After an hour's flight, the adventurers descended safely at Cliffe, in Kent County.[4]

On November 7, 1836, at 1:30 P.M. Charles Green and two companions, Messrs. Holland and Monk-Mason (also spelled "Monck"), the historian on the journey, left London in Green's balloon, the *Royal Vauxhall* with the intention of flying as far as the winds would take them. The ascent was private with only a select few invited to witness what they hoped would be an epic journey. With them the aeronauts carried upward of a ton of ballast, several gallons of brandy and wine, a large supply of coffee (with an apparatus with unslacked lime for heating it), cold fowls and ham.

They also supplied themselves with passports from the French and Dutch embassies and carried a letter for the king of Holland, should they land in any of those countries.[5]

Moving in a southeasterly direction over the plains of Kent, the aeronauts sighted the sea. Monk-Mason wrote, "It was forty-eight minutes past four that we first saw the line of waves breaking on the shore beneath us. It would have been impossible to have remained unmoved by the grandeur of the spectacle that spread out before us. Behind us were the coasts of England, with their white cliffs half lost in the coming darkness. Beneath us on both sides the ocean spread out far and wide to where the darkness closed in the scene."[6]

The wind suddenly changed direction and bore them toward German waters. Green did not feel it wise to take that route and they threw out ballast, climbing into a new current taking them over Dover. An hour later they sighted the lighthouse at Calais.

"Darkness was now complete, and it was only by the lights, sometimes isolated, sometimes seen in masses, and showing themselves far down on the earth beneath us, that we could form a guess of the countries we traversed ... the face of the earth seemed to rival the vault of heaven with starry fires."

They were three men alone on an isolated, singular, aerial vessel, staring out into the depths of space, wondering, perhaps, in their loneliness or their fear why they had ever attempted such madness and then brushing the question aside as duty called. Three human beings challenging the "final frontier" of their day, they were not unlike a trio of others who would ascend from their small blue planet in the hope and expectation of reaching and landing upon a truly foreign soil. One set of adventurers required passports to explain their presence; the others did not, for there would be no one there to receive them. Yet the Royal *Vauxhall* and the *Apollo 11* crews both faced an unknown where their footprints would forever change the face of how Mankind looked at itself in the mirror.

Traveling at a speed more than ten leagues an hour, the balloon passed over Liège at midnight. "A black profound abyss surrounded us on all sides, and, as we attempted to penetrate into the mysterious deeps, it was with difficulty we could beat back the idea and the apprehension that we were making a passage through an immense mass of black marble, in which we were enclosed, and which, solid to within a few inches of us, appeared to open up at our approach."[7]

Traveling in the pitch blackness gave them a sense of spatial dissociation, leaving the impression the wind had driven them along the coasts of the North Sea or the Baltic. As day drew near and the light of dawn brought with it the opportunity of sight, the symptoms disappeared.

The aeronauts gradually made out the Rhine and sought a place to land, dropping anchor at 7:30 A.M. After setting foot on *terra firma*, the locals informed them they had reached the Duchy of Nassau, ironically only two leagues distant from where Blanchard descended after his flight at Frankfort in 1785. In memory of the event, the three placed the flag they had carried over the sea in the ducal palace, side by side with that of Blanchard.[8]

During the course of 18 hours, the pioneers crossed England, France, Belgium, Belfort, and had passed over London, Canterbury, Dover, Calais, Ypres, Courtrai, Lille, Brussels, Namur, Liege and Coblenz. This triumphant journey was not rivaled until the end of the century.[9]

In honor of the voyage, Charles Green re-christened his balloon the *Royal Nassau*.

Monk Mason concluded, "The best answer which one could give to those who would be disposed to criticize the employment of the peculiar means which we made use of, or to doubt their efficiency, would be to state that, after having traversed without hindrance, without either danger or difficulty, so large a portion of the European continent, we arrived at our destination still in possession of as much force as, had we wished it, might have carried us round the whole world."[10]

To achieve that, the world would have to wait 166 years: incredibly, 33 years fewer than it would take Neil Armstrong, Buzz Aldrin and Michael Collins to make their historic journey to the lunar surface.

A "Monstrous" Disaster

In June 1837, Green and his "monster balloon" ascended from London. It carried up, besides the aeronaut, six other gentlemen. The balloon traveled 25 miles in 23 minutes and landed in safety.[11]

The bold type in the handbill distributed in London, July 1837, proclaimed an "Extraordinary Novelty and Combined Attraction!" Not only would Green make an ascent in the *Royal Nassau* balloon, Mr. Cocking would descend in a "Newly-Invented Parachute," appearing as an inverted cone, 107 feet in circumference. The festivities were to take place at the Royal Gardens, Vauxhall, on July 24, 1837.[12]

Robert Cocking (1776-July 24, 1837), a professional watercolor artist, witnessed André-Jacques Garnerin make the first parachute jump in England on August 26, 1802, from St. George's Parade Ground. After reading Sir George Cayley's paper, "On Aerial Navigation" published in 1809–10, Cocking spent many years developing his own version of a parachute. Cayley noted that Garnerin's parachute had swayed excessively and theorized that a cone-shaped device would be more stable. Using that untested theory, Cocking crafted an inverted cone-type parachute that connected to the balloon's basket by three hoops. Cocking approached Charles Green and his partner, Edward Spencer, who agreed to participate in the great trial.

As it worked out, the parachute hung from the car of the *Royal Nassau*, giving the appearance of four tiers: the balloon, the car containing Green and Spencer, the cone-shaped parachute and the basket holding Cocking. After ascending, the balloon rose to a height of 5,000 feet, considerably retarded by the excess weight. Over Greenwich, Green informed Cocking that he would be unable to rise higher if the descent were to be made in daylight. Cocking thus separated the parachute and began his descent.[13]

An eyewitness recounted:

> The parachute seemed to float without any oscillation, and to hang perpendicularly under the balloon. Shortly afterwards, the balloon itself was slightly agitated, and was inclined considerably more to one side than when I first saw it, and the parachute did not appear to hang so perpendicularly as at first.... In an instant afterwards I observed the balloon shooting upwards with great velocity, and the parachute, which had been suddenly separated from it, falling with great rapidity.... A sort of flapping motion was then perceptible, and the parachute appeared lessened in diameter. It then appeared turned over, and at this moment something fell out of it at a great height ... and in the succeeding instant it was seemed to have changed its flattish circular form to that of a long body, like an umbrella partially opened, or more correctly, perhaps, to a balloon very much collapsed and descending with a great velocity....
>
> I made my way through the fields in the direction in which I had seen it falling, and as I reached a spot at a little distance from where it fell I saw the lifeless body of the unfortunate gentleman placed on a hurdle to be conveyed by some labourers to an inn at Lee.[14]

Tests conducted by balloonist John Wise in 1837–38 established that Cocking's parachute would have been successful if it had been larger and better constructed. In tests on Garnerin's parachute, it was also determined that a vent in the top of the canopy would have eliminated the marked oscillation problems encountered.[15] (See chapter 24.)

A tragedy of another sort happened at Norwood, England, in the summer of 1839. An unusually large hot air balloon broke loose from its handlers, taking up five persons clinging to the ropes and sides of the car. One fell from a height of thirty feet; another's leg became tangled in the rope, suspending him, head down. When the balloon landed a mile distant, the limb was nearly severed, later requiring amputation. The balloon survived, uninjured.[16]

Novel Experiment in Aerostation

Charles Green had long cherished the idea of traversing the Atlantic and in early 1840 announced plans to cross the ocean from New York to Europe. He asserted that balloons inflated with carbonated hydrogen (as opposed to pure hydrogen, which escaped through imperceptible pores of the silk) would retain this fluid unimpaired for a great length of time. Based on observations made over the course of 275 ascents, he declared that once balloons reached the upper strata, they found one uniform current of air blowing west-north-west. Once established in that current, the altitude might be kept indefinitely.[17]

As early as 1836 Green proposed to make the experiment without monetary reward, receiving encouragement from Sir Sydney Smith, who volunteered to accompany him. In July, Green performed experiments at the Polytechnic Institution, demonstrating the feasibility of ascending and lowering the balloon without discharging gas or ballast by means of two propellers, a rudder, and a guide rope.[18]

While the elder Green worked on the project, his son, Charles, Junior, made an ascent from the grounds of the Commercial Gas Works, Stepney, with his new balloon, the *Albion*, with the intention of crossing the British Channel. Green and Mr. Bradley crossed the Thames and proceeded on course toward the Sussex coast.[19]

The same year, one of the earliest witnesses to the birth of aerostation celebrated her 110th year: Madame Montgolfier, widow of the celebrated savant.[20]

During this busy season, Charles Green made his 301st ascent aboard the *Royal Nassau* balloon from Cremorne house, Chelsea, affecting a safe landing at Hornchurch, in Essex.[21] On the 7th of August 1845, he made a night ascent in the *Albion* from the same site, discharging a quantity of pyrotechnics, displaying white, pink and green colors. He made another flight August 11th; the next night Green and his wife went up from Vauxhall gardens.[22]

Finding larger audiences abroad, Green Jr. ascended at Berlin in August 1846 to the delight of the King of Prussia.[23] The following summer, Green ascended from Cremorne gardens, accompanied by two monkeys. At a considerable elevation he set each free in two parachutes.[24]

24

American Barnstormers and
E. A. Poe's Great Hoax

Astonishing News by Express, via Norfolk!—The Atlantic Crossed in Three Days!
Signal Triumph of Mr. Monck Mason's Flying Machine!—Arrival at Sullivan's
Island, near Charleston, S.C., of Mr. Mason, Mr. Robert Holland, Mr. Henson,
Mr. Harrison Ainsworth, and four others, in the Steering Balloon, "Victoria," after
a Passage of Seventy-five Hours from Land to Land! Full Particulars of the Voyage![1]

The spring of 1838 started out on a less than auspicious note for the Americans. On
April 9, Richard Clayton (the "Western aeronaut") "lost his balloon" at Louisville, Kentucky.
During inflation, a spark from a bystander's cigar ignited the gas, producing a tremendous
explosion. Five workmen were injured, one of whom lost both eyes; Clayton was slightly
injured.[2]

Two years later, Clayton was at Pittsburg with the intention of crossing the Allegheny
Mountains. Using gas made from Pittsburg coal, he ascended on May 21, 1840, but finding
it insufficiently buoyant, he only managed to sail twenty miles.[3] Back in Louisville, he made
another voyage on September 12.[4]

After his disastrous descent in 1836, John Wise began work on a 25-foot balloon called
the *Experiment*. Unable to properly varnish it, he failed in his ascent, forcing him to release
it unmanned. "Pecuniarily bankrupt in the business, and almost so in reputation as an aeronaut," Wise retired to Philadelphia where he found employment as a scientific instrument
maker.[5]

Greatly affected by Robert Cocking's death in a failed parachute landing, Wise determined to test the design he considered a genuine advance to science. After retrieving the
Experiment, he enlarged it by adding a new mid–section so that it would hold the heavier
carbonated gas supplied by the Philadelphia Gas Works. On September 18, 1837, he launched
two small parachutes, one containing a dog and the other a cat. The trials were successful
but his balloon split at the seams, striking a three-story building. He survived by the aid
of the crowd, who held a rope while he escaped through a window.

On August 11, 1838, he ascended from the Washington Hotel carrying two small animals
and parachutes (one based on the Cocking design and the other a normal one), the success
of which "would decide the certainty and safety of my [balloon] parachute." Reaching 2,000
feet he detached the conical one with its occupant; it landed safely near Lafayette College.
Several thousand feet higher he released the oil silk parachute, "which did not descend with
that uniform velocity as the first."

After several more flights, Wise abandoned the *Experiment* because it had become brittle from varnish. Determining that linseed oil alone served the purpose of sealing the fabric, he constructed another balloon using cambric muslin. He incorporated a special design whereby the tug on a line would immediately empty gas from the envelope, the theory being that the bottom of the bag would gather in the upper hemisphere forming a parachute.[6]

Wise soon had the opportunity of testing his theory. At the height of 13,000 feet his balloon unexpectedly exploded. Fortunately, the envelope-as-parachute worked as anticipated, "the form of a concave hemisphere falling rapidly without any vibratory motion," until he reached the lower strata. In that current, with the wind blowing a gale, the machine began vibrating every ten seconds, "which now made the descent very unpleasant, every motion causing a sensation similar to that of a person dreaming of falling," a general affliction from which he frequently suffered.

Throwing out all his ballast, the car obliquely struck earth ten miles from Easton and bounced him out from a height of ten feet, bruising his shoulder.[7]

Undaunted by the experience, Wise

Balloon Ascension.

Wise's 26th Aerial Voyage, to take place on Saturday, the 24th day of April, inst., from the Prison Yard, in Hagerstown, at 2 o'clock, P. M.

"Undaunted by the experience..." (*Hagerstown Mail* [Maryland], April 9, 1841).

made a flight from Chambersburg on Saturday (August 15 or 22), landing near Shippensburg and completed his 26th ascent on September 5, also from Chambersburg.[8]

Louis Anselm Lauriat, best known for his balloon ascensions in the Northeast, had a long and successful career. Making his first flight on July 17, 1835, at the age of 50, he quickly captured the imagination of the public. Finding early success, he made numerous flights from Rhode Island, Castle Garden and Troy, New York where he went up with his son. Making it a family affair, he took his daughter with him on September 23, 1835.

In July 1838, he was challenged to a balloon race by Mr. Edge, "the pyrotechnist and aeronaut," to see who could mount the highest and travel the farthest. A prize of $2,500 was offered to the winner. The Jersey City *Advertiser* noted, "that it hopes it will be no part of the competition — to see who will come down quickest."[9]

A year later, on June 17, 1839, Lauriat ascended at Chelsea, Massachusetts, but came into immediate danger. The balloon caught against a tree and severed several cords by which it was attached to the car. Managing to hang on, the aeronaut was carried to the sea beach and dragged into the water. At length, a boat was lowered from a recently arrived schooner and Lauriat was rescued just as the balloon tore away from the netting and soared away.[10]

William Paullin was another American aeronaut destined to write his name in the annals of aerostation. Born in Philadelphia, he apparently began his career in 1833 and went on to make numerous flights from that city. On May 20, 1839, he arose from Reading and fell into an oppressively warm current of air. Attacked by a feeling of sleepiness, he fell into a stupor and remained unconscious for an hour before being roused by a singular ringing in his ears and a severe headache. The balloon had fallen close to earth but continued on its journey at a rate of 40 miles per hour before descending in New Jersey, a mile beyond Camden, after a trip of two hours.[11]

Suffering no ill effects, he returned to Philadelphia where he ascended on Monday, July 15. No word was heard from him by Wednesday and it was feared he had been carried off into the ocean. Fortunately, information eventually arrived that he had landed safely near Burlington, New Jersey.[12]

On July 4, 1840, Paullin and John Wise participated in a dual ascent from the Pennsylvania Farmer's Hotel to see who could climb the highest. Forced to go up without a basket when his new balloon could not carry the combined weight, Wise ascended first but Paullin won the contest.

The following year, Paullin left for Valparaiso, Chile, and spent the next six years flying in South America, later claiming to have made excursions in several South American countries as well as Cuba, Haiti, Puerto Rico and Mexico.[13]

James C. Patton seemed to have achieved the aeronaut's ultimate dream when he announced, on November 12, 1839, that for a $5,000 premium, he would transport an express mail regularly between New York and New Orleans in 15 hours, using a balloon that could navigate the air in any direction at pleasure, attaining speeds of one hundred miles per hour.[14] Applying to the government for a mail contract, the Senate laid the whole matter "under the table."[15]

Ballooning as a Moral Pastime

The advertisement read: "MR. WISE takes pleasure to inform the public that his long and successful experience in the practice of Aeronautics, will enable him to give general satisfaction, and make the occasion worthy of an intelligent community."[16] The wording was typical of the time and not much different in style from those selling Cholera Pills or dental services. The distinction, at least made by a gentleman in a letter to the editor, elevated the aeronaut and his profession over other promoters:

> Such exhibitions when properly conducted, cannot fail to promote the moral and sublime attributes of human intellect. When we behold a fellow-being wafted upon the wings of the wind into the wide expanded ocean of ether, it swells the admiration and leaves the pleasing impression, that "Naught was formed in vain but for admirable ends."[17]

The flight itself was almost anticlimactic. Wise ascended amid loud huzzas, attained a height one mile and circled around the town before being blown toward the Potomac. Descending near Williamsport, he took refreshment and re-ascended, drifting into Virginia.[18]

Wise ascended from Danville on June 19 and traveled 87 miles in 145 minutes, descending at Morgantown. This was indeed "Swift travelling."[19]

An exhibition was to take place on July 5 at Blossburg, but the large turnout was doomed to disappointment. In explaining his failure, Wise stated he had ordered "all necessary arrangements" for the inflation from Philadelphia, but "the boatmen who carry goods in this direction have a superstitious prejudice that all the elements of destruction are encased in the carbois which contain the sulphuric acid, and that in the accidental explosion of a part of them, their boats would be transported to the moon or some other remote planet instead of their proper destination." It took thirteen days to find any boatman daring enough to transport the material. "Hence," he concluded, "the people may judge of the difficulties of an aeronaut."[20] The disaster was doubly painful to Wise, for Mr. Boyd, who invited him to Blossburg and guaranteed his compensation, was gravely disappointed. Consequently, Wise departed for Williamsport, making his 30th voyage five days later in the *Great Eastern*. After a flight of one hour, he descended in the White Deer valley, frightening two women who took him for an evil spirit.[21]

Mr. S. Hobart, who had made several previous and perilous flights beginning in Lynchburg, Virginia, in September 1835 (where he feared being struck by "two brilliant meteors"), ascended in St. Louis with little better fortune. On October 9, 1841, he and a female passenger gained a height of nearly two miles before discovering the valve cord stuck fast in the neck of the balloon. Facing the danger of riding out the moonless night, the emergency compelled him to climb up the cords to the hoop, where he introduced head and shoulders into the neck of the balloon and disentangled the valve cord. Letting himself down, he found his companion asleep, affected by the great altitude. They descended safely eight miles from the city.[22]

The season of 1842 opened in April with Richard Clayton making an ascent from Nashville. More significantly, the Cincinnati *Enquirer* noted that in July or August Clayton proposed to launch in an open boat down the falls of Niagara, "the boat being supported and protected by the balloon."[23] Clayton made his 30th ascent from Columbus on June 4, traveling 38 miles in one hour and twenty minutes before descending near Newark.[24]

On April 22, John Wise ascended from Lewistown, Pennsylvania, and landed safely in Mexico, Pennsylvania, 19 miles distant.[25] The opening months of 1842, however, belonged to Hugh Parker. Declaring that he had always had a desire to achieve as great an elevation as possible, he ascended from Mobile in May. He may have rued his desire, for the aeronaut detailed a long list of ills which plagued him on that flight, including perspiration oozing from his skin, a ringing in his ears, a vacant feeling and difficulty in respiration; he later complained of perspiration resembling yellow oil, swollen tongue, nails and teeth loosened, every joint and all his energy relaxed.

At an altitude judged to be six miles high, a rent appeared at the top of the balloon and the gas escaped, plunging him downward. Unable to break his fall, Parker anticipated the worst until his machine fell into a pine tree and stuck. The Mobile *Register* called the story "curious," noting that the highest ascent ever made was by Guy Lussuc, who reached 23,000 feet or somewhat more than four miles, "stopping there only because it was impossible to go higher with the certainty of existence." If Parker's estimate was true, he reached 31,609 feet, or 8,000 feet higher than the Frenchman.[26]

Following a delayed departure, John Wise, "the experienced and successful Aeronaut," ascended from the Commons at York, Pennsylvania, traveling 39 miles in 58 minutes. He promised another venture on the 20th provided his expenses would be covered.[27]

Wise was soon off to Gettysburg where he proposed to fly his new black balloon, the *United States*.[28] On September 10 he made his 38th ascent, performing a scientific experiment for Professor Jacobs by studying the fact that airships invariably revolved counterclockwise.[29]

The aeronaut's next voyage, also from Gettysburg, promised the ascent of a huge balloon in the form of Atlas carrying a globe, a fish-shaped balloon, a cat let down in a parachute and six small pilot balloons.[30] These novelties assumed insignificance, however, by events that subsequently transpired. A young gentleman named John McClellan (also called "Colonel J.H. McClellan") asked Wise if two could ascend in the balloon. On receiving a negative reply, he asked what price to fly alone. Wise suggested $100, McClellan offered $50 and was accepted on the supposition he was in jest.

McClellan ascended in the tethered balloon, then cut the rope and sailed away. Wise shouted some hasty and imperfect instructions and the balloon was soon lost from sight. McClellan eventually determined to descend but pulled too violently on the valve line, tearing the valve door off its hinges where it fell into the car. Gas rapidly escaped and the balloon fell, fortunately catching sufficient air to form a parachute, coming down "*heavily like a wet sheet.*"[31]

The Comet *and the "Cloud of Terror"*

John Wise's 40th ascent in the *Comet* went far better. On May 27, he rose from Carlisle and traveled 50 miles to his hometown of Lancaster, where his unexpected appearance was viewed as one of Mr. Miller's "Signs" (predictor of a great calamity). Realizing their mistake, the aeronaut was welcomed by rejoicing. After a brief reception, Wise determined to ascend a second time, but finding the ascending power nearly equal to his own weight, he divested himself "of all his clothing but his pantaloons, even to his shoes." He remained afloat for half an hour before landing very near his place of ascent, later expressing gratitude to the people of Lancaster who "inflated my collapsed money bag."[32]

Wise's next ascent from Carlisle proved unique, but from a different perspective. Ascending on June 17 in the *Comet*, he reached the height of an immense black cloud. Wise soon regretted entering it, for he immediately encountered snow and hail, causing him great distress and sickness in the stomach. Covered with hoar frost, he anticipated the gas would condense and the balloon descend. However, it whirled upward with fearful rapidity, gyrating violently to a noise resembling the rushing of "a thousand milldams." Repeatedly swept up and down, this action caused considerable kinking and breakage of the machine, while affecting him with an almost irresistible desire to sleep, which he only overcame by the most powerful vomiting.

Admitting his own alarm, Wise grasped the sides of the car to wait out the storm. After 20 minutes the balloon descended under the "Cloud of Terror," which he ruefully noted he would avoid at all costs in future.[33] He landed five miles distant from Carlisle.[34]

"*To all the Publishers of Newspapers on the Globe*" (Republican Compiler, June 19, 1843). Thus began John Wise's petition to the world, written on June 8, 1843, from Lancaster, describing what he called "The dream of my lifetime."[35] The extraordinary letter detailed " a trip across the Atlantic Ocean in a Balloon, in the summer of 1844." He hoped, by providing advance notice, no one who chanced to be in the vicinity would suffer any fearful apprehensions for his safety.

Wise expressed his belief (one critical to the success of a trans–Atlantic flight and hotly debated in scientific circles) that a regular current of wind blew at all times from west to east with a velocity of 20–40 miles per hour. He also claimed to have "discovered a composition which will render silk or muslin impervious to hydrogen gas," so a balloon might be kept afloat for many weeks. His proposed balloon was to be 100 feet in diameter with an ascending power of 25,000 pounds; it would have a sea-worthy car attached and a crew of three persons: an aeronaut, navigator and scientific landsman.[36] J.A. Crever, Wise's partner, was listed as one of the passengers.[37]

The Philadelphia *Ledger*, echoing a theme taken very seriously, noted that should this voyage be successful and others follow, the customhouse officers would have to look out as it might become the medium for smugglers.[38]

When funds for his project were not forthcoming from the public sector, Wise petitioned Congress on December 20, 1843, asking $15,000 to cover expenses. The request went unanswered.

Making his 42nd ascent from Lancaster,[39] Wise then traveled to Winchester, Virginia (a suburb of Washington), perhaps in hope of influencing politicians. For what was billed as his 43rd ascent, he earned $300. Mr. Crever, of Carlisle, ascended with him in front of 6–8,000 persons, 1,800 of whom took "inside" tickets. His advertisement for an ascent from Lancaster on the 5th added that Wise would take a passenger for $100.[40]

Apparently no one took him up on the offer, for he ascended alone, landing on the Reading road nine miles from town. He was then towed to Earlville where he attempted a second flight, without success. While discharging gas, the balloon escaped and floated off, eventually getting caught in a tree where it was secured.[41]

Wise returned to Virginia, ascending from Fredericksburg in April 1844. While crossing the Rappahannock, "the attraction of the water kept him down" (another dire concern for 19th century aeronauts), but after jettisoning his hat, coat, and vest, he reached a considerable height and landed 13 miles distant, near Stafford Court House after a one-hour voyage.[42]

On Saturday, May 4, he ascended from Hollidaysburg, Pennsylvania, into a high wind that tore the network away from the top of the balloon. As a "bulk as large as a hogshead" protruded through the netting, he reached 4,000 feet, encountering a severe gale which increased the rupture at every surge. Throwing his weight against the valve rope, he descended, rebounding several times before getting one leg caught in the anchor rope. Hanging upside down, the balloon finally stuck in a treetop where Wise freed himself with a violent kick. The gale disentangled the balloon and it soared away, coming to earth near Catskill, New York.[43]

J.A. Crever made his own ascension on May 8, 1844, from Harrisonburg, Virginia. After a flight of one hour and ten minutes he landed 80 miles distant in Culpepper County.[44] He promptly announced an ascent from Carlisle on June 1.[45]

John Wise, presumably having retrieved his balloon, made an ascent from the Farmer Tavern below Callowhill, Philadelphia, in August. As he was rising in the tethered balloon, "some busy individual" cut the rope, causing the machine to violently strike against the chimneys and sides of buildings. After being dragged some distance, Wise descended in Wood Street.[46] On October 5, he ascended from Columbia, South Carolina, in front of the Amphitheatre. After passing over the State House, he landed five miles below the city.[47]

Edgar Allan Poe's Great Balloon Hoax Sets the Stage

The world was set soaring with the extraordinary news that "The great problem is at length solved! The air, as well as the earth and the ocean, has been subdued by science, and

In 1895, along with the Napoleonic revival, E.A. Poe became wildly popular throughout the Continent. At the same time, French aeronauts Castellani and Latruffe left Loffoden with the idea of witnessing Poe's maelstrom "as near as possible." They left on their trip April 26, 1895, and arrived in Paris on May 10, having taken half a dozen photographs of the churning sea (*The World* [New York], June 2, 1895).

will become a common and convenient highway for mankind. *The Atlantic has been actually crossed in a Balloon!*"

Written by an erstwhile reporter named Edgar Allan Poe, the notice ran in the New York *Sun*, April 13, 1844. It had the same effect on 19th century minds as Orson Welles' radio broadcast of *War of the Worlds* (1939) had on those of the 20th century. What they had in common, of course, was trickery: neither was true.

Poe concocted a story based on the expectations of Americans and Europeans that John Wise or Charles Green would soon accomplish the feat of crossing the Atlantic. Using familiar aerostatic names, he described in vivid detail the journey of the *Victoria*, claiming that after a passage of 75 hours the aeronauts safely reached the low coast of South Carolina. He concluded the "journals" of the aeronauts with, "We have crossed the Atlantic — fairly and *easily* crossed it in a balloon! God be praised! Who shall say that any thing is impossible hereafter?"

Indeed, who could now deny the miracle of the ages? But denial came quickly, forcing the editors to run a retraction, noting, "we are inclined to believe the intelligence is erroneous."[48] The *Sun* sold a lot of papers, however, and amidst the uproar, the author joined a growing caste of American pitchmen which would eventually embrace self-styled physicians, mesmerists, "professors," "artistes" and Cardiff giants.

As such, Poe's brief foray into the field of ballooning put him in good company. In 1847, one of John Wise's neighbors noted that he seemed to have no "regular employment" other than keeping a balloon tethered in a vacant lot near his house.[49] Unlike their European counterparts who enlarged their cars for the purpose of taking up numerous passengers as a means of obtaining extra income, American balloonists generally flew alone or provided space for only one or two people. That meant they required support from sponsors or a large paying crowd to cover expenses. Many, like Wise, traveled extensively to reach new audiences and eventually joined troupes making the rounds throughout the east and Midwest.

Ascensions were incorporated into regular exhibitions, and, as such, "aeronauts" were recruited from the ranks of circus people. This necessarily expanded the field to include aeronaut-performers who ascended in unmanned balloons hanging from trapezes and exhibitions featuring animal-aeronauts.

Female aeronauts also became novelty attractions. "M'lle Emma V." made several successful flights from New Orleans, one ending less agreeably, as she came down "plump" in the river "where she got a most thorough ducking."[50] In May 1848, "Mademoisell V" [sic] made her 5th ascent from Bingamont's Race Course and "Madame B" was advertised to make her "First Ascent from the Place D'Armes (New Orleans)."[51] This, apparently, did not go well. When she determined to send the balloon up alone, the indignant populace cut it to pieces with bowie knives while "Madame V" took triumph in the "discomfiture of her less courageous rival."[52]

The mainstays, of course, continued to fly, but landings continued to be an ever-present danger. J.A. Crever ascended from Wilmington, North Carolina, in July 1846 in a "silken gasometer," but landed in a swamp. Being unable to find his way out, the aeronaut spent the night "very comfortably" upon a log.[53]

When not touring, John Wise continued to fly from Pennsylvania, ascending from Lancaster in July 1846,[54] and West Chester in August.[55] Continuing his whirlwind tour, Wise ascended from Lancaster on June 5, 1847,[56] then made (by his account) his 61st flight from Auburn Garden, Buffalo, July 31. He landed a mile from Liverpool after a flight of 1 hour and 35 minutes and had the *Rough and Ready* towed to Syracuse. During passage by wagon, the top of the still-inflated balloon struck and broke a telegraph wire. In an annoyed and sarcastic tirade, Wise warned the Syracuse and Oswego Telegraph Company that, "they must remember that when they come in my way they must knock under." With the possibility of a lawsuit in mind, he added that in no way was the wire willfully broken.[57]

Wise made a second ascent soon after, from Morris' Garden, Buffalo. Although rising "under disadvantageous circumstances," the aeronaut *who never fails*[58] remained in the air 25 minutes, passing over Grand Island and Niagara Falls,[59] noting, "my mind seemed bent on a soliloquy on Niagara's raging grandeur, but it looked *too small.*"[60]

On August 6, Wise made his 63rd ascent from Morris's Garden, Buffalo. After reaching a height of 4,000 feet, he fell into a current bearing him 20 miles per hour and opened the valve. Spotting the brig *Eureka* on the lake, he hailed Captain Burnell and asked him to lower a boat to pick him up. The officer complied, Wise was rescued and the *Rough and Ready* towed him to shore, ending what he styled his "Aero-amphibious voyage." In his narrative, Wise thanked "those who paid for the sight," and apologized to those who did not as he dropped sand on their heads in his hurry to depart.[61]

Perhaps still hoping for a favorable outcome on his petition to Congress, Wise was back in Washington on May 3, 1848, where he made his 67th ascent from the rear of City Hall, landing seven miles from the city.[62] He failed to sway the politicians, but in a flight from Baton Rouge on November 20, 1848, a gentleman succeeded in "swaying" his wife. Ascending with a lady, the aeronaut took advantage of the situation by kissing her. Unfortunately for him, his wife was in the audience, having armed herself with a spyglass by which she took in the "crime."[63]

Slightly less life threatening was the descent of Dr. Morrill (also spelled "Morrel") from Boston. Having already made two ascents in his red-colored balloon, his voyage in October 1848 had two "tragic" components: he failed to take up a young lady, and after a descent into the water near Fort Independence, he nearly drowned.[64] The following month he had little better fortune. After an ascent from Niblo's Garden, New York, his balloon dropped into the river where he remained for an hour and a half until, chilled and "nearly perished from exhaustion," he was picked up by a boat dispatched from a passing light ship.[65] The trip apparently made him infamous, for in describing the balloon descent of Mr. Godard from Bologna, a newspaper mentioned that he "met the fate of Dr. Morrill," having fallen into the water and being later rescued by boatmen.[66]

A Balloon for California, an Aerial Locomotive, and Feet-First Ascents

The year 1849, with its news of gold in the far West, created another sort of gold field, but this one was given birth in New York. Inspired by the multitude of young explorers eager to try their hand in the mines and streams of the western territories, a company constructed the model of a balloon 24 feet in length and two feet in diameter, running to a point at each end. It was to fly point forward, like a fish, with a demonstration promised at the Broadway Tabernacle in March 1849.

The actual vessel was proposed to be 500 feet in length and 40 feet in diameter, with a long saloon suspended below. The steam engine used to propel it would have two screw propellers, with fans each 20 feet long. When filled with hydrogen gas, its proponents estimated it would carry 50 persons, and would travel to California in four or five days, flying only during the day and anchoring at night. It was said that 200 names had already subscribed for the voyage.[67]

On February 14, the exhibition took place before 2,500 persons. Unfortunately, "some little accident" happened, preventing an entirely satisfactory demonstration. That did not put off the investors, who were so sanguine of success, they made arrangements for constructing the immense machine.[68] Possibly the same inventors carried off another exhibition in Rochester the following year where a Mr. Clum demonstrated his model, guided by a rudder, around the room "as beautifully as a bird would skim the air."[69]

Equally inventive, was the "Aerial Locomotive." The Porter & Robjohn's prototype of a proposed full-sized model was exhibited at the Exchange, New York. Propelled by a spindle balloon "made of gold-beaters skin," about 10 feet long, a miniature steam engine turned the light paddlewheels with ease. Directed by a rudder, the craft made two full circles around the room before descending in a spiral. It "remains to be seen," the newspaper reported, "whether a large machine, similarly constructed, would safely resist the violent commotions of the open air."[70]

Robjohn continued to perfect his idea, constructing "a huge artificial dragon" at Hoboken, New York, in 1851; his balloon was cigar-shaped, 260 feet long, 24 feet its greatest diameter and 61 feet in length. It was composed of a strong, light wooden frame covered with canvas, including doors and glass windows. The machine was to be propelled by two engines of gunmetal and cast steel, of 12-horse power. The weight of the car was 4,000 pounds; the machine was designed to run 200 feet above the surface of the earth with a speed of 25–50 miles per hour. Robjohn proposed to drive the vessel by steam, derived from decomposing water.[71]

25

All Balloons, Great and Small

It is hard to tell which is the most difficult— to get a new truth into people's heads or an old prejudice out. Till a science is successful, every body looks upon it as a humbug; while it no sooner becomes successful, than everybody wonders why "some d———fool" did not think of it before.[1]

The 1850s saw a profusion of amateur balloon flights; some aeronauts made one ascent and were never heard from again; others rose from humble beginnings and performed at local fairs from one season to the next. A select few extended their territories to neighboring states, earning reputations and perhaps a few dollars along the way. The majority used balloons of their own manufacture, although occasionally they purchased discards from the more famous aeronauts.

One small town aeronaut creating a name for himself was Ira J. Thurston, who made ascensions from Batavia and Geneva, New York, in July, 1850–51.[2] As ballooning moved into the Midwest, Thurston traveled to Detroit, making an ascension in the "Clipper Balloon" *Jupiter* on October 1, 1851. Carrying enough provisions for three days, he found the wind insufficient to transport him over the lake and made a rapid descent 8 miles from his place of departure.[3] Undeterred, he went to Chicago later in the month for another demonstration.[4] There he found competition from Dr. Boynton. His balloon, containing 400 yards of silk and holding 60,000 gallons of gas, required a cost of between $300 and $400 to fill. "Of course the Dr. has no inducement to exceed this amount of money for the gratification of the public. Those who desire to witness it must foot the bill."[5]

Joshua Pusey (also spelled "Pusy"), a Pennsylvanian, was another aeronaut who "rose above his station." He made a number of ascensions from Reading, York and Wilmington in 1850–51.[6] Pusey's luck turned sour in September 1852, when he failed to ascend at Harrisburg. The irate crowd tore the balloon, owned by Messrs. Fishelman & Fox of Lancaster, to pieces.[7]

Mademoiselle Delon, a French lady, made two ascents from Philadelphia. On her first flight, in an inducement to gather a crowd, she threw out three valuable gold watches.[8] Her second voyage, June 23, drew huge crowds and went off beautifully. Her descent was less spectacular, as she landed in Lackawanna Creek.[9]

In September 1851, Samuel A. King, destined to become one of America's greatest aeronauts, emerged on the scene when he attempted his first ascent at Philadelphia. Unable to obtain enough gas to fully inflate the balloon, he undertook the risk, but struck the Wire Bridge, becoming entangled in a telegraph wire. When finally freed, the balloon fell into the Schuylkill River, rebounded several times and dunked the aeronaut before settling on the bank. The scene was a "most thrilling one," and Mr. King "not much hurt."[10]

And perhaps as much a sign of the times as anything, a balloon sailed over a town in Rhode Island on a Sunday, creating so much astonishment that the town council considered enacting an Ordinance "prohibiting strangers passing over on Sunday."[11]

John Wise Pursues His Quest

Increasing his national renown as a balloon expert, 1850 also saw the publication of John Wise's *History and Practice of Aeronautics.*[12] Now a full-time aeronaut, he began advertising in July for 6–8 persons to ascend with him from Lancaster, promising a long voyage for the fee of $150. Prior to the flight he planned to sell brief, tethered trips in his new balloon, *Hercules*, at $2 a person, so that they might "take observations." At the same time he continued to promote his theory that there existed an "upper current of air [flowing] from West to East, by which a balloonist can safely cross the Atlantic."[13]

Wise had no trouble securing passengers for his "Grand and Topical Balloon Ascensions" on August 3, but a storm came up, forcing Wise and his family to quickly take their seats. Shortly before lift off, the balloon was caught in a high wind and "rent asunder." He promised another attempt in two weeks.[14]

On Friday, August 24, after a successful morning of "topical ascensions" from Lancaster, carrying three or four persons up at a time to a height of 1,050 feet and then reeling the machine down by means of a windlass, Wise, his wife, 15-year-old son Charles and niece, Miss Denton, ascended at 3:00 P.M. They flew for 34 minutes and then descended by means of the drag rope that Wise tossed from the car. Several persons caught it and hauled them down.[15]

Following the ascent Wise wrote an article for the *Scientific American*, discussing the various cloud layers and the effect of rain in the strata, in the hope that he might assist meteorologists in perfecting the science.[16] Another of Wise's observations concerned the sensation of vertigo while looking down from a great height. He asserted that if a person were connected with the ground by anything as slight as a rope, they became giddy, but that if "entirely isolated from the earth, no such feeling or sensation can be experienced."[17]

In December 1850, John Wise declared that a trans–Atlantic voyage would be accomplished "just as certain as steam followed horse power," and renewed his petition to Congress, asking for $15,000 to fund the scheme. Traveling eastward with the wind, he speculated it would take 30–40 days to circumnavigate the globe, returning by way of the Oregon territory to Washington City.[18]

On December 30, 1850, Senator Douglass of Illinois presented his petition. Now asking for $20,000, Wise pleaded his case for an aerial circumnavigation of the globe. Well aware of history, and how close an invading British fleet came to conquering the United States in the War of 1812, he also took pains to emphasize how balloons might be used in war. Repeating an idea first conceived for the defeat of the Mexicans at Vera Cruz, Wise suggested the aerial discharge of missiles over war ships, forts or enemy troops.

"The Memorial was treated seriously by some, and with ridicule by others — and was finally referred to the Committee on Naval Affairs."[19]

Numerous articles appeared in newspapers across the country, weighing the pros and cons of Wise's proposition.[20] Perhaps the most entertaining was printed by the Albany

Dutchman, which noted, "Till his attempt to reach Europe by balloons is crowned with success, he will be looked upon as a visionary; while he will no sooner meet with success, than he will be charged with plagiarism, and perhaps cited before the Supreme Court, to show why he should not be pelted to death with deceased cats and superannuated oranges."[21]

Wise's petition died in committee.

The lack of Federal funding did not stop the intrepid aeronaut. By May 1850, the newspapers were full of stories about the "monster balloon" he was constructing, capable of holding 50,000 feet of gas and carrying 16 persons across the Atlantic. Wise proposed to have it ready for a flight from Philadelphia June 1.[22]

Putting aside his plan in order to earn a living, Wise used 1,500 pounds of Oil of Vitriol, the same amount of iron filings and a ton of ice to prepare the gas for an ascension from Columbus on July 4, part of the entertainment presented by John Kinney, proprietor of Kinney's Mammoth Pavillion, a traveling tent show. In front of 25,000 persons, Wise waved his star spangled banner, "presenting a striking example of the genius and progress which characterize the nineteenth century."[23] His 120th aerial trip[24] was made under adverse conditions as the balloon sustained a slight rupture before lifting off. With the atmosphere highly impregnated with hydrogen, Wise described it as "passing through the descriptive pains of purgatory." After expended his ballast, he came down in a hurry and landed in a wood three miles south of the city.[25]

Scientific Lectures and Mounted Ascensions

The season of 1852 began with Professor L.A. Lyon offering a series of lectures on Electricity, the Motion of the Planets and Spiritual Medicine, to be followed by the raising of a "large and Splendid BALLOON," if at least 200 persons were in attendance.[26]

John Wise was not far behind, promising to make his first voyage of the season from Portsmouth, Ohio.[27] Thinking ahead, he advertised ascents in the Midwest as far away as September[28] and promised an ascent in Lancaster *on horseback* during the present summer.[29]

On June 3rd he ascended from Portsmouth in the *Ulysses*, *sans* horse. Quickly passing into Kentucky, a hunter shot at him, one of the rifle balls striking the car. After passing through three distinct thunder and lightning storms and doused with hail, he managed a descent without ballast ten miles from Gallipolis.[30]

In rapid succession, Wise made successful ascensions from Chilicothe on June 10, Circleville (PA), Portsmouth, Newark on July 4, Mansfield on July 17, Wooster on July 24 and at Massillon on the 31st.[31]

The "Air-Ship" *Ulysses* and her intrepid pilot next arose from Ravenna, Ohio, August 14, marking Wise's 141st ascent. In his post–flight narrative, he remarked that at a height of 10,000 feet his breath produced copious clouds, while the balloon smoked at the mouth from the safety valve, stirring his thoughts into "transcendental strains" of Homeric proportions.[32]

Elevated to the title of "Professor," Wise was back with J.M. Kinney for a flight "Grand, Sublime and Novel," from Detroit on September 4.[33] After a voyage in Cleveland at the State Agricultural Fair, Wise returned to Lancaster to prepare the *Hercules* for an experimental voyage beginning at St. Louis and ending at Philadelphia or New York. The sum of $1,000 was raised to defray his expenses for the fifteen-hour trip that did not take place.[34]

In 1853, Wise was with Franconi's Hippodrome in New York, where his ascents in the

Irene were advertised on Monday, Wednesday and Friday afternoons without extra charge for those attending the "Daring Chariot Races, Gorgeous Tournements, Modern Field Sports, and other exciting and Novel Feats of the Stadium." He was scheduled to make an Independence Day voyage from Bayardstown, Pennsylvania, but it was a "total failure," due to a want of gas.[35] He had little better luck in Lancaster the same month. While repairing his balloon, some workmen inadvertently released it, and it ascended with Mr. Wise "struggling like an eel in a net." The balloon turned mouth-downward, dumping him out and causing "more bruises than any he ever received in a regular ascension." The balloon lodged on a barn without receiving any damage.[36]

From St. Louis to New York — but Not by Air

In the summer of 1853, John Wise's idea of traveling from St. Louis to New York as a preliminary to the ultimate aim of traversing the Atlantic took hold. Correspondence between the aeronaut and the Hon. Ellis Lewis made the newspapers, stirring up considerable interest in the project. Wise asked for $25,000 to prepare the necessary equipment, breaking the request down as follows:

A globular balloon, 125 feet in diameter, will require

5,000 yards of silk, at $2 per square yard	$10,000
100 gallons prepared linseed oil	200
Net works, grapnel and cordage	300
Labor	1,000
Contingencies	1,000
Sea-worthy boat, with masts and sails stowed away, (probably)	5,000
Provisions and water for eight men	100
Instruments	500
Coal gas, decarbonized, 550,000 cubic feet (probably)	2,500
Ballast	100
Total	$20,700

Allowing for hydrogen impurity, the balloon would carry 34,357 pounds:

Balloon and network	2,600 pounds
Sea boat	5,000 "
Weight of 8 men	1,280 "
Provisions	300 "
Instruments	100 "
Ascensive power	2,000 "

leaving a net total carrying power of 25,195 pounds for ballast, and mails to be deposited at Lisbon, Madrid, Minorca, Naples and Constantinople.[37]

A great deal was made of Wise's theory of prevailing wind currents and the newspapers were filled with letters to the editor, often lengthy and persuasive in nature, supporting and denying the concept.[38]

In August, Wise was in St. Louis with his mammoth balloon to make the first of his proposed trials.[39] Unfortunately, for all the long and arduous preparations, Wise overlooked the most important factor: gas. There proved to be an insufficient quantity in all of St. Louis for the purpose and the test was postponed.[40]

Wise returned to New York City in 1854, where he planned his 163rd ascent for June 9 from the "Crystal Palace," America's answer to the world exhibition in London. His unusually frenetic narrative gives a hint of how the flight went: he shot up as though he had been "projected by the force of gunpowder"; the balloon swayed "to and fro like a furious elephant"; not until he was above the clouds did he restrain "the wild aerial ship."[41]

While aloft, Wise dropped fliers, presumably at the urging of P. T. Barnum, who introduced the aeronaut to the crowd before his departure. They read:

NEWS FROM THE SKIES

This bill is dropped by Mr. Wise from his balloon which ascended from the Crystal Palace, this 9th day of June, 1854, and will be exhibited there this evening with a description of his voyage by Mr. Wise. Mr. Wise will make his second and last Grand Ascension from the Crystal Palace, on Tuesday next, 13th 3inst., at 3:00 P.M.

The reverse held an announcement of the "Musical Congress," with a request to "see the newspapers" for particulars.

Telegraphic dispatches were received giving Wise's probable location at Bridgeport or Boston[42] but neither proved correct. In fact, the trip did not last long. Reaching Flushing and in fear of being driven out to sea, Wise "came down on the run," abandoning ship and losing a front tooth in the process.[43] The balloon dashed off, forcing Wise to advertise a reward to anyone who would return it in time for his next ascent on Tuesday.[44]

Returning to the Crystal Palace, Barnum observed that Wise must have thought "Old Nick" had got hold of him, to which the aeronaut replied that he rather thought himself on a voyage of discovery to that "sable gentleman's" dominions. For those wishing a permanent reminder of the affair, "Root, the Great Daguerreotypist" took a stereoscopic view of the Balloon.[45]

The balloon landed the same afternoon at Eastford, Connecticut, in good condition with anchor, handbills &c. in the car. "The finder commenced stripping it, but several citizens arrived in time to interfere and save it."[46] Assured it would be returned, advertising for his next trip went on in earnest, noting that the voyage, "sanctified by the presence of the Palace," would add to Wise's celebrity, provided "that nothing of an untoward nature occurs meanwhile." To enhance the excitement, "President Barnum" ran the following advertisement:

THE BALLOON ASCENSION.— Mr. Wise ascends with his balloon this afternoon from the Crystal Palace. As he never fails, the experiment will be a truly beautiful one. A reward of $25 is offered to the person who will safely return him before night, when he will address the public in the Palace, and detail his romantic adventures in the clouds.[47]

Unexpectedly, Wise was forced for the "FIRST time" to disappoint the public. Although positively assured his balloon would be returned from Connecticut, it did not arrive. Wise trusted this would be the "LAST" time he failed in an engagement.[48]

Not everyone was pleased when the ascent finally came off on the 16th.[49] An editorial noted "a perfect 'Barnum'" took place, whereby 25 cents admitted the public to watch the inflation and $25 was offered for anyone to "bring up shank's mare" and return the aeronaut back to the "great glass house" the same evening, "for the benefit of science in general and the Palace in particular, and to the total disregard of his own worthless neck."[50]

The Balloon Men

Back from his South American balloon tour, William Paullin quickly took up where he left off. Advertisements and large hand bills proclaimed the man "whose daring feats, in Aerial Voyaging, are well know [sic] to the scientific world" would make a trip from Fort Wayne, Indiana, September 8, 1852. Americans loved hyperbole, and just as peddlers were called "doctors," and men of enterprise "professors," all people participating in experiments were "scientists," and were "well known to the scientific world," despite a tenuous connection. More a showman than a researcher (as opposed to Wise, who had a keen interest in aerostatic discovery), Paullin's Midwest circuit promised grand entertainment for those hitherto deprived of witnessing "great and fearful" balloon performances. Proclaiming this to be his sixth voyage after returning from South America and the West Indies, and his 46th overall, great expectations were garnered over Paullin and the *Eclipse*, augmenting a plea for men to join a subscription list to assist to defray the aeronaut's expenses.[51]

Paullin, "an intelligent and pleasant gentleman," ascended from Zanesville, Ohio, on October 23, 1852.[52] After a delay filling the balloon, all went as expected and the *Eclipse* soared over the countryside. The affair was "worthy of better patronage than it received."[53]

Calls from around the Midwest summoned Paullin to their locales: the Zanesville *Courier* of Ohio offered as an inducement the "lightest kind of Gas," supplied by the editor of the *Aurora*,[54] while the Huron *Reflector* asked the aeronaut to bring his "Inflated Animals and Oriental Images, and Fire Works," offering to "pay him well."[55] In fact, Paullin opened the season at Sandusky, ascending on June 23. After a short ride he descended into the Bay, where he was picked up by a sailboat.[56]

While performing at Columbus, Paullin met Silas M. Brooks, a former employee of P. T. Barnum, who had made a name for himself playing in the latter's "Druidish Band." Brooks bought out Barnum's share and by the spring of 1853, hired Paullin to work for him at the staggering sum of $100 a week. By 1854, Brooks had abandoned his circus and worked for Paullin as his junior partner.[57] In celebration of July 4, Paullin arranged a race between himself and Brooks that drew a crowd of 20,000 persons. Brooks started first, but was rapidly overtaken by the more experienced pilot. After passing and re-passing one another, they shared a pleasant flight of an hour, landing near each other at Manchester, nine miles from their starting point.[58]

On June 28, 1855, Silas Brooks made an ascent from St. Louis, and Independence Day, 1855, saw him in Chicago, where he did not fare as well. Brooks' balloon came in contact with the St. Louis & Rock Island telegraph wires, severing the fastenings. Consequently, the balloon went up while Brooks and the car crashed to the ground. Without his "costly and valuable" balloon, valued at $1,000 (the third one he had lost within a few weeks), he was forced to cancel a scheduled flight at Madison. The people of Chicago went about raising a subscription to repay him.[59] Brooks' mentor, William Paullin, had better luck. His ascent from Springfield on the 4th was completely successful and greeted with cheers from the spectators.[60]

By August 14, Brooks, already announced as the "great American aeronaut," made an ascent from Rockford, Illinois, reaching an altitude of nearly two miles.[61] When asked what he saw while flying, Brooks reported, "nothing but corn."[62] The comment was taken up, and in a notice about the current state of crops in Illinois and Iowa, the text concluded, "No wonder the balloon man... exclaimed when asked what he saw — corn, corn, corn. This is emphatically a corn country."[63]

Brooks made a voyage from the DeSoto House at Galena on August 31,[64] then moved on to Dubuque in September, where he had the misfortune to be shot at by some person who "mistook his aerial car for a thing of flesh and blood. Mr. B. heard the ball whistle close by him."[65]

On October 10, S. M. Brooks gave a lecture on the history of Aeronautics, afterwards ascending in the *Comet* from the city of Burlington, Iowa, in front of 1,000 inside customers (general admission 25 cents, reserved or elevated seats 50 cents) and 5,000 on the outside. His brother, George W. Brooks, oversaw the preparations which included fireworks (separate charge). He covered 21 miles in half an hour and landed near LaHarpe.[66]

The celebrated George Elliott of Baltimore quietly continued to make balloon ascents from his native city. In the seasons of 1853[67] and 1854, he made several voyages from Baltimore[68] and September 2, from Westminster.[69] His next flight was scheduled for Richmond, October 31, but after the balloon had been inflated a young man named Carrier persuaded the professor to let him go up a short distance. In a familiar scenario, Carrier cut the cords, waved his hat and sailed away. Elliott was so disappointed at his own failure to make "a magnificent aerial voyage" that he fainted dead away.[70] That seemingly put an end to his season, for Elliott's next mention was an ascent to be made May 12, 1855.[71]

By August 1855, Elliott designed a new trick to draw crowds. Although aeronautic ascensions with animals were being prosecuted in Europe by societies for the prevention of cruelty to animals, no such statutes were in force in America to prevent Elliott going up from Carr Place, St. Louis, with a horse. While not the traditional equestrian voyage (he sat some distance above the horse as opposed to sitting astride), it was entirely successful. The horse seemed "to be considerably astonished" as the earth receded, but held its dangling legs perfectly still. Reports from the steamer *Keystone* stated the balloon and its occupants landed safely at the mouth of the Missouri River.[72]

In November, "Professor" Elliott was at it again, this time from Richmond, Virginia, in his mammoth balloon, *St. Louis*. During inflation, a flaw in the material gave way, even-

Crowning TRIUMPH of All!

P. T. BARNUM'S

GREAT

ROMAN HIPPODROME!

The name P. T. Barnum conjured up images of "freak displays," fantastic circus acts and balloon ascensions to 19th century Americans. His traveling shows received worldwide attention and many famous aeronauts worked for him in the era after the Civil War (*Fort Wayne Daily Sentinel*, July 1, 1875).

tually growing so large as to collapse it "as flat as a flounder." At the time of the explosion it contained 33,000 cubic feet of gas which cost Elliott $207.[73] His next ascent was not advertised until May 12, 1856, at York.[74]

Going Up: Preaching and Practice

The article began, "The most cruel and shameful disregard of life ever recorded in this country, is in the case of an ascension by a boy of sixteen in a balloon, on the 29th of August, at San Francisco."[75] Other reports had a different slant, describing the event as "the most extraordinary balloon ascension upon record."[76] "A boy named Joseph Gates, aged 16, made a remarkable balloon ascension from Oakland,"[77] and "Our citizens were thrown into a state of excitement and indignation on Sunday afternoon by the report of a melancholy event connected with the balloon ascension at Oakland."[78]

Details in all four articles differed in some degree but it seems that an aeronaut by the name of Kelly attempted a balloon ascent but his weight proved too heavy, and after several false starts the crowd called for a boy. The car was detached, and a hoop, about an inch square and three feet in diameter, with a board about four inches in width, was lashed across the middle. Gates, a well known "match and orange vendor," either volunteered or was prevailed upon to make the flight. The craft went up so fast no one gave him any more direction than to pull the cord when he wished to come down.

An eyewitness stated that the board immediately fell away, leaving the child to hold on with hands over his head and feet dangling. The Alta *Californian* of the 30th reported that he, for whose "safe return there appeared little ground for hope," arrived in Oakland safe but for a sprained ankle. He landed in the Suisun Valley, fifteen miles from Benecia, walked five miles to the nearest house and "retained his presence of mind throughout," traveling 50 miles in the air.

The youth recounted feeling cold while in the air and wrapping one foot in a handkerchief for warmth. Confirming that the valve rope had broken and knowing his only chance of survival was to discharge the gas, he said he climbed the quarter-inch ropes twelve feet to the body of the balloon and cut a hole. The vessel gradually descended and when it reached an open plain he jumped off. Lightened of his weight, the balloon rapidly re-ascended.

The newspapers lauded, "He saw not a little danger, but his voyage will become famous, and his name will be spoken of from Europe to Australia. He can sell oranges and peanuts with a perfect rush for a few days." In 1871, the San Francisco *Morning Call* repeated the particulars of the flight, giving the name of the child as "Reddy, the newsboy," and referring to the aeronaut as a Mr. Wilson.[79]

Another child, Mademoiselle D. Loyett, aged 11 years, made an ascent from New Orleans on December 2, 1853. She went up without a car, suspended by a single cord attached to the balloon.[80]

A sign of the times, if not the age, was the proposed ascent of Miss Louisa[81] Bradley from Reading, Pennsylvania, in October 1854. After delivering four lectures on "the elevation of women, &c." she planned to ascend in a balloon from the fair grounds.[82] She had purchased the balloon from John Wise for $100[83] and may have received some instruction from the aeronaut. The ascent apparently did not go off and the following year she appeared at Easton, Pennsylvania, to follow through on her promise. Described as a "small, delicate looking woman," dressed in a Bloomer costume of scarlet and blue,[84] and as wearing "her hippodrome costume, with a French crown cap, white feather, encircled with a wreath of green and white flowers, and appearing fairy-like"[85] she fearlessly entered the car, rose twenty feet and made a short address.

The balloon, an old one with silk "so rotten it was astonishing it bore the inflation,"[86] was filled with gas from a street main. Admitting she knew very little about the business, she let out some gas, but the cracked, dry silk gave way and the balloon burst. The upper part was torn to "ribbands" and large pieces flew away. The remainder hung down below the car as the neck of the balloon blew up, turning inside out. Catching against the network, it formed a sort of parachute and she landed in a field without the slightest jar.[87] Her home town was corrected by the New York *Daily Times* as being New-London, Connecticut, which added she "exhibited a nerve and self-possession not often found in her sex."[88]

Bradley ordered a second balloon and John Wise constructed an apparatus for the generation of hydrogen gas, but she received little public support and apparently never ascended with the new machine.[89]

On June 8, 1855, William D. Bannister (also spelled "Branmistle" and "Bamistle") ascended from Adrian, Michigan, in a balloon made by aeronaut Ira Thurston, of Adrian.[90] He was not heard from for several days, causing extreme distress to his friends, but returned on the 14th, quite well except for his feet, which were badly frozen during his aerial voyage. He reported becoming seasick and so drowsy he could not manage the balloon[91] and descended on the same day atop a tree, at Redbank, Pennsylvania (50 miles from Pittsburgh), having covered 350 miles at the astonishing rate of 97 miles per hour.[92] The people of Redbank, never before having heard of a balloon, thought him either an angel or a monster bird; two hunters followed his progress and actually shot at him.[93] Another newspaper noted, "The above takes the shine off the fleetest railway travelling, and will give some idea what we would gain by ballooning. We could go from Milwaukee to New York in fifteen hours!!"[94]

The same month Bannister ascended from Cleveland, reaching a reputed altitude of three miles,[95] and advertised a flight from Toledo on July 4.[96]

Bannister next appeared in Milan, Michigan, drawing crowds of 10,000 people to "see the sights." Unfortunately, they went home without "seeing the 'elephant,'" as the wind blew too strong toward the lake. He made a slightly more successful try the next day, but the balloon failed to ascend higher than the tops of buildings before making a rapid descent to the ground.[97]

Timothy Winchester made his first balloon ascent from Milan, Iowa, in October 1855. While at an elevation of 20,416 feet his eyes pained him, he heard a crackling sensation in his ears, suffered an unnatural respiration and experienced extreme weakness. Discharging too much ballast, he rapidly descended, eventually landing on top of a tree, 95 feet from the ground.[98] His next ascent came on October 2, 1855, from Norwalk, Ohio, and made him a household name, but not in the way he would have wished. At 2:00 P.M. he stepped into the car and was borne away in a northeasterly direction. Three days later, when nothing further was heard, clairvoyants and spirit-trappers were called upon to locate him.[99]

His body was never found, but in early 1856, John Wise interested himself in the case and offered the opinion that if Winchester had landed in the Lakes, something would have been found of his aerial apparatus. He also sent a clipping to the Norwalk *Experiment*, concerning the fate of the aeronaut M. Arban, who had been believed drowned off the coast of Spain, but re-appeared two years later after having been made a slave in Africa (see chapter 26).

26

More News from the Continent

*Riding on the winds man will become God-like, and he will "become as genial as
the forces of nature, as elevated as the superior being of poetry and religion."[1]*

England was not far behind America with its bizarre balloon attractions. When the
Royal Cremorne ascended from Cremorne Gardens, Chelsea, its advertised passengers were
Lieutenant Gale and the "Lion Queen," complete with lion. The car was replaced by a den,
atop which sat Gale; inside, the Lion Queen perched "on the back of her subject." Unfor-
tunately, the combined weight proved too heavy, forcing Gale and the lion to go up alone.
They descended safely at Mortlake.[2]

Mr. Gale (presumably Lieutenant Gale of lion fame) suggested another dangerous mission in 1850 when he proposed the use of balloons to aid Sir John Franklin, the missing
Artic explorer. His idea was to send up unmanned aerostats over the polar regions. Attached
to them would be long tails holding circulars, dispatched by the use of slow matches. Presumably, Franklin would find these papers and use the information to guide his band back
to civilization.[3]

Interest in Franklin's fate was rekindled by the discovery of a small balloon falling into
the yard of Mrs. Russell of Wootton, England. A small note attached to it read:

> *Erebus*, 112 W Long
> 71 deg N Lat
> September 3, 1851
> Blocked in[4]

It proved to be a fraud, but numerous ideas surfaced over the next several years suggesting
the use of balloons to find the explorers.

News of familiar friends continued to make the newspapers as the decade of the 1850s
progressed. Margaret Graham, with three of her daughters and her son, ascended from
Bayswater in the summer of 1850, with her new balloon, the *Victoria and Albert*. She wrote
the following note to the newspapers:

> I cannot omit noticing the extraordinary admiration of my daughter, Alice, who accompanied
> me on Friday night from Vauxhall Gardens, at the astonishing view of London at midnight,
> being the first and only attempt made by females to conduct the management of a balloon
> at night, and so much pleased am I with the nerve exhibited by those of my daughters who
> have hitherto accompanied me (four in number) that, if on trial I find the others of equal

spirit, which I doubt not, I feel disposed (God willing,) to ascend with my seven daughters at the great national exhibition of 1851.[5]

Shortly after the above, a second notice ran, stating that during a night ascent from Cremorne Gardens, London, Mrs. Graham's balloon caught fire from the lamp of a spectator. The balloon was destroyed and the aeronaut badly scorched.[6]

Mrs. Graham survived to keep her word. On July 19, 1851, she and her husband ascended from the Kensington Road close to the entrance of the Great Exhibition, but the balloon struck a pole surmounting one of the buildings, creating a large aperture. The grappling irons were immediately thrown out, but the balloon drifted toward the Crystal Palace where 40,000 inside were put in peril. Fortunately, the aeronauts were able to clear the structure and drifted toward Piccadilly. The machine eventually jammed between two mansions, destroying their chimneys and parapets. The police discovered Mr. and Mrs. Graham on a rooftop, apparently lifeless, and sent them to the residence of a local surgeon, who expressed the opinion that death was not to be apprehended.[7]

A month previous (June 16), in a remarkably similar accident, Mr. and Mrs. Green had ascended from the Hippodrome. The balloon struck against the dome of the Crystal Palace, forcing the pair to discharge ballast in a frantic attempt to rise. They succeeded in flying a short distance before the machine landed on top of a house, causing $1,000 worth of property damage.[8]

The Crystal Palace continued to plague aeronauts. In August 1851, "Md'me Palmyra Garneron" (presumably a misspelling of "Garnerin") ascended from Batty's Hippodrome at Kensington and nearly lost her life. On lift-off, the car struck a projecting garret window, half inverting the car. Garnerin's feet were caught in the netting and she hung out, face downward. The balloon collapsed, leaving the aeronaut on the roof. Fortunately, she received little injury, and after recovering from faintness caused by the release of gas, waved acknowledgment to the crowd.[9]

Aeronauts' luck had proven very little better earlier in the year. The Duke of Brunswick and a party of friends ascended from Vauxhall Gardens in Charles Green's great *Nassau* balloon, intent on reaching Germany. Armed with Soyer's cooking apparatus and a large quantity of provisions, the balloon traveled over Surrey and Kent in the direction of the Continent. However, two hours into the flight, the Duke found the currents contrary to the course he wished to pursue and the balloon was brought down at Gravesend two hours after departure.[10]

Accidents in 1851 continued as a balloon burst one mile high. Luckily, the aeronauts cut the cord that attached the neck of the balloon to the car; the falling silk created a parachute, breaking the fall and the four terrified passengers reached ground with nothing more than bruises. "Mr. Sala, a young and clever caricaturist and actor, was one of the party who risked their lives for no object but a silly desire for notoriety."[11]

Charles Green had better luck taking up a company from the British Association for the Advancement of Science. Billed as the first "scientific ascent," the balloon reached 19,200 feet, where his passengers took samples of the air. The flight received dull reviews, however, remarking that "the Italian Brothers" who performed gymnastics on the trapeze below the car and M. Poitevin's Paris ascensions on horseback were far more interesting than scientific "observations" not worth recording.[12]

Not to leave the French out, M. Coste, former editor of the *Avenement*, turned aeronaut, and made two ascents in Paris in the summer of 1852 under the tutelage of M. Godard before his third had unexpected consequences. His improperly inflated balloon was described as looking more like an "S" than the normal appearance and Godard advised him not to go up. Ignoring the words of wisdom, he leaped into the car and was driven at terrific speed on a nearly horizontal passage, barely escaping the roof of the Hippodrome.

Universal belief held that he would never again be seen alive, but the balloon eventually rose to a height of 20,000 feet before precipitously dropping. It struck the earth sideways and began rebounding. He was saved by some peasants and returned to the Hippodrome as a man "risen from the dead." He subsequently went on to make a number of other ascents, remarking that he had encountered nothing yet to dissuade him from a career as an aeronaut.[13]

The Poitevins Ascend on "Poneys"

The "honor" of being the first to ascend with a live pony belonged to Charles Green (see chapter 21). A renaissance of sorts began in 1850 with the French aeronaut Poitevin. That summer he made two balloon excursions in the *Zodiac* from the Champ de Mars mounted on the back of a horse, the first on July 7.[14]

Clothed as a jockey, M. Poitevin, "who is about forty," gave the order to "let go." "The horse seemed loth [sic] to quit his mother earth, and remonstrated a little when he found that he was being taken off his feet," but soon became "quite motionless, his legs hanging as if he were held by paralysis."

In his narrative, Poitevin remarked that the height proved too great for the horse: "An abundant flow of blood took place from his mouth, resulting from the interrupted equilibrium between the internal and external pressure, by which man is less easily affected than are most other animals." During a difficult descent, the balloon was dragged along the ground for more than a league, both horse and man surviving. On the second flight, the animal "behaved himself admirably," and this latest novelty became an instant hit with Parisians.[15]

Madame Poitevin, herself an aeronaut, also ascended with a *ponette* that summer, and in October he ascended from the Hippodrome, Paris, mounted on the back of a live ostrich. "The journals designate the illustrious pair by the well merited title of 'this foolish couple.'" Not content with the novelty of live animals, Poitevin shortly thereafter ascended from Paris with three young women suspended from the car. They had wings affixed to their shoulders, and appeared as if flying in the air.[16]

The thrill of seeing such spectacles inflamed the Parisians, and as they were not content with horses and giant birds, stranger and more peculiar creatures were sought to draw the crowds. One aeronaut announced that he would "mount into the clouds bestriding a pig!" Madame Poitevin, "in the character of *Europa*," ascended on a bull, "dressed in the *model artiste* style, in silk tights and thin gauze." She was accompanied by her husband, and after passing over Paris, they descended at Aubervilliers.[17]

All was not well, however, for aeronauts flaunting their daring. Lieutenant George Gale was at Paris in 1850, where he had been engaged for twelve nights at £90 each. For his 109th ascension he used a double car of his own design for night fireworks displays.[18]

The larger, upper car resembled a large round basket; the lower, smaller car was suspended from it at a distance of 35 feet. In order to pass from one to the other, Gale raised a trap door, barely sufficient to squeeze through. Once outside, he climbed down a rope ladder to let off fireworks. Flying in the *Royal Cremorne* on September 8, 1850, his luck ran out. Forced to leave England after animal-rights groups protested the use of live animals in balloon ascents, it was alleged he was drunk when making his first mounted voyage.

Bringing out an untrained pony, Gale paraded it around the packed Hippodrome of Vincennes, at Bordeaux, before taking off without incident. On descending, however, he ran into trouble. After the horse was released from his sling, the peasants who held down the balloon misunderstood Gale's directions and let go. The anchor gave way and struck the car, with Gale clinging to the ropes as the machine re-ascended.

The following day the balloon was discovered lying on the ground several miles distant. Gale's dead body was found in a wood, all his limbs broken. He left a wife and eight children. After the accident, the Prefect of Police announced his intention of prohibiting all balloon ascents "out of the usual mode of performance."[19]

In fact, in the summer of 1851, the French police prohibited balloon ascensions with animals. Only experienced aeronauts were permitted to ascend and only for scientific purposes.[20] The intent was well meaning, but apparently not assiduously enforced.

M. Poitevin ascended on the same day as Gale, using an ass instead of a pony. The newspaper reported, "We may expect, eventually, to hear of his death in a similar way."[21]

During the summer of 1851 the principal attraction in Paris was the Sunday balloon ascents from the Hippodrome and the Champ de Mars. Poitevin and his wife compelled Leon Fauchar (presumably the Prefect of Police) to take back his prohibition, and they made an ascent on June 29 from the latter place in an open barouche. Attached by irons to a small car, two very spirited horses were placed in front, controlled by an assistant.

The couple embraced their young son and the *Globe* rose, taking a direction toward Versailles. After two hours they landed five miles from Paris. The aeronaut stated the horses snorted and "seemed to enjoy the change of atmosphere as they went up higher." On July 15 Poitevin and a friend ascended in the *Globe*, carrying with them an American flag later presented to a family who took them in.[22]

The aerostatic husband-wife duo took their act to London in August 1852 where they encountered a protest similar to that faced in France. The Society for the Prevention of Cruelty to Animals protested to the Westminster Police against the manager of Cremorne Gardens for allowing the Poitevins to ascend from the back of a pony. The application was granted, but was destined to be ignored, as the same month Madame Poitevin ascended on the back of a bull, to the delight of the "enlightened public" (quotes in original).

The bull used on this occasion was so much injured as to require its being put down; for flaunting the magistrate's order, the Poitevins and the showman from whose gardens they ascended were levied a hefty fine and warned against such acts in future.[23]

Thus relegated to playing the part of Jupiter alone, Madame Poitevin ascended on September 6, terrifying and delighting the Londoners by descending from a parachute from the altitude of a mile. Later that month, Poitevin ascended from Cremorne Gardens in his "monster" balloon with twenty-one passengers. Encountering a severe storm, they barely escaped with their lives.[24]

M. Petin's "Etherian Navigation"

With the renewed excitement for all things balloon, street vendors in Paris sold gaily colored paper parachutes that became the favorite toy of children, while the adults continued to crowd the Hippodrome and the Champ de Mars for Sunday ascensions. While the Poitevins thrilled the spectators with live animal voyages, Ernest Petin captured their imagination with his theories of aerial navigation.

Based on fifteen years of experimental study on the laws of motion and their exemplification in animals and inert bodies,[25] he created a machine for a balloon in exact imitation of the acting muscles of the wings of birds. In 1850, after a series of ruinous disappointments, Petin fabricated a miniature collection of balloons the size of Notre Dame calculated to carry as many as three thousand persons.[26]

The following year he exhibited a model in the Rue Marboeuf. The essential feature was a fulcrum or center of resistance (*point d'appus*), situated below the balloon in the "hull." The production of a continuous series of motions on inclined planes was intended to aid the wings, by which it was to be navigated. In appearance, it gave the impression of a skeleton of some enormous sea monster.[27]

On August 7, Petin, Poitevin and three others ascended with the second of his three large balloons from the Champ de Mars. The car was replaced by a boat called the *Bon Vivant*, and the limited trial was apparently successful.[28] The entire device was 102 feet long with a series of square-framed sails revolving on pivots, capable of being turned by a propeller at either end and worked by a steam engine. Over the sails were to be placed three balloons, eighty feet high, the soundness of which Petin and Poitevin tested by trial ascensions. Petin's theory was expressed:

Relative Capacity of Balloons

A balloon of	113 square yards will carry a man weighing	204 pounds
"	201	"	524
"	314	"	1066
"	70,683	"	199,700

Monetary considerations forced Petin to abandon his native soil and in 1852 he arrived in Boston, touting this theory of navigation by the use of inclined planes. Hoping to collect a large sum of money, he gave a series of lectures on his "Etherian Navigation."[29]

Between April and June, Petin's emphasis seems to have changed, for it was advertised that he planned to ascend on horseback during the New York Independence Day celebrations. A large sum was collected, but the flight on July 5 from Bridgeport ended in disaster as the balloon was cut to shreds by telegraph lines immediately after lifting off.[30] Petin made his first successful United States flight on July 15 in a 20-foot-long balloon.[31] He descended safely at River Head, Long Island, 90 miles from Brooklyn.[32]

After promoting his favorite idea to cross the Atlantic, he made another ascension from Bridgeport on September 6. His 108 foot diameter balloon contained six miles of seams, and silk manufactured for Louis Napoleon for flags, but was condemned on account of its color, the whole apparatus cost $1,500.

Petin and three passengers were rapidly carried out to sea, coming down in the ocean two miles from shore. The boat swamped and after clinging to the network for three-quarters of an hour, the aeronauts were rescued by a lifeboat.[33]

The Frenchman had better luck on September 30 when he ascended from Springfield as part of the entertainment of an agricultural and industrial fair.[34]

Christmas day 1852 saw Monsieur Petin in New Orleans. In front of two thousand persons he and three of his friends ascended in an immense balloon, but the car proved the greater curiosity. In the shape of a large skiff, it was built mostly of cork, lined around with cavities containing gas. Attached to the sides were extensive wings for guiding the craft. It rose to 18,000 feet, when owing to an accident with the valve, it plummeted into Lake Borgue[35]; another account put their descent into Lake Pontchartain. The car split in two, but they were rescued by the captain of a Montgomery steamer.[36]

Waiting for his new balloons to arrive, Petin announced he was having constructed two immense balloons with "sails, screw propellers and an electro-magnetic engine."[37] Unfortunately, when the apparatus finally arrived, vandals broke into his workshop and damaged the works. Discouraged and nearly bankrupt, he left the United States for Mexico where he had scarcely better fortune. He died miserably in France in 1878.[38]

Scientific Ballooning and the Captain of Aeronauts — As Strange as It May Appear

Early in the summer of 1850, Messieurs Barral and Basio undertook an aerial voyage from the Observatory of Paris with a view of observing and recording the meteorological phenomena of the strata at a greater height and with more precision than had previously been accomplished. Their balloon proved inadequate to resist the expansion of the gas and it burst in two places, plunging them back to earth.

Undaunted, they made a second attempt on July 27, 1850, strangely using the same worn out, threadbare balloon. This time, instead of using the more common carbonated hydrogen, they had it filled with pure hydrogen gas to provide additional buoyancy. The principal points to be studied were:

1. The law according to which the atmospheric temperature diminishes as the height increases
2. The influence of solar radiation
3. The determination of the hygrometic state of the air
4. The analysis of the air at different heights
5. The determination of the quantity of carbonic acid in the air of the higher regions
6. The examination of the polarization of light upon clouds
7. The observation of any optical phenomena in the clouds

On ascending, the car came in contact with a tree and broke one of the barometers and a thermometer. At 18,000 feet and a temperature of 13°, the balloon suffered a rent four feet in length along the lower part. After attaining its highest elevation, the balloon began a downward movement, forcing them to dispose of everything but their instruments in order to break their fall. They achieved a safe landing after a flight of one hour and 27 minutes, achieving some of their stated goals.[39]

Eugene Godard, head of an elite aerostatic family, was born in Clichy, near Paris, on August 27, 1827. Self-educated, he made his first balloon flight in a paper Montgolfier at Lille in 1847.[40] The following year found him at Bologna, where he suffered the same fate as that of Dr. Morrill (see chapter 21) by descending into the water.[41] He was rescued by some boatmen and survived to become a dominant name in aerostation in the latter part of the 19th century.

By 1851, Godard preformed regularly at the Paris Hippodrome as ballooning continued to be "all the rage." In August, a "peculiar inducement" to spectators was the descent of Godard, the "Captain of Aeronauts," in a parachute. In a planned scheme, the umbrella did not open for 100 feet, leaving the onlookers to fear the return of a "lifeless, mangled corpse stretched at their feet." Shortly thereafter, the folds gradually unfolded and Godard landed in perfect safety. An American editor jocularly noted, "The money market must be extremely 'tight' in those 'diggins,' where a man is reduced to such a mode of 'raising the wind.'"[42]

A Paris paper of October 14, 1851, described a moonlight balloon excursion on which Godard demonstrated his ability to steer the atmospheric ship as conveniently as one riding the water. He drifted over Paris and its environs, picking up his passengers as he went, fulfilling his promise with "wonderful exactness."[43]

Being famous had its consequences, and the fable made the rounds of both continents that Eugene Godard, during the off-season when aeronauts were generally believed to be out of money, had been arrested for debt and taken to Clichy. The Director of the prison refused to arrest him, for he could not be responsible for his safe keeping, as Godard's brother was also an aeronaut and might come in a balloon to rescue him.[44]

Another of the famous acrobats to perform at the Hippodrome in Paris was Thevelin, renowned for hanging by his feet and "cutting strange antics in the air." In 1851 the Frenchman ascended at Brussels, performing gymnastic exercises at a considerable height. In crossing the city he got foul of the statue of St. Michael. To save himself, he clung to the statue while his balloon floated away. By dint of extraordinary presence of mind and considerable skill, he descended 362 feet to the ground.[45]

Back in Paris, where he became a regular Sunday participant, a spectator might take in one of Thevelin's performances, watch Godard perform his feats of navi-

A STRONG NERVE.

Do you know the value of a **strong nerve**?

Do you remember the story of the aeronaut, who, when the safety valve at the top of the balloon would not work, boldly mounted the delicate netting step by step, swinging out over the vast swell of the madly thrashing balloon, hanging tooth and nail over the yawning abyss and raging sea below, until he closed the valve, stopped the escape of gas and made the airship ride again to safety?

It was *nerve* which saved him and his companion.

Would you have had the nerve to do it?

A THOUSAND TIMES NO.

This nicely crafted illustration of aeronauts struggling in the water near a collapsed balloon is actually an advertisement for "Dr. Greene's Nervura, the greatest known restorer of nerve strength," and "the best brain invigorant" (*Sandusky Daily Register* [Ohio], March 13, 1891).

gation and watch a man advertised to fly "bird-fashion, or at least flap his wings" at the Hippodrome.[46]

News of a sadder note brought information that an aeronaut named Guiseppe Tardini made his twenty-third ascension from Copenhagen on the 10th of September 1851, taking with him his eleven-year-old son and an actress. His balloon landed in the sea near the island of Amack. Cutting the cords and seizing them with both hands, Tardini was borne upward. The woman and child were rescued and the balloon was subsequently discovered near Goldberg, but the aeronaut was supposed to have drowned in the Baltic.[47]

Strangely, the same balloon taken up by Tardini on his fatal voyage was used by a Swede named M. Sivertsen, who made the first ascent from Norway. Arising from Christiana on July 25, 1852, in front of 40,000 persons, he completed a successful flight and returned to the town in triumph.[48]

Observing that "Wonderful events always take place in obscure corners," the story of a Spaniard named Antonio Moles was recounted in 1852. Using a small table instead of a car, the aeronaut ascended from a small town on the frontier of Spain. Upon his legs were two umbrellas and in each hand was a set of silken screens, opening with hinges and expanding and contracting at will. A rope around his neck communicated to the valve of the balloon, and around his body he carried seven pounds of shot for ballast. Using a swimming motion, he sailed five miles in a straight line and then returned, covering ten miles in 29 minutes.[49]

The news from Spain was made even stranger by the announcement that the aeronaut M. Arban, who made an ascent form Barcelona more than two years previous and was thought to have been carried out to sea and drowned, was found alive. The report stated that the balloon actually sailed all the way to Africa, where Arban was seized and made a slave. He had only recently escaped.[50]

27

"No Preventing Providence"

This is probably the last of Pusey's ballooning, and the public will be on their guard in future when aeronauts come around unless they are known and highly recommended.[1]

Out west in California, Wilson, "the aeronaut," proposed to run a balloon line between San Francisco and St. Louis, offering trips at thirty miles an hour, "without delay from station or break of gauge — no fear of collision and no possibility of running off the track — will bring a balloon in three days from the shores of the Sacrimento [sic] to the foot of the Alleghanies [sic], and land her freight and passengers, fresh and healthy, almost at the very threshold of their homes."[2]

While waiting for his proposition to reach fruition, Wilson offered to entertain children, preparing two small balloons for their *picnic* grounds. The demonstration was somewhat of a disaster as the balloon burned; the smoke rose, however, which amounted "to the same thing." He next advertised an ascent in El Dorado in a balloon 40 feet wide and 90 feet long; in case of another failure, the spectators might be somewhat appeased by the offer of an old-fashioned Barbecue prior to the attempt.[3]

In June, the "professor" proposed to go up with Mrs. Fountain. As they stood in a car, "an envious puff of wind" struck the machine against a post, causing a tear through which the gas escaped. Remarking there was "no preventing providence," Wilson vowed another ascent in a week. Finally able to keep his word, he made two flights in rapid succession, the first landing on the top of a pine tree and the second descending near the head of Chilian Ravine.[4]

On the opposite side of the country, A.L. Carrier (also called "L.A. Carrier") celebrated Independence Day by ascending from Fredericksburg, Virginia. He landed 30 miles below Richmond, covering 100 miles. Subsequent to this, he made a flight from the same city during a violent thunderstorm, seated on a plank across the cords, traveling 12 miles. Having little better luck in March 1857, Carrier ascended from Richmond. At 8,000 feet he encountered a severe snowstorm that almost killed him. He landed near Washington.[5]

The Milwaukee *News* urged its readers to shell "out enough of the real" to enable Professor Pusey to elevate himself "as high — as we should like to go," and make his "Unprecedented Attraction" a success! The "well known balloonist of Philadelphia," billed as "the most successful and only scientific Aeronaut now operating," and the performer famous for his "curious freaks in the air," promised (if sufficient funds were subscribed) a "Hydrogen Menagerie," where artificial animals would be sent aloft affixed with fireworks. A lady passenger would be taken up free, but a gentleman would be charged $40. Price of admission for Pusey's 35th voyage: 50 cents.

Things did not go well. On August 18, not daring to take Madame Reis due to fog, and in the presence of a rather small paying crowd, Pusey ascended, letting down a cat in a parachute before becoming lost in the atmosphere. He traveled a scant three miles before descending. He made a voyage on August 27 before perpetrating a "balloon hoax" on September 3. After mounting on the back of an artificial eagle, he made "one grand effort to ascend, then scientifically tumbled off," and let the balloon go up alone, fearing (it was speculated) it would descend in the Lake, which it did.[6]

Women were particularly angry on discovering no man was aloft and "expressed themselves in such terms of indignation, that would have endangered the Professor's hair — had he been near at hand." The citizens then called for Professor Brooks, "a celebrated aeronaut," nearby at Janesville, to make an ascent from Milwaukee, believing he would "not fail them."[7]

Ill disposed to forgive the "hoax," the *Weekly* Wisconsin ran a report of "Pusey, Prof. Pusey, humbug Pusey" in Buffalo, where he "gulled the good people" there with another disaster. During inflation the "rickety old balloon burst in three or four different places, and was abandoned by Pusey who made his escape from the crowd as best he could." When last seen, the balloon was being torn apart by boys who captured it as a "lawful prize."[8]

"Professor Pusey" survived the indignation, making several successful voyages in New England in 1857. Being referred to as "a gentleman of extended reputation as an aeronaut," newspapers urged their readers to add to the subscription being raised to bring Pusey to their cities, adding, "A balloon ascension has always held a rank among the most popular exhibitions of modern times; and when we consider the probable importance of experiments of this nature, they cannot be too favorably regarded."[9]

"Skylarking" with the Godards in America

Eugene Godard established a reputation as one of the première aeronauts of France in the period between 1847 and 1853, working as a regular performer at the Hippodrome from 1850. By late 1853 or early 1854, he, his wife and five balloons arrived in the United States, where he began the process of re-creating himself to the public.[10]

Godard's earliest known American flight came on October 22, 1854, from the Hippodrome in New York. Carried by a violent gale, he covered seven miles in five minutes. His second flight took place the following Saturday from the same locale. Although great interest was expressed, the sale of tickets was insufficient to pay for the Manhattan gas with which the balloon was inflated.[11]

Godard's flights continued in rapid succession. On November 29 he took up one of the animals belonging to the Hippodrome, sending it down in a parachute, and then performed gymnastic feats on a trapezium, hanging onto it with his chin, standing on it with both hands off the rope and then dangling by one leg. Godard also performed on New Year's Day, ascending from Congo Square, making his 233rd aerial voyage.[12]

The family then began a whirlwind tour, traveling to New Orleans, where they ascended on January 15. Godard and his passengers descended that night in a swamp near La Valacherie, requiring two days travel by pirogue, mule and railroad to return. The balloon was a good deal ruptured but Godard promised another voyage the following Sunday.[13]

On April 30, Godard again ascended from New Orleans, taking with him his assistant, M. Manduit. After an aerial tableaux, "a feast of surprise and a dessert of grandeur," they reached an altitude of nearly three miles and descended near Vicksburg, having been in the air six hours and fifty minutes, covering 160 miles at an average of 23 miles per hour.[14]

Later that season Godard appeared at Cincinnati, where he and his wife ascended on September 22 with J. C. Bellman, the self-proclaimed "balloon editor" of the Cincinnati *Gazette*. On October 1, Godard ascended with four passengers, including a reporter and the editor of the *Daily Times and Gazette* (Bellman, W.G. Crippen, Col. Latham and Captain William Hole, also spelled "Hoel"). So many people gathered to watch that the staging under a tier of seats gave way, injuring several, including a child who suffered broken legs.

On descending, the balloon struck a cornfield and rebounded half a mile, during which time Godard was thrown out, followed by Latham and Hole. Bellman and Crippen continued for some distance before being dashed against a tree and rendered unconscious. They were rescued near Waynesville, 51 miles from Cincinnati, Hole having broken several ribs, Godard with facial and leg lacerations, Latham with a sprained ankle, Bellman with several cuts and Crippen with a "skewed" neck and bruised face. The passengers determined thereafter to "rest contented upon the earth."[15]

The Godards' third ascent from Cincinnati (and 267th overall) followed quickly. This time, instead of passengers, they took with them a horse, suspended by means of belts below the car. After a short voyage, the horse (which was small and mulish) became an instant celebrity, kicking persons who crowded too near.[16]

The Godards opened the season of 1856 in Havana, Cuba, where they joined Morat, the aeronaut, who had already advertised several ascents. On Sunday, April 20, Godard went up with five gentlemen, including Mr. Perez, the "King of Awning Makers." Once aloft, the safety valve could not be opened. The aeronaut proposed two alternatives: wait until night when condensation of the gas would lower the balloon, or tear the fabric and make a perilous descent. They opted for the latter and the machine plummeted to earth. The balloon struck a palm tree and rebounded, breaking Perez's leg. Other ascents were made on May 7, May 23 (with a horse), April 27 (his 295th ascent), June 15 and June 29.[17]

The Godards celebrated July 4, 1856, at Manchester, New Hampshire, before a crowd estimated between 20,000–50,000 spectators. With Mrs. Godard in the car and her husband standing on the back of a horse, they rose to 6,000 feet. After a circuit of twelve miles they came to Londonderry, where the anchor caught in a treetop. The locals in the vicinity "thought the end of the world was coming, and the devil was riding through the air." Eventually they came out of hiding and rendered assistance.[18]

Receipts for a single Boston ascent on July 21 amounted to $3,000, and despite the total loss of the balloon *America* on August 3rd, the Godards traveled to Montreal, where they ordered the construction of a new balloon, the *Canada*. They made three flights on September 8, 15 and 22 before returning to Philadelphia, where they made several late season ascensions that November.[19]

During one flight, Godard sang a song in accompaniment with his own echoes, and at one point they were so low a gentleman put his head over the basket, giving three cheers for "Mr. Buchanan." Afterward, he strangely appeared ten years older; the mystery was solved when the aeronauts realized his teeth had fallen out![20]

Editors Ascending and the Next Generation

In boastful self-promotion, Silas M. Brooks, "who has made more successful voyages throughout the heavens than any other man living," promised an ascent on July 12, 1856, from Decatur, Illinois. Using the *Hercules*, the excursion proved successful, despite passengers having to jettison their coats, spyglass and cigars before coming down 14 miles from Evansville after a voyage of an hour and 28 minutes.

At the passengers' request, Brooks permitted them to go up a second time, while he stayed on the ground. Finding navigation not as easy as it looked, one later wrote, "To say that we were not deeply interested in the solution of the landing question, would be ridiculous." All ended safely, if not smoothly. Brooks also ascended at Ottawa, Illinois, achieving a height of three miles and traveling 18 miles before sending his agent, Major Burnell, to Janesville to arrange for a flight on September 6.[21]

Charging the usual price of 25 cents regular, 50 cents reserved or elevated seating, he promised "no failure" and fireworks. Following weather delays, Brooks went up Monday, September 8. Sadly, the "profits of the enterprise footed up on the wrong side."[22]

On Saturday, September 13, Brooks made his twelfth voyage of the year, and 69th ascent overall, from Madison, Wisconsin. The balloon required half a day to fill, and when this was accomplished, a light wicker basket the size of a nursery-wagon was attached. Brooks flew for an hour and landed near Fulton, 28 miles distant. Brooks completed another successful ascent from Dixon, Illinois, in early October, traveling 35 miles in 25 minutes.[23]

George Brooks ascended from St. Louis in September 1857, managing to discharge a dog in a parachute before encountering thick mist, hail and eventually snow. As the balloon reached ground, Brooks' arm and leg caught in the ropes and he was dragged 400 yards until becoming wedged between corn stalks. Torn to pieces by the wind, the balloon collapsed, allowing the drenched aeronaut to crawl away.[24]

John Wise continued his ascents and maintained a presence in the community by penning treatises on his favorite subjects: wind currents and weather. Among other works, he wrote "Velocity of Wind" for the *Scientific American* (October, 1855), asserting that "Neither hurricanes, tornadoes, not common thunder-storms travel as fast as the wind currents above them," and "Information About Thunder Storms," in February 1857.[25] As a sideline, Wise continued his teaching of aeronautics, his première pupil being his son, Charles E. Wise, almost inevitably referred to as "Mr. Wise, Jr."

"Charley" made his first ascent from Shannondale Springs, Virginia, September 3, 1853, at the age of seventeen, and by 1856 he was performing on his own. On July 4 he was in Boston, where he flew the *Young America* fourteen miles, landing in South Braintree. Not above a bit of hawking, during one flight, he distributed bills all over the countryside, proclaiming, "Use Redding's Russia Salve."[26]

Remaining in the area, he ascended from Newburyport in October 1856. Only four miles from the ocean, he managed to drop himself off on Plumb Island Point after only 12 minutes aloft. Freed from his weight, the machine sailed away. Captain Wheeling of the schooner *Europa* picked up the *Young America* (valued at $250) at sea. In a strange twist, the salvagers demanded $62.50 for the return of the balloon, which Wise refused to pay. The people of Newburyport donated $150 to make good his loss; in return, Wise promised to return next year and carry up his benefactors.[27]

It was reported Wise proposed to let down a Broadway belle instead of an ordinary parachute during his next ascension; voyages in September that year from New York in the

Old America were entirely successful,[28] but unfortunately, no mention was made of any "belle."

On August 12, 1857, the people of Penobscot, Maine, ran a notice soliciting funds from the public to bring "a distinguished aeronaut" to their state. Remarking that the expense was great, a large amount of money was required; interested persons were requested to procure tickets *at once.*

Wise, Sr., advertised on September 30 to go up from Bangor, Maine, in his favorite balloon, the *Old America*, with 200 flights to her name, promising to take up a pony. For whatever reason he changed his mind and brought with him the *Young America*, "much handsomer and better than the Old."[29]

Prior to visiting Bangor, Wise appeared in New Hampshire, letting down a dog named Tray in a parachute. After crossing a "volcanic crater," he landed safely near Big Falls.

This advertisement ran on September 30, 1857. Part of the text ran, "This is the balloon *Old America* one of the finest in the country and handsomely decorated, which will make the scene one of great novelty and beauty and at the same time show to the citizens of Bangor one of the greatest curiosities in the triumph of Science and Art in the navigation of the atmosphere" (*Bangor Daily Whig and Courier*, September 12, 1857).

The second northeast voyage proved less a charm for Wise Sr. He ascended on October 1, and after a voyage of 65 minutes, began his descent into a sudden squall. The force of wind drove his grapnel through the side of the car, substantially injuring it, while dragging Wise over trees, fields and a pond where he was several times submerged. Loath to leave his ship, he finally jumped into a scraggy wood and was forced to walk five miles to Old Town.[30]

The French aeronaut, "Professor" Morat, also had his eye on the northeast. On June 12, 1857, he ascended from Newark, flying over New York, Brooklyn and Jersey City before reaching the Sound. He reportedly traveled 125 miles in an hour and a half, beating the fastest locomotive.[31] That summer Morat (also called "A.J. Morant") made a flight from Burlington, Vermont, with Captain Andrews, commandant of the U.S. Arsenal at Vergennes. Covering 30 miles in an hour and a half, they took a hearty lunch and were "half-seas over" by the time they landed at Elgin Springs.[32]

After an ascent from Philadelphia on July 4, Godard reached Wilmington, Delaware. Discharging his passenger, he immediately re-ascended and seemingly disappeared. When nothing was heard from him, memories of the sad case of Mr. Winchester were evoked. Since no one ever found the aeronaut or his balloon, speculation was that Godard might have fallen into the same category.[33] Godard reappeared in time for another ascent, but it seems his reputation took something of a beating as the New London *Times* (Wisconsin) reported on August 7, 1857: "Godard, the great aeronaut, took a jackass with him in a recent balloon ascension at Philadelphia. Jack was great frightened at first, but finally simmered down and took it as cooly as the other donkey."

The dreamers and achievers continued to ascend in balloons across the country: Dr. Boynton offered a lecture on Natural Philosophy, Electro-Magnetism and a balloon ascension "with net and oar" from Milwaukee on January 12; James W. Allen made a flight from Providence on May 18 and again on July 4, as did Samuel Archer King.[34]

John H. Steiner, of Philadelphia, a German speaker with limited English, who had been on the aviation scene some time, finally made the national news with an ascent from Pottstown, Pennsylvania, on May 30, 1857. The Gas Company was only able to supply him with limited gas, and with the balloon one third full, he mounted into the air. Upon reaching 50 feet, "der mersheene" was seized with a backward motion and came down in the "Manatawny." After considerable "floundering, kicking, ballooning and shouting," the half-drowned "Professor" was pulled to land.[35]

Steiner made an ascent from Erie on June 18 but landed in the lake. Bringing down the aerostat, Captain Woodruff of the *Mary Stuart* sent out a rescue boat. Steiner was saved, but the force of the wind blew his $500 balloon (the third to suffer the same fate) away. Interestingly, a Mr. Koon had predicted a comet would destroy the world, beginning on June 13. Upon spotting the aerial car shrouded in cloud, the crew of the *Mary Stewart* [sic] took it for the Comet. "The religiously inclined portion prepared for prayers, the reckless made for the bar, and the more prudent part went to the clerk's office and drew their wages." Only after a telescopic examination did they properly identify it as a balloon.[36]

John La Mountain, the "celebrated French Aeronaut," also garnered national attention in 1857. His first notices were a "fizzle." Placards advertised a flight from Fort Wayne, Indiana, on September 16, in which he promised to take Miss E.M. La Mountain with him. The flight did not take place. Official word was that the balloon had been cut and could not be inflated. Speculation ran rampant, however, that with few paying customers, La Mountain did not care to risk his life for the gratification of outsiders. The newspaper did not blame him on that account, but held him responsible for not paying their "little advertising bill; by this he has placed himself on a level with those who sought to sponge a view of the ascension off him, and materially lessened his claim on our sympathy."[37]

28

"A Little Relief from the Ordinary Cares of Life"

BALLOON ASCENSION, &c.— By advertisement it will be seen that a great bill of attraction is presented for the 26th inst., including a regular balloon ascension by the great aeronaut Mons. Godard. We want a little relief from the ordinary cares of life just about these times.[1]

Silas A. Brooks, under the auspices of the Erickson and Hydrogen Balloon Company, performed with M. Le White, "The Great, Daring, Foreign Equiliptic [sic] Aeronaut!" in Alton, Illinois, on July 10, 1858. When the balloon was only three-quarters full, a threatening thunderstorm appeared on the horizon, so the Professor determined on an early voyage. As he weighed 180 pounds, his weight proved too much, so his brother, George Brooks, 40 pounds lighter, volunteered. All went well until the descent when a flaw struck the balloon, breaking the heavy loop above the basket and throwing George to the ground. Without a pilot, the machine sailed away.

In consequence of the premature departure, receipts were far below expenses, falling short by $100. Added to the loss of the $800 balloon, the Professor was hardly able to bear the tragedy. As his performances were no "clap-trap," the newspaper hoped the public would help him back on his feet. Four days later the balloon was found lodged in a tree near Alton, and Le White promptly secured it. Although considerably damaged, it was felt it could be repaired and made almost as good as new.[2]

Le White ascended on July 21 from Alton[3] and, as he was apparently less expensive than his well-known associate, the town of Olney, Illinois, advertised to raise $100 to bring Le White to their area.[4]

The first of two remarkable voyages took place at Centralia, Illinois, on Friday, September 17. Silas Brooks (another account stated it was G.W. Brooks)[5] was advertised to ascend but, feeling unwell, permitted Samuel Wilson, "a young man who had been traveling around with him, learning the theory and practice of ballooning," to go up in his place. After a 20-mile flight, Wilson descended in a tree on the property of Benjamin Harvey. Being helped down, the aeronaut allowed three children, a boy of three years (David Isham), a girl of eight (Martha Ann) and an older sister, play in the tethered balloon. The elder girl got out and the machine swiftly ascended.

Word spread, rousing Brooke from his sickbed. He suggested the balloon would descend within two or three hours, no further away than 30 miles. He also sent a message to the distraught parents, advising there was no danger except in landing in the woods, where they might be difficult to find. Reassurances aside, the idea took hold that the children might perish in the freezing atmosphere and the story quickly became a national incident. Hundreds of men turned out to search and the excitement "was extreme."

At 3 o'clock the following morning, Mr. Ignatius Atchison, living a mile from Mount Vernon, Illinois, saw a blazing star — the great comet — and hurried out, only to hear the plaintive cry, "Come here and let us down; we're almost froze!" He cut away several limbs of the tree to free the balloon and rescued the children. News reached Centralia on Sunday and by Monday the children were welcomed to the city by the firing of cannon.[6]

The Case of the Missing Aeronaut

It all started out innocently enough. News out of Adrian, Michigan, on September 16 stated, "Messrs. Bannister and Thurston made a splendid balloon ascension from here to-day."[7] The story would quickly develop, becoming the second national incident in a month that made "the flesh creep" and sent "a shudder through every nerve!"

W.D. Bannister (Thurston's father-in-law) and Ira Thurston were partners. On the fateful Thursday, Ira, who had not planned on going, was induced to take a seat and completed his 37th ascension, descending 18 miles west of Toledo in a new balloon jointly owned, and valued at $1,000.[8]

While packing the balloon for transport, it was turned on its side to disentangle the netting and enable the aeronauts to reach the valve in order to discharge gas. Thurston stood on the 13-inch wooden disc, holding up the collapsed portion of the envelope. With the apparatus disengaged (rope: 50 pounds; car: 25 pounds; ballast: 160 pounds) and Bannister stepping away (weight: 140 pounds),[9] the balloon shot up "with the suddenness of a rocket."[10] Thurston slid down onto the disc, the collapsed part of the balloon between his legs and his arms around it. He reportedly called, "It will be all right shortly," but the rapid ascent prevented him from jumping down.[11]

Twelve feet over his head, Thurston could not reach the envelope to cut a hole and discharge the remaining 13,000 feet of gas. The accident took place at 11:00; by 1:00 P.M. it was dimly visible going in the direction of Malden.[12]

Balloon sightings poured into Adrian.[13] Marshes were searched; rumors placed Thurston in Canada. Bannister, who had gotten lost two years earlier when he made an ascent from the same place (involuntarily making the longest trip ever in America),[14] expressed faith the aeronaut would be found alive. Even Mrs. Aldrick, of Aldrich, a Spiritual medium summoned for help, gave directions to a house where she asserted Thurston would be found alive.[15]

Joseph Marks eventually found the balloon near Baptiste Creek, stripped it on Sunday, September 19, and took the silk into his house, where Bannister collected it. It appeared the valve board on which Thurston sat had torn away, indicating Thurston's weight had been too much. In that case, he likely would have fallen to his death.[16]

The missing man's brother, S.R. Thurston, came from Livingston County, New York, to continue the search, ultimately deciding Ira had fallen alive into the marshes on Lake St. Clair but, in an exhausted condition, had perished before help arrived.[17]

On March 6, 1859, Ira J. Thurston's remains were discovered in the woods ten miles northwest of Toledo. The body had been eaten by animals: bones were scattered everywhere, the broken jaw partly buried in the earth. Among the effects were a Lepine silver watch (stopped at 11:40), jack-knife, a buckskin purse containing $1.36 and a letter directed to Thurston. The items were boxed up and taken to Adrian where they were identified.[18]

Later that month, the "French aeronaut, Monsieur Carlincourt" of Utica, New York, proposed a monument to Thurston, informing the newspaper he had written to La Mountain, Wise and other aeronauts proposing that each should give an ascension and donate the proceeds to the purchase of the monument.[19]

In an interesting side note, Dr. Boynton made a lecture in Buffalo, stating that several months previous to his death, Thurston informed him he intended to make an ascent sitting across the valve board with the slack of the balloon between his legs. If true, Boynton concluded Thurston was a victim of his own imprudence.[20]

Probably aware of Boynton's assertion, Bannister commissioned a series of large paintings to truthfully show the manner in which Thurston took his fateful ride. He also proposed to ascend in the same balloon on his tour of Michigan the coming summer.[21]

On June 7, 1859, Bannister successfully ascended from Kalamazoo in the *Adrian*, originally designed under Thurston's supervision. It cost $1,500, was 66 feet in length, and 40 feet in diameter with a 36,000 cubic foot capacity.[22] On his descent, Bannister was blown into an apple tree where he hung suspended as the balloon sped off. Three days later a 12-foot square of silk was discovered near Delaware, a small town on the Thames River in Canada.[23]

The Great Fort Wayne Balloon Debacle and, Incidentally, a Balloon Ascension

Bannister made flights at Grand Rapids on July 4 and one from Detroit before sending his agent into Fort Wayne, Indiana, with an offer to perform there for the sum of $500. In what must be described as pure Americana, what followed was an astonishing and, with hindsight, amusing glimpse into the hearts and minds of 19th century citizens.

Feeling "humiliated" they had not yet had a balloon ascension and taunted by the neighboring town of Lafayette, which could boast of John Wise having flown there, the citizens of Fort Wayne put together a committee to raise subscription funds. Encouraged by Mr. Dawson, editor of the *Daily Times*, who wrote almost hysterical daily editorials promoting the event, he gave Bannister's assurance of as long a voyage as that of Mr. Wise "before his *last* accident at Lafayette," and warned his readers against the bugbear "Hard Times," suggesting "general prosperity" would come of the project "and remove all apprehensions with regard to the future."

With funds still lacking, it was determined Bannister would go up "whether or no," with the exhibition "free to all — children half price." The date was set for August 30 and went off handsomely, albeit briefly. Passing through an electrical storm in the *Pride of America*, Bannister landed 80 miles away, at Hog Creek Marsh. On a sour note, Dawson singled out the firm of Townley & Co., observing that it took in $750 revenue from the spectators, which was "$750 more than they subscribed for the Balloon enterprise." Bannister made a point of thanking the gentlemanly editor of the *Times*, even though it appears from the following he did not come close to being paid the fee of $500.[24]

REPORT OF THE BALLOON COMMITTEE RECEIPTS.

Am't of subscriptions outside of Com.	$365.78
" Subscribed by Com. ten in No.	*52.47*
	$418.25

EXPENDITURES

Paid Bannister,	$300.00
" Gas,	46.25
" Materials of H.B. Reed,	5.30
" Music deficiency,	1.00
" Powder, Williams & Huestis,	3.25
" Distributing bills & cartage,	3.92
" Printing of Times Office,	42.50
" Cartage,	1.00
" J. Fairfield, work on balloon,	4.00
Subscriptions refused paym't,	12.00
	419.22
Deficiency paid by committee	
	$ .97

NOTE.— The subscription of the Times office was $15.[25]

Yet all was not yet over. Other editorials followed, blaming those citizens "croaking" about the short duration (only 80 miles!) of the voyage or the early hour of ascension. Not to be left out, the Toledo *Times and Herald* wrote a scathing editorial, blaming the committee for failing to put the time of ascension on its fliers and thus disappointing "thousands" who came by the Wabash Railroad and so did not arrive until after 2 P.M. This elicited a spirited defense by the editor of the *Daily Times*, remarking that the Pittsburg Railroad ran a special train on the 30th, getting spectators into Fort Wayne on time; if the Wabash refused to do so, the fault lay on them and not the committee.[26] The newspaper feud continued for a week, with the exasperated editor of the *Daily Times* finally concluding to the *Times and Herald* that on August 29 it definitively published the time of ascent as between 10 and 11 o'clock: "God help your weakness. You have eyes, read."[27]

Bannister left town on the 5th, sending the balloon with his partner, Mr. Cumming, on to Dayton.[28] Adding salt to the wound, the Fort Wayne *Weekly Republican* (September 7, 1859) observed that Professor Bannister would make several voyages from Indianapolis, the people of that city having "almost perfected" the arrangements to meet his expenses.

The *Republican* had its own axe to grind: the editor sent a letter to the Balloon Committee complaining that it was not given a share of the printing executed for the occasion. "One of the Committee" (undoubtedly Dawson) published the rebuttal, explaining the reasons the work went to the *Daily Times*, "none of which will in any wise apply to the *Republican*":

1st. A most liberal contribution on the part of Mr. Dawson (before the matter of printing was talked of,) to assist in defraying the expenses of the ascension.
2nd. The constant, free and unsolicited use of the editorial columns of the Daily and Weekly *Times* for the promotion of the balloon enterprise.
3rd. The personal assistance of the editor himself in promoting subscriptions to defray the expenses of the occasion.
   Now, what did the editor of the *Republican* do to favor the enterprise?[29]

Still seething over the insults, the *Daily Times* noted Bannister's successful flight from

Indianapolis aboard the *Pride of America* on September 23, noting he landed three miles from his place of ascent,[30] prompting a defense by the *Republican* that unpleasant weather was likely the cause.[31] Fortunately, the "Tabernacle of Amusement: Antonio & Wilder's Great World Circus" came to Fort Wayne on October 12 and took everyone's mind off past grievances.

Bannister, the innocent victim of the press war, continued his summer work by traveling to Peoria in October, where, it was noted, he landed six miles from his place of ascent. No one complained.[32]

The Geese-Man, the "Manbat" and Monkey Circuses

If missing children and a missing aeronaut were different sides of the same coin, then the case of the geese-man and the "manbat" were two sides of the same coin. Even stranger, they both took place in Arkansas.

Considerable excitement was occasioned in Columbia County, Arkansas, on February 25, 1858, by the appearance of a balloon being driven by 30 harnessed geese. The aeronaut, Ben Johnson (also called "Ben Jones"), brought them down in a field and explained he had set out from Harrison county, Missouri, and had been flying 48-hours and thought it about time to come down and "fodder."[33]

The same season, Mr. Leonard made a successful ascension from Montgomery, Alabama. A short distance from the capital he was shot at three times by a Minnie rifle — in the hands of someone who mistook him for a monster "manbat" — "no doubt a descendant of the same family which ran out to stop the first high-pressure steamboat they saw going down the river, mistaking it for a runaway sawmill. But the most probable motive was the mischievous and wicked curiosity of some idle vagabond, to see if he could not bring the balloon down with a rifle ball."[34]

At a time when every aeronaut needed an edge to attract the paying customers, the performance of Eugene Godard and family was advertised for May 15 in Alton, Illinois, to include feats of magic. Godard's brother Augustus, with the assistance of Madame Godard, using "a cabinet and apparatus costing over twenty thousand dollars," would give a grand "Soiree De Magique," with all the best Philosophical, Electrical and Magical experiments of Macallister, Anderson and Houdin (the namesake of Houdini).

Godard was also scheduled to perform in Davenport, Iowa, on May 26 with the "Great Monkey Circus, and Burlesque Dramatic Troupe." The flight never came off. A report on May 27 sourly noted the advert had been a "humbug": the "cut" of a balloon in the newspaper was meant only to draw crowds, so it "paid the showmen" to promise what they had no intention of delivering.[35]

Godard did ascend from Cleveland on July 5th in front of 35,000 spectators. (When Independence Day fell on a Sunday, celebrations took place on Monday.) Using a balloon made in Montreal, described as being 40 by 30 and 30 feet high, made of raw silk and varnished, with a car of basket work 4 feet square and 3 deep, covered inside and out with red plush, the flight went off as advertised.[36]

On Tuesday (either July 27 or August 3), Godard and his wife made a successful flight from Buffalo, New York,[37] followed by a second ascension on August 5. The voyage was an entirely successful one, save for Godard tossing over as "ballast" two bottles of *au-de-vie* that had been transported across the ocean on the British bark *Resolute*, after one of his passengers consumed too much wine. The sum of weight was given as:

Balloon and materials, lbs.	616
Passengers	618
Baggage and provisions	45
Ballast	221
Total	1,500[38]

Professor Steiner ascended from Harrisburg, Pennsylvania, in June,[39] then began writing a series of letters on his intent to cross the Atlantic in a balloon. For $20,000 he proposed to construct a machine with an ascending power of 8 tons. The car would be constructed of cedar and the balloon constructed of common twilled muslin coated with balloon varnish. He proposed to guide the machine by a drag line attached to a float in the water.[40]

In order to improve accommodations, he intended an experiment in Syracuse, New York, when he ascended there in the fall. He proposed building a small house ten feet square, capable of holding five persons to be slung beneath his balloon, the *Star of the West*, after it was greatly enlarged.[41]

The idea of a transatlantic flight was one that had dominated the minds of most aeronauts in the 19th century, but financing had always been the sticking point. As a means of raising money, balloon races were a guaranteed way of receiving press. As early as October 30, 1857, a notice ran in the Delaware *State Reporter* of a proposed race for a "$2,000 side" to take place at Buffalo between two celebrated aeronauts. Nearly a year later, details emerged: M. Godard had challenged Prof. Steiner to a race to be held at Buffalo or Rochester.[42] They were to start together and the one landing farthest from the city, without regard to time, won.[43]

The site was changed to Cincinnati and it was determined that along their route (projected to last three or four days), the aeronauts would send down "logs," containing points of interest so that citizens around the country might be kept informed by telegraph.[44]

Not everyone was enthralled by the prospect. An Iowa editor expected the aeronauts to "descend after breakfast" and suspected there was a great deal of "humbug" and "Barnum spirit" at the bottom, where both were "thinking more of the almighty dollar than of glory."[45]

On Monday, October 18, the celebrated French aeronaut in *À la Belle France*, and "our darling Young American aeronaut" (Steiner, the German) prepared for the big event.[46] Steiner stocked 600 pounds of ballast, a basket of provisions, a can of water and a bottle of wine in his balloon, the *Pride of the West*. Godard's balloon, the *Leviathan*, was larger than its rival, giving Godard the advantage of 7,860 feet of gas. Going up with him was William Hoel, who had previously gone up with the aeronaut October 1, 1855, where he sustained several broken ribs. Steiner ascended alone.

At 4:00, J. C. Bellman of the Cincinnati *Gazette* (also an alumni of the October 1855 voyage) went up in advance in a small balloon, followed by the two contestants at 4:21 P.M. The aeronauts were soon within speaking distance, and the three shared a toast, "To the Great Republic," over individual bottles of wine. Five minutes later, Steiner's balloon drove so close to Godard's that the baskets struck, forcing the latter to shove away with his hands. Tossing out ballast, the *Leviathan* rose out of danger and the real contest began.[47]

Proving the skeptic at the Davenport *Daily Gazette* correct, the race did not last nearly three days: Godard landed the same night at 10:30 P.M., 15 miles from Sandusky, and Steiner at 11:00 P.M. within one mile of that city, making Steiner the "champion balloonist of America."[48] Depending on the report, the distance traveled was 190–230 miles at a rate of 27 miles per hour.[49] The explanation of why they did not travel farther was that neither was disposed to cross into Canada.

In a preview of future events, a man seeking passage on the Ohio and Mississippi Railroad left his overcoat and carpetbag in the office. At the same time an assistant of Godard's came in for some traps; he mistakenly took the traveler's possessions with them and tossed everything into the balloon, making this the first time in aerostatic history that lost baggage became an issue.[50]

Filling in the Gaps

The news in May concerned a twenty-year-old lady named Mary Way, who proposed to make a solo ascension from New Orleans, provided the citizens subscribed money to pay her expenses.[51] The following year her name made the newspapers again when it was announced she would debate women's rights with a Kentucky lawyer and then make a grand ascension from Congo Square.[52]

A student of Samuel Wilson, Miss Way, "attended by her gallant cavalier," went up from the Placo (aka Place) d'Armes May 3, 1859, in the air-ship *Paul Murphy* (also spelled *"Morphy"*). She wore a beaver Bloomer hat, a profusion of black ringlets, a black silk dress and gray shawl, and seemed to take delight in the proceedings.[53] They landed 130 miles from New Orleans where the balloon became entangled in a tree. The pair were forced to remain there until daylight when Way climbed down and went for help.[54]

Mrs. E.W. Davis, another student of Samuel Wilson, made an ascent July 10, 1858, from Tuscumbia, Alabama, aboard the smoke balloon *American Eagle*, and a second flight from Nashville the same month. She was slightly injured by being thrown about when it landed.[55]

A less successful ascent took place in Dayton, Ohio, in May 1858. A "reckless daredevil" named Sellers, twenty-two years of age, "rigged a huge muslin concern, coated with glue and 'white-washed' with yellow ochre, in size and shape very much resembling the canvas under which circus showmen" exhibit big snakes. During inflation of his Montgolfier the balloon caught fire several times. Quickly patching the holes, he managed to reach an altitude of one mile before a precipitous descent, one mile from where he started.[56]

In Providence, several aeronauts charged $5 a head for passengers wishing to ascend in a tethered balloon,[57] while on July 3, Mr. Reynard (probably Gustave Reynauld, a French mechanic who had accompanied Ernest Petin to America in 1852 and made several ascents from Bridgeport, Connecticut) ascended from that city. Upon reaching 16,000 feet, the temperature fell to 32 degrees below zero. He also made a flight from New Haven on October 7, 1858.[58]

Another Connecticut aeronaut from Winsted, H.M. Spencer, completed a flight from Pittsfield, Massachusetts, on July 5 and again on September 18.[59] The flights gave so much satisfaction that Spencer was invited back for the Independence Day celebrations of 1859. This arrangement did not suit all parties, however, as Charles Cevor, of Albany, an engineer of the Western Railroad and a student of both La Mountain and Wise, planned his first solo flight from the same city in June. The debut, in a 66-foot high and 33-foot diameter balloon, *The Pride of America*, was to be witnessed by Wise and Edward La Mountain, brother of John. After the successful completion, Cevor intended to make a second flight on July 4th — which would be in direct competition with that of Spencer. A meeting at the Town Hall was called to consider the subject.[60] Spencer won out, for on June 24th the announcement was made that he would make an ascension in his new mammoth balloon, *Comet*, on Monday, July 4.

Cevor and Edward La Mountain's flight from Pittsfield was postponed from June 8 to 11th because of weather but came off successfully. For his second flight, Cevor had to settle for Montpelier on Independence Day. Leaving Albany on July 1, he traveled to Vermont, but found the gasometer too small to supply more than 12,000 feet of gas. Being too heavy, he sent his assistant, Edward La Mountain, 30 pounds lighter, up in his stead. Ironically, Cevor might have gone to Troy, New York, La Mountain's hometown, for the citizens there failed to secure an aeronaut for the holiday.[61]

Apparently, Troy had other things on its mind, as the editor of the Troy *Budget* took a ride on the Hudson river in a "life boat or car" built to accompany John La Mountain on his proposed trip across the Atlantic. It was described as a "model of beauty," and when beheld with its wings (the fans), looked like a "monster bird wounded and fluttering in efforts to rise."[62]

Spencer added one more flight in Pittsfield, Massachusetts, in September, when he volunteered to ascend during the Cattle Show for his own personal expenses and the cost of gas.[63] Cevor ascended from Albany on September 28. In descending, he encountered a tornado, was dashed into trees and landed with great velocity, coming away with two black eyes and a bruised hip.[64] Staying in the northeast, he flew from Northampton, Massachusetts, in October 1860, landing at Hardwick, 31 miles distant.[65]

Adding to the oddities of balloon lore, the pilot boat *Washington* chased a balloon on May 28, 1859, five miles before overhauling it. On the valve was painted, "Built and owned by Joshua Pressy [Pusey], Philadelphia, 1857."[66] Undaunted, Pusey ascended from Williamsburg in June.[67] Bad luck plagued him on July 4 at Jones' Wood, New York. Unable to obtain sufficient gas to make a holiday flight, the Nineteenth Ward was called out for his protection from an irate mob. Robert Grant of the gas company later revised the story, stating that sufficient gas was supplied, but "certain mischievous spectators perforated the balloon with bullets and otherwise — no less than seven holes and one large rent being found in the silk, through which the gas escaped." Finally, after a flight from Poughkeepsie, New York, on September 19, Pusey descended with such violence that he escaped with his life.[68]

GRAND, SUBLIME AND NOVEL EXHIBITION!

ERICSSON HYDROGEN

YOUNG AMERICA.

BALLOON COMPANY,

Will exhibit at Portsmouth, on
Thursday, September 6th, 1860,
in their Mammoth Wall Pavilion,
POSITIVELY FOR ONE DAY ONLY!

Professor William J. Shotts had his share of problems. Advertised as "The Greatest of American Aeronauts ... engaged by the Company at an immense Expense," his failures were actually more common than his successes. The Superlatives "greatest," and "immense" were commonly used in 19th century advertising and seldom reflected the true state of affairs (*Logansport Pharos* [Indiana], June 30, 1881).

And proving not all was serious, the *Democratic Standard* poked fun of William J. Shotts by giving a "blow-by-blow" description of his Ohio tribulations: "MONDAY — 4 o'clock P.M. — Began to inflate balloon — man up a tree cutting off limbs so it can spread itself — 20 minutes past — people getting mad — begin to cry, humbug! — 5 o'clock P.M. — balloon sways against tree — hole torn in — didn't go off. TUESDAY — the Balloonist ordered to vamoose the Fair Ground — WEDNESDAY — 3 o'clock — balloon going up. Balloonist waving hat — So ends the great Balloon ascent in Delaware, which has been the theme of conversation for nearly a week, miles around."[69]

29

Crossing the Atlantic — Or Not

In this nineteenth century, it will not do to laugh at any proposition, however absurd it may seem. We can, therefore, only wait, and we shall see what we shall see.[1]

In April 1858, John Wise left Lancaster, Pennsylvania, for Washington. Engaged by the Smithsonian Institution, provided instruments for the purpose, and with arrangements with the City Gas Company for a liberal supply of gas, he intended to study the feasibility of creating a squadron of balloons in the shape of a regatta. Another study was to consist of a trial where Wise would descend from a balloon with a canvas air conductor. His primary goal, however, was to establish the practicality of guiding balloons along telegraph lines, so as to steer and arrive at a given point with as much certainty as ships, "and carry on commerce with the world."[2]

By May 31, a notice ran in the newspaper that there would be a regatta and a balloon ascension at city expense for the 4th of July.[3] On the holiday, John Wise and his son both made ascensions in front of an estimated crowd of 200,000.

On August 31, 1858, John La Mountain made an ascent from Troy, New York, with Dr. Elisha Waters and a ten-year-old girl. Dropping Waters off at Lanesborough, the aeronaut and child resumed their flight to Boston.[4] Back in Troy the following month, La Mountain proposed a balloon capable of crossing the ocean, putting himself in "competition" with Wise and Steiner, asking for no money, being willing "to encounter the attendant risks without any immediate prospect of reward."[5] It is likely the Troy *Times* confused working capital for remuneration, for in a follow-up story, the aeronaut requested a loan of $25,000, promising a scheme to make stockholders amply secure.[6]

Perhaps in response to this, the Alton *Weekly Courier*, September 9, 1858, put in a word of support for the "Trans–Atlantic Steam Balloon Company," in consideration of which they asked to be one of the first passengers — "free as usual."

La Mountain traveled to Bennington, Vermont, in late 1858 to meet with Oliver Ayer Gager, proprietor of the Bennington Pottery,[7] later to be called "a wealthy citizen of Boston."[8] After a balloon ride, Gager went in on the deal, agreeing to supply the money.[9] La Mountain was in Boston in January 1859, making arrangements for his Atlantic balloon[10] and then returned to Troy. His balloon was to be powered by a "gun cotton engine," designed by a man in Springfield, Massachusetts. John Wise was said to be in consultation on the project and approved the plan.[11]

By February 25, La Mountain had ordered the construction of five miles of rope and cordage from the Troy Patent Rope Works[12] and Gager ordered fabric from a recent importation of East Indies silk. Elisha Waters, of Troy, was entrusted with getting up an apparatus for maintaining different degrees of altitude without wasting gas or discharging ballast.[13] The balloon, as proposed, was to be constructed in Lancaster upon the frames and with the apparatus used by John Wise.[14]

In reference to the temper of the times, the Troy *Whig* noted that if successful, John Bull would have "an elevated notion of America and American 'institutions.'"[15]

During the week of May 2, 1859, a Balloon Conference was held in New York City to discuss the proposed trans–Atlantic balloon flights being contemplated by La Mountain and Wise. Wise, who earlier announced an extended trip to Japan where he planned to remain four or five years, postponed the venture to take part. Among the participants was M. "Carlincourt," who reported that a test voyage to determine the practicality of crossing the ocean would take place from St. Louis. He also noted that Wise was to "take the enterprise under his direction."[16] On May 8, Wise wrote to a friend from New York that he had just completed arrangements to take his balloon, the *Nineteenth Century*, to St. Louis at his own expense.[17]

Carlincourt returned to Utica on May 12 to begin construction on a new balloon that would eclipse the *Excelsior*, to weigh only 90 pounds and carry five persons.[18]

Amid reports La Mountain, Gager and Wise had formed a partnership and that the three would perform a trial flight from St. Louis in La Mountain's balloon, the *Atlantic*, a story came out in *Harper's Weekly*, purporting to give a history of the trans–Atlantic balloon enterprise, bestowing all credit upon Wise and calling him "director-in-chief," while consigning La Mountain to a secondary position. This prompted the Troy *Times* to run a rebuttal in defense of their adopted son, stating La Mountain's plans were far advanced before Wise was brought in, adding, "Mr. Wise has not contributed a shilling to the undertaking as yet, and now he will not be permitted to do so, at least until he shall publicly disavow any connection" with the article in *Harper's* and "secure to Mr. La Mountain the credit he deserves."[19]

After making an ascension on Tuesday, June 14, Wise started for St. Louis, hoping, in part, to prove his theory of wind currents blowing from west to east. No one could have been more interested in the flight than Matthew F. Maury, the famed naval cartographer, at the time associated with the Washington Observatory. He had long proposed the idea of such a wind pattern and undoubtedly anticipated being proven correct.[20]

By June 19, Wise and Gager were in St. Louis giving interviews.[21] On July 1, 1859, La Mountain had joined them and they prepared for lift-off. At 1:00 P.M., the balloon was spread upon canvas and inflation began. A large pipe conveyed gas from the gasometer near the Seventh Street depot; 65,000 feet of gas were contracted, but only 50,000 feet were required. Fifty thousand people gathered outside but only several hundred paid to get inside the enclosure, a crowd "not sufficiently large to make the enterprise remunerative."[22] (The original idea had been to defray the expenses of the gas by ticket sales, but from the ill-chosen location, too few were able to enter.)[23] Attached to the balloon was a patent Ingersoll life-boat suspended 25 feet below the body of the balloon, between which was a willow basket, intended as a means of safety in case the balloon was dragged over trees.

Accompanying them in the $3,000 balloon *Atlantic* was William Hyde, a reporter from the St. Louis *Republican*, a sack of Express mail, $30 worth of provisions provided by the merchant Guenaudon, numerous bottles of wine and champagne donated by friends, blankets, gloves, cards of mercantile houses and candidates for office, and scientific equipment. Unfortunately, they forgot to pack water and a long delay occurred before it was delivered.

This proved to be salt water, obtained by tapping a neighboring ice cream freezer, prompting a second delay before the proper substance was secured.[24]

Wise introduced his companions to the crowd, informing them Mr. Gager had supplied the capital, La Mountain the mechanical skill, "and now he expected to perform his part of the contract, and come in for a third of the glory."[25] All went well until a visitor partook too freely of a lot of wine reserved for use by the aeronauts. Mr. Baker, the superintendent, engaged him in a scuffle and after subduing the drunkard, turned him over to police.[26]

Silas Brooks, aeronaut and manager of the St. Louis Museum, preceded the main event in his one-man balloon, the *Comet*. Attaining an altitude of 12,000 feet, he traveled 25 miles and landed in sight of the *Atlantic*, east of Edwardsville, Illinois, at 7:45 P.M.

At 6:40 P.M., the *Atlantic* ascended from Washington Square, corner of Clark Avenue and Twelfth Street, Wise in the basket and the other three in the boat. Cheered on by the spectators, the balloon took an easterly course. At 8:15 P.M., Wise went to sleep in the car. At 11:00 P.M., La Mountain called to him to open the valve. On receiving no answer he sent Gager up the ropes to "see if he were dead." Gager found Wise nearly poisoned from the discharge of gas, head dropped upon his breast, entirely insensible and breathing spasmodically. After roughly shoving him, five minutes of pure air restored Wise from what could have been a fatal accident.

Navigation proved difficult, forcing La Mountain to descend within shouting distance of land, calling out to ascertain what part of the country they were in. Receiving nothing in reply but his own echoes, he gave up in disgust, declaring, "they had passed out of the world and gone over to Canada." At 5 A.M., after reaching Lake Erie, La Mountain determined to cross, despite the perceived danger of traveling over large bodies of water. As this was held as a major deterrent to a trans–Atlantic voyage, it seemed logical to make the attempt during this "dry run." The others agreed and the balloon passed safely over, later allowing the aeronauts to claim a significant achievement.

An entire nation waited as news of the flight drifted in: "Passed Fort Wayne at 4 A.M.; Fremont, 7:00; Sandusky, Ohio 7 A.M.; Dunnville, C.W. (Canadian Wilderness), 11 A.M.; Niagara Falls 12 noon; Medina, New York, 12:30 P.M."

Low on gas and ballast, the aeronauts decided to land near Rochester and discharge Gager and Hyde, with La Mountain and Wise then continuing to the seaboard. Dropping to 300 feet, the balloon encountered a tornado. Jettisoning everything, including the mail, the propeller fan and planks from the bottom of the boat, they skirted the lake, but were blown into a stand of trees. Striking an oak, the balloon was torn to shreds, La Mountain sustaining a serious bruise on the side. With the balloon left hanging in a tree (sustaining $200 in damage), they made their way to Henderson, Jefferson County. In all, the trip began at 6:40 P.M. on Friday and ended at 2:20 P.M. Saturday; the *Atlantic*, which did not reach its namesake, traveled 1,150 miles.[27]

Wise and Gager arrived at Adams, New York, the afternoon of July 2 and spoke to a packed house; La Mountain remained behind to collect the balloon. On July 3 Gager and Hyde left for their homes; La Mountain reached Watertown the morning of July 4, announcing that when the balloon was repaired, he would make another voyage from Chicago.[28] The express mailbag was retrieved July 5 out of the lake. It contained over 40 letters, one enclosing a $1,000 draft on a New York bank.[29]

In all, the *Atlantic* was the largest balloon ever manufactured, being twenty-two hundred and fifty yards in circumference. It required six months to coat, at an average of 12 hours per day. The sewing occupied 300 days. Twenty-two hundred and fifty yards of the best Chinese oiled silk were used with six miles of cord for the netting.[30]

Was it worth the time and effort? That depended on one's point of view. One newspaper mused, "Whether any practical good is to come of it, remains to be seen."[31] Another questioned the practicality of the larger picture — that of crossing the Atlantic, by noting, "If he don't get a good ducking before he gets 1000 miles out to sea, we are greatly mistaken."[32]

Even the aeronauts had their doubts: if not about their ultimate goal, then about one another. No sooner had they gotten back to civilization when the proverbial fur started flying and the parties involved published "Cards" giving accounts of the voyage. Wise published his logbook on July 3; two days later his narrative in the New York *Tribune* gave an excellent account, even referring to La Mountain as a "hero." By July 8, however, Wise explained in a letter to the New York *Tribune* why the *Atlantic* did not reach New York City or Boston: "The reason why it was not done is, some of our party did not provide themselves with extra clothing," and "shivered with cold so that the balloon quivered with the tremor."[33]

La Mountain responded "with the most active and bitter hatred," avowing that Wise was not even a partner in the enterprise.

> Mr. Wise says we could have reached New York had I not neglected to provide myself with extra clothing!! preventing great ascent. I beg his pardon. Had he been less sleepy and more observant during the trip, he would have made no such statement. There were several reasons for the failure. 1. Mr. Wise fell asleep with a tense-rope in his hand, and the nap cost us 5,000 feet of gas. 2. During all the night upper and lower currents were blowing north-east, and carrying us on an angle toward Nova Scotia, though twice, on awakening and rubbing his eyes, Mr. Wise insisted that we were going south-east. 3. During most of the forenoon the local and upper current were east. 4. We had too many passengers. 5. The tornado we encountered was blowing north-east, and we could not rid ourselves of extra ballast to escape it. I did not once descend from any altitude on account of cold, and Mr. Wise knows it....
>
> From first to last I have been robbed of just credit, slandered, ridiculed, and placed in a false position by this man, whom I allowed to accompany me. He has conveyed every where the idea that I was a fellow of some pluck, but of no scientific knowledge of ballooning, and that his wisdom barely compensated for my blunders. This course is my apology for referring to matters I should else have forgotten. — *Lafayette Courier*.[34]

The newspapers quickly latched onto the story, eclipsing the achievement and leaving a sense of unease. On July 16, the New York *Times* noted, "There is trouble between Mr. WISE and Mr. LA MOUNTAIN, the aeronauts, who went up harmoniously together in their balloon, but came down at sword's-points." After publishing La Mountain's challenge to Wise where they would pit their relative prowess in a race from San Francisco to the Atlantic seaboard (Troy, July 11), the Racine *Daily Journal* of July 25 pleaded, "It will not do for these aerial navigators to *fall out!* They should be *above* quarrels.—But this challenge to aerial race is worth considering. Why should they not be backed for $10,000, as in the case of the rival billiard players?" But the Davenport *Daily Gazette*, July 19, spoke for many when it added, "We feel a deep interest in the subject of these aeronautic experiments, and with much regret we have noticed a boyish quarrel between two men, which must injure both without benefiting either, and probably throw great obstacles in the way of this trans–Atlantic experiment. Let them become reconciled and work together."

William Hyde returned home and wrote a detailed account of the journey without commenting on "the objects attained by the results to be anticipated from the voyage."[35] He later went on to have "prolific hair breadth escapes." After his perilous balloon voyage, Hyde came near being shot by a policeman and nearly drowned in the Missouri while giving his dog a bath.[36] O.A. Gager wrote his own card, drawing the less than encouraging conclusion, "there is no reason to believe that the supposed regularly westerly current exists, or that a balloon can be guided at pleasure."[37]

Without doubt, however, the best response to the flight came from Mr. Dawson, editor of the Fort Wayne *Daily Times*. Writing an inspired satire on the event, entitled "Narrow Escape of the Aeronauts!!!" he wrote of the fictitious voyage of the *Belle*, going up from Fort Wayne with the four famous aeronauts "at great expense" to the citizens. Playing on the various published cards, he included such gems as, "La Mountain among other things, requested some one to pay his bill at Dawson's office, if he should die on the trip," and "Mr. Hyde describes his feelings as reaching a point of elevation equal to that produced by six glasses of 'lager.'" He concluded, "their descent was facilitated by the ignition of the aerial ship, by contact with the colored lanterns attached which furnished quite a pyrotechnic exhibition to the b'hoys."[38]

Wise ignored La Mountain's challenge, remarking in a card published in the St. Louis *Democrat* that his thoughts were turned to crossing the Atlantic, "and with a precision much better than was the trip from St. Louis to New York."[39] Well might he take that attitude, for he now seemed to be in sole possession of the titles "hero of 'Ballooning." As such, he traveled to St. Louis, joining his son, Charles E. Wise, who had left Lancaster on the 21st,[40] writing an explanatory note to the *Evening Bulletin*. Remarking that a subscription was underway to defray his expenses, he added that the use of ill-conditioned balloons had hitherto impeded scientific research. They were "no more adapted to the great end of aerial navigation than a pleasure yacht to the navigation of the Pacific Ocean," and promised to shortly bring a properly constructed one into use.[41]

Wise and his son made the elder's 231st flight on July 30 from Washington Square in the *Jupiter*, under the direction of Silas and George Brooks[42] but only reached Ridge Prairie, Illinois. His intent had been to reach Terre Haute, Indianapolis or Lafayette, replenish his supply of gas and continue eastward, thus showing the practicality of stopping and supplying along the way.[43] Had he reached the latter city, it would have gone a long way to proving his theories of wind currents, but the balloon was beaten down by rain.

Wise hurriedly departed for Lafayette, Indiana, where he had been promised $1,000 for an ascent.[44] Meeting his son Charles, they ascended on August 16, but after striking telegraph wires, the balloon rapidly came down. The following day Wise had better luck, landing south of Crawfordsville.[45] Despite Wise's protests, the newspapers declared this flight, like the one from St. Louis, a "failure," because it was announced as a "Voyage to the Atlantic."[46]

La Mountain's Strange Adventure

For a brief time after the failed trans–Atlantic voyage, money seemed to be falling from heaven. Toward the end of July, several capitalists of New York offered La Mountain $5,000 to construct a proper balloon for the voyage,[47] while it was reported the Hon. Thaddeus Stevens offered Wise "sufficient pecuniary aid" for the same end, on condition he ignore La Mountain's challenge of a race.[48]

For his part, La Mountain promised to construct a balloon to take him across the ocean after a spate of flights from upstate New York. Completing a 4-hour inflation from a vacant lot near Stone Street, Watertown, he ascended alone on August 12 (some accounts list it as August 11), in the repaired and significantly reduced *Atlantic*. Due to an insufficient supply of gas, he achieved an abbreviated flight of 12 miles.[49] He made a second flight from Saratoga on September 1, landing near Laxton River, Vermont, having made 100 miles in an hour and a half.[50] La Mountain made one more voyage September 8 from Watertown, landing at North White Creek, Washington County.[51]

The "fate of Thurston" reared its ugly head later that month. On September 22, 1859, La Mountain and his friend, John Haddock of the Watertown *Reformer*, ascended from that city at 5:23 P.M. Within thirty minutes, after reaching an altitude of three and a half miles, the temperature fell from 84° to 24° and they lost sight of earth. Twenty minutes later darkness fell. Having lost all bearings, they eventually descended into a dense wilderness. The balloon caught in a tree and they remained in the car, enduring a cold and rainy night.

Finding it impossible to re-ascend the next morning, they climbed down the tree and started walking, La Mountain bidding a tearful good-bye to his aerostat. In what became one of the strangest balloon adventures ever recorded, the pair traipsed off without provisions or means of making a fire. With only a compass to guide them, the going proved slow and arduous. Finding no humans but only the remnants of an old campfire with a box marked "Mess Por —P.M.— Montreal," they deduced the *Atlantic* had taken them into Canada, but exactly where they could only surmise.

Spending the first night in a lumber shanty, they ate two tiny white frogs for "food." The following day they devised a raft and set out down a stream, hoping to be carried to civilization. Two more days of exposure to cold, hardship and privation brought them to the brink of collapse, La Mountain later writing, "We were dying, starving, perishing by inches. And yet something whispered to me that we should be saved. It seemed as if I co'd hear a voice telling me that I must live to cross the ocean in a balloon." Hearing several gunshots revitalized their spirits and in what may be considered a miraculous escape, they came upon an Indian boy who brought them to a "generous-looking Scotsman" named Angus Cameron who offered all kindly assistance.

The aeronauts discovered they were 150 miles north of Ottawa, having gone 390 miles in a course due north from Watertown. The loss of the balloon cost La Mountain $3,000.[52]

During their absence, various reports surfaced, including a supposed note from La Mountain stating that Haddock had gone insane; another recounted a conversation between La Mountain and his wife, where the aeronaut supposedly said that if she did not hear from him, he had taken his balloon and gone over the Atlantic, not wanting to be done out of the honor by an upstart named "Carlincourt" who was in New York preparing for a trans–Atlantic voyage.[53]

It did not take long before the finger wagging began, primarily by those who observed that the flight path, due north, "strikes a hard blow at the favorite theory of a steady easterly course in the upper strata of the atmosphere."[54] La Mountain was quick to point out that he did encounter the easterly current at an altitude of 2½ miles, and if he had kept to it, he would have been carried out to sea.[55]

John A. Haddock, capitalizing on his fame, went on to become Deputy Clerk of the Assembly in 1860.[56]

Professor Lowe — By Any Other Name

The aeronaut most associated with the Civil War was a late arrival on the scene. Having made a number of unpublicized ascensions as early as 1856, he flew in Ottawa to celebrate the laying of the first Atlantic cable in 1858. Back in the United States, "Carlincourt" went up in the *Excelsior* at Utica, New York, on April 2. Landing at Litchfield, he promised a flight on horseback, which apparently did not come off.[57] By June 14, Carlincourt was still in Utica when his partner, Charles Coe, concluded that Oswego wasn't ready to pay for an ascension, so they "can't have one."[58] The citizens there must have come up with the money, for Coe (referred to as a former associate of Carlincourt and proprietor of the *Excelsior*) went up from that city on July 4.[59]

Carlincourt ascended from Portland, Maine, July 4, 1859, and then dedicated his time to the perfection of the air machine. Monsieur Carlincourt's name came to public attention when he suggested a monument to the late aeronaut Ira Thurston, and later when he attended the Balloon Conference in May 1859. During this period he was considered a French aeronaut, possibly due to the fact he had married a French woman, Leontine Gachon, daughter of an officer of Louis Philippe's Royal Guard.

Carlincourt's actual name was Thaddeus Sobieski Constantine Lowe. He adopted a corruption of his middle name for his early work, and only after his brother, Pembroke G. Lowe, wrote letters of protest, remarking that the change was "sheer affectation and pretense," did he discard the "high-sounding French name."[60]

As Lowe became more renowned, an article entitled "The Explosion" offered his background:

> Prof. Lowe, who has been the round of the newspaper kingdoms as about to cross the Atlantic in a balloon, turns out to be nobody but a man who traveled through the west as a performer in feats of legerdemain. About three years ago, he performed in Freeport one or two evenings, gave out that he would entertain an audience the next evening, but before "daylight dawned," the Hall was cleared of his traps, and Mr. CARLINCOURT was gone. His tools were not all shipped however, and an attachment was issued, his cannon and some other articles seized, so that the rent was secured. He figured for a while in Utica as Prof. somebody, and now in New York as Prof. LOWE. A fee is charged for "looking" at his balloon, and as long as people will be duped, he is willing to take their quarters.[61]

By the time of La Mountain's disastrous voyage from Watertown, Lowe had been constructing a balloon for a voyage across the Atlantic since spring. On September 10, now referred to as "Mr. T. S. C. Lowe, a New Hampshire man, who has made thirty-six ascensions," the aeronaut proposed an October trip in the *City of New York*, projecting a flight to London in 48–64 hours.[62]

The machine was constructed in an open space of grassland five miles distant from the city. On September 22, Lowe was granted temporary use of Reservoir Square by the Board of Alderman,[63] with an account observing, "The profane have not yet been admitted to the knowledge of the mystery which surrounds the mighty heap of cloth and cord, and the jealous eye of a faithful watchman has kept at bay the inquisitive stranger." Six thousand yards of twilled cloth, or nearly eleven miles, went into the construction of the balloon, employing seventeen sewing machines to stitch the pieces together.

The varnish was a secret composition of Lowe's, applied in four coatings to prevent gas leakage. The netting was designed of flax, equal to a resistance of 160 tons; the basket was of rattan, 20 feet in circumference and four feet deep. A lime stove, invented by Mr. Gager, was presented to Lowe expressly for the trip. It was calculated that after outfitting, the balloon would have a lifting power of 19 tons, but Lowe determined to limit the company to eight or ten persons.[64] The cost of the enterprise was estimated at $20,000.[65]

While Albert H. Nicolay ran ads for the sale of "two choice seats" in the car of the

This illustration, taken from *Harper's Weekly*, September 24, 1856, depicts an artist's rendition of how the great balloon might appear on its maiden voyage to cross the Atlantic in 1859. Huge publicity was generated, but unfortunately, the project proved a "bust" and never made the trip (by permission of the National Air and Space Museum, Smithsonian Institution, Washington, D.C.).

balloon *Atlantic*, under the guidance of Professor La Mountain, other notices advised Professor Wise would ascend from Hamilton Park accompanied by reporters and a photographer to take stereoscopic views of the city.[66] All eyes, however, were on Lowe, who had suddenly become a household name. And while there were skeptics ("Most wonderful fact, if he *does* accomplish it, but we cannot help doubting"),[67] others dared not say the project was impossible.

On Saturday, October 29, "Carlincourt" Lowe (now used as a first name, "Carlincourt" would continue to stick to Lowe for some time) brought his mammoth balloon from Hoboken to the ground on Sixth Avenue formerly occupied by the Crystal Palace. He intended to begin inflation immediately, but owing to a mistake in conveying the articles required to Palace Garden[68] and the fact the subterranean pipes in 42nd Street were not fully laid by the Manhattan Gas Company, the process had to be delayed until Monday, when the grounds were to be opened to the public.[69] A fifteen-foot high fence was placed around a huge tent under which the balloon was spread. A gigantic gasometer, in the form of a cylinder, 8 feet in diameter and 12 feet long, capable of registering half a million cubic feet of gas a day, was installed to measure usage.[70] Seven days were required to fill the balloon, at a cost of $3 per thousand cubic feet, estimated to reach $2,275.[71]

Lowe was described as tall and slender, blue eyed, with black hair and moustache, dark complexion (like that of an Indian), possessing a soft, low voice, conversing in a low, gentlemanly manner, looking more like a professional citizen than an intrepid aeronaut. Huge numbers of spectators, including John La Mountain, were reputed to have come to gawk at the proceedings.[72] In a card dated October 29, Lowe attempted to explain his theory of air currents, first developed by Charles Green of London twenty years since. Remarking that the current was found at various altitudes, not merely at a point 2 miles above the earth, he attempted to correct misconceptions about the project by declaring he was not "insane, rash, or a seeker after fame." Placing a thin line between "seven-eights" of those engaged in aerostation who were "not practical investigators, but merely exhibitors," interested only in "pecuniary reward," he justified his own public exhibition by stating the trial would otherwise overtax his personal means.[73] By late November, 30,000 persons were said to have paid their quarter for a sight of the "monster."[74]

All was progressing according to schedule until the night of November 10, when a storm blew up, dragging the balloon and its heavy sand bag weights "like puppet dolls." The balloon was blown into a sharp pole, creating a hole in the muslin, through which gas poured out. In a few minutes, 68,000 feet of gas escaped, giving Lowe $3,000 "in dead loss."[75] Lowe promised to repair the damage and try again.

The Charleston *Mercury* reported that a young businessman from Utica, New York, Mr. Gilbert, was the principal backer of the enterprise. His interest lay in the establishment of a regular balloon express to Europe carrying important business papers and goods ten days faster than if they had gone by steamer. The balloon would then be sent back by steamer and the process repeated. Other investors were listed as Benjamin and Henry Wood of "Col. Wood's Museum of Great Wonders," New York.[76]

The four Wood brothers were interesting and somewhat shadowy characters. Fernando, the chief of the "institution," became mayor of New York City in 1855; Ben was the "great lottery and police man," who had under his influence nearly all the lotteries in the United States; next came Henry, "the minstrel man, former partner of George Christy," who had a Midas touch with everything except the "big balloon." The fourth brother remained out of the limelight, heading the well-known firm of Wood, Miebther & Co.[77]

Receiving a splendid outfit of furs from J.N. Genin of Broadway and presented an anerold and mercurial barometer from Lieutenant Maury on behalf of the United States government, Lowe made an ascent in an experimental balloon, the *Pioneer*, November 17,[78] then announced he would ascend on next Saturday on his trans–Atlantic trip. When the flight did not come off, the New York Board of Councilmen declared the project a "hum-bug," and withdrew his privilege of inflating the balloon in Crystal Palace Square.[79] For all of that, it was reported Lowe cleared $4,000 by the "No Go."[80]

Realizing it best to postpone the flight until next spring, Lowe packed up and moved to Charleston to spend the winter, leaving behind the newspapers to poke fun of his mis-adventures. The last two stanzas of a poem read:

> I've heard it whispered, Mister Lowe —
> I re'ly hope it isn't so —
> I'm sure I do n't pretend to know:
> They *say*—you never meant to go.
>
> A man is lucky that's got brass —
> A man is lucky that's got gas:
> With brass and gas, and backers, too,
> A smart man ought to wriggle through![81]

Not to be forgotten in the "Cross the Atlantic" craze was "Professor" John Steiner. Before Lowe's name became a household word, he, too, proposed crossing the ocean. From Xenia, Ohio, he detailed his plan of constructing an air ship 300 feet long and 80 feet in diameter, tapering toward each end in a cigar-shape, to be propelled by paddles or fans. He wished Congress to aid him "but if he waits for that he will probably never cross the ocean, save in imagination."[82]

Possibly Steiner read the reviews, for he escaped to Toronto, making a flight in the *Europa* on August 25, 1859.[83] He had less fortune in Milwaukee, when his ascension was advertised for October 1, during the final day of the Fair. Steiner showed up with his balloon but inexplicably no arrangements were made to inflate it. Of significance, what did "come off" was a speech by the Honorable "Abram" Lincoln." "Abe Lincoln, of Illinois" gave a written and extemporaneously delivered talk on the benefits of Agricultural Fairs, bringing together large numbers to "form new friendships and strengthen old ones."[84] An interesting addendum to one report mentioned that Lincoln had inquired about a seat in the aerial car to distribute his circulars while sailing through the clouds.[85]

The project was eventually abandoned, and Steiner declared a humbug.[86]

While the World Was Looking Elsewhere

La Mountain and Lowe captured the world's attention with their plights, but other aeronauts were still actively involved in their profession. Charles Coe, late associate of "Car-lincourt," made a double ascent (he in the *Excelsior*) with Silas Brooks (from St. Louis, in the *Comet*) at Ithaca, New York, on August 31.[87] At Rome, New York, on September 29, 1859, Coe discovered the safety valve of his balloon to be "deranged." The balloon exploded and plummeted half a mile, swaying madly before the aeronaut managed to form a parachute from the remnants of the envelope and land atop a tree.

Coe recovered the balloon, ascertaining that the safety valve of his own invention had been damaged before the flight. While in the tree attempting to dislodge the balloon, he fell and broke his wrist, bones protruding from the skin. Two weeks later his arm was amputated to save his life.[88] Silas Brooks stayed in the area, making a flight on September 15 in the *Comet* from Oswego, New York, and arranged for another voyage from Ithaca on Friday, the 23rd.[89]

John A. Light, "the successful young aeronaut," made an ascent at Hagerstown on August 6, and another from Chambersburg on the 27th, letting off a dog in a parachute. Crossing the mountain in a direct line for Gettysburg, he fell into another wind current and landed six miles south in Freedom Township, Adams County.[90] In December 1860, his death (erroneously) was reported, stating his balloon came in contact with some object, by which he was thrown out and broke his neck.[91]

In another dual ascent, James Allen, in his balloon, the *Frolic*, went up on July 4, followed by Samuel King in the *Queen of the Air* from Boston Common. Allen left his passenger, Mrs. Allen (the aeronaut's sister-in-law), near the Agricultural grounds and reascended, coming down in Dorchester.[92] By July, Allen and King had determined on a three-balloon race with Mr. Turner of New Orleans (alternately spelled "Turrene," "Turene" and "Turrenne") if they could raise $500 for expenses. The idea of a race was abandoned and on August 28, Allen went up from Newport but was thrown out by high winds; the following day King and Turner ascended in the *Louisiana*, landing beyond Fairhaven.[93]

"Little ascensions" of the period included the "balloon editor" of the Cincinnati *Gazette*, J.C. Bellman from Dayton, Ohio[94]; George Burford (the "enterprising pyrotechnist, taxidermist and fruit seller") at Racine[95]; and Q.E. (Quince) Andrews (who would later team with Charles Coe), who ascended from Seneca Falls, New York on October 6, traveling 50 miles in 45 minutes.[96] Expanding the scope of aerostation, the Navy sent a force to investigate the possibility of constructing a shipping canal across the Isthmus of Darien, sending a balloon and experienced aeronaut for the purpose of making aerial observations.[97]

For those keeping track, a balloon containing 18,000 feet of gas cost between $300–$350. By 1859, there were ten or twelve major balloonists in the United States, of whom John Wise was the oldest, "though perhaps not the *wise*-est."[98]

30

Higher Than Anyone Had Gone Before

*Let the reader imagine that he has been riding on the engine, with the fire roaring
in the furnace, has suddenly leaped into the air, and he will get some faint notion
of the situation.*[1]

In Europe, the decade of the 1850s reflected an uneasiness toward aerostation and a
divide between those interested primarily in performing and others dedicated to the pursuit
of science. While not completely diverse, their alliance was an uneasy one, occasionally
crossing but never reconciled. With the newness of ballooning worn off, newspapers generally
considered ascensions as little more than local concerns, leaving aeronauts to capture headlines where they could — often at greater risk, or from some voyage gone awry.

Such was the case in the summer of 1853, when the Godard brothers ascended from
the Champs Elysées, one in the balloon and the other in his parachute. The gymnast dangling
from the aerostat narrowly avoided contact with the trees before a proper height was
obtained. On discharge, his contrivance swung so wildly the oscillations became frightful.
The parachute eventually fell into the Seine where Godard was rescued.

An eyewitness offered an insightful reflection of the times:

> I knew that he was an enthusiast in his profession, and would be glad to educe good from
> it if he could. I knew he was daring, cool, skillful, patient. But I could not find a motive
> sufficient to excuse and justify such exposure and personal risk. The Hippodrome had paid
> him five hundred francs for the descent, and next Sunday, for five hundred francs more, he
> will consent to run the same risk, or a worse risk, again. I could have wished that he had
> saved a woman from the flames — that he had rescued some one from sudden death, or that
> he had discovered a new planet when suspended in mid–sky,— something to ennoble his
> courage, to dignify the risk, to palliate the coolness of nerve with which he had affronted
> the perils of the air.[2]

In America, however, where enthusiasm had not dwindled, the Godards were considered
"the acme of aerostatic achievement" when one descended in a parachute on horseback.[3]

Lamenting the use of balloons for no greater good than public entertainment and dis-
tressed by the haphazard results of scientific experiments, the French Academy of Science
directed Messieurs Arago and Launay to draw up a program of aeronautic experiments. The
famed balloonist M. Poitevin offered his entire catalog of aerostatic material, including four
immense balloons,[4] but received little encouragement. Departing for St. Petersburg, he left
behind his famous aeronaut pony (see chapter 26), which was subsequently sold for $20
for back upkeep. By 1855, Poitevin had relocated to Italy, reduced to charging $4 for tethered

balloon rides. The sad career of the once-popular balloonist ended in September 1858, when he drowned in the sea near Malaga, Spain.[5] Left on her own, Madame Poitevin, billed as "the balloon woman," made an ascent at Rouen, France, in September 1859.[6] On a more quasi-scientific voyage, in July 1859, M. Garvini traveled in an aerial machine, "part balloon, and part flying machine," from Paris to Algiers and back, 15,000 miles from his starting point, in eighteen hours, making 83 miles per hour.[7]

By 1853, with the Crimean War in the headlines, talk centered around the idea of discharging missiles from the sky, with Louis and Eugene Godard volunteering their expertise.[8] Experiments were made at Vincennes but proved unsuccessful.[9]

June 1859 found the two Godard brothers in Italy, first at Peschiera reconnoitering enemy positions from a balloon and then at Castelnedolo. Difficulties in inflation, danger to the aeronauts and the near impossibility of transmitting information to commanders on the ground, even with telegraph wires attached to the aerostat, offset the usefulness of balloons during battle.[10]

In late November 1858, the famous French photographer Félix Tournachon (better known as "Nadar") became the first person to take aerial photographs in a balloon. Ascending with Godard from Paris, he achieved the goal of capturing the city and surrounding countryside from a bird's eye view.[11]

The big news in 1863 was the autumn completion of Nadar's luxury balloon, *Le Géant*. The car of the monster balloon was fitted with glass windows and every comfort for the wealthy and famous. The first flight occurred on October 9, but the passengers proved so rowdy, tossing glasses and champagne bottles overboard, that the aeronaut was forced to publish the *Reglement de Bord*, or rules and regulations by which it was hoped to avoid future accidents.[12]

The second flight occurred on Sunday, October 18. Among the passengers were Nadar and his wife, the Prince of Wittgenstein and the Princes de la Tour Auvergne (who paid 1,000 francs for the privilege), M. Delessert, the two Godard brothers, M. Tirion (great-grandson of Montgolfier), M. De St. Félix and Alexander Chevalier, the aeronaut. The party ascended from the Champ de Mars, Paris.[13]

The balloon passed Erquelines, on the Belgian frontier,[14] but in descending, was caught in a gale and blown across a railway line in the path of an oncoming train. The engineer was able to brake and *Le Géant* escaped, rebounding ten miles before coming to ground in a small wood at Hanover. Nadar, the Princess, St. Félix and Delessert were injured, while Chevalier sustained broken bones.[15]

The Limit of Human Existence

On September 5, 1862, James Glaisher, an English meteorologist, and aeronaut Henry Coxwell performed one of the most extraordinary feats in aerostation when they ascended from Wolverhampton, attempting to reach a higher altitude than any before.

At the height of two miles they reported the temperature had fallen to the freezing point; at three miles it reached 13°; at four miles, the thermometer read 8° and at five miles it registered -2°. At the calculated elevation of 5 miles, Glaisher's eyesight failed and he could not read the instruments; shortly thereafter he could not hold up his head. Coxwell, returning from the ring, lost the use of his hands, which, when inspected, were nearly black. Fighting off the feeling of insensibility, he attempted to open the valve. Unable to move his fingers, he grabbed the line between his teeth and pulled until the balloon took a turn downward.

The meteorologist determined that "five miles from the earth is very nearly the limit of human existence," concluding, "whenever the barometer reading falls as low as 11 inches, open the valve at once; the increased information to be obtained is not commensurate with the increased risk."[16]

James Glaisher began the season of 1863 by ascending on March 31 from the Sydenham Crystal Palace near London.[17] He made his eleventh voyage on June 26, reaching an altitude of four miles. He ascended again from Wolverhampton on September 23, 1863.[18] Glaisher continued his aeronautic scientific experiments over the next several years, making night ascensions on October 2 and December 2, 1866. The observations he made on clouds added considerably to the 19th century conception of atmosphere and weather.

Henry Coxwell also continued to fly, making a voyage from the Crystal Palace in the fall of 1863[19] and from Belfast, Ireland, in the summer of 1865, losing his balloon after a difficult landing.[20]

Eugene Godard left France for England where he set up shop at Cremorne Gardens in July 1864, with his Montgolfier-type "fire balloon," the *Eagle*. Bragged to be larger and grander than Nadar's "Giant" balloon, it was 118 feet; 7 inches in height; 95 feet, 9 inches in circumference, 2,005 pounds in weight; with 498,556 cubic feet in contents. Three cylinders were designed by Godard to counteract the radiated heat upon the occupants of the car. The fuel burned was rye straw compressed into blocks. Inflation required between 30–45 minutes.

On July 20, Godard ascended with three passengers. Despite precautions, the heat from the fire proved "almost painful," and "at no time did that ugly, roaring, crackling clamor cease!" Never achieving more than half a mile altitude, Godard brought it down in a "nasty dive."[21]

31

Great Plans, Tragedies and a Civil War

We regard every man in our midst an enemy to the South who does not boldly declare that he or she believes African slavery to be a social, moral, and political blessing.[1]

Little was heard of T. S. C. Lowe during the winter of 1859–60, which he spent in Charleston, but he maintained plans for a trans–Atlantic crossing in the spring with the *City of New York* balloon, "when, as everything is in the most complete and perfect order, I shall (my life and health being spared) solve the problem."[2]

Charleston was a peculiar destination for the aeronaut, and if Lowe went south to please his backers, the trip did not have the desired effect. On June 8, he wrote a card to the New York *Times*, laying the blame for his failure of 1859 on those with a pecuniary interest. Against his wishes but according to his contract, he permitted an exhibition to be opened in his name in an effort to raise money for the investors. After the disaster on November 18, he took it upon himself to suspend operations. He added that many people supposed he had made a fortune out of the exhibition; aside from the "comparatively small sum" he did make, the rest went to repay those involved in the enterprise.

These investors promised him continued support, at least as far as paying for the gas, but soon reneged, throwing him wholly upon his own resources. "By diligent perseverance," he found the chance whereby he realized his dream, and promised a flight in the summer.[3]

In May 1860, the Board of Aldermen at Philadelphia received a request to give a balloon exhibition in the presence of visiting Japanese ambassadors.[4] William Paullin was chosen to give a private performance at the expense of the city.[5] At some point, Lowe was also invited to participate. Two weeks later, after unconscionable delays waiting for the delegation to arrive on the scene for the ascensions (it was later explained they were shopping and touring the Mint), representatives of the Princes finally showed up and the aeronauts "Let her rip." The dual ascensions were successful, although there were considerable complaints about sand from ballast bags nearly striking the spectators and covering everyone with dust.[6] The cost for the ascension was placed at $150.[7]

Still preparing for his trans–Atlantic flight, Lowe made an ascension from Philadelphia on June 29.[8] The flight was a success, but his return to the glory held the previous summer was a long way off. John Wise kept in touch with Lowe during 1860, but he had his own projects underway. In an interesting opinion published at the tail end of 1859, Wise discussed his idea for a balloon made of sheet copper. He calculated that at a weight of one pound per square foot, he could design a vessel with a lifting power of over two million pounds.[9]

By January 1860, reports stated that Wise was engaged in construction of a balloon to be flown from Kingston, Canada, May 24, the Queen's birthday, and that he had put forth plans to ascend from Boston in a trans–Atlantic voyage to start from that city July 4. John La Mountain had not forgotten his dream of crossing the ocean, either, but concentrated his efforts toward the creation of four new balloons at Lansingburgh, New York, to be used for local ascensions.[10] By March, reports out of Boston stated that Wise and La Mountain both proposed trans–Atlantic trips from that city, the former to London (starting July 4) and the latter to Paris in May. La Mountain asked the city for $4,000 and Wise requested $6,000.[11]

By April, Wise was in New York promoting the construction of a huge balloon. His success rode on the fact he "was no Professor Lowe."[12] On April 19 he ascended from Palace Garden in the *Ganymede* in front of several thousand spectators. Assisting the balloonist were La Mountain and a 25-year-old man named Augustus M. Conner (occasionally referred to as "O'Conner" and "Connee"). Professor Lowe and P. T. Barnum were mentioned as being spectators.[13]

Conner, a pupil of John Wise and from whom he bought his balloon, was scheduled to make his first solo ascent in the *Venus*. Despite violent gusts of wind he insisted on going up. No sooner had the aerostat ascended when it was dashed against a concert saloon facing Palace Garden. The basket was hurled against a skylight, collapsing the balloon. Conner was discovered on the roof with internal injuries. He remained insensible and expired at 11 P.M. that night. Conner's wife, who witnessed the calamity, might have shared the same fate, for it had been her intention to go up with her husband, had the machine possessed enough ascending power. She was terribly shocked at witnessing the tragedy and fell to the ground in a faint.[14]

Such a tragic death did not reflect positively on Wise, who had not only instructed Conner but had sold him the clearly unserviceable *Venus*. In fact, Conner had commenced a suit against the professor, alleging that their contract called for Wise to supply a machine capable of accommodating two persons. Before making his fateful voyage, he was reputed to have told Wise, "I'm going up today, and I suppose you'll be glad if I never come back." Whether fabricated or not, the story goes on to tell of a hole being found in the balloon prior to ascent. The aeronaut supposedly tied it up with a piece of twine, and "laughingly said, 'it might cause the balloon to burst and spill him out.'"[15]

In his own defense, Wise declared Conner had been a headstrong pupil who chose to use his own, inadequate network, rather than the one supplied with the balloon.[16] On June 5, Wise ascended from Palace Garden in the *Ganymede* as a benefit for Conner's family.[17]

On August 15, another of Wise's pupils, Mr. O.G. Maynard, made a successful ascension under the supervision of George Wise (John's son) from Palace Garden in the new balloon *Skylark*. He landed safely on Long Island.[18]

Leaving New York behind and in the midst of secessionist talk throughout the country, Wise went to Petersburg, Virginia, making an ascent on September 20. When attempting to descend, a hole at the top of the balloon split, causing the balloon to strike the ground with terrible force. He escaped with only slight injury.[19] It was no wonder that life insurance companies began inserting clauses in their policies, prohibiting subscribers from risking their necks by "ballooning or tight rope performances."[20]

Professor Lowe and Other Balloonists of Notoriety

On July 23, 1860, the New York *Times* reported that T. S. C. Lowe was in Philadelphia "and had actually persuaded some of the citizens to advance him funds" for his trans–

Atlantic flight. By September, the newspapers were writing, "We see that Prof. Lowe, of balloon notoriety, has turned up again. In Philadelphia this time-when we last heard from him he was in Charleston, S. C."[21] Such skepticism did not bode well for the venture, but worse followed. On September 7, Lowe began inflating his balloon at the Point Breeze Gas Works, Philadelphia, proposing to start his oceanic voyage the following day.

In a letter penned September 9, John Wise remarked to Lowe that he considered the plan and machinery "too incongruous," and thus his refusal to accompany him on the proposed flight in 1859. He added that in a conversation with William Paullin he learned the balloon was "somewhat dilapidated" and unfit for use with the ponderous machinery.[22] The letter came too late to be of use, however. On September 8, high wind caused the balloon to burst. "Reporters, and citizens generally, are indignant."[23] Thus put an end to the grand scheme that merited a mere five lines in the New York *Times*.

Like Wise and La Mountain before him, the affair reduced Lowe to the status of barnstormer. On the eve of Civil War he found himself in Albany, September 1, 1860, making a balloon flight from the County Fair Grounds. The brief mention in the newspaper sandwiched the notice between the resignation of the President's private secretary and counterfeit $3 bills being circulated in New York City.[24]

La Mountain, lost in the shuffle of the more "newsworthy" aeronauts, made small ascensions from Troy, New York, on July 4; a flight in celebration of the Battle of Bennington, in Vermont on August 16; an ascent in the *Atlantic* from Albany on September 21. This proved to be somewhat more than an adventure, as he was caught in a tornado, thrown out of the car and knocked unconscious for half an hour. On October 26, he completed his year with a successful trip from Potsdam, New York.[25]

Although being declared a "humbug," John Steiner returned to Milwaukee, Home of the Non-Ascents, for the 4th of July celebrations of 1860. This time, everything went as planned, except for the poor remuneration Steiner received from the gate. The flight in the *Europa* (his 89th overall) was described as "sublime" and the event of the day. The Professor landed in Lake Michigan, but managed to re-ascend after detaching the car, eventually reaching shore at Kalamazoo, Michigan. The basket floated in the following day but was plundered of its contents.[26]

Earlier in 1860, Richard Wells ascended from New York, nearly losing his life when the wind blew his balloon into the kitchen of Coosa Hall. Wells, by that time hanging by his hands, leapt onto the roof just as the machine rebounded away, escaping certain death.[27] At the end of August he ascended from Richmond, Virginia, in a caloric balloon.[28] He flew again from the same city in November, traveling 96 miles in 2 hours.[29]

Charles Cevor, another of Wise's pupils (who, like Wells, would later offer his services to the Confederacy), ascended from Savannah, Georgia, March 16. Cevor descended into Callaboga Sound, where he was rescued after a flight of 13 minutes, covering 40 miles. The balloon, worth $700, was subsequently blown out to sea and lost.[30] The citizens gave the aeronaut $300 toward replacing it, of which $150 was donated by the Central Railroad Company, Cevor being a former railroad man.[31]

The "air line" of Messrs. King and Allen unexpectedly dropped in on the citizens of Portsmouth during a trip from Providence, in June 1860.[32] It had been their plan, while aloft, to duplicate the efforts of the French photographer Nadar, who, in 1860 (see chapter 30), became the first person to successfully take aerial images from a balloon. Their attempt proved unsuccessful, but they repeated it from Boston in October aboard the *Queen of the Air*. Accompanied by Mr. Black, an eminent photographer of the firm of Black &

Batchelder, they first tried a tethered ascent, then set themselves free in order to obtain a wider field.

Gas flowing from the neck of the balloon neutralized the effect of light and turned the coating on the glass plate a dark brown color. Neutralizing the effect by reaching a high altitude, Black created two amazingly sharp photographic images.

In writing of this voyage, Samuel A. King noted that neither he nor his partner, James Allen, believed a balloon could be successfully navigated with any greater precision than had already been done. "The worse than foolhardy scheme of crossing the Atlantic is another overreach of these visionaries, and can never be accomplished while the laws of nature remain the same." But, he continued, voyages such as the one just accomplished, proved balloons could be made useful when employed in a legitimate manner.[33]

Samuel Wilson, whose name became synonymous with the balloon accident involving two children at Centralia, performed at Chicago and Pittsburg before ascending at Harrisburg on August 4, 1860. When no word was heard from him, fears were entertained for his safety. It was ultimately discovered that Wilson managed a landing near Butler, sustaining no material injury but losing his balloon.[34]

Proving that he, too, had been bitten by the trans–Atlantic bug, Wilson offered to make an oceanic voyage from Boston if the gas company could supply sufficient gas. For the trip he had prepared the *Great Western* and the *American Eagle*.[35] Not to be left out, Charles C. Coe announced his plans to make a balloon voyage to Europe in October 1860, bragging his monster balloon, the *United States*, was "three times larger than Lowe's."[36] Neither plan got off the ground.

Another one of the "ten or twelve balloonists in the United States," Silas Brooks "left our mundane sphere" to soar among the clouds. Avoiding the waters of the Wallkill, he maneuvered the machine to descend in full view of his starting point, a mile east of Phillipsburg. He made another voyage in the *Eclipse* September 4, using manufactured hydrogen gas.[37]

In light of the pending crisis in the United States, it is peculiar the Brooks brothers, Silas and George, wrote to Garibaldi, offering their services "for the purpose of reconnoitering the positions of the Neapolitans." They received a personal letter from Garibaldi accepting their services, and were to leave for Italy in November.[38]

The Coming War

Abraham Lincoln ran for President of the United States amid the terrible threat of Southern secession. As American as speeches, bonfires, rockets and fireworks, balloons were part of the campaigning; many unmanned vessels were sent "towards the North Star" with red, white and blue ribbons, inscribed with such sentiments as "Honest Old Abe."[39]

After his monumental victory, balloons were also used in celebration, so it was perhaps apropos that they should have been enlisted into the service of their country. Much has been written about the use of balloons during the Civil War: Lowe, Wise, La Mountain, James Allen and William Paullin offered their services to the Stars and Stripes; Charles Cevor and Richard Wells went with the Stars and Bars. After limited success and much controversy, a 13-word sentence appeared in the newspaper:

> Washington, June 19.— The Aeronautic corps of the army of the Potomac has been dispersed with.[40]

Possibly the best summary appeared in the New York *Times*, July 12, 1863.

Use of Balloons in War. — An item of news, received from Washington a short time since, was to the effect that the "Aeronautic Corps" of the Army of the Potomac had been dispensed with, and the balloons and inflating apparatus had been sent back to that city. It does not appear whether it is intended, but it is evidently implied by the form in which this announcement is made, that balloons have been found of no value in the conduct of military operations, or at least not of sufficient value to justify the expense and trouble of them. This will excite some surprise, for the public has been led to put considerable confidence in balloon reconnoisances from facts heretofore given....

An Aeronautic corps was organized in the early months of the war, and it has followed the army in all its wanderings, from the Potomac to the Peninsula and back again, and all through the Maryland and Rappahannock campaigns, until last week, when it appears to have been sent to the rear in disgrace.... It will be found, perhaps, that the use of balloons has not been wholly barren of results, and that the partial failure, if such is the final judgment of our military leaders, is owing to the heavily wooded character of the State of Virginia, where they have been used, whose dense forests screen so much of the movements of armies from view.

There are three specific achievements, we now call to mind, of the Aeronautic corps of the Army of the Potomac. 1. It was a balloon reconnaissance that first made known the abandonment by the rebels of the batteries that had so long blockaded the lower Potomac. 2. It was by means of balloon reconnoissances that the configuration and strength of the rebel works at Yorktown were obtained, and McClellan's approaches governed. 3. And it was by the same important aid, by the acknowledgment of Gen. McClellan, that the battle of Fair Oaks was fought and won. The aid of balloons in this great struggle was of incalculable value.... An incident of aeronautic and telegraphic achievement marked the close of the battle of Fair Oaks.

The balloons advanced with the army to the front of Richmond, and hovering in the air day after day, seemed to the anxious people of the long beleaguered city the sure presages of an evil fate soon to burst upon their devoted town. The presence of these aerial observatories never failed to rouse the ire of rebel artillerists, whether on the Potomac, Chickahominy or Rappahannock; and many a rifled cannon shot has been sent hurtling through the air in the effort to puncture them. From first to last, however, they have been unharmed, and no loss of life, it is believed, has attended their use in all the time of their employment by the Army of the Potomac.

32

Civilian Ballooning During and After the Civil War

The necessary frailty of the air chariot, the possibly hidden defects in the material,
the treachery of the upper air currents, the inevitably fatal results of any accident—
make the life of the aeronaut one of romantic peril.[1]

Early in the War, T. S. C. Lowe offered his professional services to the Union, and under his direction the Balloon Corps was organized. On October 11 he recruited William Paullin. John Steiner joined in December 1861, followed by Ezra Allen (brother of James) in January 1862; James followed in March. John La Mountain, whose relationship with Lowe had been strained to the breaking point, was not considered. He applied independently, securing personal testimonials and offering to supply his own balloon. Although not officially part of the Army, he was summoned by General Benjamin Butler to bring his apparatus to Fortress Monroe, Virginia.

La Mountain overestimated his readiness to supply the requisite equipment, including a portable apparatus for inflating balloons in the field, and significant difficulties arose. On July 24 he did make an ascension near Hampton, and his flight of July 31 is considered the first effective use of observation balloons in the American Army.[2] The manufacture of hydrogen gas continued to be a serious drawback. When his brother Edward, also an aeronaut, applied to join him in June, his application was ignored.

General Fitz John Porter, himself an advocate of balloon reconnaissance, was ordered to try and reconcile La Mountain and Lowe, but animosity and personal jealousy persisted and the two never worked together. The government eventually bought La Mountain's two balloons, *Atlantic* and *Saratoga*, but on November 11, the *Saratoga*, the larger of the two, was lost due to inexperience of the crew and inclement weather. La Mountain was eventually given charge of a company he could train, but his relationship with Lowe continued to deteriorate. Lowe's appointment as Chief Aeronaut did not improve the situation, and on February 19, General McClellan issued orders that La Mountain be dismissed. It was an unfortunate end to a man who had dedicated great energy to the cause.

La Mountain returned to New York. On March 27, 1867, a report mentioned he had recently been divorced from his wife, whom he had met while taking her up in a balloon.[3] Two years later a short notice appeared that he was busily engaged in Troy manufacturing a balloon to carry him across the Atlantic,[4] but the trip never came off.

John La Mountain died at South Bend, Indiana, February 14, 1870. His obituary stated his life "was full of daring adventures and of incidents, which were frequently more interesting than agreeable." Calling him "among the most fearless aeronauts in this or in any other country," it added, "He was compelled to make balloon ascensions for the public amusement as a means of support, but he hoped to make his experiments useful in the advance of science and the development of meteorological theories.... He finally died poor at the age of 41."[5]

William Paullin was assigned to General William Hooker's troops at Budd's Ferry on the lower Potomac. After a number of ascensions, Lowe discharged him in January 1862 for neglect of duty by running an ambrotype business on the side. He returned to civilian life and abandoned ballooning.

The other aeronauts engaged by Lowe for his Balloon Corps were John B. Starkweather of Boston, Ebenezer Mason, Jr., of Troy, New York; Ebenezer Seaver of Philadelphia, John R. Dickinson and Jacob C. Freno. None were extensively experienced in aerostation although each played his part in the War. Starkweather joined in November 1861 and served under Brigadier General Thomas Sherman at Port Royal, South Carolina until mid–summer, 1862. In 1863 he was reassigned to General Quincy Gillmore at Charleston. He resigned after his duties were completed. Mason was a balloon-maker whose his first assignment was to oversee the construction of two army vessels, the *Eagle* and the *Excelsior*. During the spring of 1862 he accompanied Lowe to the Peninsula. When he complained about his salary being a month and a half overdue, Lowe dismissed him.

Seaver joined in November 1861 and served along the Potomac lines until being sent to replace Paullin at Budd's Ferry. Like Mason, he was dismissed during the "strike for pay."

Dickinson remains an unknown, garnering only one mention in a dispatch as an assistant in charge of the *Union* balloon at Washington. Freno, originally enlisting as a soldier, was charged with cowardice at Harper's Ferry and promptly applied to Lowe, with whom he was familiar before the War. He credibly served along the Potomac lines but was dismissed by Lowe for gambling and disloyal sentiments. He returned to Washington, maliciously damaging the balloon *Washington* being stored there for overhaul.[6]

John Steiner served under Brigadier General Charles Stone's Corps of Observation on the Upper Potomac until February 1862, when he was ordered to report to Cairo, Illinois, where he made several ascensions at Island No. 10. His service, although valuable, went largely ignored by his superiors, and more than anything, proved the futility of utilizing aerial observations without the support or interest of the commanders. He returned to the Army of the Potomac and resigned in December 1862 because of difficulty in receiving his pay.[7]

"A Man in a Mighty Hard Fix"

In the early days of the war, civilian interest was centered on a quick and decisive victory. As the months dragged into years, their interest if not their spirits waned, and they needed respite from the daily grind. After the disburdenment of the Balloon Corps in 1863, it seemed an appropriate time to renew that form of entertainment. It was not long before the same names that appeared with such regularity in the newspapers before 1860, populated the print columns once again.

By the first week in July 1863, John Steiner returned to his civilian pursuits with the *Hercules*. From his base in Milwaukee, he traveled across the state, offering exhibitions for

$400.[8] On August 21 from Milwaukee, Steiner took up the German, Count de Zeppelin.[9] Zeppelin was very taken with Steiner's ideas, particularly his design for a new type of reconnaissance craft less susceptible to the varieties of wind. Steiner's plan called for a small, two-person craft of a long, thin shape. With the addition of a strong rudder, he felt he could effectively navigate the balloon. Over half a century later, Zeppelin would recall his visit with Steiner and write that this was when the idea of aerial navigation and the first "Zeppelin" came to him.[10]

Steiner also used the *Star of the West*, a balloon he constructed the previous winter, composed of silk oilcloth, 95 feet in circumference. During a voyage from Dubuque in November 1863, the valve cord broke, leaving the balloon unmanageable. Landing in a field and calling for help, a farmer inquired, "Vot in hell you bees?" to which he replied, "A *man* in a mighty hard fix." The answer did the trick and help was forthcoming.[11]

Steiner and his wife opened the 1864 season at Fort Wayne. Editor/owner Dawson of the *Daily Times* became his champion, just as he had done for the ill-fated "humbug Pusey" in 1856 (see chapter 27). The flight went off well and he spent the next several summers giving "army ascensions" and free flight in the *General Grant*.[12]

In September 1867, after receiving his balloon, the *City of New York*, in damaged condition, Steiner purchased 342 yards of canvas from Johnson & Co. and his wife began sewing it on a Wilcox & Gibbs Sewing machine, while at the same time taking care of her six month old child. In less than three days the balloon was finished; it was varnished the following day and christened the *First National*.[13]

Receiving an invitation to make an ascension in Milwaukee on July 4, 1871, Steiner ordered his balloon from Chicago, where it had been kept in storage. Upon receipt, however, he discovered it had been consumed by spontaneous combustion.[14] Creating an entirely new balloon named the *City of Milwaukee*, he completed his 308th flight, being borne directly over Lake Michigan. When no word was heard from him it was feared he had fallen into the water and drowned, but fortunately, he managed a safe landing near Kalamazoo, two hundred miles away.[15]

After assisting in the inflation of the Wise-Donaldson trans–Atlantic *Daily Graphic* in September 1873, Steiner appeared in Chicago with his own experimental balloon being tested for an ocean voyage. He was not sanguine that any practical good could come from air navigation, or that ocean trips could be accomplished except at particular times, but he was willing to make the trip "in good faith."[16] The cost was borne by a "party of scientific gentlemen"[17] from the Meteorological Society of Philadelphia. Trials were set for June 19 and 23, in that city, but Steiner opted to take the monster balloon *Trans–Atlantic* to Milwaukee, where it was put on exhibition.

The flight on July 7 was a limited success. The ascension was perfect, but with the heavy load and inferior gas, Steiner and his passengers only traveled seventeen miles, far short of the advertised Atlantic Coast voyage.[18]

"A Time for All Things"

In 1866, Emperor Dom Pedro offered T. S. C. Lowe the opportunity of going to Brazil and taking charge of a Balloon Corps. Brazil, Argentina and Uruguay were at war with Paraguay and wished to use aerostats for military purposes. Lowe turned the offer down, but suggested James and Ezra Allen might accept the position.[19] They did, and after making hundreds of flights for the cause and receiving the appreciation of Dom Pedro, returned to the United States by April 1868. Not long after they dissolved their partnership.

Through 1869–72 James Allen worked the northeastern states. On July 4, 1871, he was in Troy, New York, marking his 250th voyage in the new aerial ship *Jupiter Olympus*.[20] Although he anticipated a three-day trip, the balloon landed in Greenfield that evening. The same day James K. Allen, his son, made his first solo ascent in a small balloon named *Empyrean*, landing at Putnam, having traveled 100 miles in two hours.[21] Ezra Allen also worked the holiday, ascending from Boston with Professor George A. Rogers, C. W. Emerson of the Boston *Herald* and F. W. Whiteman of Cambridge.[22] (Ten years later, Professor Rogers, of Malden, was fatally injured at Lynn Beach, Massachusetts, after falling 100 feet from his balloon.)[23]

Samuel King, who had been omitted by Lowe when he assembled his Balloon Corps, applied for military work in the summer of 1862, but no action was taken on his application. Resuming his civilian occupation, he ascended from Boston Common on Independence Day, 1863, in *The Star Spangled Banner*.[24] In November, proving the war was still very much on everyone's minds, he left Bangor, Maine, and observed along his trip a woman ushering her children into the house, crying, "There's one of Jeff. Davis's big bomb shells."[25]

Another flight, this time from Bangor, Maine, had an unintentionally amusing ending. Ascending in August 1869, the balloon landed in a deserted field after dark. Calling for help, a man approached. Failing to secure the rope, he shouted to his companions, "Say! you blasted, golldurned, cowardly sneaks, come out and help me: the darned thing 'ill kill me." Never having heard of a balloon, the backwoodsmen slowly ventured forth, one inquiring, "Ah yer skedadlers?" King assured him they were not, and they eventually assisted in tying down the "big coach."[26] King went on to make numerous flights in the *Hyperion* and the *Aurora*.

After his war service, Lowe returned to his civilian pursuits in Philadelphia. Perhaps trying to be amusing, he sullied his name when he dropped a straw figure of a man from his balloon, frightening those below who believed it real.[27] By 1865 he was advertising ascensions in his "Army Balloon" from Central Park, New York, "every day and evening," by which spectators could arise 1,000 feet for a view of the city[28] for "$15 a head."[29] During this time he fitted up a bridal car, and on November 9, Miss Mary West Jenkins (other accounts give her name as "Allen") of St. Louis and Dr. J. F. Boynton of Syracuse went through a ceremony, although having actually been married the day previous.[30]

For several years, "Balloon Weddings" became the rage, and small notices of nuptials being performed "in the region of the clouds" were found from Bennington to Fort Wayne. In most cases, ministers took the precaution of having the aerostats firmly tethered before reading the service. The New York *Times* drolly noted, "the next thing in order is a balloon funeral."[31]

Lowe opened the ballooning season on June 20, 1866, from his Amphitheatre on Fifth Avenue, promising a brilliant year, replete with new sensations, including the tightrope specialist Harry Leslie, of Niagara Falls fame, performing feats on ropes suspended from the vessel. Lowe's war balloon, the *Washington* (which he purchased from the government as war surplus), was not capable of generating sufficient ascending power for the entertainments, so he arranged for the manufacture of pure hydrogen on the premises. Aside from Leslie's performances, most of Lowe's ballooning consisted of tethered flights in which he took up eight to ten persons at one time. He made aerial flights on July 4 and 8 and the same month inaugurated a journal called the *Balloon Pictorial*.[32] A less than generous review

"Balloon ascension in Binghamton, New York, 1865. After the Balloon Corps was disbanded in 1863, all but one of the military aeronauts went back to civilian ballooning. Although much of the freshness had gone out of the sport, crowds continued to be attracted by the sight of a brightly colored globe floating across the sky. In this photograph, T.S.C. Lowe sails over the countryside in the *United States* (by permission of the National Air and Space Museum, Smithsonian Institution, Washington, D.C.).

stated, "Professor Lowe, the balloon man, issued a pictorial of the same size as Harper's, devoted to glorifying Lowe, and illustrating the indefinite 'science' of ballooning."[33]

The remainder of the summer he spent giving tethered ascensions, losing one balloon that was torn from its moorings and blew up in Central Park during a storm.[34] Later that year Lowe abandoned aerostation and went into other business opportunities. In 1873, it was reported he had introduced to the South a new industry — the manufacture of ice by artificial means, establishing several ice factories in Atlanta, Charleston and New Orleans.[35]

John Wise also offered his services to the Union, and after having constructed a balloon for reconnaissance, he was ordered to report to General McDowell's headquarters on July

19, 1861. Delays prevented him from moving until the 21st, by which time the (First) Battle of Manassas (Bull Run) had already been fought. Wise and his son Charles continued on their way but when attempting to move the inflated balloon through a narrow passage (there being no inflation apparatus at the front), the envelope was torn and the gas escaped. In June, Wise proposed a system of field inflation using the water decomposition method first employed by Captain Coutelle 67 years before, but ultimately it was considered too cumbersome and expensive. After repeated efforts to establish himself as a military aeronaut, Wise left Washington on August 13, 1861, bitterly disappointed. At Lancaster he raised a cavalry regiment but soon after his health declined and he resigned.[36] Between his army service and 1869, Wise rarely made balloon ascensions.

Resurfacing in the summer of 1869, Wise ascended from Memphis, confirming his theory that when ascending, a balloon always made a whirling motion from right to left; when descending, from left to right; and at equilibrium it remained stationary. He also repeated his recommendation that anyone suffering from disorders of the stomach or liver seek relief by aerial voyages. A confirmed dyspeptic before he began his career, Wise evinced a complete medical cure from his occupation.[37]

By the fall of 1869 John Wise was traveling with his son, Charles E. Wise. Of particular note was the latter's ascension from Lancaster on September 18. Having two vacant seats in the *Jupiter*, Wise offered them for sale and received two $50 bids. A third party resolved to go up "if the price rose as high as a thousand dollars"; accordingly, an offer was made, to which Wise requested payment. His wife, Louisa, the high bidder, replied that she had paid in advance, "by numerous charges against him for darning stockings and sewing on his buttons for ten years past." He made no appeal, and she accompanied him on the voyage. They landed safely nine miles distant after a trip of one hour and ten minutes, proving there was "a time for all things."[38]

Professor John Wise ascended from Chicago on July 4, 1870, making his 444th balloon trip. Afterward, he stated his belief that the clue to practical aerial transit was not in the improvement of the balloon, "but in actual flight by means of wings." Such a subject was under consideration by the British Aeronaut Society, operating under the Duke of Argyll, and to whose aim Wise had determined to devote his fortune.[39]

Spending much of his time writing scientific articles, including another paper on his idea of balloons constructed of copper,[40] he proposed making a number of summer ascensions for meteorological observations.[41] On July 29 he made his 445th flight from Chambersburg, and encountered a snowstorm that caused him excruciating pain.[42]

"Rather Anxious and Nervous"

In what would become more and more common as the decade advanced, Charles Coe laid aside plans for a trans–Atlantic voyage, putting together "Professor C. Coe's Champion Fair," offering a wide variety of entertainment including sports, horsemanship and balloon races, with purses as high as $500 to the winner. By 1873, Coe was in San Francisco, partnering with the aeronaut Lay to sponsor numerous ascensions from Woodward's Garden.[43]

John A. Light, whose premature death had been reported in 1860, made a re-appearance on the scene in 1866. In his balloons the *Flying Cloud* and the *Albion* he made flights throughout Maryland and Pennsylvania, achieving his 100th voyage by 1870, and charging the stan-

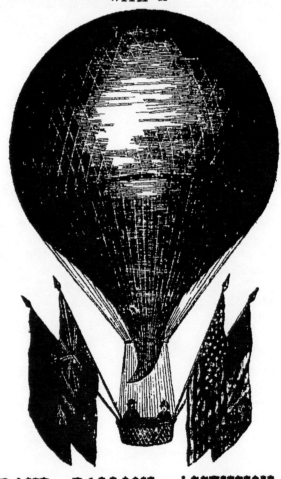

Professor S.S. Thurston was one of the fortunate aeronauts who prolonged his career over several decades. For the 4th of July celebrations in 1881, this advertisement promised partial ascensions during the day for those who wished to go up in a "Mammoth Silk Balloon, Holding 15,000 feet of gas," operated by a "well known aeronaut" (*Greenville Advance Argus* [Pennsylvania], June 23, 1881).

dard fare of 50 cents for adults and 25 cents for children.[44] By 1871, Light claimed 114 flights and the devotion of "nineteen years to the science."[45]

Neither Silas nor George Brooks served as aeronauts during the war, but they remained somewhat active as civilian aeronauts during those long years. On one scientific expedition, Brooks made a flight from Memphis, July 3, 1869, with a mechanical contrivance for descending without ballast or gas.[46]

An aeronaut who had made 68 previous ascents but received no national attention found his name in the newspapers for a brief period in the late 1860s, although it was alternately spelled "Wilbur," and "Wilber." Apparently his history was such that when he did ascend, his trips were so abbreviated his balloon was followed by hundreds of small boys, each hoping to be the first to arrive where "the thing lit."[47]

Professor Wilbur's career came to a tragic end on September 30, 1871. At Paoli, Indiana, George Knapp, editor of the Paoli *Union*, apparently convinced Wilbur to let him fly alone, fortifying his courage with "bad whisky." At the height of 30 feet Knapp jumped out and Wilber, determined the balloon should not go up alone, snatched a hanging rope and attempted to climb into the car. He failed and the balloon continued to ascend. Eventually losing his grip, he struck the ground, his poor wife crying out, "O, my God, he will die — he will be killed."

Unfortunately, she was correct. "His head was mashed into an indistinguishable mass and his body was bruised and crushed horribly." The body made a hole eight inches deep and rebounded four feet from where it struck.[48]

July 4, 1866, saw the emergence of S. S. Thurston, a local man of Meadville, Pennsylvania. On his first flight he was "rather anxious and nervous," but managed to make a credible voyage, to which the reporter remarked, "Now that Thurston made such a successful ascent, I suppose he will have balloon on the brain till he has made enough ascensions to deprive sky-navigation of all novelty."[49] The prophesy proved true, for the aeronaut made other trips around Pennsylvania during the next several years, occasionally offering the *Bridal Chariot* to wedding parties and giving tethered trips "for a consideration."

In June 1870, when Professor H. D. Squire made his first balloon ascent from Poughkeepsie, New York, in the *Flying Cloud*, a fifteen-year-old boy named Byron Bird begged to go with him. Owing to insufficient ascending power, he was left behind. On July 4, 1870, Bird convinced Squire to let him go up alone and proceeded to make a successful flight until jumping out and losing the balloon. Finding himself the darling of the media, Byron attempted another ascent at Cottage Hill August 20, but the balloon did not go up owing to a lack of gas. Undeterred, the "youngest aeronaut in the United States" promised to travel across the continent in a balloon of his own design.[50]

A balloon race was part of the July 4, 1871, celebrations in Poughkeepsie, pitting Professor Squire in the *Atlantic* against another of his pupils, Miss Nellie Thurston. A "well-educated young lady of nineteen," and a student at a prominent institution of learning, she had already made 20 ascensions with her uncle, Ira Thurston (the unfortunate aeronaut who lost his life in 1858), as well as several voyages that season. For the race, Squire kept low to the earth while Thurston reached a height of "at least four miles." He landed later in the day and Nellie proved the clear winner, descending near Redfield at nightfall. When her balloon settled on top of a large tree she remained in the car and "camped out." In the morning she jumped the last twenty feet to the ground and walked two miles for help.[51]

The decade of the 1860s had been a tumultuous one for the nation: civil unrest had turned to civil war; lives had been tragically sacrificed; faith, economy and principals were stretched beyond the breaking point and a new Constitutional Amendment was baptized in blood. Balloonists who had gone to war came home, some picking up their former occupations, others drifting away from a sport that promised more danger than remuneration. Civilians who stayed home to make names for themselves as quickly vanished, and as with all wars, past and present, the paradox that life changed and life remained the same proved itself once again.

Perhaps in compiling the balloon news, two events best represent the decade. At Kewana, a proposed ascension did not take place, the weather proving unfavorable. Irate spectators tore it to shreds and the aeronauts had an attachment placed on the balloon by the arm of the law. The owners were compelled to leave a gold watch and the remnant of the balloon "in soak," departing Logansport "in the worst possible humor."[52] Finally, in a sad yet gallant note, a man who had lost both arms in the war was treated by the citizens of Belton, Texas, to a balloon ascension on the night of July 6, 1868.[53]

MAGNIFICENT

BALLOON ASCENSION

—IN—

Driving Park, Winnipeg,

—ON—

WEDNESDAY, SEPTEMBER 20, 1882.

Between 3 and 5 p.m., by and for the benefit of

MISS NELLIE THURSTON,

The famous female aeronaut Nellie Thurston's career began in 1871. Learning her craft as a child from her uncle, aeronaut Ira Thurston, Thurston was tutored by Professor Squire, who traveled with her during a career that lasted into the 1880s (***Winnipeg Free Press***, September 18, 1882).

33

Of Songs, Circuses and "No-goes"

The project of crossing the Atlantic with a balloon is being revived by the aeronauts.
All are willing to have someone else try it.[1]

Anyone who has seen Angela Lansbury's inspired flirtation with Charles Boyer in the film *Gaslight* (1944) will recall the tune immediately:

> Up in a balloon, boys,
> Up in a balloon.

Unfortunately, that was all she sang. The song actually originated in 1869. In its entirety, the rest of the song goes:

> Up among the little stars,
> Sailing round the moon:
> Up in a balloon, boys,
> Up in a balloon,
> What a jolly place to go
> And spend your honey moon.[2]

For the cost of five cents, the 19th century lady or gentleman of fashion could obtain a copy from "Hitchcock's Half Dime Music," No. 98 Spring Street, New York, printed on heavy paper, with colored title, music and words. The ditty became a staple at music halls and around parlor pianos, while the first two lines were frequently used when referring to anyone considered odd or an aeronaut who had disappeared. Various amended versions made the rounds of local taverns, including:

> Up in a balloon, boys,
> Up in a balloon,
> Take a glass of sherry
> Up in a balloon."[3]

America was ready for aerial navigation, and coming from "this comparatively obscure corner of the globe," better known as San Francisco, they were enticed by the ideas of Frederick Marriott, incidentally owner of the San Francisco *News Letter*, one of the most popular publications on the West Coast. Having his own organ by which to promote his ideas (and an independent fortune) went a long way toward bringing attention to his cherished project—that of constructing a machine capable of independent movement against the wind.

Beginning a series of editorials in 1867, Marriott wrote, "Our soul expands with the thought of the triumphs of geographical, meteorological, astronomical discovery which will be opened up to the enterprise and daring of man!"[4]

The first trial of the *Avitor* was held July 2, 1869, with shareholders in the Aerial Steam Navigation Company present. Described as being a balloon in the shape of a cigar, 95 feet long, height 10 feet, width at the center 7 feet, the ship contained a rudder placed at the rear, with the propelling force supplied by a small engine.[5] Word soon came out that a party of "shrewd men" had joined the project, projecting a trip to New York and back in sixty to ninety days.[6] Nothing came of it.

The *Avitor*'s fame outlived the ship, and throughout the latter half of the 19th century other inventors presented equally outlandish ideas for balloon navigation. Unable to get away from the concept of using an aerostat, they typically devised one-man vessels that looked similar to a man riding a bicycle suspended under an inflated globe. By means of peddling, they supplied power—as long as their energy lasted. More advanced plans incorporated the use of steam engines, rightly supposing leg-power incapable of propelling a craft (to say nothing of cargo) any significant distance. None were ever completely successful and most were relegated to the category of mere curiosities before they ever got off the ground.

On a sad note, John La Mountain's brother, Edward (whose last name was occasionally misspelled "Lafontaine"), a sometimes aeronaut, made an ascension from Ionia on July 4, 1873, in a poorly prepared hot air balloon, "the worse for being filled with heated air too often." The basket was attached to the balloon by eight long, unevenly spaced ropes that separated during flight, causing the globe to invert. La Mountain was thrown out and struck the ground feet first, splintering and grinding his bones to powder. Edward was a jeweler by trade and was said to have remarked before ascending that he planned on taking the train home immediately after his flight as his wife was very sick. "He himself had not had his clothes off for ten days."[7]

The Great Sensation—Circuses Come to Town

In one sense, the Civil War brought an end to the innocence of American ballooning. The fascination of watching men ascend into the sky and then return to *terra firma*, offering wondrous insights into their perilous journeys, lost its freshness. Irritation at long delays, the uncertainty of weather and the too soon disappearance of the aeronaut led spectators to seek newer, more thrilling modes of entertainment. Traveling circuses were quick to capitalize on this and their numbers proliferated. Owners soon absorbed ballooning into their repertoire, but aeronauts were often relegated to positions behind Paragons of Beauty, Charming Equestrians, Trained Ponies, elephants and hippos. They did occasionally manage to find their name in the full-column advertisements, as did Miss Lottie St. Claire ("The Only Female Aeronaut in the World"), if she happened to look between the "Comic Trick Mules" and the "Wild Horse of Tartary," performing for "The Great Sensation Circus,"[8] but she was the exception rather than the rule.

In a few short decades, those of science and careful preparation from the European school of aerostation were replaced by a "catch as catch can" attitude. Experience gave way to necessity, and many of the "name" stars did not go up as advertised, primarily because they had been injured during a previous flight and someone less qualified was sent up in their place.

COMING!

BY RAIL

THE GREAT

CALIFORNIA

CIRCUS

When it became financially unfeasible for individual aeronauts to make a living free-lancing, many joined circuses. This offered multiple benefits. Rather than relying on ticket sales, they received a salary or a fee from the manager and also saved on travel and advertising expenses (*Stevens Point Daily Journal* [Wisconsin], June 11, 1881).

Although George W. De Haven's circus was recognized in the West "as one of the best circuses that ever travelled,"[9] accidents were common, often carrying serious consequences. A typical sequence of events took place *in one month* during May 1870. A balloonist from De Haven's ascending from Rock Island, Illinois, fell through the roof of a summer house; the unnamed aeronaut suffered internal injuries.[10] Another fell into the Mississippi; one ascending from Dubuque descended "more rapidly than was comfortable… and was not of a kind to inspire people with much confidence."[11] Finally, at McGregor, Iowa, on May 23 an aeronaut "was speedily dumped" into the river. He attempted to swim to shore but his strength gave out. The report added:

This man thus drowned was not the regular aeronaut, who had not yet recovered from the severe fall he experienced at Davenport a week ago. We presume this man was one of the tent men, as it was one of those sent up in the balloon from Dubuque.[12]

Inexperience and shoddy, ill-kept equipment played a large part of circus accidents, but of more importance was the cheap, quick and dangerous method used for filling the aerostat, called "smoke inflation" (and the balloons, "smokies"). A hole was dug in the earth in which was placed the iron apparatus for manufacturing gas, with a flue leading upward. On either side of the hole were positioned two immense poles secured with numerous guy ropes. The balloon, a mere cotton or muslin bag lacking any mechanical valves or apparatus, was fastened to the poles by pullies and tackle, the mouth of it being placed directly over the fire. Thick smoke sealed the fabric and under the blazing fire, inflation required little more than fifteen minutes. Once filled, the poles were quickly removed and the balloon shot up like a rocket.[13]

The aeronaut had no substantial car, no dragline and no ballast, thus sailing at the mercy of the wind. When the air cooled, he dropped without the least control.

Some circus aeronauts achieved their own fame: Professor Smythe in his balloon, the *Carrier Pigeon* from the Great New York Circus; Reluault and

Renno (who nearly burned to death in a balloon accident in May 1871) from Wootten & Haught's Mammoth New York Circus and Menagerie; Professor Hayden, associated with De Haven and Stone & Murray's Circus; Blondin; and the Parisian Paul Le Gand of James Robinson's Circus and Champion Show. Others remained anonymous, and when the newspaper's eye was not upon their employers, the injured were often left behind, as was the case at Council Bluffs in May 1871. There, an aeronaut fell from his balloon and was badly injured. No one but a few working men even went to see if he were alive, and when Lake's Circus pulled up stakes, the unfortunate's belongings went with them, leaving him at the mercy of strangers with no more than the thin muslin suit he wore during the performance.[14]

When all was said and done, perhaps the best paragraph written on American circus ballooning is contained in the following:

> The crop of small boys in town blossomed out yesterday in full force to see the circus and balloon ascension. When the latter occurred, the "air ship" was followed by hundreds of youngsters who raced through the fields, and annihilated the seats of their trousers on fences and underbrush, in their desire to see the aeronaut smashed.[15]

It started out innocently enough: a small paragraph in a New York newspaper in April 1869, declared, "The price of a balloon passage from New York to Europe is fixed at $250, and the plucky French aeronaut, M. Chevalier, who will make the trip this month, says he has already one hundred applications for the passage."[16]

Although New Yorkers, remembering "Prof. Lowe's money-making fiasco in a similar project," were quick to pronounce the present venture a "humbug," Alexander Chevalier, (of *Le Géant* fame) cared little about skeptics. A French aeronaut with 165 balloon ascensions to his credit, he had recently arrived in America with a plan. Working at Landsman's Park, the aeronaut was described as a "quiet, unobtrusive, yet prepossessing young man of 33 years; of dark complexion and with black hair and mustache." With kindly black eyes and a countenance indicating no fear, he conversed and wrote excellent English, French, German and Russian.

Chevalier's own invention of a "compensator," or reserve balloon, set to receive excess gas discharged from the main balloon during expansion at high elevations, was to eliminate loss of buoyancy and thus permit the machine to travel long distances. The balloon, named *L'Espérance* survived trial flights on May 29 and June 19 but never made it across the water. It would not be long before another "humbug" presented itself.

The Tight Rope Walker and "Magician"

Washington Harrison Donaldson, a gymnast and tightrope walker, made his first ever balloon ascent on August 30, 1871, from Reading, Pennsylvania. The self-styled "magician" went up again September 4, performing amazing feats on the trapeze 300 feet above the earth. His career as an aeronaut nearly ended the same day when, on his descent, the trapeze struck the roof of a house. The balloon rebounded and landed in a field, with Donaldson turning a somersault to save himself from a hard fall.

Finding the prospect of aerial gymnastics appealing, he went on to make numerous ascensions, earning the erstwhile praise, "Donaldson, the intrepid aeronaut, seems determined to kill himself, or else he would discontinue his perilous balloon adventures astride a trapeze bar."[17] His safety record was hardly one to commend him, and on one occasion he was said to have died after he reportedly fell from his balloon at the height of one half mile.[18]

In a description remarkably similar to that of Chevalier, Donaldson was described as "a short, thick-set man, about thirty-two years of age, dark complexion, dark eyes and black hair, with a gaudy moustacho, waxed and twisted in a most Napoleonic manner," who never drank nor used tobacco.

He expressed his taste for the dramatic by stating, "People demand sensational spectacles. Their tastes must be gratified." When questioned about danger, Donaldson was quoted as saying, "People call me reckless and crazy, but they forget that I value my life as much as they do, and that I know exactly what I am about.... I have been lost, given up as dead, found again, bruised, scratched, landed in the Atlantic, and baptized in Lake Michigan, but am here to-day, with not a bone broken nor a mark visible. I have lost two balloons, have had one burst under me when two miles high, and have damaged three."

Donaldson's most compelling dream, however, had to do with his plan to cross the Atlantic in a balloon to be called *North America*, that he proposed to have ready by June, 1873. His balloon was to cost $5,000 and travel 2,600 miles in two and a half days.[19]

Donaldson's ambition was likely inspired by Chevalier and fired by an interview given by John Wise to the Philadelphia *Star* in December 1872, where the venerable aeronaut stated his renewed plan to orchestrate a trans–Atlantic flight in the summer of 1873.[20] By February, Donaldson was close to closing an agreement with John Wise, who was to accompany him to Europe. If successful, Donaldson anticipated establishing a balloon mail and passenger line round the world.[21]

Wise and Donaldson's plans seemed to fall into place in May when the Boston Common Council passed an order approving $3,000 for the venture.[22] A subsequent article noted that $3,000 was to be raised by an appeal to the wealthy men of Boston,[23] and another reported that Wise and Donaldson were both in Boston in June, where their proposal had been passed by the "Committee on the Fourth of July," but required final action by the Council.[24]

Some took the project less seriously:

> Prof. Wise promises to cross the ocean from Boston in a balloon next month, if the city will allow him $3000 for expenses. Expenses? Are there railroad porters and hotel porters, and worst of all, hotel clerks in that undiscovered country through which his balloon will pass? If so, it is to be hoped that aerial navigation will continue to be a failure.[25]

By June 15, after the great fire in Boston and sudden contraction of its currency, the city withdrew its support, forcing the partnership to try the wealthy gentlemen of New York.[26] This brought out the "old fogies," who hoped Wise might find his modest sum in the city "as the surest means of ridding itself once and forever of so irresponsible a dunner."[27]

Wise and Donaldson hit pay dirt the last week in June when the articles of agreement between themselves and the *Daily Graphic* Company of New York were signed. The *Graphic* agreed to pay for the construction of a balloon, "not less than 130 feet in height and 100 feet in diameter," to be ready by August 20. In return, the aeronauts promised "to have nothing to do with other balloon enterprises," and to superintend the construction.[28] In a letter written June 26 to the Lancaster *Intelligencer*, Wise noted, "The arrangement for the transatlantic balloon voyage is now definitely settled, and settled in such a way as not to embarrass the integrity of its successful termination by any pecuniary considerations."[29]

The balloon, now named the *Daily Graphic*, was put on display, much as had been done in 1859. Numerous articles promoting the activities were published by the *Daily Graphic* newspaper, with the editors even establishing a new weekly called *The Balloon Graphic*.[30]

The Domestic Sewing Machine Company volunteered to do the sewing free of charge, running up 14,080 yards of sewing and 4,316 yards of cloth for the envelopes.[31] The material was unbleached sheeting, of a thick, coarse quality of the brand known as "Indian Orchard," purchased from Eldridge, Dunham & Co. Twelve seamstresses were to use thread of silk and cotton, the top spool being silk.[32] For this consideration, the Domestic Company received free publicity and was loaned a bird of prey, affixed with gold anklet, to put on display.[33]

The weight of the balloon was:

Balloon	4,000 lbs
Net and ropes	800
Car	100
Boat	1,000
Drag rope	600
Anchor and grapnels	300
Sundries	300
Total	7,100 lbs

4,500 pounds allowed for passengers and ballast.[34]

Work on varnishing the cloth was done at the Brooklyn navy yard using linseed oil, boiled very thick, reduced by benzene and laid on with calcimining brushes. The strips required three coats, one inside and two outside, and was performed by six men over the course of six weeks. Work on the car was entrusted to R. Hoe & Co.[35]

Not surprisingly, "The other New York dailies do not have much to say about this novel undertaking, because they recognize it as an ingenious advertising dodge, and do not care about lending their columns to the service of a competitor."[36] It did not matter, for "that enterprising sheet is getting plenty of advertising out of its $10,000 investment if nothing else."[37]

Indeed, the proprietors of the *Daily Graphic* Company knew what they were about. Swatches of oiled balloon sheeting were sent to newspaper editors across the country, along with invitations to attend the ascent. Additionally, it seemed invitations to cross the Atlantic were offered by the Company to every notable man in America, including George B. McClellan, Benjamin F. Butler and Charles A. Dana. They all begged to be excused on the grounds of "previous engagements."[38]

These invitations, more than anything else connected with the endeavor, elicited humorous responses in dailies around the country. The most reprinted was:

> If there is room for one more in that balloon of the *Graphic*'s there is a young man in Danbury who can fill it. He lives opposite us and plays the accordion. He might object to the risk, but he could be stunned by a blow on the head, and got into the balloon before he recovered.[39]

By July, the *Graphic* was compelled to write that judging from the number of applications, "about one half of the people of the United States wish to go to Europe by balloon," but due to the limited capacity, only two aeronauts, a navigator and an artist from the newspaper were to be included.[40]

When Wise asked Professor Joseph Henry of the Smithsonian his opinion of the flight, he expressed a wish that a voyage be conducted from San Francisco to New York in order to fully explore the theory of an eastern air current. Wise responded he would rather risk the ocean than the Rocky Mountains.[41]

Fifty carrier pigeons were sought to fetch back dispatches from the balloon,[42] and on August 24, J. H. & C. M. Goodsell, Managers of the *Daily Graphic*, assured the public that no "money has been spared, to adopt every part of the plans and wishes of the aeronauts," adding it had been their intent "to avoid anything like public display in the matter."[43] That said, after the date of departure was changed to September 10, they advertised that viewing was to be held on the Capitoline Ground, Brooklyn, from September 6–10. All connected with the expedition, were to be on exhibition, including the carrier pigeons.

Daily Graphic Measurements

Length of 9 great sections, each:	176 feet:
Un-inflated	
Width:	36 feet
Inflated	
Width:	115 feet
Diameter:	110 feet
Circumference:	335 feet
Length from crown to keel:	348 feet
Length of boat: 160 feet	
Height of car:	15 feet
Length of lifeboat:	24 feet

In their advertisement for "The Transatlantic Aerial Voyage," the *Graphic* listed the cost as being nearly $15,000.[44]

"Something Rotten in Denmark"

Rumors of Wise's dissatisfaction began to surface, particularly in the Philadelphia *Herald*; those he emphatically denied.[45] Allegations that he was upset about the use of cotton rather than silk[46] proved accurate. Interestingly, a less publicized bone of contention between the aeronaut and the *Graphic* Company concerned "a misunderstanding" about Wise's writing, which he alleged they wished to control. In August, he arranged for a new edition of his book, under the title, *Through the Air: A Narrative of Forty Years Experience as an Aeronaut*, to be printed by the To Day Publishing Company, Philadelphia.[47] Wide deduced this displeased the *Graphic* and was the reason "many of his wishes in preparing for the balloon voyage were not respected."[48]

It would get worse. The idea to have three balloons was abandoned, leaving only one large aerostat. The graphic artist who was to accompany the aeronauts pulled out at the last minute. Wise voiced complaints about the stitching, using cotton instead of silk; that the *Graphic* hired an incompetent superintendent who altered his ideas. He complained that the balloon had been exposed to open air for weeks and had become rotten. The lifeboat was half a ton heavier than he wished. In an interview with the New York *Herald*, Wise expressed the opinion that Donaldson was "a reckless, daredevil fellow who is chiefly anxious to make a sensation, and who is rather pleased with the idea of going up in a balloon that is reported to be unsafe."[49]

Not insensitive to the growing unrest, Donaldson declared he would go alone or solicit volunteers, should Wise join the artist in backing out.

Odds on the Success of the Voyage

The balloon would not get half way across the ocean					19:1
"	"	"	"	travel 100 miles	9:1
"	"	"	"	stay up a single day **	5:1
"	"	"	"	find the wind current **	3:1
The entire project would fizzle					2:1
The balloon would burst **					Even[50]

On September 10, the day of the grand ascension, Donaldson and six men reported for work at 3:00 A.M. By 8:00 A.M. Wise had not made an appearance and by 9:00 the attempt was abandoned due to high wind. Donaldson cut a six-foot hole in the unmanageable balloon to let out the gas, which would require hand stitching to repair. The safety valve was said to have been out of order.[51]

Headlines read "THE BALLOON — DISAPPOINTED" and "Balloon Scheme Supposed to be Bursted."[52] Other headlines read, "Prof. Wise thinks the balloon seriously damaged,"[53] and "Professor Wise denies the rumor that he has refused to accompany the balloon."[54]

The common joke in New York became that if someone wished to make himself generally disagreeable, he should pass through the streets and ask every man he met if the balloon was going up that day.[55]

News broke that Wise and Donaldson had a serious quarrel the morning of the non–ascent. Wise charged Donaldson with incompetence and announced he would "shoot Donaldson if insubordinate." Donaldson countered by accusing Wise of being afraid and threatened to ascend with Captain Lunt, who was to serve as navigator.[56]

A strip of muslin was sewn over the holes, and aided by Wise's niece, Mrs. Ihling, covered with several coats of varnish and declared ready for a second attempt.[57] Donaldson slept in the car of the *Daily Graphic* balloon the night of September 11, and on the 12th, the second inflation began under the direction of newly employed John Steiner. Charles Wise, who had joined his father in New York after an abortive attempt to make a transatlantic voyage in his own balloon from Philadelphia, went with the latter to the Capitoline Grounds sometime around 9 A.M. After initially being denied entrance (Wise had not been there since Wednesday), he and his son entered, only to have Charles Goodsell of the *Graphic* order the younger Wise out. A row began in earnest. In order to keep the squabbles private, Steiner took them to the ticket office. Leaving Charles outside, he, Wise and the Goodsells conversed for half an hour, ending cordially enough that Wise remarked he should be called at 21 City Hall Place when the balloon was inflated. Since he had not overseen the inflation, his actual participation was clearly in doubt.

Tempers flared. The incensed Charles gave a "wrathful" interview, remarking, "The Goodsells can see a ten-cent piece at the bottom of a well with the naked eye, but I'm — — — if they could see an atom of honor or decency in any body else with a telescope."[58]

The prospects for success did not improve. An easterly wind, opposite that required to start a European voyage, blew up a gale. Donaldson, Lunt, a reporter from the *Sun* and eight workmen attempted to hold down the violently swaying craft. By the time the envelope had filled to one-third capacity and had risen forty feet, it became unmanageable. Help was solicited from men on their way to work and one hundred of them attempted to get the aerostat under control, but a sudden jerk ripped the neck of the balloon from the gas pipe, tearing the muslin.

At 9:00, with the weather worsening, Donaldson scaled the ropes and opened the valve. When no relief was imminent, he pulled the ripcord, designed to tear a slit in the fabric and allow gas to escape during emergency procedures. A six-foot tear appeared and the gas escaped, nearly suffocating Inspector Folk, Goodsell and Police Commissioner Briggs.

Despite an announcement of the disaster, ticket gates remained open, and by afternoon, as many as 30,000 spectators had paid their fifty cents to witness the ascension.[59] Speculation ran as high as a $20,000 income for the combined ticket sales.[60] After Steiner declared no further inflation could be made that day, the crowd turned mean, making a general rush toward the balloon with the intent of tearing it to shreds. A strong police force held them back.[61]

Finger pointing began immediately. Rumor had it Wise sold a seat in the balloon for $500; the *Graphic* accused Wise of having no intention of going. Wise called the balloon "rotten."[62] Steiner stated it was his belief "a balloon of cotton of this size can never be made that will stand the strain of inflation."[63] Charles Goodsell called Charles Wise "a deadbeat," who was "employed on the balloon until we discharged him." He called John Wise "dilatory and fickle-minded," and remarked that Wise was angry because Alfred Ford, a journalist at the *Graphic*, was to go on the trip instead of Wise's friend Haughton, who had promised the aeronaut $500.[64]

The aftermath grew ugly. In an interview given the night of the 12th, Wise claimed the Goodsells had spent no more than $4,000 on the balloon and, lacking sufficient funds, had asked for contributions. A scientific society sent Wise a check for $1,200 that he turned over to the managers and got "nothing out of it." He charged the Goodsells of recovering their upfront money by ticket sales and avowed he had received nothing but $195 for expenses. Significantly, "he particularly dwelt upon the treatment of the managers in relation to his book, which he had contracted to write and publish." The *Graphic* had "advertised by implication that he was to edit this book in conjunction with some of the people connected with them," which alarmed his publishers.[65]

All goods to have been used in the flight, including the cages of carrier pigeons, were stored in the buildings on site, and the Goodsells promptly offered to construct Donaldson a new balloon, this one of silk. He readily accepted.[66]

In defending himself, Wise wrote to the New York *Herald*:

> It is a sad thing for me, when I thought that the great dream of my life was about to be realized, to behold such an inglorious conclusion; but I feel no blame can attach to me in the matter, and that an impartial public will only blame me for not having abandoned the enterprise long ago.[67]

Typical of the newspapers was: "The balloon trip to Europe is indefinitely postponed. The postponement carries Professor Wise's obituary with it."[68]

While P. T. Barnum was proposing to build his own trans–Atlantic balloon, the Goodsells prepared a new balloon for Donaldson. To make sure John Wise kept his distance, the *Graphic* people let it be known he was "neither courageous, consistent, temperate nor truthful."[69]

The "Impotent Conclusion"

Pre–publicity began almost immediately. After initially refusing to participate, Donaldson finally agreed to ascend on October 4 in the *Magenta*. Accompanying him were Alfred Ford (*Graphic* journalist) and G.A. Lunt (*Graphic* artist correspondent), the inflation overseen by newly recruited Samuel King.[70]

On October 6 at 9:00 A.M. the same trio began their trans–Atlantic flight in the quickly assembled balloon. Donaldson stated "the advice of the best aeronauts in the country" had been solicited and that he believed this time he could not fail. Alfred Ford sent off two carrier pigeons along the way with jolly notes on their progress. Passing Norwalk at an altitude of 5,080 feet, they struck the eastern current, but by noon a violent storm set in; at 1:15 P.M. their situation became perilous. The balloon began to descend with frightening velocity, spinning over the trees. At 1:25 P.M. when over New Haven, Connecticut, Donaldson gave the order to abandon ship; he and Ford jumped but Lunt was not quick enough, and he remained inside as the vessel shot up. Unable to open the valve cord, he eventually leapt into the top of a tree but lost his balance as the balloon scraped his hands, plummeting to the ground. None of the three appeared badly injured, and the aerostat was recovered "in a sadly demoralized state" a mile beyond Lunt's fall.[71] The men who captured the balloon at Caanan stripped it of everything potable, including the aeronaut's personal belongings, and the farmer on whose land it descended put in a heavy claim for damages. To secure these claims, the sheriff attached the property for $800.[72]

The claimants came down slightly from their demands, and thus ended the great hope for a trans–Atlantic flight with "a most impotent conclusion."[73]

Sadly, George A. Lunt died in May 1874 of injuries received when jumping from the *Graphic* balloon.[74]

34

The "Impossibility" of Aerial Navigation

An overly optimistic agreement was called for "which may prevent the pure air of heaven from being made the scene of bloodshed. Earth and sea are already consecrated to deeds of violence and death — surely the air may [by] mutual consent, be neutralized.[1]

Napoleon III's ambition to conquer Prussia gave Bismarck the opportunity to unite the southern and northern German states. After the disputed candidature for the French throne, the Elms Telegram, sent by Wilhelm I of Prussia refusing French conditions, provoked the latter to declare war. The Prussians moved in and a month later, the French were trapped at Metz (east of Paris). In an attempt to relieve the city, the French army was trapped at Sedan on the Belgium border.

Ballooning became integral during the Franco–Prussian War, first as weapons reputedly used by the Prussians to shower balls of gutta-percha filled with nitroglycerine on the enemy.[2] It was not long before daily ascensions were launched from Paris for reconnoitering in enemy territory.[3]

The fear factor and eyewitness observations played their role (Nadar kept his balloon *Neptune* permanently inflated during the siege of Paris),[4] but a greater contribution came in the form of transporting the post between beleaguered cities and the outside world. Between September 23 and November 30, 1870, 30 rudely constructed balloons of home manufacture were dispatched by the mail service. Made of cotton, sewed by machines, coated with varnish or linseed oil and litharge, and filled with ordinary coal gas, they performed remarkably well. In all, 64 aeronauts left Paris between September 23 and January 28. They conveyed 91 passengers, 354 carrier pigeons, about 3,000,000 letters and a large number of dispatches. Of these, five balloons fell into the hands of the Germans (including the *Vauban, Galilee* and the *Daguerra*) and two were lost at sea (the *Jacquard*, sent up November 28, presumably lost over the British seas, and the *Richard Wallace*, which left Paris January 27, 1871, piloted by M. Lucaze and destined for Bordeaux).[5] On November 21, the *Archimede* launched from Paris, caught a veering wind and eventually landed in Holland. On the 24th, M. Rollier and M. Bezière, aboard the *Villa d'Orléans*, left Paris for Tours. After being caught in a current, they were pushed over the German Ocean and finally touched ground in Christiana, Norway, having covered 750 leagues in less than fifteen hours, surpassing the distance covered by the *Nassau*.[6]

On October 30, 1870, Metz capitulated; resistance in Paris continued but orders were issued that all Americans and Englishmen were to be evacuated.[7] To accommodate this end, two private balloon companies were established, one under Nadar (who resigned late in the year), the other under Jules and Eugene Godard. The latter opted to charge 2,000 francs ($400) to wealthy foreigners for the chance to escape beleaguered Paris. Jules D. Hasler, the baritone in Adelaide Phillipps' concert company, escaped, as did five female dancers, whose fare was paid by Henry D. Jarrett, who planned to have them appear in his Broadway theater that winter.[8]

Despite a fierce resistance, Paris was forced to surrender in January 1871 and the war came to a close with the Treaty of Frankfurt. One of the first topics under discussion had to do with the question of aeronauts. A number captured by the Germans were charged with a breech of military law and sent before courts-martial boards. Inasmuch as aeronauts carried military packets, it was suggested aeronauts be treated similar to naval crews running a blockade.[9]

In 1874, at the Brussels Congress concerning the laws and customs of war, an attempt to make permanent the status of captured aeronauts was presented by making the distinction between espionage and reconnaissance. The article stated, "persons captured while engaged in balloon voyages are to be regarded as prisoners of war."[10]

Europe after the War and Beyond

On March 22, 1874, acting on the ideas of de Fouvielle, M. Croce-Spinelli and M. Sivel ascended from La Villette in the balloon *Étoile Polaire* (*Polar Star*), hoping to ascertain if the respiration of highly oxygenized air would mitigate the suffocating effects of high altitude. They achieved an altitude of 7,400 meters, where the temperature registered 22° below zero, and the aeronauts would have perished without the "air respirator," carried in bags.[11]

The aerostatic news of 1868 was the completion of the Giant Captive Balloon at Ashburnham Gardens, London. Ninety feet in diameter with a capacity for 363,000 cubic feet of gas, it was intended for scientific research and tethered flights. Owned and operated by a French company, the outlay was £28,000; to recoup their investment, one shilling was charged for a visit within the enclosure and one-pound sterling required for "aeronauts" to go up in the "apparently safe and commodious car."

The balloon was held to the earth by a cable, worked by steam generated in a drum 21 feet long and 7 feet in diameter, passing underground to the vessel. The pure hydrogen used to inflate the monster was manufactured with 200,000 pounds of sulfuric acid and 110,000 pounds of iron filings. The first manned ascent was taken by Godard, son of the aeronaut, and Mr. Youens, who had a large share in the management of the enterprise.

On September 11, only a week after operations began, a spark from the Merryweather steam engine ignited bags filled with iron. The flames traveled to the barrels where the gas was generated, causing sixteen of them to explode. The barrelheads and the zinc pipes by which they were connected to the gasometer were blown away, scattering debris everywhere. Further ascensions were postponed until the following year.[12]

Flights continued in 1869, which included a nice story about Mrs. Hogg, an inmate of St. George's Workhouse, Chelsea. On attaining a milestone birthday she was asked how she would like to celebrate the event and replied, "Send me up in the great balloon, that I may admire the world I have lived 100 years upon." Her wish was transmitted to Godard and on August 5 she made the trip, going up 2,000 feet in the air. At that altitude she was given wine and biscuits and presented with a medal to commemorate the event.[13]

In 1874, Gustave De Groof, a Belgian who claimed to have perfected a flying machine, immigrated to England. Dubbed "The Flying Man," he created a simple machine with 35-foot long wings by which he imitated the action of a bird. After one successful demonstration, he attempted to repeat the experiment a week later. At the height of 4,000 feet he detached his winged machine. Set free at a dangerous angle, the "Flying Man" was unable to right himself and fell "with a terrible thud," smashing his skull. A mob of men and boys tore up the mangled craft and ran off with the pieces.[14]

All of these events, in one way or another, touched the Aeronautical Society of Great Britain, established in 1866 under the leadership of His Grace the Duke of Argyll. With the motto "Onward and *upward*," the society (with the vigorous support of John Wise) investigated and encouraged alternate methods of flying. One of their studies critiqued the process of a winged velocipede, and the inventors of the *Avitor* sent a model of their airship from San Francisco.

The members also seriously entertained the idea of flying with wings propelled by a steam engine, and to promote inventions along those lines, they arranged to hold an exhibition at the Crystal Palace in 1868.[15] The nine-day fair "was a decided failure," losing considerable prestige by the explosion of the Captive Balloon, for which the members issued placards, inviting aid for the owner, who suffered the entire loss.[16]

Declaring aerial navigation in balloons "an impossibility," the members turned away from balloons and toward "flying machines." The Duke of Sutherland offered £100 to the inventor of a machine (not a balloon or kite) that would raise a person to the height of 120 feet. "The great aim, in a word, is to get an engine by which the exercise of its own power, aided by the strength of the man or men upheld by it, shall support itself in the air and move about."[17]

35

News That Shocked the World

The Washington Chronicle considers balloon ascensions public nuisances, and wants a law made to prevent them.[1]

For the 4th of July celebrations in Boston in 1872, Samuel A. King prepared a new balloon. Requiring five months to complete, the 1,200 feet of Lyman mills cloth was then coated with oil-varnish. The name *Colossus* was printed on the side in seven-foot high letters.

A comparison with King's other balloons justified the name.

Colossus	100,000 cubic feet capacity	
Hyperion	65,000	"
Star Spangled Banner	50,000	"
Queen of the Air	33,000	"
General Grant	15,000	"[2]

Unfortunately, the *Colossus* was destroyed by "spontaneous combustion" on June 6 at the aeronaut's residence in Chelsea, Massachusetts. King was in Philadelphia at the time, making arrangements for construction of a "novel car" for the balloon. Receiving news of the disaster by telegraph,[3] he hurried home and set about replacing the envelope. The new *Colossus* was ready in time for the 4th of July celebrations, for which he was to be paid $1,000 on his 164th ascent.

After 80,000 feet of gas had been pumped into the aerostat, a horrific storm arose. With preternatural darkness falling, the balloon exploded with a tremendous report, leaving it "a dirty mass of cotton shreds, dragged and slimy in the rain and mud." King was overwhelmed and reported to be out $2,000.[4]

In a fascinating aside from his aerial duties, King was hired by a New York company to measure the discharge from a gas well in Ontario County, New York. This gas, conveyed to Rochester by pipes 26 miles distant, was then mixed with illuminating or street gas for city use. The company suspected a leak but could not determine whether it came from the source or somewhere along the line. Using two balloons, of 20,000 and 13,000 feet capacity, King measured the flow at the mouth. His calculations met expectations, proving the leak came from somewhere down the line.[5]

In what would turn out to be an extraordinary adventure, Samuel King and the Boston journalist Luther Holden set off at 4:00 P.M. on Thursday, September 26, 1872, from the Grafton County Fair, Plymouth, New Hampshire, little suspecting what lay in store. Unable to pinpoint their location due to cloud cover, they were compelled to stay aloft all night for fear of descending into a mountain. At daylight they descended in the midst of a dense forest, anchored the balloon to a tree and climbed down. Working their way out of the wilderness, they found themselves near Sayabec, Quebec, having covered 500 miles at 50 miles per hour.[6]

Hardly silent on the prospects of Wise and Donaldson's pending ocean voyage, Samuel King remarked it was "impossible to cross the Atlantic in a balloon,"[7] adding he would not accept a free pass to Europe from the Graphic Air Line Company.[8] His faith did extended to overland flights, and King prepared another mammoth balloon in Buffalo, named after that city. "Tastefully ornamented under the direction of Fred. Stanfield, the well-known scenic artist," with seven-foot high letters in carmine, black and green and with scrollwork framing the name[9] the balloon ascended before 75,000 people on September 16, 1873. Landing his passengers at Hornby, New York, he spent the night and arose alone the following day, reaching Post Creek Valley, six miles from Carring. On September 25, he made his 171st ascent alone from the Fair Grounds at Plymouth, New Hampshire, using hydrogen gas manufactured for the occasion.[10]

Notwithstanding his criticism of trans–Atlantic flight, he traveled to New York City to oversee the inflation of the *Graphic* balloons between October 2 and 6. Professor King subsequently made one of the longest recorded American flights when he ascended from Buffalo in the *Buffalo* on July 4, 1874. Taking with him James Albro of the *Commercial Advertiser*, Luther L. Holden of the Boston *Journal* and Walter T. Chester, the aeronauts sailed over parts of New York, Maryland, Delaware, New Jersey and Pennsylvania, remaining aloft all night at a variable rate between 25 and 80 miles per hour. After floating for thirteen hours and covering a circuitous route of 400 miles, they landed near Salem City, New Jersey.[11] He continued to make ascents and by 1875, was charging the staggering sum of $1,500 for a 4th of July voyage from Cleveland.[12]

P. T. Barnum Gets into the Act

P. T. Barnum, the quintessential American showman, knew a good thing when he saw it, and never quibbled about reaping a reward from another's failure. In wake of the *Daily Graphic* balloon disasters, Barnum pitched into the fray, meeting with John Wise, his son and Dr. Parisel at the Astor House on October 13, asking their requirements for a trans–Atlantic balloon, regardless of cost. With those notes in his pocket, Barnum set sail for Europe the following day.[13]

After spending 1873 performing, Washington Donaldson's path crossed that of the great American operator and they soon struck a deal. At the Grand Inauguration of P. T. Barnum's Mammoth Balloon Enterprise from the Great Roman Hippodrome, New York, July 7, 1874,[14] the aeronaut ascended in a silk balloon designed for "scientific purposes." Twelve trips were planned, but as the affair "looks very much like one of Barnum's advertising dodges," it attracted little attention.[15] The cost of the balloon was given as $2,000.[16]

Numerous flights were taken at the Hippodrome with similarly constructed balloons (one of which was called the *Barnum*), after which the traveling show opened in Boston August 3.[17] Thus began a series of flights where local reporters were given rides in the expectation of free publicity.[18]

As a full-fledged member of Barnum's circus, Donaldson's voyages were ostensibly billed as scientific experiments "to settle the idea of an eastern current preparatory to making a voyage across the Atlantic." During the season he ascended from Boston, Allentown, Philadelphia, Baltimore and Pittsburg. At Cincinnati, two of Barnum's attachés were married in his balloon, the affair arranged by Donaldson's assistant, Harry Gilbert.[19]

Barnum's Roman Hippodrome (also known as the "Traveling World's Fair") set out its itinerary for the coming season that included daily balloon ascensions with a car large enough to hold twelve persons, at a cost to the entrepreneur of $500 per day.[20] During a descent on April 21 from Philadelphia, Donaldson was forced to cut loose the basket, thereby losing the balloon.[21] That evening, a telegram was sent under the name "Dr. Spencer," stating the aeronaut had been killed.[22] After originally denying knowledge of "Dr. Spencer," Donaldson confessed on the 22nd that he sent the telegram under a fictitious name as a scheme to advertise himself. The story played out rapidly and subsequent reports made him out to be a hero for surviving the ordeal.[23]

On July 7 Donaldson made his 132nd voyage from Fort Wayne, having taken in his career, to date, 219 passengers, 40 of whom were women and children, the youngest being three years of age. His numbers rapidly escalated as his contract called for him to make an ascent at every town visited by the Hippodrome where gas was available. At his disposal were seven balloons, called, respectively, "1" to "7"; #4 cost $800.[24]

Under the Direction of Mr. Donaldson

Donaldson's daredevil flying quickly made him a legend. His style of skimming along the earth's surface with a trailing drag rope to regulate the balloon's speed enabled him to "hitch up" refreshments along the way, but the rope also struck fruit trees and crashed window-panes, causing substantial damage. In 1875, on a voyage from Worcester, his drag rope caught on a passing train and only the stalwart effort of the crew succeeded in releasing it before lives were endangered.[25]

Perhaps his reputation began to get on his nerves. In late June he was quoted as saying that he expected to be killed that summer on a balloon trip.[26] The premonition would prove eerily correct. On Thursday, July 15, 1875, Donaldson made his 136th ascension from Chicago with Newton S. Grimwood, a young reporter from the *Evening Journal*. After they ascended, no word was forthcoming and speculation ran rampant that their balloon had been blown into the lake during a nighttime gale.

As was usual in such cases, an expert was solicited for his opinion. Professor John Steiner stated he had seen the balloon Donaldson used in Philadelphia that spring and remarked, "the bag had been subjected to a good deal of hard usage," and had a lot of patches. He felt it was "a very inferior one to use in the neighborhood of these lakes."[27] Steiner's comments were widely published and drew harsh criticism down on Donaldson's absent head. Barnum's press agent, D. S. Thomas, continued to give out positive assessments: the aeronauts were safe, but probably blown ashore in some remote district.

Days passed without word. The Chicago *Tribune* charged Barnum with "serious responsibility" if the ascension turned out to be a disaster. Donaldson was reputed to have been nervous at the outset, "whistling vacantly to himself," and taking frequent observations of the wind. Described as "sunburnt, dusty, and restless," he kept to himself without speaking to reporters. When someone shouted "You'd better get out," he replied, "I wish to Christ I could!"[28]

On July 17, with an eye toward the concept that "the show must go on," another balloon ascended from the Hippodrome with Dave Thomas, the press agent (and Donaldson's friend), as aeronaut. It was his first flight and "was probably the first and only balloon ascension ever made in silence." He landed safely and that ascent ended the balloon season in Chicago.[29]

On the 18th, Barnum thought Donaldson "was safe," but chartered the tug *Burton* to scour the lake and shores for the bodies. Thomas denied the affair was "an advertising dodge," and artfully complained of Steiner's observations, adding that perhaps he "has not been treated with as much consideration by our people as he thinks he deserves." Steiner replied on July 19 by issuing a card published in the Chicago *Tribune*, noting he was "not in the habit of asking favors from Barnum or his hirelings."[30]

No one belonging to the Hippodrome believed the disappearance a publicity stunt; a man named Coop responded to the charge by saying, "Great God! Donaldson wouldn't do anything of that kind. Do you think he would rend the hearts of his best friends by playing this as a dodge?... I tell you he has the heart of a woman."[31] Although rewards as high as $700 were offered, not one credible lead was substantiated. A clairvoyant, Professor O.W. Baker, predicted the aeronauts were alive and would shortly be heard from.[32] A mind reader named J.R. Brown predicted the two men were concealing themselves, awaiting the sensation their loss would create in the public mind.[33]

On July 21, before any credible news concerning the fate of Donaldson and Grimwood had been received, Barnum callously "sent to the East for a new aeronaut," Professor Samuel King. By July 24, King had already begun making ascensions in the *Buffalo*."[34] Perhaps in response to public sentiment, an attaché of Barnum's put out the story that Donaldson was not dead, but had rejoined the show before it reached St. Louis and was in hiding because he "lost Grimwood." "King," he said, "did the balloon business" until that time when his contract expired and "Hurd wouldn't pay his price any longer." Donaldson then resumed flying under the name "Sailor Ned."[35] Although generally disbelieved, the name "Sailor Ned" stuck to Donaldson and clouded his reputation.

By July 23, newspapers reported, "the world has grown rather tired" of the speculation and predicted ballooning would soon be abandoned "when all the balloonists have been killed off."[36]

A Long and Discouraging Month

Humor, despair, anger, hope, disinterest. Nearly three and a half weeks passed without a substantial lead before a bottle was discovered containing a card on which was written:

A typical newsprint advert alerting people to the acts being offered. The well known Donaldson was one of Barnum's main attractions (*The World* [New York], July 30, 1874).

This wet-plate albumen Cabinet Card photograph depicts aeronaut James Allen (on the platform above the car) with a bride and groom. The ceremony took place at the State Fair Grounds, Providence, Rhode Island, September 27, 1888. Being married "among the clouds" became the rage after the Civil War and was frequently incorporated into balloon acts attached to circuses (by permission of the National Air and Space Museum, Smithsonian Institution, Washington, D.C.).

July 16, 2 A.M. We cannot stay up more than an hour longer, as the gas is rapidly escaping. N.S.G.

The handwriting was pronounced to be Grimwood's.[37] And then, 33 days after their disappearance, the body of Grimwood was discovered. A mail carrier named Beckwith, traveling the area between Stony Creek and Montague, noticed a peculiar smell and came upon a human being lying face down on the beach. Decomposition, "horrible to the senses," had set in: the hair was nearly all gone and the face badly disfigured. Fastened around the waist was a broken life preserver retaining no sustaining power and in the pockets were found a diary, library card, letters and a watch, stopped at 20 minutes past 11. The body was fully clothed except for boots and hat, with the top buttons tightly fastened, implying Grimwood had prepared to swim.

Burying the body where it lay, the effects were brought back to Chicago. It was presumed Donaldson's body would wash to shore near that of the newspaperman's but when the "floater" was not found, many expressed the belief that Donaldson had remained in the balloon after Grimwood left, and might still be alive, although hiding.

At Minneapolis, where Barnum's Hippodrome exhibited to 12,000 people, management read the Associated Press report on the discovery of Grimwood's body. "It created intense excitement, as did also the appearance of Miss Taylor, Donaldson's affianced, who immediately afterward participated in a hurdle race."[38] It was later stated she was one of the principal riders and was obliged to appear, "although her tearstained cheek was plainly visible to all."[39]

An inquest was held August 18 and rendered a verdict of accidental drowning.[40] On August 20, a large quantity of silk and netting, supposed to belong to the lost balloon, was found in Green Bay.[41] Finally, in an exclusive that broke on August 23, the Cincinnati *Times* announced that Donaldson had been found alive. According to a Mr. Wilson, editor of the Pembroke (Ontario) *News*, he and a party of friends on a fishing trip fifty miles from Lake des Quinzes discovered Donaldson, left leg and arm broken, in the final stages of starvation.

In a bizarre deathbed confession, the aeronaut described the horrific storm that nearly drove them into the lake. Grimwood, becoming "completely unmanned," threatened to lighten the balloon of his companion's weight. Donaldson responded in "self defense" by tossing the reporter overboard.

Once relieved of Grimwood's weight, the balloon shot up and pursued a course into Canada. Donaldson passed out and only awoke as the machine crashed into the treetops. Wilson concluded, "Once in the hands of his fellow-beings, and his story told, the will which had sustained him seemed to fail, and a quiet death soon followed."[42]

Reaction was swift. The New York *Graphic* accused the Chicago newspapers of making the story up.[43] The New York *World*, on August 24, called the report a hoax, poking holes in the story. No positive identification of the body was ever made. More likely, the remains of a man discovered November 22, 1876, in Newaygo County, Michigan, were those of Donaldson.[44]

August 20, 1875, P. T. Barnum published a card in the New York *Sun* relieving himself of all blame, and while deploring the loss, stated that "we have the satisfaction of knowing that nothing was spared to render all his ascensions safe and agreeable."[45]

For a while, at least, balloons in the air were considered "flying Dutchmen,"[46] and the expression, "Donaldsoned" became synonymous with being drowned. In a less than touching effort "to keep the memory of the aeronaut fresh in the minds," tiny balloons with Donaldson and Barnum's pictures were offered for sale at every city in which the Hippodrome stopped.[47]

In a strange ending, if ending it is, in 1880, a junk dealer bought a load of bottles kept in a liquor warehouse, gathered about the city around 1875. In one of them was found a card on which was penciled:

> The hurricane is upon us. Our sand is all exhausted. A few moments and the balloon will be in the water. Tell Barnum to give the balance of my salary to Molly. Good-bye. Grimwood behaves nobly. DONALDSON.

D. S. Thomas identified the handwriting as Donaldson's. He said "Molly" referred to Barnum's highest-salaried hurdle rider, Maggie Taylor, to whom the aeronaut was engaged and gave the pet name.[48] The note presented a far better view of Donaldson and Grimwood than the cruel hoax perpetrated by editor Wilson.

Professor King continued to make ascensions for Barnum in the *Cloud Nymph* until the end of the season, when he left to devote his time in preparing two balloons for the coming centennial.[49]

36

Seekers after the Philosopher's Stone

Barnum is going round telling people about "The World and How to Live in It."
The way not to live in it is to go up in one of his balloons.[1]

The attrition of balloonists continued in horrific numbers, primarily among the untrained, whether independent operators or attached to circuses. By the summer of 1874 flights were occasionally attended by "accident agents." A passenger making a tethered ascent could buy $3,000 worth of life insurance for 25 cents, "so that in case of disaster the heirs of deceased may have some substantial consolation."[2] Even "Sailor Ned" (the name reputed to have been used by Donaldson) was not immune. On September 29, 1875, an aeronaut by that name ascended from Cincinnati in one of Barnum's balloons. In attempting to land, he was dragged a long distance, the balloon being torn to shreds. He was thrown out, but fortunately survived.[3]

Events coming out of San Francisco were at least different. In February 1874 James Allen arrived in San Francisco by the steamer *Montana* from Panama with two balloons, one holding 65,000 cubic feet of gas and the other a smaller one serving to provide tethered ascensions. He proposed to give instructions in balloon management.[4] His arrival was heralded as being that of "The first aeronaut of long, tried professional experience that has ever visited the Pacific Coast." Described as "an elderly man," he made captive ascensions from Woodward's Gardens.[5]

John Steiner, then making his residence in Oakland, was called upon to take part in the 25th anniversary of California's admission to the Union. On September 9, 1875, he sat on a swing under the aerostat and managed to cross the Contra Costa Mountains, where he landed 30 minutes later near Moraga Valley. After disembarking, the balloon re-ascended without him.[6]

On September 26 he made an hour and a half flight from San Francisco, arriving at Contra Costa. In descending, the basket became separated from the balloon, dropping him to the ground with a terrible shock. He lost his second balloon but survived with a concussion to the body. Returning home to his wife, Steiner observed, "the Pacific coast is not the most delightful place in the world for ballooning."[7]

"Hanging on" toward the Centennial

The grand balloon ascension of Professor Denniston was advertised as being the event of the day for the July 4, 1875, celebrations at Eau Claire. A local man named Edward

Carmichael was induced to put up $1,000 for the project. For this sum, Denniston paraded about town "in gay livery turnouts," buying whisky for himself and his friends. On the promised day, however, he attempted to take his leave (in a carriage) without so much as a "'Thank you my friends, 'Good day,' 'Go to thunder,' or an apology of any sort." The townspeople then ordered him to make of a go of it, which he made with reluctance, and "with fear and trembling" gave the word. The balloon rose 100 feet in the air and promptly came down to the ire of the spectators.[8]

The extended Wise family continued performing, with Lizzie Ihling making an ascent from Philadelphia on July 5, 1875. At a considerable height her basket began violently oscillating; then the balloon exploded and began a rapid descent. She fainted, remembering nothing until helped out of the car.[9] John Wise made his 453rd balloon ascent from Philadelphia in September, followed by Lizzie, who made a voyage in the *Republic*, narrowly escaping death when she became overcome by escaping gas. Wise's grandson John made the third ascent of the day, landing near Holmesburg.[10]

An advertisement for Professor Dennison's balloon ascent in 1874 from eau Claire, Wisconsin. The flight apparently went off well, for he was invited back in 1875. Presumably the offer was not extended in 1876 (*Eau Claire Weekly Free Press* [Wisconsin], June 25, 1874).

For the Centennial year, Wise was in Philadelphia, with a scheme to "symbolize the progress of our country's life" by furnishing the corporate authorities with "a fleet of balloons" in which to cross the Atlantic."[11] He then supervised Lizzie's ascension, who went up in her classic costume impersonating the Goddess of Liberty. For her services she required $250 from the city to supply the gas. Mother Nature intervened, however and just as she stepped into the car a tremendous storm broke and the balloon burst.[12]

Ihling did make an ascension from Huntingdon on August 12, under John Wise's supervision. She traveled fifteen miles and landed safely at Franklinville. One of the scientific projects she carried was "ozone paper," which changed from white to brown during the course of the flight.[13]

Centennial celebrations around the country were in full swing by the fall of 1875. Among the most ambitious were those under the management of Samuel King. He proposed an "aeronautic observatory," in Buffalo, where a number of balloons would be kept on hand during July for captive ascents.[14]

The bizarre events of January 19, 1876, changed his plans. While in Buffalo attending to details, he went to the office of Dr. Dayton to obtain his signature on a petition. At the office was a nine-year-old girl who subsequently returned home and reported the aeronaut had made improper advances. Her parents immediately instituted prosecution. King was arrested at the Erie Railroad depot and taken into custody, charged with assault and "intent to commit rape."

At an inquest before Judge King, the aeronaut "responded with great feeling, 'Not guilty, so help me God.'" He testified that he has caressed the child "as any man would naturally do," but denied any improper act or intent. He was given the choice of being tried for rape, or taking proceedings to trial for indecent assault. By advice of council he took the latter alternative and was fined $50. King, a married man with children, wept with evident intense emotion when professing his innocence. "The tender age of the child, in the opinion of the justice, precluded the possibility of her statement being a fabrication."[15]

King left for Philadelphia and pitched his idea to operate a dozen first-class balloons in Fairmount Park during the Centennial. He required $30,000–40,000 expenses and the passenger fees for his profit.[16] His proposed ascension on the 4th was cancelled due to rain.

The Centennial proved unlucky for aeronautics around the country, especially so for the Allens. James intended to carry up a large party, but the gas was poor, forcing him to ascend alone. James K. (his son) made an attempt from New Bedford but the balloon was dashed against a pump and burst; Ezra was scheduled to fly from Newport, Rhode Island, but the balloon struck some telegraph wires and got caught in a tree.[17]

Professor Thurston ascended at Ravenna, Ohio, on the 4th without a basket and Nellie Thurston made an ascent at Odonsburg the same day.[18] Not to leave anyone out, J.C. Bellman, the "balloon editor," ascended from Indianapolis with a company of others on July 25. Two years later he was still performing in the state, making an ascension at the State Fair.[19]

In a strange, two-line obituary on July 21, 1876, a short blurb noted that aeronaut John A. Light "was killed a few days ago, at New Paris, Ill., in a row. A woman is said to have been at the bottom of it."[20] In a not unusual twist of fate, his wife, Lizzie L. Light, took to the skies. By 1877 she had made three successful ascensions.[21]

In scientific news, the re-discovery of Leverrier's planet was announced. "Vulcan" was described as the youngest of the planets, continually floating in a sea of unimaginable light, making a revolution around the sun in 23 days.

Aeronaut Harry Gilbert, Donaldson's friend, became attached to the Exposition of the Tradesmen's Industrial Institute and was scheduled to make balloon ascensions in the *Don-*

"THE DAY WE CELEBRATE."

GRAND BALLOON ASCENSION

GRAND FOURTH of JULY DEMONSTRATION

AT LOGANSPORT, INDIANA.

Balloon ascensions quickly became in integral part of the Independence Day celebrations, although ironically, it seemed more accidents and "no goes" occurred on July 4 than any other day (*Logansport Phars* [Indiana], June 30, 1881).

aldson every day for the first two weeks, beginning August 16, 1876.[22] He spent 1877 in Cincinnati offering captured flights for $2 each[23]; in June 1878 he was in Logansport offering to ascend on July 4 if money could be raised to justify the exhibition.[24]

A triple race was scheduled from Cincinnati on September 1 between Helen A. Thiers in the *Erkenbrecher*, Gilbert and a party in the *America* and Hayden with his party in the *Leo Steele*. Thiers rose highest; The *America* was the first to land near Newtown, Thiers went further, descending at Batavia and the *Leo Steele* traveled the greater distance, landing at Mount Carmel.[25] Another race between Thiers and Gilbert was to come off in Indianapolis on October 1, but owing to bad weather, he refused to let Thiers proceed. To appease the crowd Gilbert attempted to ascend in the smaller balloon but it was released before he was ready. The car was dashed against a tree, the envelope was split and he jumped out, falling thirty feet. He sustained a fracture to his left knee and internal injuries.[26] Hayden continued ballooning, ascending in the Midwest. In 1882, he went up from Cincinnati in the *Mabley*.[27]

Another of Donaldson's friends, D. S. Thomas, still listed as Barnum's Press Agent, ascended alone in the new balloon, *W.H. Donaldson*, from Bridgeport, Connecticut, October 3, 1876. Losing his anchor and being without a "rip-cord" to collapse the balloon, he endeavored to wreck it in the woods. In doing so, the basket was overturned, throwing him out. Thomas narrowly escaped death after his successful sixty-mile flight, completed in fifty minutes. He went on to write a book of his 34 balloon voyages, entitled *Reminiscences of an Amateur Aeronaut*, in 1895.[28]

In one of the more novel enterprises using balloons, Ferdinand Habermann of New Zealand proposed sending up a number of 7-foot balloons filled with canisters of powder. When they reached cloud level, they were to be ignited by a fuse, the explosions hopefully breaking the clouds to make rain.[29] The idea of seeding reappeared in 1880 when General Daniel Ruggles of Virginia proposed to send up skeleton balloons filled with dynamite, exploded by fuses or magneto electricity, supposing the concussions and vibrations might consolidate mists into raindrops.[30]

Samuel King, now referred to as "Professor King of Philadelphia," barnstormed over the south in 1877. The season of 1878 saw him making voyages in Trenton and Philadelphia while advertising in Milwaukee, asking $1,000 for expenses[31] and writing letters to Dubuque newspapers, lowering his price to $300.[32]

Charles Francis Ritchel (variously misspelled in the newspapers) of Corry, Pennsylvania, first hit the national scene in March 1878 with his "flying machine," then being constructed at Bridgeport. It consisted of a black silk cylinder 24 feet long and 12 feet diameter, holding 3,000 feet of gas. In front of the seats were two hand-operated cranks attached to a wheel, which in turn was connected with an upright shaft at the lower end, which operated a fan similar to the screw of a propeller. At the front was another fan capable of being turned in any direction.

Ritchel claimed to have been working on the idea since 1871 and had advanced far enough in seven years to interest even P. T. Barnum, who was present at a test of the model on March 14. It failed when the fan broke.[33]

In May, the machine was exhibited at the new Permanent Exhibition in Philadelphia; on June 12 a successful test was made, with the aeronaut maneuvering backward, forward and against the wind at will.[34] In Boston on July 4, another trial of the hydrogen-filled flying machine was made. The operator, Mark Quinlan, shot up 2,000 feet and quickly discovered that the gearing would not work. After a daring repair job of crawling under the machine, he discovered a loose screw. Upon tightening that, the fans worked and he landed at Farnumsville. A second trial the same day proved a failure as the machine would not fly against a strong current.[35]

Despite Fanny Irvine's enthusiastic poem and some success displaying the machine as a novelty, the idea ultimately proved unworkable.

> The telephone a great wonder has been,
> But what is that to the flying machine?

We are born, we're married, and buried T'ween,
All done in a flash, thro' the flying machine.[36]

Ballooning around the Country

Aeronaut Nellie Thurston, still traveling with Professor Squires, made an ascension near Syracuse, New York, in September 1877, landing safely near Cortland, and in October another successful flight was made at Baldwinsville, landing 33 minutes later in McFranville, 60 miles distant.[37]

Professor Kinney, of Kinney's Balloon Museum fame, was still operating in 1878, employing another familiar name, William J. Shotts, and Professor Lapere, a trapeze artist.[38]

In a lighter vein, Signor Pedanto was another of the traveling aeronaut-gymnasts making the Midwest circuit in 1878. Billed as the "man-fly," his notoriety was walking on a rope head downward like a fly walks on the ceiling. In October he was promised $275 to perform certain specified ascensions. After completing the first of two flights, he took off in his balloon, leaving his manager, J. M. Clark, to pay his creditors. Clark attempted to collect Pedanto's pay but discovered the aeronaut had already drawn most of it. Some $89 was owed for the gas and an equal amount to the hotel where Pedanto stayed. Lawsuits were issued fast and furiously. Clark was held accountable for the sums, but owing to a clerical error his name was misspelled on the contracts and he was relieved of responsibility, leaving the gas-man and the hotel owner "to carry on the contest in courts over all that is left of Sig. Pedanto."[39]

In less grim news, toy balloons continued to be a popular and occasionally useful amusement. In 1877, the "Squawk! Squawk" of new toy balloons were envisioned as "the meanest sort of revenge" if the earsplitting noisemakers could be supplied to the children of one's enemies.[40] Balloons were also sold formed into the shape of men. A device on the back, wound up with a key, made them twist and turn in the air like real men.[41] And for those not brave enough to be an aeronaut, they might seek an ancillary career as a balloon vendor: for a mere $20, a gas machine plus two gross of toy balloons could be had.[42] There were risks, however, as those holding stock in the World's Fair Captive Balloon Company discovered when it went into receivership.[43] Finally, in India, captive balloon flights were offered to sick people who could not afford to leave home. After a few days in the air, the pure atmosphere braced the most languid individuals.[44]

37

"Paddy-Whacks" but "No Balloon Rackets!"

When a professor, a newspaper reporter, and a bear go up together in a balloon, and any accident occurs by reason of which it becomes necessary to lighten the machine, we think the professor should be thrown overboard first, and the reporter next, in the humane endeavor to save the bear.[1]

The world was changing. Balloon ascensions were illuminated by electric light.[2] Thomas Edison reproduced the human voice; the National Bell Telephone Company was licensed. Gasoline was being manufactured. Refrigerators and Singer Sewing Machines were being sold. Elevators were built in New York City hotels; electric house bells and burglar alarms were put in wealthy homes. Lea & Perrin's Worcestershire Sauce was stocked on grocer's shelves alongside Carter's Little Liver Pills. The day of the independent businessman was being eclipsed by monopolies. A man named Mr. Johnson from New Orleans developed a method by which a rural scene in miniature, including a working windmill and a balloon conveying two aeronauts toward the clouds, was seen moving across a 3-foot-square backdrop.[3] Medicine warned that most virulent diseases of the blood were capable of being transmitted from person to person by means of toy balloons, as they passed through the mouths of three or four workmen before the sale.[4] A different sort of science practiced dropping torpedoes from aerial machines.

Nothing would ever be the same. Private aeronauts could be engaged for as little as $100 for a 4th of July performance.[5] Glossing over numerous accidents and "no goes," circuses boldly proclaimed "No Balloon Rackets!"[6]

> Knick-knack Paddy-whack;
> Give the dog a bone;
> This old man came rolling home.

Human life was cheaper than rhyme. In the late 1870s, the "monstrosity of a circus," the great Arabian Paddy-Whack Circus and Balloon Show, "ran up a horrendous record of accidents." In Phenixville, Pennsylvania, a trapeze performer by the name of Robert Hoagland, going by the stage name "Bob Cavella," fell from a balloon in September 1878. In May, after being given up by his doctors, his family removed him from St. Barnabas Hospital and carried him home to die.[7]

With ballooning literally falling into the realm of gymnasts and amateurs, only one goal remained for the old guard — that of crossing the Atlantic — and even that seemed a moot point. After so many expensive failures, technology was expanding in other directions. Most educated people believed that when aeronautics became truly practical, it would be from a direction far removed from balloons.

Samuel A. King knew those facts. Yet he could not abandon the dream without one last try. By early 1879 his plans were fixed. He proposed two spherical balloons, each 65 feet in diameter with a capacity of 150,000 cubic feet of gas, to be inflated with hydrogen. He would use a cable 1,000 feet in length to elevate and lower the balloon, worked by a steam hoisting apparatus. After numerous tests, he proposed to go in the spring or fall of 1880.[8]

King's plan included making captive balloon ascents from Coney Island; he avowed, "I believe that if I meet with no accidents, you can count on the ocean voyage as good as made."[9] With the American Aeronautic Society expending $75,000 for the experiment, King's first balloon, the *Pioneer*,

An advertisement for an illuminated balloon proved a novel excitement for spectators in Fort Wayne for the 4th of July, 1887 (*Fort Wayne* June 9, 1887).

ascended from an amphitheater on Manhattan Beach. Passengers were to be allowed to accompany the aeronaut on subsequent ascensions "at a special price."[10]

The idea went up with a "boom" on August 18, 1879, when the *Pioneer* burst, putting an end to the American Aeronautic Society, which suffered $5,000 in claims filed against the bankrupt company.[11] The New York *Times* sarcastically noted, "It was reported that Prof. King was sitting in the rain, with a big darning needle, mending up his captive balloon, but as the door of the inclosure [sic] was locked, the report could not be verified. The festive balloon that goes up when it gets ready, and comes down with a whack is named the Pioneer, but unscrupulous little Coney Island boys have nicknamed it the Pie an' Beer. No extra charge is made for a rapid descent, and $5 'ascension fee' paying all expenses, both up and down."[12]

Nor did the idea of navigating balloons go away quietly. In April 1879, two engineers from Montreal, Richard W. Cowan and Charles A. Page, invented an aerial car with paddlewheels to be used for propelling a balloon. They became associated with Professor Charles H. Grimley, an Englishman previously working the New York and Canadian circuit.[13] After Cowan's airship, *Canada*, failed to ascend on June 21, 1879, from the Shamrock Lacrosse grounds,[14] the actual test came on July 31. This time, the *Canada* was filled with a light gas made especially for the purpose by the Montreal Gas Company. Grimley, Cowan, Page and three reporters went up, Page taking possession of the crank. Assisted by the reporters, they succeeded in descending and ascending by means of the rudder. On landing, Grimley pulled the escape valve and was finally forced to use the rip-line. They effected a safe arrival at Fami.[15]

Newspaper accounts of the voyage were mixed: in one, it was stated the steering apparatus had a "perceptible effect." Another noted, "The aerial car does not seem to have any appreciable effect in steering the balloon."[16]

By 1880, Grimley professed no faith in any apparatus for guiding balloons, continuing his free ascensions from Montreal.[17]

Ballooning on a smaller scale continued to maintain its public popularity, as evidenced by illustrations used to fill the *Young Folks News*, "the best Juvenile Newspaper for the price." The *Peanut* (4 inches by 5) was another such publication. The editor's comment in an 1879 edition was purely adult, however. When he requested a pass for Woodward's Gardens to watch an ascension, he received in reply a written permission to stand outside and see the balloon go up. In the next morning's issue, the reporter wrote, "We noticed Mr. Woodward sunning himself on Kearny street yesterday. We suppose they are cleaning his cage."[18]

Daredevil, fool or a little of both, men and women continued to make flights whenever they could make a booking. Superlatives helped. In May 1879, the "world-renowned aeronaut," Harry Gilbert, brokered a deal for a balloon race between himself and "the most daring lady aeronaut in the world," Helen A. Thiers, to be performed September 23rd from Fort Wayne.[19]

Nellie Thurston made a balloon ascent from Carthage, New York, September 5, 1879. In an extraordinary adventure, she landed in the depths of Lowville, and with night coming on, opted to sleep in the woods. Next morning, Thurston trekked seven miles, found a log cabin and obtained directions on how to reach civilization. Although followed by a bear, Nellie never lost her calm, finally reaching Lowville by 5 P.M. that evening.[20]

"The Safest Mode of Traveling in the World"

The years 1877–78 were something of a family affair for the Wise clan. Lizzie Ihling worked throughout the period under the direction of her agent, John M. Kinney. Johnny Wise, aged 16, and his sister Helen, aged 13, celebrated July 4 by ascending from Philadelphia, landing "somewhere in New Jersey." Two days later, Johnny went up with brother Paul, aged 10. John Wise superintended the flights, as he did the semi-weekly ascensions at the Permanent Exhibition.

In an interview given during the celebration, Wise declared that ballooning was the safest mode of traveling in the world, "for it is now, with modern appliance, an easy matter to land the air-ship; and even if it should burst, the friction of the atmosphere on the immense spread of canvas would be sufficient to prevent the aeronaut from dropping too suddenly."[21]

On July 21, Charles Wise made his first ascension in two years, ascending from Philadelphia.[22] John Wise traveled to St. Louis where his niece, Lizzie Ihling Wise (as she was often called), made her 20th solo aerial voyage from the Grand Avenue Base Ball Park on October 14. Described as being a tall, fine-looking lady between 25–30 years of age, she was one of her uncle's earliest pupils, first going up with him at age eight. Proving a fearless aeronaut, on this trip she nearly ended up in the river, but even though she could not swim, she handled the *Amazon* with great calmness, finally bringing it down in a nighttime descent. She made her 21st ascension from Bodermann's Grove, St. Louis, August 30, 1878, in the *Amazon*, landing near the Gravois road.[23] In July 1879, she was married in that city to Charles J. Helfenstine, formerly of Lancaster, Pennsylvania.[24]

Professor Wise continued to give interviews throughout 1879, remarking on the feasibility of balloon voyages to the North Pole and hinting that he might try another trans–Atlantic voyage; preliminary experiments were already being tried out on Manhattan Beach, New York.[25] When Mayor Overstoltz, of St. Louis, heard of Wise's desire, he promised a good "send off," which Wise accepted. On August 15, 1879, Wise and his nephew, editor of the *Journal*, set off for that city.

The original plan called for a new balloon to be constructed exclusively for the purpose, with Wise, James F. Downey (Wise's son-in-law) as assistant, Charles G. Gonter (an old friend of Wise's), and a reporter to make the trip.[26] The expenses for the balloon were borne by Mr. Mabley, a St. Louis clothier.[27]

Plans changed, for on September 28, 1879, the 71-year-old John Wise made his 463rd ascent with only one person, George Burr, teller of the St. Louis National Bank, who had purchased a seat in the small car. Burr had made three previous ascensions, one in 1878, which badly crippled him by the too-sudden descent of the balloon. They ascended in the new balloon, *Pathfinder*, "solely in the interest of science, particularly meteorology," from Lindell Park.

The weather was not ideal with a stiff wind blowing. As the balloon was let go, it bounded away at a slant, barely avoiding the trees. Several men in the crowd foolishly caught hold of the three-quarter inch, 1,800-foot drag rope, giving the machine a great shock and causing a brief diagonal descent. The accident tore the netting (admitted by both Wise and John Jr. as being "light"), forcing Wise to sever the rope at the basket. This act proved significant as the drag rope (along with stacks of railroad advertisements he had been contracted to distribute), were the only ballast taken.[28]

Regaining equilibrium, the balloon took a northerly direction, crossed the Mississippi River near the mouth, and passed east of Alton. By September 30, no word had been received from the aeronauts. Because the lifting power was not considered equal to a long voyage, concern was raised for their safety.[29]

Balloon "sightings" became almost as common as speculations on the fate of the two unfortunates. By October 2, it was feared Wise and Burr had met the same tragic end as Donaldson and Grimwood, perishing in Lake Michigan. Inevitably, rumors circulated that the *Pathfinder* had been old and rotten, forcing Downey (who lived in Louisiana, Missouri) to publish a card October 3, stating the aerostat was new and made of the best material.[30]

William E. Burr, president of the St. Louis National Bank and brother of the missing aeronaut, offered a $250 reward for recovery of the body or information leading to its recovery.[31] John Wise, Jr., and a party left St. Louis on October 4, exploring the Macoupin creek bottoms. They were able to track the flight of the balloon by circulars found along the way, indicating the aeronauts had flown northeast in an almost straight line through three counties. One, labeled "Dropped from Prof. Wise's transcontinental balloon, the Pathfinder," was found at Carlinville, proving they had not wandered south and been lost in the dense forests.[32]

Similar to the Donaldson case, many people believed Wise was retaliating against the St. Louis newspapers, which he felt had not properly advertised his trip, by hiding out to increase suspense. Lending credence to this belief was Mabley's statement that Wise felt the investor had not received a just return for his outlay, but "the advertisement would prove a greater one than he had expected."[33]

Louis Faber and John Bulla of the Lake Shore and Michigan Southern Railroad stated that on Monday the 29th, they saw a balloon go overhead in the direction of Lake Michigan; on October 13, the Alton *Telegraph* reported that "a number of scientific men" were of the opinion a balloon found near Milwaukee was Wise's, and that the aeronauts had drowned in the lake.

Guesswork ended on October 25, when the body of George Burr was washed ashore near Miller's Station, Indiana, 30 miles from Chicago. It was badly decomposed and could only be identified by clothing, the teller's name appearing very plainly on his stockings. The body had neither coat nor boots, leading to the inference Burr had prepared to swim. The coroner's inquest resulted in the simple determination, "Found drowned."[34]

The discovery of the missing aeronaut in Lake Michigan, coupled with various sightings, led to the conclusion the *Pathfinder* reached the lake about 11 P.M., September 28, having traveled from St. Louis a distance of 300 miles in six hours. It was probable the balloon struck the water about that time, not far from shore and that Burr either jumped or was washed out of the car. Relieved of this weight, the balloon then re-ascended, perhaps carrying Wise, which would account for the well-corroborated reports that a balloon, with the car hanging to one side, was seen at 4 o'clock Monday morning in Michigan, 100 miles due north of Miller's Station.[35]

Assuming that to be true, it never explained why Wise did not land the balloon before reaching the lake, which would have been visible to him on the clear, moonlit night, at least 30 miles in advance. Charles Wise was among those left wondering. His father surely would have known the balloon could not pass over Lake Michigan, as the amount of gas taken in at Lindell Park could not have sustained it more than six hours, the precise time it took to reach the lake.[36]

Ironically, Donaldson and Wise, whose names were inextricably connected, met the same tragic fate. Like Donaldson, John Wise's body was never found, and no definitive answers were ever forthcoming.

In January 1880, John Wise, Jr., wrote a letter to the Whiteside County Agricultural Society, stating the entire affair was the fault of a man he did not name, "for his own financial benefit, and to satisfy his vanity." After failing Wise and Mr. Mabley on the advertising side, this person left the inflation to the elderly aeronaut. Since this was beyond his capabilities, Wise asked his grandson to handle the business. Clearly rankled by the affair, Wise, Jr., continued by stating that the flight "never would have been undertaken had it not been for the influence exercised by Mr.—on my grandfather in reference to outside matters."

Junior asserted the original plan called for him to ascend in the *Pathfinder*; that the elder Wise had made but one ascension in the past ten years not supervised by him or his father, and that one overseen by the individual in question. On that voyage, John Wise nearly lost his life and did lose his balloon. Wise Jr. concluded that the St. Louis voyage was poorly attended to, most specifically in the improper amount of ballast taken, adding that any descent at night was perilous and always attended by accident.[37]

Writing again a year later, Wise Jr. stated his belief that the tragedy was owing to the fact the senior aeronaut put the balloon in the hands of Burr while he took a nap and the banker failed to wake him. Burr, Wise asserted, an aeronaut himself, had purchased a balloon from Wise Sr. just before their ascent, promising to pay him $375 when the descent was made.[38]

The story was not quite over. Sightings of Wise's lost balloon continued toward the end of the decade, making it a sort of Flying Dutchman, "the name given by sailors to a spectral ship imagined to cruise in storms off the Cape of Good Hope, under full sail, when all honest vessels are fain to try bare poles." The newspaper concluded, "When such stories are rife, it is plainly only a step to the supernatural; and should the Wise mystery remain unsolved, out of it will likely come a wild spectral air-ship, drifting forever in the skies, and portending storms."[39] Watch the heavens.

In light of the disaster, the St. Louis *Globe-Democrat* called for a ban on balloon ascensions. The plea not only went unheeded, an aeronaut named Neil Brayton ascended from St. Charles, just west of St. Louis, on October 25, 1879, less than a month after the Wise disaster. James Downey, Wise's son-in-law, assisted with the inflation. Clad only in tights and hanging onto the rings, Brayton hung head downwards, barely missing several houses before reaching 500 feet. The balloon crossed the Mississippi and landed near Grafton, Illinois, 60 miles distant.[40]

The Coney Island Bat-Frog Monster

With his own failure still fresh, Samuel King gave a lengthy interview to the New York *Express* on the state of aerostation. He bluntly stated, "The day will never come when balloons will be made to navigate the air against the currents. That can only be done by flying machines having momentum, which a balloon is without." His view of the future held that a "flying machine will have wide, strong wings, and will be propelled by some great force — it may be nitroglycerine, it may be with gun-powder, and it may be hydrogen and oxygen gas, or it may be something else, that will give it momentum; but whatever it is, it will be light and compact, so that a handful of it, so to speak, will last a whole day."[41]

As with the death of Donaldson, balloonists ignored the fate of others and continued in their professions. Professor Carl Myers, formerly a photographer from Hornellsville, New York, returned in October 1879 after numerous ascensions in Ohio and Massachusetts. During the process of re-varnishing his balloon, the *Homing Antwerp*, he offered to make a flight with his wife, Mary (who later used the stage name "Carlotta"), for a nominal fee, "just for the sake of drawing a crowd into town and making a bit of a stir." Myers rarely made ascensions himself, typically acting as an aeronautic-engineer for a corps of aeronauts who he managed in the different states and Canada.[42]

Even more wondrous, Thomas A. Edison was "puzzling his brain to devise a bridge to span the 'mighty deep,'" the structure to consist of pipes through which gas was fed to large balloons placed short distances apart to support the aerial wonder,[43] and from Onondaga, New York, a marriage ceremony was to be performed in a balloon with a telephone strung to the ground so the congregation might hear the ceremony.[44]

In New York, torpedo balloons were experimented with, carrying 50-pound cans of nitroglycerine, released by clockwork after a lapse of time to carry the boat "over the populous area."[45] In Ohio, where piped gas was not plentiful, the recipe for concocting gas was supplied to would-be aeronauts:

> A. Place a quantity of zinc scraps in a bottle, pour over them a mixture of sulphuric acid and water, and hydrogen gas will be rapidly evolved.
> B. Convey this gas through a wash bottle to your balloon. This experiment should not be performed in the vicinity of a light or fire.[46]

If there were any doubt about women holding their own against men, the Whiteside County Agricultural Society put it to rest, at least in Illinois, when the committee engaged Nellie Thurston "at greater expense than any balloonist that has ever been in the state." Her balloon, *Satellite*, inflated under the supervision of Professor Squires, was open to public on September 11, drawing a huge crowd cheering her as the "Only Successful Lady Aeronaut in the World." On landing, the balloon rebounded several times before local men came to her assistance, afterward collecting small handfuls of sand ballast as mementos. The newspaper proclaimed, "We thought last years ascension, managed by the lamented Prof. John Wise, could never be equaled, but it has been, and many think the last ascension the best."[47]

Among all the ascensions of 1880, one deserves special note. In September, an apparition was observed over Coney Island. Several reputable witnesses described a deep, black-colored monster with bat's wings and improved frog's legs, soaring 1,000 feet in the air. They identified the alarming creature as a man flying toward New Jersey. A month previous, the exact creature was spotted over St. Louis by a number of persons "who happened to be sober," and later, reports of it came from Kentucky. "It is without doubt the most extraordinary and wonderful object that has ever been seen, and there should be no time lost in ascertaining its precise nature, habits and probable mission."[48]

38

Flying Too High

No doubt balloons have hitherto been very subject to accidents, and the bare idea of anything going wrong at the height of thousands of feet above the earth, has in it something very appalling.[1]

The French Aerial Navigation Society arranged a series of night ascents for the purpose of spectroscopic and electrical observations, sending up their balloon the *Zenith* on March 23, 1875, from Paris. The aeronauts were Captain Sivel, Croce-Spinelli, Gaston and Albert Tissandier, and Jobert. Following an eventful 23-hour journey, they alighted on the desert tracts near Arcachon, 300 miles distant.[2]

On April 15, Gaston Tissandier, Sivel and Croce-Spinelli made a second ascension for the object of making experiments on the lungs at an extremely high altitude. An hour and 20 minutes into the flight the *Zenith* reached the height of 7,000 yards, with a temperature of 50° Fahrenheit. Tissandier felt weak and took some of the oxygen they carried in little balloons, designed under the direction of Dr Paul Bert. At 8,000 yards altitude, Tissandier became powerless to use the oxygen and passed out. When he awoke two hours later, the balloon was rapidly descending and his companions lay insensate at the bottom of the car. He fainted again and was aroused by Croce, who ordered him to throw out more ballast to break their freefall. He did so and relapsed into insensibility. When he reanimated, the others were crouched down, heads covered by their cloaks. On attempting to wake them, he observed Sivel's face was black and his mouth full of blood. Croce-Spinelli's eyes were shut and his lips blood-stained.

Eventually reaching earth, Tissandier faced the grim truth that his friends had perished from asphyxiation (or died from "apoplexy, the consequence of insufficient atmospheric pressure in the higher regions of the air").[3] Suffering a fit of feverish excitement, Tissandier "sobbed to suffocation," and was taken to Ciron, near Le Blanc, almost dead.[4]

The two aeronauts were buried in Paris on April 20, with Mr. Lomat, a representative of the Smithsonian, tendering the homage of that institution to the martyrs of science.[5] By October, $15,000 had been collected for their families.[6]

If proof were needed that advertising throughout the ages has been in bad taste, a short promotion appeared in an American newspaper stating that the uncontrollable ascent of the balloon containing the two unfortunate aeronauts "was occasioned by their carrying too large a stock of Peerless Baking Powder in their stores for a short trip."[7]

On May 2, M. de Fonville made a balloon ascent from Paris to determine whether the air at five miles was insufficient to sustain human life. At 12,000 feet, he experienced no

difficulty breathing, but a bird suspended in a cage near the mouth of the balloon was suf-
focated by inhaling the escaping gas, leading him to conclude a similar occurrence aboard
the *Zenith* actually killed Sivel and Croce-Spinelli.[8] Interestingly, that May, M. Trove, a
civil engineer, offered to ascend to the height of seven miles. If breathing became difficult,
he proposed putting on an India-rubber diver's dress, provided with an airtight mask for
the face. The mask had two tubes inserted between the teeth: one for a supply of pure air
from a reservoir and the other for the expulsion of vitiated air.[9]

A less hazardous voyage for Eugene Godard, at least, occurred on May 16, when the
aeronaut let down his frequent companion, Jack the monkey, in a parachute. Jack, a famous
gymnast in his own right, was unfortunately blown into the pond at the Zoological Garden.
After struggling mightily and close to drowning, he was fished out by a net and saved.[10]

During the French Exhibition of 1867, a huge captive balloon became one of the main
attractions at the Champ de Mars. Capable of reaching 800 feet, with a capacity of 176,660
cubic feet of gas, the "monster" was maneuvered by means of a steam engine dubbed the
"injector," invented by Henry Giffard, who made a fortune from it. An even greater balloon
was planned for the upcoming Paris Exhibition of 1878. Gaston Tissandier submitted the
proposal to the French commissioners. The balloon was to be made of a solid material
impermeable to hydrogen gas, manufactured alternately with sheets of linen and caoutchouc
and protected by varnish. Attached to earth by eight cables, the car was to hold 40–50 persons and be reached by two movable gangways.[11]

While activities for the Exhibition were underway, the French government auctioned
the last four balloons constructed for the siege of Paris. Considered unfit for service, an
appropriation of $40,000 was placed in the budget for new military balloons.[12] The gov-
ernment was proven correct in its assessment; on Easter Monday, 1879, the aeronaut L'Estrange (Blondin's stage name) ascended from Australia in the *Aurora*, the same balloon used
to convey dispatches during the Franco–Prussian War. After ascending nearly two miles,
the well-patched aerostat burst, sending L'Estrange zigzaging to the ground. He struck a
tree and survived with only bruises.[13]

After losing out on a space at the Champ de Mars, the Monster Captive Balloon created
for the Exhibition of 1878 was established at Tuilleries, the proprietors paying a ground rent
of $3,000. On July 20, 1878, the maiden voyage of Giffard's balloon reached 700 yards
before drawn down by a steam windlass. By far the largest balloon ever made, its diameter
measured 118 feet, with a total cubic capacity of 882,900 feet. It was reported to have cost
$150,000, with Giffard paying the entire sum.[14]

On July 19, the balloon was opened to the public for the cost of 20 francs ($4) per
person. A typical ascent took 20 minutes. Passengers remained airborne another 20 minutes
before descending, making each trip approximately one hour's duration. A voyager described
his wonder at the quiet that quickly surrounded the ascending balloon and the utter lack
of any sensation of motion, unless he happened to look down. It was, he wrote, worth the
three-hour wait in line.[15]

After two weeks, the new construction proved successful, for no gas had escaped. On
some days as many as seventeen ascents were made and by September, receipts totaled
£8,000. By October 8, 748 ascensions had been made, totaling 21,604 passengers, while
another 250,000 paid one franc for admittance to the yard, for a total receipt of $128,625.20.
After nearly three months, no loss of gas was reported and the varnish remained intact.[16]

The famous Sarah Bernhardt became one of the most famous persons to ride in the
Monster, by some reports ascending three times a day. She also made a free balloon ride,

alighting fifteen miles east of Paris. Another person, this one made famous by association, was a boy born while his mother was aloft. At the conclusion of the Exhibition, the balloon was sold to an Englishman for $20,000.[17]

In April 1879, it was announced that another captive balloon, 11 feet high, would be set up at Tuilleries Garden, charging only $2 per person. It proved so successful that even Victor Hugo made his first aerial trip in July, and the proprietor began offering night flights, some of which were situated so as to allow the passengers to view the sunrise.[18] On the afternoon of August 17 (other reports give the date as the 15th), a squall came up and the balloon burst with a noise like a thunderclap. The vessel was empty at the time and only one employee was injured.[19]

As the century drew on, the International Exhibition of Electricity opened in Paris on August 10, 1881. Among the wonders was a model balloon created by M. Tissandier with a propeller run by a Siemens dynamo-electric machine that operated a screw, creating a speed of ten feet per second. The aeronaut proposed to create a colossal balloon on the same principal, capable of lifting a 26-ton load and traveling at 25 miles per hour. The success of storing electricity in Gaston Plante and Chouille Faure's batteries also prompted the idea of driving balloons by these devices; M. Trouve demonstrated its practicality by employing the Plante battery to propel a tricycle along the streets of Paris.[20]

"John Bull" Takes On a New Meaning

While France was preparing for the Great Exhibition, not a little excitement was occasioned in England on August 28, 1876, when two aeronauts, J. Morton and Silyanus Tanner ascended from Alexandria palace. After crossing the Thames they descended in a field. As Morton alit, a large bull gave a tremendous bellow and charged them. The aeronauts quickly discharged ballast, but failed to escape the horns of the infuriated animal that tore the grapnel line. Tanner grabbed his partner, heaved him into the car and they miraculously escaped.[21]

On May 21, 1877, one of the worst balloon accidents occurred at Hull, England. Aeronauts J. Medcalf and J. Whitaker were ascending in the *Queen* when it came in contact with a striking machine, ripping the fabric. The aerostat blew over a bogie fire belonging to one of the stall-keepers, igniting the gas. The balloon exploded, casting sheets of flame over the spectators. In four minutes, over eighty-three people were burned, six dangerously.[22]

In perhaps a page from history, two peasants in Leicestershire, England, came upon the remnants of a balloon. Inside the car was a skeleton, on the finger of which was a ring inscribed, "Allen Fern, 1467."[23]

The idea of exploring the North Pole by balloon gained new popularity in 1877, when Captain John P. Cheyne, a retired British naval officer and a veteran of three polar expeditions in search of the missing Franklin party, volunteered to conduct an aerial party over the frozen regions. Not to be left out, in early 1878, the United States Senate passed a bill appropriating $50,000 to promote Captain Howgate's colonization scheme, whereby fifty men were to establish a colony at Lady Franklin Bay and extensively explore the polar icecap.[24]

The London Balloon Society inaugurated their winter session of 1881 with an address by W. H. Le Fevre on an electric stationary balloon invented by Jules Godard and de Fonvielle. To prevent a balloon from gyrating, an electric current was transmitted from one side to the other, countering the motion and placing the car in equilibrium. The Plante-Faure battery that produced the electric current would, at the same time, act on a shaft running at the bottom of the car, turning a screw. The balloon would thus neither ascend nor descend.[25]

The advance of technology may have frightened an eccentric, 83-year-old man of Lincolnshire, England, who became convinced the world was coming to an end. He ordered a balloon made by means of which he hoped to ascend and witness the destruction of the planet without sharing its fate. Where he proposed to land remained unclear.[26]

Godard's stabilizer might have come in useful when the War Office balloon *Saladin* captained by Templer, of the Royal Engineers, and accompanied by Walter Powell, Member of Parliament from Malmsburg and Mr. Gardner, ascended from Bath December 10, 1881. On descent, Templer and Gardner were thrown out but Powell, unable to escape, was carried out to sea.[27] A £200 reward was offered for information and various sightings were reported; later in the month, a broken thermometer belonging to the aeronaut was found on the Dorsetshire coast, leading to the conclusion Powell drowned.[28] The balloon, with Powell's body inside, was eventually found on January 21, 1882, in the Sierra Pedrosa.[29]

By November 1, 1881, having failed to obtain sufficient funds for his polar expedition, Commander Cheyne was in New York, seeking donations equaling $75,000–$180,000 to enable himself and Lieutenant Schwatka to make the journey.[30] On December 12, from Canada, he spoke of an "Anglo-American expedition," whereby each country would donate $40,000 to pay for the construction of three balloons, each costing $4,000. Cheyne continued to promote his idea through 1882, noting it would go through three stages: suggestion, ridicule and adoption.[31] He was correct about the first two.

"Gentleman, We Are One Too Many"

Mr. Simmons Lynn made a balloon flight from Calcutta on January 29, 1878, that had an unusual twist. Lynn had planned on taking with him Blondin (L'Estrange), the aeronaut, but owing to the poor quality of gas, went up alone. Drifting over the jungle, he had no option but to attempt a landing or remain aloft all night. Bringing the balloon down, he found a relatively clear spot and he came within 50 yards of the ground before observing a huge crocodile in the bulrushes moving toward him. After calling "lustily for help," some natives waded through the mud and after much persuasion, were induced to drag the balloon three miles away to a clearing where the aeronaut got out in safety.[32]

Fair wind or foul, nothing, it seemed, could keep the Godards down for long — or in one place. Fanny Godard and M. Keril both had their arms broken by an accident during a balloon ascension at Amsterdam in 1879; in 1881, Eugene Godard ascended from Vienna on a Sunday evening in September. After narrowly escaping death by being trapped between two thunderstorms, the aeronaut, accompanied by three journalists, brought the vessel down toward what he believed to be safety, only to discover they were in imminent peril of descending into the Danube. Godard cried out, "Gentlemen, we are one too many," inferring that a reporter ought to save the others by self-sacrifice. The "offer" went unheeded and every unresisting article was thrown overboard. This enabled the car to skim over the top of the waves long enough for assistance to arrive.[33] Eugene Godard ascended again at Berlin in 1882, making his 1,867th ascent. It was estimated that in his career, he traveled over 1,000 leagues in the air.[34]

With each year seemingly beginning or ending with a report of war, a Nihilist plot was foiled by Russian police when they arrested a number of people attempting to assassinate the Czar. The plan involved bringing a balloon filled with dynamite and explosive fireballs down near Gatschina. After the explosives set the palace on fire, the terrorists hoped to seize the ruler and his family.[35]

39

"A Ridiculous 'Flunk'"

It is to be hoped that the voyage of Prof. King may demonstrate the safety and utility of the balloon. We must have some way of getting across the state of Missouri without being robbed and murdered.[1]

Captain Cheney's North Pole Expedition went through two of three stages: suggestion and ridicule. Samuel A. King's plans took him to the third stage of adoption, but just barely.

Colonel S. W. King, casting about for a "supreme attraction" to open the Minneapolis Fair, hit upon the idea of asking aeronaut S. A. King to make a pre–trans–Atlantic flight during the proceedings. The colonel offered to cover the immense expense of hydrogen gas and King accepted, hoping that if all went well, to make his ocean voyage from New York to London at the height of the September trade winds.[2]

Samuel King received a draft for $3,000 on August 12 and promised to leave for Minneapolis by September 1. He proposed taking Charles M. Faye of the Minneapolis *Tribune*, Winslow Upton of the Signal Service, Luther L. Holden of the Boston *Journal*, W.G. Nicholas of the Chicago *Times*, E.B. Johnson of the St. Paul and Minneapolis *Pioneer Press* and Mr. Chester of the New York *Spirit of the Times* (later replaced by W. Greemer of the New York *Herald*). King predicted the balloon, *The Great Northwest*, would reach New York in perfect safety, in one of the "most thrilling voyages ever made."[3]

Providing each aeronaut with a suit of rubber clothing, a compass, an automatic lamp and flask of corn juice to guard against snake bites,[4] the great aerostat ascended Monday, September 12, carrying seven persons and 500 pounds of ballast. It traveled only a few miles before King was forced to bring it down near Fort Snelling, St. Paul, claiming, "the gas failed." King eventually called the flight off, had the balloon collapsed and sent east, reportedly being "deeply chagrined" at the failure. So, too, was Colonel King, who spent $8,000 on the voyage (Freeborn County Standard).[5] The much-advertised trip was ultimately styled "a ridiculous 'flunk'" and a "fizzle." The rainy-week fair ended $18,000 in arrears.[6]

Overlooked on the program for the fair were the husband-wife team of Carl Myers and "Carlotta," who were to ascend on the last day of the fair, he in the *Flying Cloud* and she in the *Aerial*.[7]

The Bismarck *Tribune* of October 7, 1881, satirized King's next attempt:

Prof. King, the balloonist, who made such a complete failure at the Minneapolis fair, has begun operations at Chicago. He is to go up a hundred feet or so for a clothing house as an advertising scheme. He bamboozled Minneapolis out of a fine silk balloon, and he is probably now working for a suit of broadcloth.

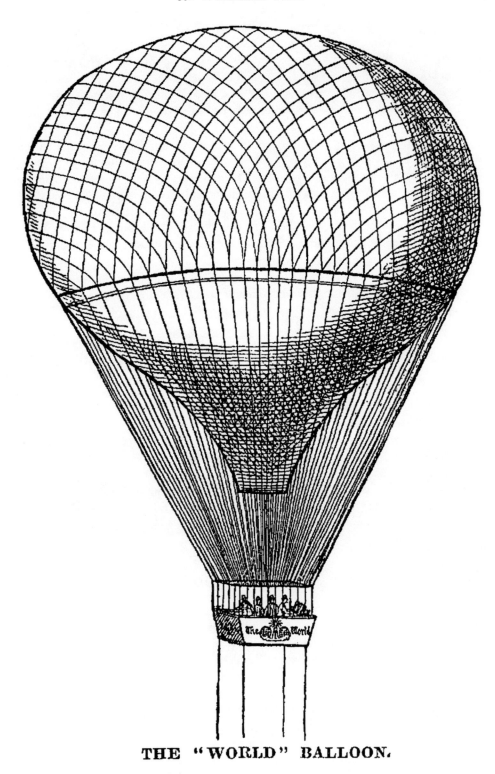

THE "WORLD" BALLOON.

The World Balloon was yet another in a long series of "flunks" (*The World* [New York], June 5, 1887).

King did make a voyage from the Chicago lakefront on Thursday, July 13, in company with Mr. Hashagen, a Signal Service representative aboard the *A. J. Nutting*. The balloon was caught in a stiff southwesterly breeze; by 9:00 P.M. it was sighted at Princetown, Illinois; by 7:00 Friday morning it appeared over Sparta, Wisconsin, where King spoke to the people below but refused to come down, saying he was "O.K."[8] No authenticated news arrived on the 16th and it was feared the aeronauts had met with disaster, possibly falling into Lake Superior.

Annoyed by newspapermen, Mrs. King left for the east, expressing confidence in her husband and his safety. By October 17, when no further information was forthcoming, the opinion was freely expressed that King "had fallen victim to the Prince of the Power of the Air,"[9] the same antagonist who worked against the unlucky Barrett in 1802.

Having taken with them only 24-hours'-worth of rations: two roasted chickens, six sandwiches, one piece of pie, two slices of cake, four slices of bread and butter, two sticks of celery, a gallon of water and a little fruit, anxiety turned to concern that they might starve, no word coming after a week of silence.[10]

Inevitable rumors began that King had purposely secluded himself to further the purpose of the Nutting company that sent him aloft as a flying advertisement. Fortunately for the reputation of the aeronaut, a telegram was received from Chippewa Falls, Wisconsin:

> We are all safe. Just out of the woods. King, Balloonist.

The story developed that after leaving Chicago, the balloon moved southwest, becoming becalmed over Peoria. Early Friday morning, it was over Spring Valley, Wisconsin, where a settler fired at them. The gas becoming exhausted, it eventually descended on the west bank of the Flambeau River, 65 miles from Chippewa Falls, after a trip of twenty-two hours. It required four days for the aeronauts to work themselves out of a cranberry bog, finally reaching some workmen on the 18th "in a ragged, dirty and hungry condition."[11] It did not take long for the popular song, "Up in a balloon, boys," to have a new tag added: "Down in a cranberry bog."[12]

King's balloon cost $5,000 and required $500 to repair. A.J. Nutting, the clothier, paid him $1,500 for the trip, which gave him a "fair profit." If, however, the balloon remained many weeks in the bog it would prove a total loss, leaving King a deficit of $3,500.[13]

While Professor King Was Not Going to New York...

John M. Kinney, "the Barnum in this line," was at Atchison, Kansas, with the Circus Royal, arranging for a balloon ascent for the 4th of July. Among Kinney's performers were Signor Pedanto and Lizzie Wise. It was later advertised that J. P. Pomeroy might ascend with either Wise or Pedanto, whoever was "the coolest and bravest."

As Kinney described it, "everything went wrong." Pomeroy went up alone (being shot at as he descended), and Kinney was held responsible for the disappointment. Pomeroy was said to have lost $200 on the enterprise, the gas alone costing him $101. On August 11, Pomeroy advertised a balloon for sale.[14]

Nellie Thurston continued her astonishing career, ascending at Syracuse in September 1881, and again, accompanied by Professor Squire, from the same city during the 4th of July celebrations, 1882.[15] Under the heading of "New Career," Luther L. Holden, of the Boston *Journal*, retired after 30 years and took up ballooning. During his career as a journalist he made 28 balloon flights and apparently decided forming excursions provided a more exciting, if not steady, employment.[16] Seemingly in agreement, Professor White abandoned ballooning and began touring with a slight-of-hand and trained dog show.[17]

In a sad story, toy balloons found their way to the Executive Mansion, where President Garfield lay dying from an assassin's bullet. His son James made his own balloon out of paper and paste and promised that as soon as the President was out of danger, he intended to have a grand ascension on the ground behind the White House.[18]

In September 1883, the horrific burning of the Exposition Building at Allegheny City, Pittsburgh, was reputedly caused by Canadian aeronaut Harry Warner. After his balloon burst on September 15, it was taken to the boiler room for repairs. Pouring boiling linseed oil on the canvas to strengthen the fabric, he then used benzene as a drying agent. The evaporating chemical was ignited by a gas jet, causing $150,000 damage, of which insurance covered $40,000.[19]

Continuing with the dangerous procedure of "smoke balloons," Professor A. L. Tolbert nearly lost his life at Chicago when he ordered cupfuls of kerosene and gasoline added to the fire in expectation of increasing the heat. On ascending, his balloon was seen to be ablaze. Unaware of his peril, Tolbert performed on the trapeze until the aerostat burst at 1,000 feet. The balloon plummeted to earth, but fortunately, Tolbert was flung out, landing on a telegraph wire that broke his fall. He eventually dropped to earth, sustaining serious but not fatal injuries.[20]

In February 1886, Samuel King was appointed "balloonist" in the office of the Chief Signal Officer.[21] He made several meteorological ascents, using the *Great Northwestern* and the *Eagle Eyrie*.[22] He also proposed another trans–Atlantic voyage in 1888, explaining his desire to "demonstrate the usefulness of the balloon," by making meteorological observations. He required $14,000 for the effort.[23]

In 1893, King was at the World's Fairgrounds, Chicago, making ascents. On September 22, he went up in the *Eagle Eyrie* with a young woman named Josie Morris. Caught in a rapid air current, the balloon was carried over the lake and the aeronauts were feared lost. Fortunately, they were rescued by the cutter *Andy Johnson* and taken safely to shore.[24] Two years later, King proposed yet another trans–Atlantic flight, this time from Philadelphia, using a 500,000 cubic foot "gasbag," a 5,000-pound drag rope and water anchors.[25]

The French aeronaut M. L'Hoste had already proven the usefulness of water anchors when he succeeded in crossing the English Channel in 1886. His "contrivance" dragged in water from a rope suspended from his balloon. This helped maintain a stable altitude, and when drawn up, served as a form of renewable ballast.[26]

With armed conflict breaking out across the globe, attention was again directed toward aeronautics. In 1885, General Russell Thayer, inventor of the "Dirigible War Balloon," received an order from the War Department to create a vessel in the shape of a cigar, 60 feet through by 185 feet high, costing $10,000.[27] Addressing the necessity of inflating aerostats in the field, a new method was developed by heating slaked lime and powdered zinc and enclosing the gas in cartridges for safe transportation. By heating the cartridge, enough hydrogen was obtained to fill a balloon in three hours.[28]

While war efforts were proceeding, "a distinguished officer of the United States navy" remarked, "War will soon become impossible because it will signify not merely great losses of life and destruction of property, but annihilation," but adding, "In case of necessity, an aerial ship can be constructed that will destroy London or any other city in the world with which the United States may be at war."[29]

R. G. Wells and the Cuban Club of Harlem proposed sending "4th of July balloons" filled with dynamite over Cuba, hoping to have them explode over the invading Spanish, destroying their works.[30] The same idea was suggested for other theatres of warfare, with one "crack" observing that if the dangerous aerostats were blown back over the attackers, "the army would have to get up and run like —."[31]

On tragedy of a smaller scale, aeronaut Parker A. Van Tassell (also spelled "Van Tassel") and his wife, an accomplished trapeze artist, were the headliners on the West Coast for several years. A dreamer beyond his means, he developed plans for the balloon *Eclipse* to sail across the Rocky Mountains.[32] The victim of "hard luck,"[33] he "fizzled" as often as succeeded,[34] at one point earning $800 in subscriptions and at others being in arrears for his hotel room.[35]

On November 16, 1889, Van Tassell was in Honolulu for the occasion of the King's birthday. Unfortunately, his balloon was blown over the ocean. Attempting to bring it down, his parachute opened and he was catapulted out. Boats were sent to his rescue, but his body was never found and it was presumed he had been eaten by sharks.[36]

Professor Hazen said: "The balloon voyage, though short, has been eminently successful in the cause of science."[37] The St. Louis *Globe-Democrat* gave it a different slant: "The best way to land that balloon safely in New York would be the way in which it came from New York — on a freight train."[38]

The immense *World-Post Dispatch* balloon ascended from Sportsman's Park, St. Louis, on June 18, 1887, on a scientific mission to benefit the Signal Service in predicting weather from the effects of air currents.[39] Aboard the vessel was Professor H. Allen Hazen of the Signal Service, Alfred T. Moore, aeronaut; John P. Doughty, photographer; and Edward Duffy, chronicler. The project garnered national attention and citizens from the Midwest to the Atlantic seaboard were encouraged to be on the lookout as the *World* traveled overhead.[40] After several "no goes," the balloon finally departed the ill-fated city, Mr. Pulitzer of the *World* hoping to give the "town a little boom for that day."[41] Moore received a serious hand wound on take-off. This injury and the "giving out of the gas" proved disastrous and the *World* voyage terminated "ingloriously in the wilds of Illinois."[42] Although reaching 16,000 feet, the highest record in America[43] the aeronauts left their vessel in the company of a watchman[44] and slunk into Centralia, where they registered under assumed names and refused to be interviewed.[45] Later finger pointing noted that the balloon had aboard six gallons of brandy and whisky, which was "pretty well used up" at the end of the voyage.[46]

A more tragic flight transpired on July 16, 1889, from Brooklyn. Professor Edward D. Hogan, reportedly "not over confident"[47] ascended in a $2,500 experimental vessel made by Carl Myers and designed by Peter C. Campbell with a steering apparatus operated by a hand crank.[48] Immediately after ascension the propeller fan, used for raising and low-

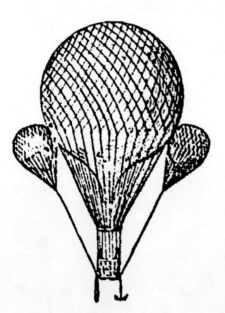

Illustration of L'Hoste's balloon (*Cedar Rapids Standard* [Iowa], February 2, 1888).

ering the balloon, fell off. The envelope inverted and Hogan was seen hanging by netting.[49] The balloon was later sighted floundering at sea. Despite rumors of being found alive, it was ultimately determined Hogan perished in the ocean.

Edward's brother George ("Jack") Hogan also died in a ballooning accident on August 29, 1891, when he lost his grip on the trapeze bar at Detroit and plunged to his death.[50]

In July 1891, Eugene Godard and Pillus Pinas (also spelled "Panis") were to operate a captive balloon similar to the one used in Paris. Applying to the Custom's House for the purpose of securing their balloon free of duty under the "tools of trade" rule, they were informed that as aeronautics was an "art" and aeronauts "professors," they were not subject to contract labor laws.[51] Finally securing their property, they were floating over the park on July 7, when the balloon was struck by lightning, reducing the vessel to "a pile of ashes and a strong odor of gas." The aeronauts survived but lost the $25,000 balloon that was only partially insured.[52]

An American dynasty was having its own problems. In October 1889, Professor Ezra Allen (son of James) was contracted to ascend from Fitchburg, Massachusetts. During the inflation the balloon was blown against a signboard, causing a rent from top to bottom. Allen was overcome to the point of tears and his wife wept at the news, offering to repair it herself.[53] A year later, James Allen accused his son of being "incompetent to conduct a balloon ascension"[54] stemming from the Fitchburg disaster. Ezra won a defamation of character suit and James was imprisoned at Cranston, Rhode Island, because of his inability to pay the judgment of $47. He was eventually released when Ezra allowed the board bill at the jail to lapse.[55]

On July 4, 1891, Ezra ascended from Boston. Reaching a height of almost three miles, he let out too much gas and violently struck the water off Marblehead Neck. A rescue was affected before they drowned.[56]

James K. Allen (James' more successful son) completed his 182nd ascent in the *City of Manchester*, from Smithville, Massachusetts, July 4, 1895. By this time, James had retired, completing 380 ascensions in his career.[57] In October 1895, during an ascent from Lowell, Massachusetts, James K. nearly lost his life when he fell unconscious in the perch above the basket. His companions kept him from falling overboard, eventually succeeding in bringing down the aerostat. The cause of Allen's distress was attributed to gas poisoning.[58]

In the last decade of the century, two "lady parachutists" merit note among the many women who flocked to the sport. Renowned in London, Mme. Crawford remarked, "I don't know what impelled me to become an aeronaut. Just my uncontrollable passion for adventure, I suppose," adding the only stock required for the business was "nerve." In over one hundred

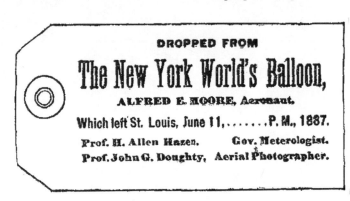

It was common practice to drop advertising circulars or souvenir "tickets" during balloon flights. In one instance, such circulars were actually used to track the progress of a lost balloon (*The World* [New York], June 5, 1887).

ascensions, she sustained only one accident when her parachute descended into a tree. Crawford broke three ribs but avowed never to have felt fear.[59] Louise Bates, of Brooklyn, declared, "About the best friend I have in the world is a parachute." Using the smallest one ever made, measuring a mere 16 feet in diameter, she completed her first drop as a child from East Enterprise, Indiana. Her particular method was to descend in a willow and rattan basket hanging 15 feet below the parachute she designed and made. Nearing land, she stretched herself flat across the top of the basket and came to rest so gently she claimed to hardly know when she touched ground. Born in Germany, her mother died when she was ten years old, and Louise was adopted by aeronaut Harry Gilbert.[60]

In scientific news, Dr. Berson ascended from Germany on December 3, reaching an altitude of 5½ miles, using "artificial oxygen" carried in bags, eclipsing the record set by Glaisher of 8,500 metres in 1862.[61]

The idea of an aerial exploration over the North Pole was resurrected in 1895, when Swedish explorer S.A. Andrée obtained approval from the Swedish Scientific Society and the International Geographical Congress, as well as a liberal contribution from King Oscar of Sweden, to make the attempt.[62] Finally departing from Spitzbergen on July 1, 1897, he was never heard from again and in 1904, a Stockholm court pronounced him "dead in law." Contemporary accounts determined Andree and his companions were killed by Eskimos.[63] Rounding out the decade, Count Zeppelin introduced his flying machine with an aluminum motor capable of sustained travel for weeks or months.[64]

The End of an Era

In hindsight it is easy to see where aeronautics was leading. Visionaries were placing gas engines in balloon-like devices; aluminum had been invented; propellers, cranks and gears were all in place. Even with foresight, the future was clear. An article in *McClure's Magazine*, 1893, began:

> Of course the air ship of the future will be constructed without any balloon attachment. The discovery of the balloon undoubtedly retarded the solution of the flying problem for over a hundred years.[65]

The march of aeronautics had been inspiring and at the same time discouraging. As the 19th century progressed, science gave way to entertainment. In that transformation, the solo flier went from aeronaut to professor and from professor to barnstormer. Trapeze artists took over from the "ascenders," who were quickly superseded by the "jumpers." Balloons were used in rainmaking schemes and in mining, where aeronauts inspected mountain cliffs for otherwise inaccessible deposits of ore. In peace, toy balloons continued to fascinate children and in war, to destroy them.

Men and women became famous and men and women perished in pursuit of their quests. In the dreams of many, balloons were to have provided rapid and safe transit between local destinations and to exotic cities around the world. Destiny would prove otherwise as the Wright brother's famous flight was just around the corner.

If balloons did not live up to man's lofty expectations, they brought excitement and inspiration to countless millions. By 1900, many achievements remained unfulfilled. The Atlantic was never crossed. Despite the bizarre and the creative, the "gas bag" never succumbed to the navigational desires of her pilot. The great debate on the Upper Air Current remained unsettled and the North Pole unexplored by air. Yet, as balloons faded from the scene, perhaps one question among the many puzzles was finally answered. On July 4, 1892, a balloon named *Omaha* came down in New York City. No one ever learned who owned it.[66] Forty-seven years later an aeronaut may finally have claimed it. He was called a wizard and he flew the *Omaha* away from Oz, leaving a little girl and her dog to get home by another form of travel: the flight of fancy. And all of a sudden, the world was in color.

Appendix: Glossary

accident agent: Insurance agent

air balloon: A small explosive often used in conjunction with other types of fireworks during celebrations.

anchored balloon: A tethered balloon; commonly used in the 1880s

"Army" ascent: A tethered ascent; it came into use during the American Civil War.

avoir du poids: Weight; heaviness

Bengal light: (aka Bengola) A kind of firework giving off a blue flame and used for lighting or signaling

brazier: The small stove used aboard a balloon, which was inflated by rarefied air to re-inflate the balloon during the flight.

British pound: (Money) One British pound equaled approximately 20 French francs

cadis: Wool cloth, used in construction of the envelope. It was less prone to catching fire than linen and used primarily in the 1700s.

caoutebone: A solution of India rubber used to varnish the balloon envelope

carpoy: A large bottle used for storage

captive flight: A tethered ascension used in the 1870s and beyond

Castle Garden: New York; waterfront property at the toe of Manhattan, bordering Battery Park

collapse line: ripcord

curricle: A light, open two-wheeled carriage pulled by two horses side by side. *Origin*: from L. *curriclum,* "course, racing chariot"

cwt: Hundredweight

dragline: A rope suspended from the balloon, used to control rotary motion and altitude; invented by Charles Green

envelope: The balloon itself; referring to the globe inflated by either rarefied or inflammable air

experiment: Typically used to mean a balloon ascent in the 18th and 19th centuries

fire balloon: Typically, any type of small balloon inflated by rarefied air. Many were classified as toys and were inflated by a candle set in a tiny basket. As such, they were a great fire hazard when landing near any inflammable material. The term was occasionally used for large balloons as well.

gallery: Another word for basket or car in describing the vessel in which the aeronauts stood during an ascension.

German mile: Equals 6 British miles

German Ocean: The North Sea

grill: Used interchangeably with "brazier"

gutta-percha: A latex made from several Malaysian trees resembling rubber but containing more resin than rubber; used in the 1850s to make small toy balloons. Filled with hydrogen gas, they were sold as children's toys.

halyard: A rope or tackle for hoisting and lowering something, like a flag

inflammable air: A gas possessing buoyant properties created from chemicals, usually vitriol poured over metal shavings.

lawn: A fine sheer linen or cotton fabric

"Lawn balloon": A derisive term for an old, worn-out balloon

maroon: *chiefly Brit.:* a firework that makes a loud bang, used as a signal or warning. *Origin* (in the sense of "chestnut"); from Fr. *marron*; so named because the firework makes the noise of a chestnut bursting in the fire.

osier: A small willow of damp habitats with long flexible shoots used in basketwork.

picquet: Variant spelling of *picket* (a soldier or small body of troops sent out to watch for the enemy)

posting: Advertising taken out in newspapers and fliers distributed around the countryside in anticipation of a balloon ascent

puncheon: *Historical:* a large cask for liquids or other commodities, holding from 72 to 120 gallons

ripcord: A rope used during emergency landings to tear a slit in the envelope and allow for the rapid escape of gas

shinty: A Scottish twelve-a-side game resembling hockey, played with curved sticks and taller goalposts and derived from hurling

sky-lark: Going up in a balloon

smack: A single-masted sailing boat used for coasting or fishing

squib: A small firework that hisses before exploding

tilbury: A light, open, two-wheeled carriage

toifel: A measurement of distance; one toifel equaled 6 British feet

topical ascensions: Tethered balloon ascents

vitriol: Sulfuric acid

whin: *Brit.:* furze; gorse (a yellow flowered shrub of the pea family; the leaves of which have the forms of spines). Also: hard, dark basaltic rock

Chapter Notes

Preface

1. *London Times*, August 30, 1811.
2. *Ibid.*, October 11, 1811.
3. *Northern Vindicator* (Iowa), October 12, 1888.

Chapter 1

1. Alexander Jamieson, L.L.D., *A Dictionary of Mechanical Science* (London: Henry Fisher, Son, and Co., London, 1829).
2. *Daily Universal Register*, October 20, 1786.
3. *London Times*, August 17, 1790.
4. *Edinburgh Advertiser*, May 4, 1784.
5. *London Times*, August 25, 1816.
6. "What Is the History of Hot Air Balloons?" www.wisegeek.com/what-is-the-history-of-hot-air-balloons.htm.
7. "Early History of Flight," Part 1, http://inventors.about.com/library/inventors/blearyflight.htm.
8. "Lighter Than Air: Chemists," http://chm.bris.ac.uk/webprojects2003/hetherington/final/balloonychemists.html.
9. *Onondaga Standard* (Syracuse, NY), October 7, 1829.
10. Jamieson, *A Dictionary of Mechanical Science.*
11. *Jackson County Banner* (Wisconsin), August 26, 1858.
12. "Montgolfier Brothers," www.solarnavigator.net/history/montgolfier_brothers.htm.
13. *Ibid.*
14. Faujas de Saint-Fond, Report made by the Academie des Sciences, "Première suite de la description des expériences aérostatique," Paris, 1784.
15. "Montgolfier Brothers."
16. *Journal de Paris*, 27 Juillet 1783, de la Lune le 29.
17. de Saint-Fond, "Première suite de la description des expériences aérostatique."
18. "The History of Ballooning," http://www.oreivystescentras.lt/eng/hot_air_balloons/the_history_of_ballooning/.
19. *Journal de Paris*, 27 Juillet 1783.
20. *Edinburgh Advertiser*, September 30, 1873.
21. "Report submitted to the Académie des Sciences," Paris, December 23, 1783.
22. *Edinburgh Advertiser*, September 30, 1783.
23. "Montgolfier Brothers"; see also *Ibid.*
24. Edita Lausanne, *The Romance of Ballooning* (New York: Viking Press, 1971), p. 18.

Chapter 2

1. *Journal de Paris*, December 2, 1783.
2. Frederic-Melchoir Grimm, "The Philosopher's View," *Correspondance littéraire* (Paris, August 1783).
3. *Journal de Paris*, August 28, 1783.
4. *Mercure de France*, No. 37 (September 13, 1783).
5. Avertissement au Peuple, De Paris, 27 Aout, 1783.
6. Edita Lausanne, *The Romance of Ballooning* (New York: Viking Press, 1971), p. 22.
7. "Montgolfier Brothers," www.solarnavigator.net/history/montgolfier_brothers.htm.
8. *Edinburgh Advertiser*, October 24, 1783.
9. *Ibid.*, November 4–7, 1783.
10. *Journal de Paris*, November 22, 1783.
11. *Edinburgh Advertiser*, December 9, 1783.
12. "Francesco Zambeccari Bolognese," Zambeccari's letter of November 28, 1873, *Notizie biografiche del conte.*
13. *Edinburgh Advertiser*, November 28, 1783.
14. *Ibid.*, December 16, 1783.
15. *Ibid.*
16. *Journal de Paris*, December 2, 1783.
17. *Edinburgh Advertiser*, December 16, 1783.
18. "Rapport fait a l'Académie des Sciences," December 23, 1783.

Chapter 3

1. *Journal de Paris*, August 28, 1783.
2. Fulgence Marion, *Wonderful Balloon Ascents, or the Conquest of the Skies* (New York: Charles Scribner, 1870), p. 92.
3. *Mercure de France*, No. 3 (February 17, 1784).
4. *Journal de Paris*, No. 92 (April 1, 1784).
5. *Ibid.*
6. *Edinburgh Advertiser*, March 16, 1784.
7. *Ibid.*, March 19, 1784.
8. *Ibid.*, May 21, 1793.
9. L. Lecornu, *La Navigation Aérienne* (Paris, 1903).
10. Pilatre de Rozier, "Première expérience de la montgolfière construite par order du Roi," Paris, 1784.

Chapter 4

1. *Edinburgh Advertiser*, September 24, 1784.
2. *Journal de Paris*, No. 123 (May 2, 1784).
3. *Edinburgh Advertiser*, September 24, 1784.
4. *Ibid.*, September 21–24, 1784.
5. *Journal de Paris*, June 26, 1784.
6. Tom D. Crouch, *The Eagle Aloft* (Washington, DC: Smithsonian Press, 1983), p. 68.
7. *Maryland Journal and Baltimore Advertiser*, June 25, 1784.
8. *Journal de Paris*, No. 194 (July 12, 1784); extract from a contemporary print, Bibliothèque Nationale, Paris, July 11, 1784.
9. *Edinburgh Advertiser*, August 10, 1784.
10. *Ibid.*, August 3, 1784.
11. *Ibid.*, August 27, 1784.
12. *Ibid.*, September 3, 1784.

Chapter 5

1. *Edinburgh Advertiser*, September 17, 1784.
2. Vincent Lunardi, "An Account of the First Aerial Voyage in England" (London: printed for the author, 1784).
3. *Ibid.*
4. Fulgence Marion, *Wonderful Balloon Ascents, or the Conquest of the Skies* (New York: Charles Scribner, 1870), p. 137.
5. *Edinburgh Advertiser*, September 11, 17, 21, 22, 23, and 24, 1784.
6. *Ibid.*, September 24, 1784.
7. "Flights of Fancy," Part 3, www.printsgeorge.com/ArtEccles_Aeronauts3.htm.
8. *Edinburgh Advertiser*, October 12, 1784.
9. "Flights of Fancy."
10. *Ibid.*
11. "James Sadler," www.viswiki.com/en/James_Sadler_(balloonist).
12. *Edinburgh Advertiser*, October 19 and 22, 1784.
13. *Ibid.*, September 24, 1784.
14. *Ibid.*, October 1, 1784.
15. *Ibid.*, October 8, 1784.
16. *Ibid.*, November 30, 1784.
17. *Ibid.*, December 3, 1784.
18. *Ibid.*, December 21, 1784.

Chapter 6

1. Extract from Dr. Jeffries' letter, Calais, January 1785, in the British Museum, London.
2. "Flights of Fancy," Part 3, www.printsgeorge.com/ArtEccles_Aeronauts3.htm.
3. John Jeffries, "A Narrative of Two Aerial Voyages of Doctor Jeffries with Mon. Blanchard" (London, 1786).
4. *Ibid.*
5. Fulgence Marion, *Wonderful Balloon Ascents, or the Conquest of the Skies* (New York: Charles Scribner, 1870), p. 144.
6. *Ibid.*, pp. 181–84.
7. *Ibid.*, p. 184.
8. Frederic-Melchoir Grimm, "The Philosopher's View," *Correspondance littéraire* (Paris, August 1783).
9. Marion, *Wonderful Balloon Ascents*, p. 186.
10. *Daily Universal Register* (London), October 14, 1786.
11. Louis Guilbert, *La formation du vocabulaire de l'aviation* (Paris: Larousse, 1965).
12. Mertens, Joost. "Technology as the science of the industrial arts: Louis-Sebastien Lenormand (1757–1837) and the popularization of technology." In *History and Technology: An International Journal*, 18:3. (Ox-

ford: Taylor & Francis Journals/Routledge, 2002), pp. 203–31.
13. *Star and Republican Banner* (Pennsylvania), January 1, 1833.
14. *Journal de Paris*, No. 242, August 30 and September 7, 1785.

Chapter 7

1. *Daily Universal Register*, September 30, 1786.
2. *Ibid.*, April 26, 1786.
3. *Ibid.*, June 3, 1786.
4. *Ibid.*, September 15, 1786.
5. *Edinburgh Advertiser*, August 25, 1786.
6. *Ibid.*, September 22, 1786.
7. *Daily Universal Register*, September 22, 1786.
8. *Ibid.*, September 25, 1786.
9. *Ibid.*, September 27, 1786.
10. *Southport Telegraph* (Wisconsin), September 16, 1845.
11. *Daily Universal Register*, August 1, 1787.
12. *Ibid.*, August 2, 1787.
13. *Ibid.*, August 4, 1787.

Chapter 8

1. Selle de Beauchamp, *Mémoires d un officer des aerostiers aux armies de 1793 à 1799* (Paris: Ledoyen et P. Giret, 1853).
2. *Edinburgh Advertiser*, July 23, 1790.
3. *Ibid.*, August 10, 1784.
4. de Beauchamp, *Mémoires d un officer.*
5. *Ibid.*
6. *Grimshaw's England*, reprinted in the *Adams Sentinel* (Pennsylvania), June 20, 1821.
7. *Wilmingtonian & Delaware Advertiser* (Delaware), August 17, 1826.
8. *London Times*, August 15, 1794.
9. *Ibid.*, September 25 and October 11, 1794.
10. *Edinburgh Advertiser*, December 22, 1797.
11. Edita Lausanne, *The Romance of Ballooning* (New York: Viking Press, 1971), p. 68.
12. *London Times*, August 8, 1798.
13. *Edinburgh Advertiser*, January 18, 1799.
14. André-Jacques Garnerin, wikipedia.com. "History of Aviation: Andre Jacques Garnerin," http://www.spartacus.schoolnet.co.uk/Avgarnerin.htm.
15. *Edinburgh Advertiser*, July 5, 1799.
16. *Ibid.*, November 10, 1812; see also *Torch Light & Public Advertiser* (Maryland), January 15, 1829.

Chapter 9

1. *Wochentliche Nacbrichten aus*

dem Berichthaus zu Basel, May 8, 1788.
2. A. Sircos and T. Pallier, *Histoire des Ballons* (Paris, 1876).
3. *Journal des Débats*, August 3, 1800.
4. *London Times*, June 16, 1802.
5. *Ibid.*, June 16, 1802.
6. *Edinburgh Weekly Journal*, July 7, 1802.
7. *Edinburgh Advertiser*, July 7, 1802.
8. *London Times*, June 29, 1802.
9. *Edinburgh Weekly Journal*, July 7, 1802.
10. *London Times*, July 3, 1802.
11. *Edinburgh Advertiser*, July 6, 1802.
12. *London Times*, July 7, 1802.
13. *Ibid.*, July 21, 1802.
14. *Edinburgh Weekly Journal*, August 11, 1802.
15. *London Times*, August 4, 1802.

Chapter 10

1. *London Times*, August 13, 1802.
2. *Edinburgh Weekly Journal*, August 11, 1802.
3. *London Times*, August 13, 1802.
4. *Ibid.*, August 14, 1802.
5. *Ibid.*, September 16, 1802.
6. *Ibid.*, September 28, 1802.
7. *Ibid.*, October 22, 1802.
8. *Edinburgh Advertiser*, October 12, 1802.
9. *Ibid.*, October 12, 1802.
10. *London Times*, October 22, 1802.
11. *Ibid.*, October 19, 1802.
12. *Ibid.*, November 22, 1802.
13. *Ibid.*, November 23, 1802.

Chapter 11

1. *London Times*, October 28, 1802.
2. *Ibid.*, August 23, 1802.
3. *Ibid.*, August 26, 1802.
4. *Ibid.*, August 25, 30, and September 6, 1802.
5. *Ibid.*, September 10, 1802.
6. *Ibid.*, September 17, 1802.
7. *Ibid.*, September 20, 1802.
8. *Ibid.*, September 24, 1802.
9. Ibid, September 24, 25, and 28, 1802.
10. *Ibid.*, April 9, 1803.
11. *Ibid.*, September 2, 1803.
12. *Ibid.*, August 31, 1803.
13. Fulgence Marion, *Wonderful Balloon Ascents, or the Conquest of the Skies* (New York: Charles Scribner, 1870), p. 145.
14. T.C. Guasti, *Francesco Zambeccari, aeronauta*, Police Report of Zambeccari's Ascent (Milano, 1932).
15. Marion, *Wonderful Balloon Ascents*, p. 149.

16. *London Times*, December 5, 1803.
17. L. Lecornu, *La Navigation Aérienne* (Paris, 1903).
18. *London Times*, October 10, 1804.
19. *Ibid.*, October 7, 1805.
20. *The Centinel* (London), July 2, 1806.
21. *London Times*, October 10, 1804.
22. *Centinel*, October 28, 1807.
23. *London Times*, January 15, 1805.
24. "The Coronation Balloon," *Le Moniteur Universal* (Paris), December 4, 1804.
25. *Edinburgh Weekly Journal*, October 28, 1807.
26. *London Times*, September 8, 1808.
27. *Ibid.*, May 28, 1806.
28. *Centinel*, July 16, 1806.
29. *London Times*, May 2, 1806.
30. *Ibid.*, May 28, 1806.
31. Marion, *Wonderful Balloon Ascents*, p. 186.
32. *London Times*, May 28, 1806.
33. *Centinel*, October 19, 1808.
34. *London Times*, October 26, 1809.

Chapter 12

1. *London Times*, August 30, 1811.
2. *Ibid.*, July 9, 1810.
3. *Edinburgh Advertiser*, July 18, 1810.
4. *London Times*, July 9, 1810, July 4, 1811.
5. *Ibid.*, July 10.
6. *Edinburgh Advertiser*, July 18, 1810; *London Times*, September 26, 28, and 29, 1810.
7. *London Times*, February 20, 1811.
8. *Ibid.*, August 14, 1811.
9. *Ibid.*, August 30, 1811.
10. *Ibid.*, August 31, 1811.
11. *Ibid.*, October 17, 1811.
12. *Ibid.*, October 11, 1811; *Edinburgh Advertiser*, October 15, 1811.

Chapter 13

1. *London Times*, July 16, 1814.
2. *Ibid.*, September 25, 1815.
3. *Ibid.*, May 3, 1816.
4. *Ibid.*, July 31, 1816.
5. *Ibid.*, September 20, 1816.
6. *Ibid.*, August 28, 1816; *Edinburgh Advertiser*, September 3, 1816.
7. *London Times*, September 5, 1816.
8. *Edinburgh Advertiser*, July 14, 1818.
9. *London Times*, October 2, 1810.
10. *Ibid.*, September 26, 1811.
11. *Ibid.*, December 23, 1811.
12. *Ibid.*, May 9, 1814.
13. *Ibid.*, October 2, 1817; *Edin-*

burgh Advertiser, October 7, 1817, and July 16, 1819.
14. *Le Moniteur Universal*, July 8, 1819.
15. *Edinburgh Advertiser*, July 16, 1819.
16. "The Journal of Norwich Duff," July 6, 1819.
17. *London Times*, July 13, 1819; *Edinburgh Advertiser*, July 16, 1819; *Le Moniteur Universal*, July 8, 1819.
18. *London Times*, September 17, 1819.
19. *Ibid.*, August 7, 1816.
20. *Ibid.*, September 12, 1816.
21. *Edinburgh Advertiser*, September 27, 1816.
22. *London Times*, October 16, 1818.
23. *Ibid.*, October 18, 1818.
24. *Ibid.*, October 20, 1818.
25. *Ibid.*, November 13, 1818.
26. *Ibid.*, November 27, 1818.
27. *Munchener politische Zeitung*, No. 233, "Wilhelmine Reichardt's Ascent," October 2, 1820.
28. *London Times*, November 9, 1812; *Edinburgh Advertiser*, November 12, 1812.
29. *Ibid.*, October 5, 1821, and October 9, 1821.
30. *Ibid.*, August 8, 1823.

Chapter 14

1. *London Times*, July 12, 1819.
2. *Edinburgh Advertiser*, July 14, 1812.
3. *London Times*, August 15, 1812.
4. *Ibid.*, November 9, 1812.
5. *Ibid.*, October 6, 1812; *Edinburgh Advertiser*, October 6, 1812.
6. *Ibid.*, September 9 and 10, 1813.
7. *Ibid.*, November 6, 1813.
8. *Ibid.*, July 15, 1814.
9. Forster, T., *Annals of Some Remarkable Aerial and Alpine Voyages* (London: Keating and Brown, 1832).
10. *London Times*, July 16 and 19, 1814.
11. *Ibid.*, July 23, 1814.
12. *Ibid.*, July 29, 1814.
13. *Ibid.*, September 12, 1816.
14. *Ibid.*, November 11, 1816.
15. *Ibid.*, July 29, 1817; *Edinburgh Advertiser*, July 29, 1817.
16. *Ibid.*, August 29, 1817; *Ibid.*, August 26, 1817.
17. *Ibid.*, October 4, 1819.
18. *Edinburgh Advertiser*, January 14, 1820.
19. *London Times*, November 26, 1802.
20. *Edinburgh Advertiser*, October 11, 1822.
21. *Wisconsin Free Democrat*, August 15, 1855.
22. *Janesville Morning Gazette* (Wisconsin), July 1, 1857.
23. *Salt Lake Tribune*, July 6, 1895.

Chapter 15

1. *London Times*, June 4, 1823.
2. *Torch Light & Public Advertiser* (Maryland), September 18, 1821.
3. "Gas Light and Coke Company," http://en.wikiperia.org/wiki/Gas_Light_and_Coke_Company.
4. *Edinburgh Advertiser*, July 27, 1821.
5. *London Times*, August 2, 1821; *Edinburgh Advertiser*, August 7, 1821.
6. *Ibid.*, September 10, 1821.
7. *Ibid.*, October 3, 1821.
8. *Edinburgh Advertiser*, October 9, 1821.
9. *London Times*, October 8, 1821.
10. *Edinburgh Advertiser*, October 26, 1821.
11. *London Times*, August 1, 1821.
12. *Ibid.*, August 2, 1822.
13. *Ibid.*, August 3, 1822.
14. *Edinburgh Advertiser*, August 9, 1822.
15. *London Times*, August 30, 1822.
16. *Ibid.*, September 13 and 14, 1822.
17. *Ibid.*, September 17, 1822.
18. *Ibid.*, June 2, 1823.
19. *Ibid.*, June 5, 1823.
20. *Ibid.*, June 16, 1823.
21. *Ibid.*, August 4 and 12, 1823.

Chapter 16

1. *London Times*, August 15, 1823.
2. *Ibid.*, August 19, 1823.
3. *Ibid.*, August 20, 1823.
4. *Ibid.*, September 8, 1823.
5. *Ibid.*, September 6, 1823.
6. *Ibid.*, September 12, 1823.
7. *Ibid.*; *Edinburgh Advertiser*, September 12, 1823.
8. *Edinburgh Advertiser*, September 9, 1823.
9. *London Times*, September 13, 1823.
10. *Ibid.*, September 25, 1823.
11. *Ibid.*, September 26, 1823.
12. *Ibid.*, September 27, 1823.
13. *Ibid.*, September 29, 1823.
14. *Ibid.*
15. *Ibid.*, October 3 and 4, 1823.
16. *Ibid.*, November 15, 1823.
17. *Ibid.*, December 27, 1823.
18. *Edinburgh Advertiser*, March 12, 1824.
19. *Ibid.*, April 27, 1824.

Chapter 17

1. *London Times*, June 1, 1824.
2. *Ibid.*, May 28, 1824.
3. *Ibid.*, May 26, 1824.
4. *Ibid.*, May 27, 1824.
5. *Edinburgh Advertiser*, June 1, 1824.
6. *London Times*, May 27, 1824.
7. *Ibid.*, May 28, 1824.

8. *Ibid.*, May 27, 1824.
9. *Ibid.*, May 28, 1824.
10. *Ibid.*, May 27, 1824.
11. *Ibid.*, May 28, 1824.
12. *Ibid.*, May 27, 1824.
13. *Ibid.*
14. *Ibid.*, May 28, 1824.
15. *Ibid.*, June 1, 1824.
16. *Ibid.*
17. *Ibid.*
18. *Ibid.*, June 4, 1824.
19. *Ibid.*, June 25, 1824.
20. *Ibid.*, July 2, 1824.
21. *Sandusky Clarion* (Ohio), July 24, 1824.

Chapter 18

1. *London Times*, June 3, 1824.
2. *Ibid.*, May 27, 1824.
3. *Ibid.*, June 2, 1824.
4. *Ibid.*, June 3, 1824.
5. *Ibid.*
6. *Edinburgh Advertiser*, June 11, 1824.
7. *London Times*, June 18, 1824.
8. *Ibid.*, June 19, 1824.
9. *Edinburgh Advertiser*, June 29, 1824.
10. *Ibid.*, June 29, 1824; *London Times*, July 6, 1824.
11. *London Times*, July 6, 1829.
12. *Edinburgh Advertiser*, July 2, 1824.
13. *Ibid.*, July 9, 1824.
14. *Ibid.*, July 24, 1824.
15. *London Times*, August 6, 1824.
16. *Ibid.*, July 12, 1824.
17. *Ibid.*, July 22, 1824.
18. *Edinburgh Advertiser*, July 20, 1824.
19. *London Times*, August 26, 1824.
20. *Ibid.*, August 26, 1824.
21. *Ibid.*
22. *Ibid.*, August 27, 1824.

Chapter 19

1. *London Times*, August 27, 1824.
2. *Ibid.*, September 1, 1824.
3. *Ibid.*, September 6 and 7, 1824.
4. *Ibid.*, May 28, 1824.
5. *Ibid.*, September 22, 1824.
6. *Ibid.*, September 27, 1824.
7. *Edinburgh Advertiser*, September 28, 1824.
8. *London Times*, October 4, 1824.
9. *Ibid.*, October 5, 1824.
10. *Ibid.*, October 9, 1824.
11. *Ibid.*, October 11, 1824.
12. *Ibid.*, October 15, 1824.
13. *Ibid.*, October 19, 1824.
14. *Ibid.*, October 20, 1824.
15. *Ibid.*, October 27, 1824.
16. *Ibid.*, October 28, 1824.
17. *Ibid.*, October 27, 1824.
18. *Ibid.*, October 28, 1824.
19. *Ibid.*, November 12, 1824.

20. *Edinburgh Advertiser*, January 8, 1825.

Chapter 20

1. *London Times*, June 24, 1825.
2. "Charles Green," www.1902en cyclopedia.com/A/AER/aeronautics-22.html.
3. *Edinburgh Advertiser*, May 17, 1825.
4. *Ibid.*, June 7, 1825.
5. *Republican Compiler* (Pennsylvania), July 27, 1825.
6. *London Times*, June 14, 1825.
7. *Ibid.*, July 12, 1825.
8. *Edinburgh Advertiser*, August 19, 1825.
9. *London Times*, June 29, 1826.
10. *Ibid.*, June 29, 1826.
11. *Ibid.*, April 5, 1825.
12. *Edinburgh Advertiser*, May 17, 1825.
13. *London Times*, May 12, 1825.
14. *Ibid.*, June 15, 1825.
15. *Ibid.*, June 24, 1825.
16. *Cambridge Chronicle* (England), July 5, 1825.
17. *Edinburgh Advertiser*, July 19, 1825.
18. *London Times*, August 11, 1825.
19. *Ibid.*, August 10, 1825.
20. *Ibid.*, September 6, 1825.
21. *Edinburgh Advertiser*, September 6, 1825.
22. *London Times*, August 30, 1825.
23. *Republican Compiler*, September 6, 1825.
24. *London Times*, September 5, 1825.
25. *Edinburgh Advertiser*, October 7, 1825.
26. *Ibid.*, October 25, 1825.
27. *London Times*, October 26, 1825.

Chapter 21

1. *Delaware Patriot & American Watchman*, June 6, 1828.
2. *London Times*, November 19, 1825.
3. *Ibid.*, November 19, 1825.
4. *Ibid.*, November 23, 1825.
5. *Ibid.*, November 19, 1825.
6. *Ibid.*, November 23, 1825.
7. *Ibid.*, March 30, 1826.
8. *Edinburgh Advertiser*, April 4, 1826.
9. *London Times*, May 17, 1826.
10. *Ibid.*, June 19, 1826.
11. *Sandusky Clarion*, September 30, 1826.
12. *Edinburgh Advertiser*, July 7, 1826.
13. *London Times*, July 4, 1826.
14. *Ibid.*, July 22, 1826.
15. *Edinburgh Advertiser*, August 1, 1826.

16. *Ibid.*, August 22, 1826.
17. *Ibid.*, September 19, 1826.
18. *London Times*, October 18, 1826.
19. *Ibid.*, April 18, 1827.
20. *Ibid.*, May 21, 1827.
21. *Ibid.*, June 9, 1827.
22. *Ibid.*, May 28, 1827.
23. *Ibid.*, June 11, 1827.
24. *Ibid.*, June 21, 1827.
25. Ibid, July 19, 1827.
26. *Ibid.*, July 30, 1827.
27. *Essex Herald*, October 12, 1827.
28. *London Times*, November 17, 1827.
29. *Edinburgh Advertiser*, June 30, 1827.
30. *London Times*, August 23, 1827.
31. *Ibid.*, April 12, 1828.
32. *Edinburgh Advertiser*, May 30, 1828.
33. *London Times*, July 5, 1828.
34. *Ibid.*, July 21, 1828.
35. *Ibid.*, July 30 and August 1, 1828.
36. *Norwalk Reporter & Huron Advertiser* (Ohio), November 15, 1828.
37. *London Times*, September 15, 1828.
38. *Ibid.*, August 22, 1828.
39. *Ibid.*, September 23, 1828.
40. *Ibid.*, October 22, 1828.
41. *The Tiles* (London), June 12, 1829.
42. *London Times*, July 6, 1829.
43. *Ibid.*, July 25, 1829.
44. Tom D. Crouch, *The Eagle Aloft* (Washington, DC: Smithsonian Press, 1983), p. 146.

Chapter 22

1. *Edinburgh Advertiser*, October 12, 1824.
2. *Republican Compiler*, June 21, 1820.
3. *Ibid.*, October 25, 1820.
4. *Adams Centinel* (Pennsylvania), December 6, 1820.
5. *Republican Compiler*, July 15, 1834.
6. *Adams Centinel*, September 1, 1824; *Brooklyn Star*, September 4, 1824.
7. *New York National Advocate*, July 11, 1825.
8. *New York Tribune*, February 10, 1853; *New York Times*, October 1, 1856.
9. *Ibid.*, September 6, 1825.
10. *Commercial Advertiser* (New York) October 21, 1825; see also *Torch Light & Public Advertiser*, November 1, 1825; *Republican Compiler*, November 2, 1825.
11. *Adams Sentinel*, October 4, 1826.
12. *Ohio Repository*, June 7, 1827.
13. *Torch Light & Public Advertiser*, October 9, 1828.

14. *New York Statesman*, October 23, 1828.

15. *Sandusky Clarion*, November 8, 1828; *Adams Sentinel*, November 5, 1828; *Baltimore Chronicle*, October 27, 1828; *Torch Light & Public Advertiser*, November 13, 1828.

16. Tom D. Crouch, *The Eagle Aloft* (Washington, DC: Smithsonian Press, 1983), pp. 149–50.

17. *Sandusky Clarion*, September 25, 1830.

18. *Adams Sentinel*, July 15, 1833.

19. *National Gazette and Literary Register* (New York), September 25, 1831.

20. *New York Standard*, August 26, 1831.

21. *New York Gazette*, May 17, 1832.

22. *New York Advertiser*, May 30, 1833.

23. *Commercial Advertiser*, May 31, 1833.

24. *Huron Reflector* (Ohio), June 25, 1833.

25. *Republican Compiler*, July 2, 1833.

26. *Albany Evening Journal* (New York), August 16, 1833.

27. *Republican Compiler*, September 24, 1833.

28. *Baltimore Gazette*, September 26, 1833.

29. *Adams Sentinel*, September 30, 1833.

30. *The Mail* (Maryland), October 4, 1833.

31. *Adams Sentinel*, October 7, 1833.

32. *Republican Banner*, October 22, 1833.

33. *The Mail*, October 25, 1833.

34. *Adams Sentinel*, August 11, 1834.

35. *Baltimore Visitor*, September 28, 1834.

36. Crouch, *The Eagle Aloft*, pp. 157–58.

37. *Newport Daily News* (Rhode Island), March 5, 1873.

38. *The Mail*, April 11, 1834.

39. *Torch Light & Public Advertiser*, April 10, 1834.

40. *Adams Sentinel*, April 14, 1834.

41. *The Mail*, May 9, 1834.

42. *Adams Sentinel*, May 5, 1834.

43. *The Mail*, May 9, 1834.

44. Crouch, *The Eagle Aloft*, p. 159.

45. *Hagers-Town Free Press*, June 25, 1834.

46. *Torch Light & Public Advertiser*, July 3, 1834.

47. *Adams Sentinel*, July 7, 1834.

48. *Torch Light & Public Advertiser*, July 3, 1834.

49. *The Mail*, October 17, 1834.

50. *Adams Sentinel*, November 10, 1834.

51. *Hagers-Town Free Press*, June 11, 1834.

52. *Ibid.*, June 11, 1834.

53. *Baltimore Chronicle*, July 8 and 12, 1834.

54. *Torch Light & Public Advertiser*, July 31, 1834.

55. *National Gazette*, August 13, 1834.

56. *Adams Sentinel*, August 25, 1834.

57. *Ibid.*, September 1, 1834.

58. *The Mail*, September 12, 1834.

59. *Ibid.*, November 7, 1834; *Huron Reflector*, November 18; *Adams Sentinel*, November 3; *Republican Compiler*, November 11, 1834.

60. *Republican Compiler*, November 18, 1834.

61. *Ibid.*, November 18, 1834.

62. *Adams Sentinel*, November 17, 1834.

63. *Hagers-Town Mail*, January 30, 1835.

64. *Adams Sentinel*, February 9, 1835.

65. *Republican Compiler*, May 12, 1835.

66. *People's Press* (Pennsylvania), June 12, 1835.

67. *Adams Sentinel*, June 15, 1835.

68. *Ibid.*, July 20, 1835.

69. *Ibid.*, July 27, 1835.

70. *Ibid.*, August 24, 1835.

71. Crouch, *The Eagle Aloft*, p. 164.

72. *Adams Sentinel*, July 20, 1835.

73. *People's Press*, April 24, 1835; *Huron Reflector*, May 12, 1835.

74. *Ibid.*, May 1, 1835.

75. *Republican Compiler*, May 5, 1835.

76. *Adams Sentinel*, May 11, 1835.

77. *People's Press*, May 29, 1835.

78. *Huron Reflector*, June 23, 1835.

79. *Ibid.*, July 14, 1835.

80. *Adams Sentinel*, September 7, 1835.

81. *Huron Reflector*, July 18, 1835.

82. *Adams Sentinel*, September 7, 1835.

83. *Ibid.*, February 29, 1836.

84. *Bangor Daily Whig and Courier*, September 21, 1837.

85. Crouch, *The Eagle Aloft*, pp. 169–70.

86. *Republican Compiler*, May 31, 1836.

87. *Huron Reflector*, May 9, 1837.

88. *Hagerstown Mail*, May 19, 1837.

89. *Daily Pittsburg Gazette*, September 5, 12, 14, and 16, 1837.

Chapter 23

1. *Star and Republican Banner*, August 11, 1837.

2. *Ohio Repository*, July 8, 1831.

3. *Hagerstown Mail*, October 28, 1831.

4. *Republican Compiler*, October 25, 1836.

5. *Adams Sentinel*, January 23, 1837.

6. Fulgence Marion, *Wonderful Balloon Ascents, or the Conquest of the Skies* (New York: Charles Scribner, 1870), p. 157.

7. *Ibid.*

8. *Ibid.*, p. 158.

9. A. Sircos and T. Pallier, *Histoire des Ballons* (Paris, 1876).

10. Marion, *Wonderful Balloon Ascents*, p. 158.

11. *Republican Compiler*, July 4, 1837.

12. www.scienceandsociety.co.uk/results.asp?image=10410986&www flag=2& imagepo.

13. "Robert Cocking," www.en.wikipedia.org/Robert_Cocking.

14. *London Times*, July 25, 1837.

15. "Robert Cocking."

16. *Adams Sentinel*, July 1, 1839.

17. *Madison Express* (Wisconsin), February 8, 1840.

18. *Southport Telegraph* (Wisconsin), July 14, 1840.

19. *Bangor Daily Whig and Courier*, September 8, 1843.

20. *Adams Sentinel*, July 24, 1843.

21. *Ibid.*, August 25, 1845; *London Nonconformist*, July 2, 1845.

22. *London Nonconformist*, August 13, 1845.

23. *Ibid.*, September 2, 1856.

24. *Southport Telegraph*, August 4, 1847.

Chapter 24

1. *New York Sun*, April 13, 1844.

2. *Republican Compiler*, April 24, 1838; *Hagerstown Mail*, April 27, 1838.

3. *Adams Sentinel*, May 4, 1840; *Milwaukee Advertiser*, May 23, 1840.

4. *Freeman and Messenger* (New York), October 8, 1840.

5. Tom D. Crouch, *The Eagle Aloft* (Washington, DC: Smithsonian Press, 1983), p. 187.

6. John Wise, *Through the Air: A Narrative of Forty Years Experience as an Aeronaut* (Philadelphia: To-day Printing and Publishing Co., 1873), pp. 304–10.

7. *Hagerstown Mail*, August 24, 1838.

8. *Adams Sentinel*, August 31 and September 14, 1840; *Freeman and Messenger*, October 8, 1840.

9. *Hagerstown Mail*, August 24, 1838.

10. *Huron Reflector*, July 9, 1839; *Adams Sentinel*, July 1, 1839.

11. *Star and Republican Banner*, June 4, 1839; *Adams Sentinel*, May 27, 1839.

12. *Adams Sentinel*, July 22, 1839.

13. Crouch, *The Eagle Aloft*, pp. 190–91.

14. *Wisconsin Democrat*, November 12, 1839.

15. *Southport Telegraph*, July 7, 1840.

16. *Hagerstown Mail*, August 9, 1841.

17. *Ibid.*, April 16, 1841.

18. *Ibid.*, April 30, 1841.

19. *Star and Republican Banner*, June 22, 1841.

20. *Tioga Eagle*, July 28, 1841.

21. *Ibid.*, July 28, 1841.

22. *The Experiment* (Ohio), November 17, 1841; *Adams Sentinel*, November 1, 1841; *Bangor Daily Whig and Courier*, October 28, 1841.

23. *The Independent Treasury* (Ohio), April 13, 1842; *Bangor Daily Whig and Courier*, April 12, 1842.

24. *Huron Reflector*, July 12, 1842.

25. *Ohio Repository*, May 12, 1842.

26. *Southport Telegraph*, May 24, 1842.

27. *Adams Sentinel*, August 8, 1842.

28. *Ibid.*, August 22, 1842.

29. *Republican Compiler*, September 19, 1842.

30. *Adams Sentinel*, September 26, 1842.

31. *Hagerstown Mail*, October 14, 1841.

32. *Republican Compiler*, June 5, 1843.

33. *Adams Sentinel*, June 26, 1843.

34. *Republican Compiler*, June 26, 1843.

35. John Wise, *Through the Air: A Narrative of Forty Years Experience as an Aeronaut* (Philadelphia: To-day Printing and Publishing Co., 1873), p. 426.

36. *Ohio Repository*, June 29, 1843.

37. *Adams Sentinel*, August 28, 1843.

38. *The Experiment*, July 5, 1843.

39. *Milwaukee Democrat*, September 29, 1843.

40. *Adams Sentinel*, July 24 and August 28, 1843.

41. *Republican Compiler*, September 4, 1843.

42. *Ibid.*, April 22, 1844.

43. *Ibid.*, May 20, 1844; *Lorain Republican* (Ohio), May 29, 1844.

44. *Adams Sentinel*, May 20, 1844.

45. *Republican Compiler*, May 27, 1844.

46. *Racine Advocate* (Wisconsin), August 13, 1844.

47. *Adams Sentinel*, October 28, 1844.

48. Clarence S. Brigham, *Poe's Balloon Hoax* (Metuchen, NJ: American Book Collector, 1932).

49. Crouch, *The Eagle Aloft*, p. 202.

50. *Newport Daily News*, February 16, 1848.

51. *Watertown Chronicle* (Wisconsin), May 17, 1848.

52. *Ibid.*, May 24, 1848.

53. *Adams Sentinel*, June 29, 1846.

54. *Ibid.*, August 3, 1846.

55. *Janesville Gazette*, September 5, 1846.

56. *Republican Compiler*, June 14, 1847.

57. *Southport American*, August 14, 1847.

58. *Buffalo Express*, August 1, 1847.

59. *Sandusky Clarion*, August 10, 1847.

60. *Madison Express* (Wisconsin), August 17, 1847.

61. *Buffalo Commercial Advertiser*, August 7, 1847.

62. *Republican Compiler*, May 8, 1848.

63. *Adams Sentinel*, December 18, 1848.

64. *Weekly Wisconsin*, October 11, 1848.

65. *Janesville Gazette*, November 1, 1848.

66. *Racine Advocate*, November 1, 1848.

67. *National Intelligencer*, February 10, 1849.

68. *Ibid.*, February 21, 1849.

69. *Watertown Chronicle*, July 24, 1850.

70. *Lorain Argus*, April 3, 1849.

71. *Scientific American*, reprinted in the *Prairie du Chien Patriot* (Wisconsin), August 13, 1851.

Chapter 25

1. *Albany Dutchman*, January 31, 1851.

2. *Milwaukee Daily Sentinel and Gazette*, August 6, 1850, and July 29, 1851.

3. *Marshall Statesman* (Milwaukee), October 15, 1851.

4. *Milwaukee Daily Sentinel*, October 22, 1851.

5. *Weekly Wisconsin*, November 5, 1851.

6. *Star and Banner* (Pennsylvania), September 20, 1850; *Republican Compiler*, September 29, 1851; *New York Daily Times*, July 7, 1852.

7. *Adams Sentinel*, September 6, 1852.

8. *Burlington Hawk-Eye* (Iowa), June 12, 1851.

9. *Republican Compiler*, June 30, 1851.

10. *New York Daily Times*, September 27, 1851; *Adams Sentinel*, October 6, 1851.

11. *Daily News* (Rhode Island), October 7, 1851.

12. *Star and Banner*, May 24, 1850.

13. *Ibid.*, July 19, 1850; *Republican Compiler*, July 22, 1850.

14. *Ibid.*, August 9, 1850; *Adams Sentinel*, August 12, 1850.

15. *Republican Compiler*, August 19, 1850; *Zanesville Courier* (Ohio), September 7, 1850.

16. *Zanesville Courier*, September 12, 1850.

17. *Republican Compiler*, December 16, 1850.

18. *Star and Banner*, December 27, 1850.

19. *Sauk County Standard* (Wisconsin), January 30, 1851.

20. *Oshkosh Democrat* (Wisconsin), March 28, 1851.

21. *Kenosha Telegraph* (Wisconsin), January 31, 1851.

22. *Star and Banner*, May 16, 1851; *Adams Sentinel*, May 19, 1851.

23. *Elyria Courier* (Ohio), July 8, 1851.

24. *Huron Reflector*, July 15, 1851.

25. *Elyria Courier*, July 15, 1851.

26. *Milwaukee Daily Sentinel*, April 21, 1852.

27. *New York Daily Times*, May 19, 1852.

28. *Daily Commercial Register* (Ohio), May 27, 1852.

29. *Star and Banner*, June 4, 1852.

30. *Weekly Wisconsin*, August 4, 1852.

31. *Zanesville Courier*, June 29, 1852; *Adams Sentinel*, August 16, 1852.

32. *Elyria Courier*, August 24, 1852.

33. *Wisconsin Weekly*, September 1, 1852.

34. *Adams Sentinel*, September 27, 1852.

35. *Zanesville Courier*, July 8, 1853.

36. *Star and Banner*, July 22, 1853.

37. *New York Daily Times*, July 29, 1853.

38. *Republican Compiler*, July 25, 1853; *New York Daily Times*, August 15, 1853.

39. *Alton Daily Telegraph* (Illinois), August 10, 1853.

40. *Ibid.*, August 12, 1853.

41. *Athens Messenger* (Ohio), June 23, 1854.

42. *New York Daily Times*, June 10, 1854.

43. *Adams Sentinel*, June 12, 1854.

44. *Waukesha County Democrat* (Wisconsin), June 21, 1854.

45. *New York Daily Times*, June 10, 1854.

46. *Ibid.*, June 12, 1854.

47. *Ibid.*, June 9, 1854.

48. *Ibid.*, June 14, 1854.

49. *Weekly Wisconsin*, June 21, 1854.

50. *Milwaukee Daily Sentinel*, June 16, 1854.

51. *Fort Wayne Times*, September 1, 1852.

52. *Zanesville Courier*, October 21, 1852.

53. *Ibid.*, October 25, 1852.

54. *Ibid.*, May 11, 1853.

55. *Huron Reflector*, June 14, 1853.

56. *Elyria Courier*, June 29, 1853.

57. Tom D. Crouch, *The Eagle Aloft* (Washington, DC: Smithsonian Press, 1983), pp. 208–10.

58. *Weekly Wisconsin*, July 19, 1854.

59. *Daily State Journal* (Wisconsin), July 13, 1855; *Weekly Wisconsin*, July 11; *Wisconsin Free Democrat*, July 11; *Daily Davenport Gazette* (Iowa), July 7, 1855.

60. *New York Daily Times*, July 7, 1855.

61. *Dixon Telegraph* (Illinois), August 22, 1855; *Janesville Gazette*, August 25, 1855.

62. *Daily Hawk-Eye and Telegraph*, September 18, 1855.

63. *Illinois Reporter*, August 16, 1856.

64. *Independent American* (Wisconsin), August 24, 1855.

65. *Daily Davenport Gazette*, September 12, 1855.

66. *Daily Hawk-Eye and Telegraph*, October 2, 11, and 12, 1855.

67. *Adams Sentinel*, October 31, 1853.

68. *Tioga Eagle* (Pennsylvania), June 22 and 29, 1854.

69. *Wisconsin State Journal*, September 6, 1854.

70. *Daily Globe* (Washington, DC), November 4, 1854.

71. *Republican Compiler*, April 23, 1855.

72. *Davenport Daily Gazette*, August 25, 1855.

73. *Republican Compiler*, December 3, 1855.

74. *Ibid.*, April 28, 1856.

75. *Davenport Gazette*, October 13, 1853.

76. *Kenosha Democrat*, October 17, 1853.

77. *Adams Sentinel*, October 10, 1853.

78. *Hornellsville Tribune* (New York), October 13, 1853.

79. *Titusville Herald*, October 26, 1871.

80. *Adams Sentinel*, January 16, 1854.

81. The *Daily Globe, Adams Sentinel, State Reporter, Oshkosh Courier* (Wisconsin), February 14, and the New York *Daily Times* of January 26, 1855, all used the first name "Louisa." Only the *Times* article of February 8 used the name "Lucretia."

82. *Daily Globe*, October 12, 1854.

83. Crouch, *The Eagle Aloft*, p. 204.

84. *Delaware State Reporter*, February 6, 1855.

85. *New York Daily Times*, February 8, 1855.

86. *Adams Sentinel*, February 5, 1855.

87. *Delaware State Reporter*, February 6, 1855.

88. *New York Daily Times*, February 8, 1855.

89. Crouch, *The Eagle Aloft*, p. 204.

90. *Daily Free Democrat*, June 14, 1855.

91. *Dixon Telegraph*, July 4, 1855.

92. *Milwaukee Daily News*, June 19, 1855.

93. *Manitowas Tribune* (Wisconsin), July 17, 1855.

94. *Weekly Wisconsin*, June 20, 1855.

95. *Daily Argus and Democrat* (Wisconsin), June 20, 1855.

96. *Daily Free Democrat*, June 25, 1855.

97. *Ibid.*, September 7, 1855.

98. *Weekly Hawk-Eye and Telegraph*, October 10, 1855.

99. *Hornellsville Tribune*, October 18, 1855; *Daily Davenport Gazette*, October 23, 1855; *Adams Sentinel*, October 15, 1855; *Marysville Tribune* (Ohio), November 14, 1855.

Chapter 26

1. *New York Daily Times*, October 8, 1851.

2. "Bell's Life in London," reprinted in the *Potosi Republican* (Wisconsin), November 30, 1848.

3. *Prairie Du Chien Patriot*, March 16, 1850.

4. *New York Daily Times*, October 27, 1851.

5. *Wisconsin Statesman*, September 12, 1850.

6. *Weekly Wisconsin*, September 4, 1850.

7. *Davenport Gazette*, August 14, 1851.

8. *Milwaukee Daily Sentinel and Gazette*, July 7, 1851.

9. *London Nonconformist*, August 13; *Weekly Wisconsin*, September 3, 1851.

10. *Weekly Wisconsin*, April 9, 1851.

11. *New York Daily Times*, September 25, 1851.

12. *Daily Commercial Register* (Ohio), October 4, 1852; *New York Daily Times*, September 18, 1852.

13. *Dixon Telegraph*, October 9, 1852.

14. *Watertown Chronicle*, August 28, 1850.

15. *Ibid.*, August 28, 1850; *Adams Sentinel*, July 22, 1850; *Weekly Wisconsin*, September 4, 1850; *Star and Banner*, August 9, 1850.

16. *Daily Free Democrat*, October 28, 1850; *Weekly Wisconsin*, November 6, 1850; *Newport Daily News*, November 11, 1850.

17. *Republican Compiler*, November 11, 1850; *Weekly Wisconsin*, December 18, 1850.

18. "Who's Who in Ballooning," http:www.ballooninghistory.com/whoswho/who's who-g.html.

19. "Who's Who in Ballooning"; *Star and Banner*, October 18, 1850; *Republican Compiler*, October 14, 1850; *Adams Sentinel*, October 7, 1850.

20. *Milwaukee Daily Sentinel and Gazette*, July 21, 1851.

21. *Zanesville Courier*, October 10, 1850.

22. *Kenosha Telegraph*, August 15, 1851; *Republican Compiler*, July 21, 1851; *New York Daily Times*, October 11, 1851; *Wisconsin Express*, September 11, 1851.

23. *London Nonconformist*, September 1, 1852; *New York Daily Times*, September 20 and October 2, 1852.

24. *Ibid.*, September 29; *Daily Commercial Register*, September 25, 1852.

25. *New York Daily Times*, October 14, 1851.

26. *Daily Sanduskian*, March 11, 1850.

27. *New York Daily Times*, October 14, 1851; *Fort Wayne Times*, September 25, 1851.

28. *Ibid.*, September 26, 1851.

29. *Ibid.*, April 7; *Star and Banner*, March 12, 1852.

30. *Star and Banner*, June 25, 1852.

31. *Daily Commercial Register*, July 12, 1852.

32. *Hornellsville Tribune*, July 24, 1852.

33. *Weekly Wisconsin*, August 4, 1852.

34. *Alton Weekly Courier*, August 20, 1852; *Adams Sentinel*, October 4 and 18, 1852.

35. *Daily Argus and Democrat*, October 12, 1852.

36. *Zanesville Daily Courier*, January 11, 1853.

37. *New York Daily Times*, January 4, 1853.

38. *Adams Sentinel*, May 16, 1853.

39. Tom D. Crouch, *The Eagle Aloft* (Washington, DC: Smithsonian Press, 1983), pp. 219–20.

40. *Daily Free Democrat*, November 6, 1850.

41. Crouch, *The Eagle Aloft*, p. 220.

42. *Racine Advocate*, November 1, 1848.

43. *Wisconsin Tribune*, August 21, 1851.

44. *New York Daily Times*, November 7, 1851.

45. *Ibid.*, February 9, 1853.

46. *Kenosha Democrat*, November 29, 1851.

47. *New York Daily Times*, November 6, 1851.

48. *Weekly Wisconsin*, October 29; *Marshall Statesman*, November 19, 1851.

49. *New York Daily Times*, August 28, 1852; *Hornellsville Tribune*, October 30, 1852.

50. *Bangor Daily Whig and Courier*, December 29, 1853.

Chapter 27

1. *Weekly Wisconsin*, October 8, 1856.
2. *Daily Hawk-Eye and Telegraph*, April 21, 1856.
3. *Mountain Democrat* (California), May 17, 24, and 31, 1856.
4. *Ibid.*, June 21 and 28, 1856.
5. *Adams Sentinel*, June 16 and July 21, 1856; *Janesville Morning Gazette*, April 1, 1857.
6. *Daily Milwaukee News*, August 13 and 18, 1856; *Daily Milwaukee Sentinel*, August 13 and 14, 1856; *Daily Free Democrat*, August 15, 1856.
7. *Ibid.*, September 3, 1856; *Weekly Wisconsin*, August 27 and September 10, 1856; *Milwaukee Daily American*, September 3 and 5, 1856; *Weekly Wisconsin*, September 10, 1856.
8. *Weekly Wisconsin*, October 8, 1856.
9. *Newport Daily News*, July 16, 1857.
10. Tom D. Crouch, *The Eagle Aloft* (Washington, DC: Smithsonian Press, 1983), pp. 221–22.
11. *Adams Sentinel*, October 23, 1854; *Daily Free Democrat*, October 28, 1854.
12. *Republican Compiler*, December 4, 1854; *New York Times*, January 20, 1855.
13. *New York Daily Times*, January 29, 1855.
14. *New Orleans Crescent*, May 3, 1855.
15. *Weekly Argus and Democrat*, October 22, 1855; *Hornellsville Tribune*, October 18, 1855; *Weekly Wisconsin*, October 10, 1855; *Daily Free Democrat*, October 6, 1855; *Maquoketa Sentinel*, October 25, 1855.
16. *Newport Daily News*, October 29, 1855; *Davenport Daily Gazette*, November 10, 1855.
17. *New York Daily Times*, April 21, 23, 30, May 14, June 23 and July 7, 1856; *Fountain City Daily Herald*, May 13, 1856; *New York Daily News*, May 23, 1856.
18. *Wisconsin Mirror*, September 16, 1856; Crouch, *The Eagle Aloft*, p. 226.
19. *Daily Hawk-Eye and Telegraph*, November 5, 1856; *Democratic Expounder* (Michigan), November 13, 1856.
20. *Daily Courier*, November 11, 1856; *Weekly Wisconsin*, November 19, 1856.
21. *Illinois State Chronicle*, July 3, 1856; *Davenport Daily Gazette*, July 8, 1856; *Daily Democrat*, September 9, 1856.
22. *Janesville Gazette*, August 30 and September 13, 1856; *Weekly Democratic Standard* (Wisconsin), September 1, 1856.
23. *Ibid.*, October 18, 1856; *Daily State Journal*, September 17, 1856; *Milwaukee Daily American*, September 17, 1856.
24. *Davenport Daily Gazette*, October 15, 1857.
25. *Hornellsville Tribune*, November 15, 1855; *Monroe Sentinel* (Wisconsin), June 17, 1857.
26. Crouch, *The Eagle Aloft*, p. 205; *New York Evening Times*, July 5, 1856; *Whitewater Gazette*, August 21, 1856; *Adams Sentinel*, October 13, 1856.
27. *Adams Sentinel*, October 13, 1856; *Daily Wisconsin Patriot*, October 21, 1856; *Weekly Wisconsin*, October 22, 1856.
28. *Daily Hawk-Eye and Telegraph*, February 12, 1857; *Racine Daily Journal*, September 5, 1857.
29. *Bangor Daily Whig and Courier*, August 12, 1857, September 12 and 30, 1857.
30. *Baraboo Republic* (Wisconsin), October 29, 1857; *Bangor Daily Whig and Courier*, October 2, 1857; *New York Daily Times*, June 15, 1857.
31. *The Agitator* (Pennsylvania), June 25, 1857; *Progressive Age* (Ohio), July 1, 1857.
32. *Daily Wisconsin Patriot*, August 22, 1857.
33. *Daily Argus and Democrat*, July 24, 1857; *Fond Du Lac Journal* (Wisconsin), July 25, 1857; *Richland County Observer*, August 11, 1857.
34. *Milwaukee Daily Sentinel*, January 10, 1857; *New York Daily Times*, May 19, 1857; *Alton Weekly Courier*, July 9, 1857.
35. *The Compiler* (Pennsylvania), June 1, 1857.
36. *Janesville Morning Gazette*, June 25, 1857; *Maquoketa Sentinel*, May 14, 1857; *Democratic Expounder*, June 25, 1857; *Davenport Daily Gazette*, June 26, 1857.
37. *Fort Wayne Sentinel*, September 19, 1857.

Chapter 28

1. *Davenport Daily Gazette*, May 20, 1858.
2. *Alton Weekly Courier*, July 15, 1858.
3. *Ibid.*, July 22, 1858.
4. *Olney Times* (Illinois), August 13, 1858.
5. *Adams Sentinel*, October 11, 1858.
6. *Milwaukee Daily Sentinel*, September 25 and 27, 1858.
7. *Daily Milwaukee News*, September 17, 1858.
8. *Janesville Morning Gazette*, September 27, 1858.
9. *Democratic Expounder*, September 23, 1858.
10. *Marshall Statesman*, September 22, 1858.
11. *Democratic Expounder*, September 23, 1858.
12. *Marshall Statesman*, September 22, 1858.
13. *Janesville Morning Gazette*, September 20, 1858.
14. *Milwaukee Daily Sentinel*, September 22, 1858.
15. *Alton Weekly Courier*, October 14, 1858; *Whitewater Register*, October 23, 1858.
16. *Ibid.*, September 24, 1858; *Janesville Morning Gazette*, September 27, 1858.
17. *Detroit Free Press*, October 23, 1858.
18. *Hornellsville Tribune*, March 10, 1859; *Central City Daily Courier* (New York) March 14, 1859.
19. *Central City Daily Courier*, March 28, 1859.
20. *Marshall Statesman*, April 20, 1859.
21. *Sheboygan Journal*, May 7, 1859.
22. *Grand Traverse Herald* (Maryland), June 17, 1859.
23. *Wisconsin Patriot*, July 2, 1859.
24. *Dawson's Fort Wayne Daily Times*, August 17, 18, 19, 20, 22, 30, 31 and September 1, 1859.
25. *Ibid.*, September 1, 1859.
26. *Ibid.*, September 2, 1859.
27. *Ibid.*, September 7, 1859.
28. *Ibid.*, September 5, 1859.
29. *Ibid.*, September 10, 1859.
30. *Ibid.*, September 22 and 28, 1859.
31. *Fort Wayne Weekly Republican*, October 5, 1859.
32. *Burlington Daily Hawk-Eye*, October 26, 1859.
33. *Kenosha Times*, April 8, 1858; *Superior Chronicle* (Wisconsin), April 13, 1858.
34. *Lorain County Eagle*, June 16, 1858.
35. *Davenport Daily Gazette*, May 26 and 27, 1858.
36. *Progressive Age*, July 21, 1858.
37. *Alton Weekly Courier*, August 5, 1858.
38. *Hornellsville Tribune*, August 26, 1858.
39. *The Compiler*, June 21, 1858.
40. *Democratic Alleganian* (Maryland), July 3, 1858.
41. *Delaware State Reporter*, July 30, 1858.
42. *Janesville Morning Gazette*, September 24, 1858.
43. *Berkshire County Eagle* (Massachusetts), October 1, 1858.
44. *Milwaukee Daily Sentinel*, October 12 and 18, 1858.
45. *Davenport Daily Gazette*, October 16, 1858.
46. *Cincinnati Gazette*, October 10 and 12, 1858.
47. *Ibid.*, October 19, 1858.
48. *Racine Daily News*, October 21,

1858; *Fort Wayne Sentinel*, October 23, 1858.

49. *Berkshire County Eagle*, October 22, 1858.

50. *Burlington Daily Hawk-Eye*, October 25, 1858.

51. *Ibid.*, May 14, 1858.

52. *Cedar Valley Times* (Iowa), April 21, 1859.

53. *Weekly Hawk-Eye and Telegraph*, May 10, 1859.

54. *Democratic Expounder*, May 19, 1859.

55. *Weekly Gazette and Free Press* (Wisconsin), July 25, 1858.

56. *Kenosha Times*, May 27, 1858.

57. *Baraboo Republic*, May 27, 1858.

58. *Athens Messenger*, July 23, 1858; *Newport Daily News*, October 8, 1858.

59. *Berkshire County Eagle*, September 24, 1858.

60. *Ibid.*, June 3, 1859.

61. *Ibid.*, June 10, 17, 22, 24, July 1 and 8, 1859.

62. *Ibid.*, July 1, 1859.

63. *Ibid.*, September 22, 1859.

64. *Ibid.*, September 29, 1859.

65. *Dubuque Herald* (Indiana), October 21, 1860.

66. *Berkshire County Eagle*, June 3, 1859.

67. *New York Times*, June 24, 1859.

68. *Ibid.*, July 6, 11, and September 22, 1859.

69. *Marysville Tribune* (Ohio), November 3, 1858.

Chapter 29

1. *Troy Times* (New York), February 19, 1859.

2. *Daily Milwaukee News*, April 27, 1858.

3. *The Compiler*, May 31, 1858.

4. *Berkshire County Eagle*, September 3, 1858.

5. *Whitewater Register*, October 30, 1858.

6. *Hornellsville Tribune*, November 4, 1858; *Baraboo Republic*, November 18, 1858.

7. *Weekly Hawk-Eye*, March 29, 1859.

8. *Eau Claire Free Press* (Wisconsin), January 27, 1859.

9. Tom D. Crouch, *The Eagle Aloft* (Washington, DC: Smithsonian Press, 1983), p. 248.

10. *Central City Daily Courier* (New York), January 12, 1859.

11. *Hornellsville Tribune*, January 20, 1859.

12. *Lorain County Eagle*, April 13, 1859.

13. *Weekly Hawk-Eye*, March 29, 1859.

14. *Central City Daily Courier*, February 25, 1859.

15. *Lorain County Eagle*, April 13, 1859.

16. *Compiler*, May 16, 1859.

17. *Tyrone Daily Herald* (Pennsylvania), June 4, 1859.

18. *Progressive Age*, June 1, 1859.

19. *Central City Daily Courier*, June 18, 1859.

20. *Ventral Daily Courier* (New York), May 5, 1859.

21. *St. Louis Republican*, June 20, 1859.

22. *St. Louis Democrat*, July 2, 1859.

23. *St. Louis Republican*, July 2, 1859.

24. *Illinois State Chronicle*, July 7, 1859.

25. *St. Louis Democrat*, July 2, 1859.

26. *Illinois State Chronicle*, July 7, 1859.

27. *Daily Milwaukee News*, July 6, 1859; *New York Times*, July 7, 1859.

28. *New York Times*, July 6, 1859.

29. *Wisconsin Daily State Journal*, July 6, 1859.

30. *Daily Milwaukee News*, July 7, 1859.

31. *La Crosse Independent Republican* (Wisconsin), July 6, 1859.

32. *Marysville Tribune*, February 9, 1859.

33. *Davenport Daily Ledger*, July 12, 1859.

34. *Dawson's Fort Wayne Daily Times*, July 23, 1859.

35. *Janesville Daily Gazette*, July 14, 1859.

36. *Newport Daily News*, December 24, 1859.

37. *Janesville Daily Gazette*, July 14, 1859.

38. *Dawson's Fort Wayne Daily Times*, July 21, 1859.

39. *The Compiler*, July 25, 1859.

40. *Illinois State Chronicle*, July 27, 1859.

41. *Bangor Daily Whig and Courier*, August 1, 1859; *New York Times*, August 2, 1859.

42. *St. Louis Bulletin*, July 30, 1859.

43. *Eau Claire Free Press*, August 4, 1859.

44. *Davenport Daily Ledger*, July 26 and August 4, 1859; *Dawson's Fort Wayne Daily Times*, August 3, 1859.

45. *Milwaukee Daily Sentinel*, August 29, 1859.

46. *Banner of Liberty* (New York), August 24, 1859.

47. *Racine Daily Journal*, July 30, 1859.

48. *Grand Traverse Herald*, September 2, 1859.

49. *New York Times*, August 16 and 18, 1859.

50. *Ibid.*, September 2, 1859; *Milwaukee Daily Sentinel*, September 3, 1859.

51. *Ibid.*, September 9, 1859.

52. *Fort Atkinson Standard* (Wisconsin), October 12, 1859; *Burlington Daily Hawk-Eye*, October 12, 1859.

53. *Burlington Daily Hawk-Eye*, October 12, 1859.

54. *Dawson's Fort Wayne Daily Times*, October 8, 1859.

55. *Fort Atkinson Standard*, October 12, 1859.

56. *Hornellsville Tribune*, January 19, 1860.

57. *Banner of Liberty*, April 6, 1859; *Cedar Valley Times*, April 28, 1859; *Badger State*, April 30, 1859.

58. *Badger City Daily Courier*, June 14, 1859.

59. *Hornellsville Tribune*, July 14, 1859; *New York Times*, August 11, 1859.

60. F. Stansbury Haydon, *Military Ballooning during the Early Civil War* (Baltimore: Johns Hopkins University Press, 2000), p. 154.

61. *South Western Local* (Wisconsin), December 2, 1859.

62. *New York Times*, September 10, 1859.

63. *Ibid.*, September 23, 1859.

64. *Ibid.*, September 10, 1859.

65. *Wisconsin Daily Patriot*, September 23, 1859.

66. *New York Times*, September 28 and 29, 1859.

67. *Democratic Press* (Wisconsin), October 12, 1859.

68. *Oshkosh Courier*, November 4, 1859.

69. *Milwaukee Daily Sentinel*, November 2, 1859.

70. *Oshkosh Courier*, November 4, 1859.

71. *Racine Daily Journal*, November 8, 1859.

72. *Wisconsin Patriot*, November 5, 1859; *Milwaukee Daily Sentinel*, November 2, 1859.

73. *New York Commercial Advertiser*, October 28, 1859.

74. *Wisconsin Patriot*, November 26, 1859.

75. *Milwaukee Daily Sentinel*, November 12, 1859.

76. *Ibid.*, November 16; *Central City Courier*, May 4, 1859.

77. *Janesville Morning Gazette*, January 2, 1860.

78. *Weekly Gazette and Free Press*, November 18, 1859.

79. *Racine Daily Journal*, December 3, 1859.

80. *Janesville Daily Gazette*, December 15, 1859.

81. *Newport Daily News*, December 5, 1859.

82. *Burlington Daily Hawk-Eye*, January 29, 1859.

83. *Daily Milwaukee News*, August 27, 1859.

84. *Daily State Journal*, October 3, 1859.

85. *Milwaukee Daily Sentinel*, October 4, 1859.

86. *Ibid.*, October 5, 1859.

87. *Banner of Liberty*, September 7, 1859.

88. *Milwaukee Daily Sentinel*, October 8, 1859; *Newport Daily News*, October 8, 1859; *Racine Daily Journal*, October 21, 1859.

89. *Banner of Liberty*, September 21, 1859.

90. *Adams Sentinel*, August 22 and 29, 1859; *The Compiler*, August 29 and September 5, 1859.

91. *The Compiler*, December 17, 1859.

92. *New York Times*, July 7, 1859.

93. *Ibid.*, July 26, 1859; *Newport Daily News*, July 25 and August 31, 1859; *Dawson's Fort Wayne Daily Times*, August 13, 1859; *Loraine County Eagle*, August 17, 1859.

94. *Davenport Daily Ledger* (Iowa), July 16, 1859.

95. *Racine Daily Journal* (Wisconsin), July 4, 1859.

96. *Hornellsville Tribune* (New York), October 13, 1859.

97. *New York Times*, August 23, 1859.

98. *Hornellsville Tribune* (New York), October 27, 1859.

Chapter 30

1. *New York Times*, August 7, 1864.

2. *Ibid.*, July 23, 1853.

3. *Racine Daily Advocate*, September 28, 1853.

4. *New York Daily Times*, May 16, 1853.

5. *Ibid.*, July 17, 1854, and January 19, 1855; *Adams Sentinel*, September 20, 1858.

6. *Dawson's Fort Wayne Daily Times*, September 29, 1859.

7. *Weekly Hamilton Telegraph* (Ohio), July 29, 1859.

8. *New York Daily Times*, August 4, 1854.

9. *Ibid.*, August 25, 1855.

10. *London Nonconformist*, July 6, 1859.

11. *Alton Weekly Courier*, December 2, 1858.

12. Edita Lausanne, *The Romance of Ballooning* (New York: Viking Press, 1971), p. 102.

13. *Whitewater Register*, December 11, 1863.

14. *London Nonconformist*, October 21, 1863.

15. *New York Tribune*, May 25, 1869.

16. *Norwalk Reflector*, October 28, 1862.

17. *Whitewater Register*, May 1, 1863.

18. *London Nonconformist*, July 8, July 29, and September 23, 1863.

19. *Dubuque Democratic Herald*, November 13, 1863.

20. *Democratic Expounder*, August 31, 1865.

21. *New York Times*, August 7, 12, and 28, 1865.

Chapter 31

1. *Newport Daily News*, February 1, 1860.

2. *Fort Atkinson Standard*, February 23, 1860.

3. *New York Times*, June 9, 1860.

4. *Ibid.*, June 1, 1860.

5. *The Compiler*, June 11, 1860.

6. *New York Times*, June 15, 1860.

7. *Ibid.*, July 20, 1860.

8. *Burlington Daily Hawk-Eye*, June 30, 1860.

9. *Dawson's Fort Wayne Weekly Times*, November 26, 1859.

10. *New York Times*, February 2, 1860.

11. *The Compiler*, March 26, 1860.

12. *Dawson's Fort Wayne Daily Times*, April 10, 1860.

13. *New York Times*, April 19 and 20, 1860.

14. *Ibid.*, May 11, 1860; *Adams Sentinel*, May 21, 1860.

15. *Weekly Times* (Iowa), May 24, 1860.

16. John Wise, *Through the Air: A Narrative of Forty Years Experience as an Aeronaut* (Philadelphia: To-day Printing and Publishing Co., 1873), 543.

17. *New York Times*, June 6, 1860.

18. *Ibid.*, August 16, 1860.

19. *Fort Atkinson Standard*, October 11, 1860.

20. *Manitowoc Herald* (Wisconsin), April 19, 1860.

21. *Fort Atkinson Standard*, April 19, 1860.

22. Tom D. Crouch, *The Eagle Aloft* (Washington, DC: Smithsonian Press, 1983), p. 275.

23. *New York Times*, September 8 and 10, 1860.

24. *Milwaukee Daily Sentinel*, September 22, 1860.

25. *The World* (New York), September 22, 24, and October 26, 1860; *Berkshire County Eagle*, September 27, 1860.

26. *Racine Daily Journal*, July 6, 1860; *Milwaukee Daily Sentinel*, July 6 and 7, 1860.

27. *Banner of Liberty*, March 21, 1860.

28. *Racine Daily Journal*, October 3, 1860.

29. *Independent Democrat* (Ohio), November 28, 1860.

30. *Janesville Daily Gazette*, March 4, 1860.

31. *Berkshire County Eagle*, May 10, 1860.

32. *Newport Daily News*, June 7, 1860.

33. *The World*, October 19, 1860.

34. *Milwaukee Daily Sentinel*, June 28 and August 4, 1860; *Marshall Statesman*, August 8, 1860; *Burlington Weekly Hawk-Eye*, August 11, 1860.

35. *Weekly Standard* (North Carolina), September 5, 1860.

36. *Adams Sentinel*, October 10, 1860.

37. *Banner of Liberty*, August 15 and September 5, 1860.

38. *Ibid.*, November 28, 1860.

39. *Berkshire County Eagle*, September 13, 1860.

40. *Wisconsin State Journal*, June 20, 1863.

Chapter 32

1. *Dubuque Democratic Herald*, October 10, 1863.

2. F. Stansbury Haydon, *Military Ballooning During the Early Civil War* (Baltimore: Johns Hopkins University Press, 2000), p. 94.

3. *West Eau Claire Argus*, March 27, 1867.

4. *Hornellsville Tribune*, February 11, 1869.

5. *Dubuque Daily Herald*, March 13, 1870.

6. Haydon, *Military Ballooning*, pp. 263–68.

7. *Ibid.*, p. 263.

8. *Wisconsin State Journal*, July 7 and 9, 1863.

9. *Semi-Weekly Wisconsin*, August 28, 1863.

10. Tom D. Crouch, *The Eagle Aloft* (Washington, DC: Smithsonian Press, 1983), p. 284.

11. *Dubuque Democratic Herald*, September 24, October 1, 4, 7, 9, 10, and 18, 1863; *Cedar Falls Gazette*, October 9, 1863; *Janesville Daily Gazette*, November 9, 1863; *Weekly Gazette Free Press*, November 13, 1863.

12. *Dawson's Fort Wayne Daily Times*, March 24, 26, April 20, 23, May 5, 24, 25 and June 4, 1864; *Dawson's Fort Wayne Weekly Times*, March 30, 1864; *Fort Wayne Weekly Sentinel*, March 26, May 28, and June 3, 1864.

13. *Wisconsin State Journal*, September 27, 1867.

14. *Daily Milwaukee News*, June 25, 1871.

15. *Janesville Gazette*, July 11, 1871.

16. *Sterling's Gazette* (Illinois), June 2, 1875.

17. *Fort Wayne Daily Sentinel*, June 5, 1875.

18. *Milwaukee Daily News*, July 8, 1875.

19. *Newport Daily News*, March 12, 1866.

20. *Titusville Herald*, July 6, 1871.

21. *Boston Herald*, July 8, 1871.
22. *New York Times*, July 5, 1871.
23. *Fitchburg Sentinel* (Massachusetts), September 9, 1881.
24. *New York Times*, July 7, 1863.
25. *Dubuque Democratic Herald*, November 25, 1863.
26. *Daily Gazette* (Iowa), August 27, 1869.
27. *Janesville Daily Gazette*, December 14, 1864.
28. *New York Times*, August 13, 1865.
29. *Marshall Statesman*, September 20, 1865.
30. *Janesville Gazette*, November 21, 1865; *Burlington Daily Hawk-Eye*, November 9, 1865; *New York Times*, January 16, 1866.
31. *New York Times*, July 15, 1867.
32. *Ibid.*, June 21 and July 2, 1866.
33. *The North-West* (Illinois), July 26, 1866.
34. *New York Times*, July 19, 1866.
35. *Decatur Local Review* (Illinois), July 10, 1873.
36. Haydon, *Military Ballooning*, pp. 64–81.
37. *Bangor Daily Whig and Courier*, July 26, 1869.
38. *Herald and Torch Light* (Maryland), October 6, 1869.
39. *Edwardsville Intelligencer* (Illinois), July 14, 1870.
40. *Hornellsville Tribune*, June 9, 1871.
41. *Huntingdon Journal* (Pennsylvania), April 26, 1871.
42. *Herald and Torch Light*, August 9, 1871.
43. *Syracuse Daily Courier and Union*, June 10, 1865, and June 1, 1866; *Tyrone Daily Herald* (Pennsylvania), March 15, 1873.
44. *Gazette and Bulletin* (Pennsylvania), May 18, 1870.
45. *Huntingdon Journal*, July 19, 1871.
46. *New York Times*, July 4, 1869.
47. *Cambridge City Tribune* (Indiana), May 19, 1870.
48. *New Albany Standard* (Indiana), September 30, 1871; *New York Herald*, October 3, 1871; *Titusville Herald*, October 11, 1871.
49. *Titusville Herald*, July 10, 1866.
50. *Poughkeepsie Eagle*, July 5 and 7, 1870; *New York Herald*, August 22, 1870; *New York Times*, August 23, 1879.
51. *New York Times*, July 5, 1871; *Waukesha Plaindealer*, July 25, 1871; *Evening Gazette* (New York), September 14, 1871; *Weekly Wisconsin*, July 26, 1871.
52. *Democratic Pharos* (Indiana), August 25, 1869.
53. *Galveston Daily News*, July 18, 1868.

Chapter 33

1. *Decatur Republican*, October 15, 1868.
2. *Fort Daily Gazette*, March 27, 1869.
3. *New York Herald*, April 19, 1869.
4. *Morning Oregonian*, February 8, 1867.
5. *San Francisco Alta*, July 5, 1869.
6. *Galveston Daily News*, August 19, 1869.
7. *Dubuque Herald*, July 8, 1873.
8. *Ibid.*, May 17, 1870.
9. *Daily Gazette* (Iowa), May 10, 1870.
10. *Janesville Gazette*, May 20, 1870.
11. *Dubuque Daily Herald*, May 24, 1870.
12. *Ibid.*, May 24, 1870.
13. *Daily Gazette* (Iowa), May 10, 1870.
14. *Cedar Rapids Times*, May 25, 1871.
15. *Titusville Herald*, September 6, 1871.
16. *Janesville Gazette*, April 9, 1869.
17. *New York Tribune*, May 25, 1869; *New York Times*, June 20, 1869; *Elyria Independent Democrat*, October 11, 1871; *Janesville Gazette*, April 9, 1869.
18. *Portsmouth Times* (Ohio), September 28, 1872.
19. *Titusville Herald*, January 15, 1873.
20. *Cambridge Jeffersonian* (Ohio), December 19, 1872.
21. *Dixon Sun* (Illinois), April 30, 1873.
22. *Daily Kennebec Journal* (Maine), May 31, 1873; *New York World*, June 3, 1873.
23. *Janesville Gazette*, June 6, 1873.
24. *New York World*, June 7, 1873.
25. *Galveston Daily News*, June 12, 1873.
26. *Daily Republic* (Illinois), June 16, 1873.
27. *Dubuque Herald*, June 22, 1873.
28. *Fitchburg Sentinel*, July 3, 1873.
29. *Huntingdon Journal*, July 2, 1873.
30. *Paxton Weekly Record* (Illinois), July 31, 1873.
31. *Marshall Statesman*, July 9, 1873.
32. *Waterloo Courier* (Ohio), July 17, 1873.
33. *New York Times*, August 2, 1873.
34. *Waterloo Courier*, July 17, 1873.
35. *Dubuque Herald*, July 26, 1873.
36. *Salt Lake Daily Tribune*, August 28, 1873.
37. *Cedar Rapids Times*, August 7, 1873.
38. *Fort Wayne Gazette*, August 1, 1873.

39. *Ibid.*, August 15, 1873.
40. *Dixon Sun*, July 30, 1873; *Bucks County Gazette*, August 28, 1873.
41. *Gazette and Bulletin*, July 21, 1873; *Daily Leader* (Iowa), July 17, 1873.
42. *The Advance* (Pennsylvania), August 21, 1873.
43. *Daily Graphic*, August 24, 1873.
44. *Salt Lake Daily Tribune*, August 31, 1873.
45. *Daily Democrat* (St. Louis), August 29, 1873.
46. *Fitchburg Sentinel*, September 10, 1873.
47. *Fort Wayne Gazette*, August 23, 1873.
48. *Galveston Daily News*, September 30, 1873.
49. *Newport Daily News*, September 11, 1873.
50. *Dubuque Herald*, September 10, 1873.
51. *Fitchburg Sentinel*, September 10, 1873.
52. *Atlanta Constitution*, September 11, 1873.
53. *Fitchburg Sentinel*, September 11, 1873.
54. *Daily Kennebec Journal*, September 11, 1873.
55. *Gazette and Bulletin*, September 12, 1873.
56. *Fort Wayne Gazette*, September 12, 1873.
57. *The Advance*, September 25, 1873.
58. *New York Sun*, September 13, 1873.
59. *Ibid.*, September 12, 1873.
60. *Hutchinson News* (Kansas), September 25, 1873.
61. *Janesville Gazette*, September 13, 1873.
62. *Daily Kennebec Journal*, September 15, 1873.
63. *Ohio Democrat*, September 19, 1873.
64. *New York Sun*, September 13, 1873.
65. *Titusville Herald*, September 15, 1873.
66. *Ibid.*, September 16, 1873.
67. *Dubuque Herald*, September 19, 1873.
68. *Daily Kennebec Journal*, September 12, 1873.
69. *Dubuque Herald*, September 23, 1873.
70. *The World*, September 30, October 2 and 5, 1873.
71. *Janesville Gazette*, October 8, 1873.
72. *Morning Oregonian*, November 6, 1873.
73. *Newport Daily News*, October 8, 1873.
74. *Logansport Weekly Journal*, May 16, 1874.

Chapter 34

1. *Waukesha Plaindealer*, January 31, 1871.
2. *New York Times*, August 11, 1870.
3. *New York Herald*, September 14, 1870.
4. *Ibid.*, October 7, 1870.
5. *New York Times*, April 6, 1871; *Democratic Pharos*, August 16, 1871.
6. *Ibid.*, January 5, 1871.
7. *Dubuque Daily Herald*, December 17, 1870.
8. *Wisconsin State Journal*, October 27, 1870.
9. *Waukesha Plaindealer*, January 31, 1871.
10. *The World*, July 14, 1874.
11. *Semi-Weekly Wisconsin*, April 18, 1874.
12. *Edinburgh Evening Courant*, September 17, 1868; *Tioga County Agitator*, November 4, 1868.
13. *Ibid.*, August 13, 1869.
14. *Logansport Star* (Indiana), August 4, 1874.
15. *Edinburgh Evening Courant*, July 19 and October 2, 1867; *Waukesha Freeman*, August 3, 1871.
16. *Ibid.*, June 30, 1868.
17. *New York Times*, April 12, 1868.

Chapter 35

1. *McKean County Miner* (Pennsylvania), October 16, 1873.
2. *Titusville Herald*, May 23, 1872.
3. *Fort Wayne Daily Sentinel*, June 19, 1872.
4. *New York Herald*, July 5, 1872.
5. *Titusville Herald*, August 23, 1872.
6. *New York World*, October 5, 1872.
7. *Daily Kennebec Journal*, June 10, 1873.
8. *Titusville Herald*, August 16, 1873.
9. *Ibid.*, August 21, 1873.
10. *Bangor Daily Whig and Courier*, October 1, 1873.
11. *Buffalo Express*, July 6, 1874.
12. *Steuberville Daily Herald* (Ohio), June 2, 1875.
13. *Morning Oregonian*, October 14, 1873.
14. *The World*, July 7, 1874.
15. *Galveston Daily News*, July 9, 1874.
16. *Janesville Gazette*, July 9, 1874.
17. *The World*, July 16, 1874.
18. *Daily Times* (New Jersey), July 27, 1874; *Dubuque Herald*, July 29, 1874; *Titusville Herald*, July 31, 1874.
19. *Hamilton Examiner*, September 10, 1874; *Steubenville Daily Herald*, October 24, 1874.
20. *Janesville Gazette*, March 26, 1875.

21. *Fitchburg Sentinel*, April 22, 1875.
22. *Logansport Star*, April 22, 1875.
23. *Newport Daily News*, April 23, 1875; *Semi-Weekly Wisconsin*, May 1, 1875.
24. *Fort Wayne Daily Sentinel*, July 8, 1875.
25. *The World*, May 28, 1875.
26. *Cambridge City Tribune*, July 1, 1875.
27. *Janesville Gazette*, July 17, 1875.
28. *Dubuque Herald*, July 18, 1875.
29. *Milwaukee Daily News*, July 18, 1875; *Fort Wayne Daily Sentinel*, July 19, 1875.
30. *Dubuque Herald*, July 21, 1875.
31. *Fort Wayne Daily Sentinel*, July 21, 1875.
32. *Janesville Gazette*, July 21, 1875.
33. *Waterloo Courier*, July 28, 1875.
34. *Burlington Daily Hawk-Eye*, July 24, 1875.
35. *Logansport Weekly Journal*, September 11, 1875.
36. *Hagerstown Mail*, July 23, 1875.
37. *Steubenville Daily Herald*, August 3, 1875.
38. *Janesville Gazette*, August 18, 1875.
39. *Chicago Times*, August 17, 1875.
40. *Milwaukee Daily News*, August 20, 1875.
41. *Fort Wayne Daily Sentinel*, August 21, 1875.
42. *Petersburg Index and Appeal* (Virginia), August 25, 1875.
43. *Cambridge City Tribune*, September 9, 1875.
44. Reprinted in the *Janesville Gazette*, December 18, 1876, from the *Inter Ocean*; it subsequently became known as the "Inter Ocean letter."
45. *Milwaukee Daily News*, August 26, 1875.
46. *Dubuque Herald*, July 30, 1875.
47. *Racine County Argus*, September 2, 1875.
48. *Fitchburg Sentinel*, November 2, 1880.
49. *Indiana Progress*, October 6, 1875.

Chapter 36

1. *Decatur Daily Republican*, November 19, 1875.
2. *Fort Wayne Daily Sentinel*, June 23, 1874; *Ohio Democrat*, July 17, 1874.
3. *Ibid.*, September 30, 1875.
4. *Ibid.*, February 5, 1874.
5. *Titusville Herald*, March 13, 1874.
6. *Fort Wayne Daily Sentinel*, September 24, 1875.
7. *Oakland Tribune*, September 23 and 28, 1875.
8. *Eau Claire Weekly Free Press*, July 9, 1875.

9. *Milwaukee Daily News*, July 21, 1875.
10. *Ohio Democrat*, September 16, 1875.
11. *Oshkosh Daily Northwestern* (Wisconsin), May 12, 1876.
12. *Huntingdon Journal*, June 16, 23, and July 4, 1876.
13. *Ibid.*, August 18, 1876.
14. *Newport Daily News*, November 16, 1875.
15. *Burlington Daily Hawk-Eye*, January 21, 1876; *Evening Gazette* (New York), January 25, 1876.
16. *Athens Messenger*, February 10, 1876.
17. *Newport Daily News*, July 6 and 12, 1876.
18. *The Advance*, July 6, 1876.
19. *Logansport Journal*, July 25, 1876, and October 3, 1878.
20. *Huntingdon Journal*, July 21, 1876.
21. *Decatur Daily Republican*, July 13 and 31, 1877.
22. *Ohio Democrat*, August 10, 1876.
23. *Portsmouth Times*, July 14, 1877.
24. *Logansport Journal*, June 23, 1878.
25. *Weekly World* (New York), September 5, 1878.
26. *Sedalia Daily Democrat* (Maryland), October 3, 1878.
27. *Miami Herald* (Ohio), May 11, 1882.
28. *Bangor Daily Whig and Courier*, October 5, 1876; *Fitchburg Sentinel*, July 18, 1895.
29. *Hancock Herald* (Iowa), December 30, 1876.
30. *New York Times*, February 12, 1880.
31. *Milwaukee Daily News*, June 25, 1878.
32. *Dubuque Herald*, July 27, 1878.
33. *Burlington Daily Hawk-Eye*, March 15, 1878.
34. *New York Herald*, June 12, 1878.
35. *Boston Advertiser*, July 6, 1878.
36. *Warren Ledger* (Pennsylvania), November 15, 1878.
37. *Syracuse Standard*, September 22 and 24, 1877; *Daily Kennebec Journal*, October 8, 1877.
38. *St. Louis Post*, July 5, 1878.
39. *Oshkosh Daily Northwestern*, October 15, 1878.
40. *Evening Gazette* (New York), May 16, 1877.
41. *Salt Lake Daily Tribune*, July 10, 1878.
42. *Morning Oregonian*, September 13, 1878.
43. *Decatur Daily Republican*, July 6, 1878.
44. *Marion Daily Star* (Ohio), September 19, 1878.

Chapter 37

1. *Hornellsville Tribune*, August 30, 1878.
2. *Dubuque Herald*, September 26, 1879.
3. *Iowa State Reporter*, October 20, 1875.
4. *Wellsboro Agitator* (Pennsylvania), July 8, 1879.
5. *Fort Wayne Sentinel*, June 21, 1879.
6. *Syracuse Standard*, June 23, 1879.
7. *Daily Nevada State Journal*, June 28, 1879; *Weekly Reno Gazette*, July 3, 1879; *Daily Times* (New Jersey), May 13, 1879.
8. *Burlington Daily Hawk-Eye*, April 11, 1879.
9. *Indiana Progress* (Pennsylvania), May 15, 1879.
10. *Janesville Gazette*, July 7, 1879.
11. *Decatur Daily Review*, August 19, 1879.
12. *New York Times*, August 18, 1879.
13. *Dubuque Herald*, April 4, 1879.
14. *Daily Constitution*, June 26, 1879.
15. *Decatur Daily Review*, September 2, 1879.
16. *Bucks County Gazette*, August 14, 1879.
17. *Winnipeg Free Press*, November 6, 1880.
18. *Weekly Reno Gazette*, June 26, 1897.
19. *Fort Wayne Sentinel*, May 28, June 2, 3, and 4, 1879; *Racine Argus*, August 21, 1879.
20. *Daily Free Press* (Wisconsin), September 16, 1878.
21. *Bucks County Gazette*, July 12, 1877.
22. *Ibid.*, July 26, 1877.
23. *Logansport Journal*, September 3, 1878.
24. *Huntingdon Journal*, July 18, 1879.
25. *Newport Daily News*, May 14, 1879.
26. *Sterling Gazette*, August 23, 1879.
27. *Fort Wayne Sentinel*, October 4, 1879.
28. *Janesville Gazette*, October 1, 1879; *Daily Constitution*, October 5, 1879.
29. *Alton Daily Telegraph*, September 29, 1879; *McKean County Miner*, October 16, 1879.
30. *Fort Wayne Daily Gazette*, October 4, 1879.
31. *Salt Lake City Tribune*, October 5, 1879.
32. *Davenport Daily Gazette*, October 7, 1879.
33. *Fort Wayne Weekly Sentinel*, October 8, 1879.
34. *Janesville Gazette*, October 27, 1879.
35. *Bangor Daily Whig and Courier*, October 31, 1879.
36. *Fort Wayne Daily Gazette*, November 13, 1879.
37. *Sterling Gazette*, January 24, 1880.
38. *Alton Daily Telegraph*, July 28, 1881.
39. *Titusville Morning Herald*, December 12, 1879.
40. *Sterling Gazette*, November 1, 1879.
41. *The Advocate*, November 21, 1879.
42. *Hornellsville Tribune*, October 17, 1879.
43. *Titusville Morning Herald*, August 4, 1880.
44. *Syracuse Standard*, August 11, 1880.
45. *Salt Lake City Daily Tribune*, September 11, 1880.
46. *Marion Daily Star* (Ohio), December 9, 1880.
47. *Sterling Gazette*, February 7, August 7, 21, 28, September 11 and 18, 1880.
48. *Fitchburg Sentinel*, September 14, 1880.

Chapter 38

1. Dr. William Pole in *Fortnightly Review*, reprinted in the *Colorado Springs Weekly Gazette*, February 19, 1881.
2. *Staffordshire Sentinel* (U.K.), March 29, 1875.
3. *Logansport Star*, May 13, 1875.
4. *Fort Wayne Daily Sentinel*, May 6, 1875.
5. *The World*, April 21, 1875.
6. *The Constitution*, October 14, 1875.
7. *Janesville Gazette*, March 1, 1876.
8. *The World*, May 28, 1875.
9. *Winnipeg Free Press*, June 1, 1875.
10. *Aiken Courier Journal* (South Carolina), July 3, 1875.
11. *Iowa State Register*, October 18, 1876.
12. *Chester Daily Times* (Pennsylvania), February 7, 1877.
13. *Decatur Daily Review*, June 27, 1879.
14. *Daily Constitution*, August 31, 1878.
15. *Decatur Daily Review*, November 12, 1878.
16. *The World*, October 25, 1878.
17. *Winnipeg Free Press*, December 20, 1878.
18. *Ibid.*, August 22, 1879.
19. *Galveston Daily News*, September 5, 1879; *Daily Kennebec Journal*, August 18, 1879.
20. *Fort Wayne Daily Gazette*, August 19 and October 12, 1881; *Decatur Daily Review*, December 24, 1881.
21. *Logansport Journal*, September 16, 1876.
22. *Davenport Daily Gazette*, May 22, 1877; *Burlington Daily Hawk-Eye*, June 13, 1877.
23. *Stevens Point Daily Journal* (Wisconsin), August 3, 1878.
24. *Freeborn County Sentinel* (Minnesota), March 7, 1878.
25. *Galveston Daily News*, October 9, 1881.
26. *Sunday Herald* (New York), July 24, 1881.
27. *Janesville Daily Gazette*, December 12, 1881.
28. *Bismarck Tribune* (North Dakota), December 23, 1881.
29. *Salt Lake Daily Tribune*, January 22, 1882.
30. *Winnipeg Free Press*, December 1, 1881.
31. *Salt Lake Daily Tribune*, December 28, 1881.
32. *Janesville Gazette*, March 1, 1878.
33. *Winnipeg Free Press*, October 1, 1881.
34. *Palo Alto Reporter* (Iowa), June 10, 1882
35. *Bangor Daily Whig and Courier*, November 26, 1881.

Chapter 39

1. *Atlanta Constitution*, September 16, 1881.
2. *Bismarck Tribune*, August 5, 1881.
3. *Burlington Daily Hawk-Eye*, August 22, 1881.
4. *Olean Democrat*, September 15, 1881.
5. *Freeborn County Standard*, September 15, 1881.
6. *Janesville Daily Gazette*, September 21, 1881.
7. *Burlington Daily Hawk-Eye*, September 1, 1881.
8. *Ibid.*, October 15, 1881.
9. *Ibid.*, October 18, 1881.
10. *Helena Independent* (Montana), October 20, 1881.
11. *Marshall Statesman*, July 27, 1881.
12. *Logansport Pharos*, November 16, 1881.
13. *Weekly Wisconsin*, November 2, 1881.
14. *The Globe* (Kansas), June 7, 9, 10, 11, 15, 16, 21, 25, 27, 28, 30, July 5, 6, 7, 9, 22, August 2 and 11, 1881.
15. *Syracuse Standard*, August 27, 1881; *Titusville Morning Herald*, November 16, 1881; *Olean Democrat*, June 27, 1882.
16. *Reno Evening Gazette*, November 30, 1881.

17. *Cambridge Jeffersonian*, April 13, 1882.

18. *Fort Wayne Daily Gazette*, July 10, 1881.

19. *Warren Weekly*, September 20, 1883; *Janesville Daily Gazette*, October 4, 1883; *New York Times*, October 6, 1883.

20. *Logansport Pharos*, August 3, 1885.

21. *Marshall Statesman*, February 5, 1886.

22. *The World*, August 14, 1887; *Indiana Democrat* (Pennsylvania), July 12, 1888.

23. *Daily News* (Mississippi), November 16, 1888.

24. *Cedar Rapids Standard*, September 28, 1893.

25. *Delphos Daily Herald* (Ohio), February 9, 1895.

26. *Galveston Daily News*, October 7, 1886.

27. *Star and Sentinel* (Pennsylvania), May 19, 1885.

28. *Dunkirk Observer-Journal* (New York), February 19, 1889.

29. *Warren Ledger*, February 2, 1894.

30. *Evening Democrat* (Pennsylvania), July 13, 1895; *Alton Evening Telegraph*, August 1, 1895.

31. *Freeborn County Standard*, July 24, 1895.

32. *New York Times*, December 1, 1884.

33. *Morning Oregonian*, October 5, 1888.

34. *Salt Lake Daily Tribune*, August 23, 1888.

35. *Morning Oregonian*, January 3 and 4, 1889.

36. *New York Times*, November 24, 1889.

37. *San Antonio Daily Express*, June 21, 1887.

38. *Ibid.*, June 22, 1887.

39. *Decatur Daily Review*, June 19, 1887.

40. *Janesville Daily Gazette*, June 10, 1887.

41. *Ibid.*, June 10, 1887.

42. *Titusville Morning Herald*, June 20, 1887.

43. *Salt Lake Daily Tribune*, June 19, 1887.

44. *Daily Index-Appeal* (Virginia), June 20, 1887.

45. *Piqua Daily Call*, June 20, 1887.

46. *Janesville Daily Gazette*, June 20, 1887.

47. *The World*, July 17, 1889.

48. *Syracuse Daily Standard*, July 26, 1889.

49. *The World*, July 17, 1889; *Sandusky Daily Register*, July 18, 1889.

50. *Newark Daily Advocate*, August 31, 1891.

51. *Salem Daily News* (Ohio), July 2, 1891.

52. *Centralia Enterprise and Tribune*, July 11, 1891.

53. *Fitchburg Sentinel*, October 7 and 14, 1889.

54. *Herald and Torch Light*, June 19, 1890.

55. *Fitchburg Sentinel*, June 27, 1891.

56. *Lowell Sun*, July 11, 1891.

57. *Fitchburg Sentinel*, July 9, 1895.

58. *Newark Daily Advocate*, October 10, 1895.

59. *Logansport Journal*, April 23, 1893.

60. *The World*, June 22, 1893.

61. *Journal of Aeronautics and Atmospheric Physics*, reprinted in the *Cedar Rapids Standard*, July 11, 1895.

62. *Morning News* (Maryland), July 31, 1894.

63. *Covina Argus* (California), March 15, 1902; *Rock Rapids Reporter* (Iowa), November 17, 1904.

64. *The World*, August 9, 1896.

65. *Sioux County Herald*, July 5, 1893.

66. *Olean Democrat*, July 12, 1892.

Bibliography

"André-Jacques Garnerin." http://en.wikipedia.org/wiki/Andr%C3%A9-Jacques_Garnerin.

"Avertissement au Peuple." Des Paris, le 27 Aout, 1783.

"Ballooning History." http://www.ballooninghistory.com/whoswho/who'swho-g.html.

Beauchamp, Selle de. "*Extraits des Mémoires d'un officer des aerostiers aux armies de 1793 à 1799.*" Paris: Ledoyen et P. Giret, 1853.

Brigham, Clarence S. "Poe's Balloon Hoax." Metuchen, NJ: American Book Collector, 1932.

"Charles Green." www.1902encyclopedia.com/A/AER/aeronautics-22.html.

Cocking, Robert. See Robert Cocking.

Crouch, Tom D. *The Eagle Aloft.* Washington, DC: Smithsonian Press, 1983.

de Rozier, Pilatre. "Première expérience de la montgolfière construite par order du Roi." Paris: De l'imprimerie de monsieur, 1784.

de Saint-Fond, Faujas. Report made by the Académie des Sciences. "Première Suite de la description des expériences aérostatiques. Paris, 1784.

"Early History of Flight." Part 1. http://inventors.about.com/library/inventors/blearyflight.htm.

Evans, Charles M. *War of the Aeronauts: A History of Ballooning in the Civil War.* Mechanicsville, PA: Stackpole Books, 2002.

"Flights of Fancy." Parts 3 & 6. www.printsgeorge.com/ArtEccles_Aeronauts3.htm.

"Francesco Zambeccari Bolognese." Zambeccari's letter of November 28, 1873. Tprino, *Notizie biografiche del conte*, 1847.

"Gaslight and Coke Company." http://en.wikipedia.org/wiki/Gas_Light_and_Coke_Company.

Grimm, Frederic-Melchoir. "The Philosopher's View." *Correspondance littéraire.* Paris, 1783.

Guasti, T.C. "Francesco Zambeccari, Aeronauta; Police Report of Zambeccari's Ascent." Milano, 1932.

Guilbert, Louis. *La Formation du Vocabulaire de l'aviation.* Paris: Larousse, 1965.

Haydon, F. Stansbury. *Military Ballooning during the Early Civil War.* Baltimore, MD: Johns Hopkins University Press, 2000.

"Histoire des Balloons." Paris, 1876. Thomas Knowles Collection, Special Collections, Akron-Summit County Public Library, Akron, Ohio.

"History of Aviation: Andre Jacques Garnerin." http://www.spartacus.schoolnet.co.uk/Avgarnerin.htm.

"The History of Ballooning." http://www.oreivystescentras.lt/eng/hot_air_balloons/the_history_of_ballooning/.

"James Sadler." www.viswiki.com/en/James_Sadler_(balloonist).

Jamieson, Alexander. *A Dictionary of Mechanical Science.* London: Henry Fisher, Son, and Co. Newgate-Street, 1829.

Jeffries, John. *A Narrative of Two Aerial Voyages of Doctor Jeffries with Mon Blanchard.* London, 1786.

Lausanne, Edita. *The Romance of Ballooning, the Story of the Early Aeronauts.* New York: Viking Press, 1971.

Lecornu, J. *La Navigation Aérienne.* Paris, 1903.

"Lighter Than Air: Chemists." http://www.chm.bris.ac.uk/webprojects2003//hetherington/Final/balloonychemists.html.

Lunardi, Vincent. "An Account of the First Aerial Voyage in England." London: printed for the author, 1784.

Marion, Fulgence. *Wonderful Balloon Ascents, or the Conquest of the Skies.* New York: Charles Scribner, 1870.

Mertens, Joost. "Technology as the science of the industrial arts: Louis-Sebastien Lenormand (1757–1837) and the popularization of technology." In *History and Technology: An International Journal,* 18:3. Oxford: Taylor & Francis Journals/Routledge, 2002.

"Montgolfier Brothers." www.solarnavigator.net/history/montgolfier_brothers.htm.

"Newly Invented Parachute." www.scienceandsociety.co.uk/results.asp?image=10410986&wwwflag=2&imagepo.

"Rapport de l' Academie des Sciences." Paris, December 23, 1873.

"Robert Cocking." www.en.wikipedia.org/wiki/Robert_Cocking.

Spann, Edward K. *The New Metropolis: New York*

City, 1840–1857. New York: Columbia University Press, 1981.

The War of the Rebellion: A Compilation of the Official Records of the Union and Confederate Armies. Washington, DC: Government Printing Office, 1899.

"What Is the History of Hot Air Balloons?" www.wisegeek.com/what_is_the_history_of_hot_air_balloons.htm.

"Wilhelmine Reichardt's Ascent." Munchener politische Zeitung, No. 233 (October 2, 1820).

Wise, John. *Through the Air: A Narrative of Forty Years Experience as an Aeronaut.* Philadelphia: Today Printing and Publishing Co., 1873.

"Wochentliche Nacbrichen aus dem Berichthaus zu Basel." May 8, 1788.

Index